Designing User Interfaces With a Data Science Approach

Abhijit Narayanrao Banubakode
MET Institute of Computer Science, India

Ganesh Dattatray Bhutkar
Vishwakarma Institute of Technology, India

Yohannes Kurniawan
Bina Nusantara University, Indonesia

Chhaya Santosh Gosavi
MKSSS's Cummins College of Engineering, India

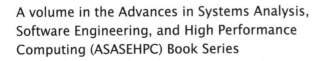

A volume in the Advances in Systems Analysis,
Software Engineering, and High Performance
Computing (ASASEHPC) Book Series

Published in the United States of America by
IGI Global
Engineering Science Reference (an imprint of IGI Global)
701 E. Chocolate Avenue
Hershey PA, USA 17033
Tel: 717-533-8845
Fax: 717-533-8661
E-mail: cust@igi-global.com
Web site: http://www.igi-global.com

Library of Congress Cataloging-in-Publication Data

Names: Banubakode, Abhijit, DATE- editor.
Title: Designing user interfaces with a data
  science approach / Abhijit Banubakode, Ganesh Bhutkar, Yohannes
  Kurniawan, and Chhaya Gosavi.
Description: Hershey, PA : Engineering Science Reference, [2022] | Includes
  bibliographical references and index. | Summary: "This book provides
  chapters that demonstrate an understanding of human-computer interface
  guidelines, principles and theories combined with data science
  techniques investigating user-centered designs of applications across
  domains while analyzing user data with a data science approach for
  effective and user-friendly user interfaces"-- Provided by publisher.
Identifiers: LCCN 2021047656 (print) | LCCN 2021047657 (ebook) | ISBN
  9781799891215 (h/c) | ISBN 9781799891222 (s/c) | ISBN 9781799891239 (eISBN)
Subjects: LCSH: User interfaces (Computer systems)
Classification: LCC QA76.9.U83 H344 2022 (print) | LCC QA76.9.U83 (ebook)
  | DDC 005.4/37--dc23/eng/20211120
LC record available at https://lccn.loc.gov/2021047656
LC ebook record available at https://lccn.loc.gov/2021047657

This book is published in the IGI Global book series Advances in Systems Analysis, Software Engineering, and High Performance Computing (ASASEHPC) (ISSN: 2327-3453; eISSN: 2327-3461)

British Cataloguing in Publication Data
A Cataloguing in Publication record for this book is available from the British Library.

For electronic access to this publication, please contact: eresources@igi-global.com.

Advances in Systems Analysis, Software Engineering, and High Performance Computing (ASASEHPC) Book Series

Vijayan Sugumaran
Oakland University, USA

ISSN:2327-3453
EISSN:2327-3461

MISSION

The theory and practice of computing applications and distributed systems has emerged as one of the key areas of research driving innovations in business, engineering, and science. The fields of software engineering, systems analysis, and high performance computing offer a wide range of applications and solutions in solving computational problems for any modern organization.

The **Advances in Systems Analysis, Software Engineering, and High Performance Computing (ASASEHPC) Book Series** brings together research in the areas of distributed computing, systems and software engineering, high performance computing, and service science. This collection of publications is useful for academics, researchers, and practitioners seeking the latest practices and knowledge in this field.

COVERAGE

- Engineering Environments
- Virtual Data Systems
- Performance Modelling
- Distributed Cloud Computing
- Computer System Analysis
- Enterprise Information Systems
- Metadata and Semantic Web
- Software Engineering
- Network Management
- Computer Graphics

IGI Global is currently accepting manuscripts for publication within this series. To submit a proposal for a volume in this series, please contact our Acquisition Editors at Acquisitions@igi-global.com or visit: http://www.igi-global.com/publish/.

Titles in this Series

For a list of additional titles in this series, please visit: www.igi-global.com/book-series

Technology Road Mapping for Quantum Computing and Engineering
Brojo Kishore Mishra (GIET University, India)
Engineering Science Reference • © 2022 • 305pp • H/C (ISBN: 9781799891833) • US $225.00

Advancing Smarter and More Secure Industrial Applications Using AI, IoT, and Blockchain Technology
Kavita Saini (Galgotias University, India) and Pethuru Raj (Reliance Jio Platforms Ltd., Bangalore, India)
Engineering Science Reference • © 2022 • 309pp • H/C (ISBN: 9781799883678) • US $245.00

Deep Learning Applications for Cyber-Physical Systems
Monica R. Mundada (M.S. Ramaiah Institute of Technology, India) S. Seema (M.S. Ramaiah Institute of Technology, India) Srinivasa K.G. (National Institute of Technical Teachers Training and Research, Chandigarh, India) and M. Shilpa (M.S. Ramaiah Institute of Technology, India)
Engineering Science Reference • © 2022 • 293pp • H/C (ISBN: 9781799881612) • US $245.00

Design, Applications, and Maintenance of Cyber-Physical Systems
Pierluigi Rea (University of Cagliari, Italy) Erika Ottaviano (University of Cassino and Southern Lazio, Italy) José Machado (University of Minho, Portugal) and Katarzyna Antosz (Rzeszow University of Technology, Poland)
Engineering Science Reference • © 2021 • 314pp • H/C (ISBN: 9781799867210) • US $225.00

Methodologies and Applications of Computational Statistics for Machine Intelligence
Debabrata Samanta (Christ University (Deemed), India) Raghavendra Rao Althar (QMS, First American India, Bangalore, India) Sabyasachi Pramanik (Haldia Institute of Technology, India) and Soumi Dutta (Institute of Engineering and Management, Kolkata, India)
Engineering Science Reference • © 2021 • 277pp • H/C (ISBN: 9781799877011) • US $245.00

Handbook of Research on Software Quality Innovation in Interactive Systems
Francisco Vicente Cipolla-Ficarra (Latin Association of Human-Computer Interaction, Spain & International Association of Interactive Communication, Italy)
Engineering Science Reference • © 2021 • 501pp • H/C (ISBN: 9781799870104) • US $295.00

Handbook of Research on Methodologies and Applications of Supercomputing
Veljko Milutinović (Indiana University, Bloomington, USA) and Miloš Kotlar (University of Belgrade, Serbia)
Engineering Science Reference • © 2021 • 393pp • H/C (ISBN: 9781799871569) • US $345.00

701 East Chocolate Avenue, Hershey, PA 17033, USA
Tel: 717-533-8845 x100 • Fax: 717-533-8661
E-Mail: cust@igi-global.com • www.igi-global.com

Dedicated to our beloved family members and parents.

Table of Contents

Section 1
Human-Computer Interaction and Applications

Priyadarshan Dhabe, Vishwakarma Institute of Technology, India
Vedika Hatekar, Vishwakarma Institute of Technology, India
Sagar Wankhade, Vishwakarma Institute of Technology, India
Ishwari Kulkarni, Vishwakarma Institute of Technology, India
Rishabh Chaudhary, Vishwakarma Institute of Technology, India
Divya Deepak Patwari, Vishwakarma Institute of Technology, India

Tomasz Zawadzki, Arkin University of Creative Arts and Design, Cyprus
Rob Kitchin, Maynooth University, Ireland

Lamya Anoir, Abdelmalek Essaâdi University, Morocco
Mohamed Khaldi, Abdelmalek Essaâdi University, Morocco
Mohamed Erradi, Abdelmalek Essaâdi University, Morocco

Ganesh D. Bhutkar, Vishwakarma Institute of Technology, India
Mishail Shailendra Singh, Vishwakarma Institute of Technology, India
Yohannes Kurniawan, Bina Nusantara University, Indonesia

Section 2
Human-Computer Interaction and Data Science

Detailed Table of Contents

Section 1
Human-Computer Interaction and Applications

Chapter 1
Priyadarshan Dhabe, Vishwakarma Institute of Technology, India
Vedika Hatekar, Vishwakarma Institute of Technology, India
Sagar Wankhade, Vishwakarma Institute of Technology, India
Ishwari Kulkarni, Vishwakarma Institute of Technology, India
Rishabh Chaudhary, Vishwakarma Institute of Technology, India
Divya Deepak Patwari, Vishwakarma Institute of Technology, India

Most of the crimes that happen these days don't reach the police either because nobody reports them or there is no real time proof. The citizens don't have the real-time images, videos related to the crime, and hence, it goes unreported. This chapter presents a real-time video call-based crime reporting system, where the crime victim or an eye witness can start an end-to-end encrypted video call with the police present in the nearest police station. A data science approach is used to find the nearest police station. Once the police officer picks up the call, he will get the location of the crime and nearest route to reach the crime spot. Police can even catch the criminals or handle the crime while it is happening. After the video call ends, a recording of that call will also be available to the police.

Chapter 2
Tomasz Zawadzki, Arkin University of Creative Arts and Design, Cyprus
Rob Kitchin, Maynooth University, Ireland

In this chapter, the authors detail how six commercial products have sought to provide 3D spatial media solutions for the planning domain, and set out their own approach to developing an interactive, multi-platform city information model (CIM) for desktop/WebGL (on a PC), VR (HTC Vive), and MR (Microsoft HoloLens) for Dublin informed by user requirements elicited through interviews with professional urban planners. They demonstrate how a Unity game engine solution can be used to build and manage a multi-platform CIM project from initial stage to the final build. They discuss issues concerning the handling geographic data, data integration, UI development, multi-platform support, interaction types (controllers, gestures, etc.), and potential application. They present core interactive simulations, including shadow analysis, flood resilience, visibility analysis, importing building models, and run-time modeling tool, which are crucial for city information modeling.

Chapter 3

    Lamya Anoir, Abdelmalek Essaâdi University, Morocco
    Mohamed Khaldi, Abdelmalek Essaâdi University, Morocco
    Mohamed Erradi, Abdelmalek Essaâdi University, Morocco

In the face of technological innovation, the field of education has undergone a progressive evolution through the use of technology. Among the techno-pedagogical trend, the authors find the adaptive E-learning which is a new reform. This trend consists in providing personalized learning adapted to individual and collective needs, both in terms of learning pace and content. Through this chapter, they try to link personalization and adaptation. In a first step, they define adaptive e-learning after giving a historical overview of the different adaptive systems from open distance learning to e-learning as well as the components of adaptive systems. In the second part, they define the notion of personalization in adaptive e-learning and the pedagogical scenario. Finally, in the last part of the chapter, they propose an approach to design a personalized and adaptive learning system based on the pedagogical scenarios during the different types of pedagogical activities.

Chapter 4

    Ganesh D. Bhutkar, Vishwakarma Institute of Technology, India
    Mishail Shailendra Singh, Vishwakarma Institute of Technology, India
    Yohannes Kurniawan, Bina Nusantara University, Indonesia

Due to rapid digitization in India, a large section of the Indian population has gained access to fast and affordable internet services such as online food ordering. It offers a fascinating opportunity to research the way Indian people utilize food ordering apps. This chapter provides an interesting study based on contextual inquiry of Indian food ordering app users. The collected data, in interviews and other minute observations, have been documented into five work models, which explain various facets of the food ordering and delivery process and related user experience of Indian users. The identified user-types reveal insights into the unique mindset of Indian users when using and navigating these apps. The analysis of the work models and various top food ordering apps have also highlighted various subtle but important cultural implications of ordering food.

Chapter 5

    Nina Lyons, Technological University Dublin, Ireland
    Matt Smith, Technological University Dublin, Ireland

This chapter outlines an operational definition for a range of experiments that will examine a number of visual aesthetics to identify ways to influence mental models to test how well they will communicate to the user. Utilising principles for semiotics and visual communication, the aim is to create a number of small interaction experiments that will be meaningful and resonate with the user so that they will understand how users want to interact with objects without relying on conventional interaction paradigms. As these experiments will be a mixed methods approach with equal emphasis on quantitative and qualitative data and will utilise a code book of visuals, the operational definition becomes the blueprint that will ensure a consistent procedure that will contain a full description of procedures and actions required to observe and measure the experiments. This will allow for a high level of transparency and replicable set of experiments.

Chapter 6

Software engineering is the extensive study of how to build a software product using software development life cycle stages, beginning with requirement analysis phase to the last phase of testing and maintenance. This approach in the development of software application ensures completion of the project within the stipulated period without compromising quality of the software with effective utilization of resources. The most important is to develop a quality product. Case studies make readers understand the concept in a more impartial and tactile manner; one can make use of this experience in real-life circumstances for providing solutions to the complex problems. The significance of this case study is to represent the authors' experience of developing software by using method of software engineering, understanding how to apply them to build an application. This chapter gives a holistic review of the development of an Android application titled Vaccination Management System (VMS) "Vacc-IT" as a comprehensive case study.

Section 2
Human-Computer Interaction and Data Science

Chapter 7

Diseases such as cancers, pneumonia, and COVID really need to be detected at the right time. If early detection and treatment of such diseases get started as soon as possible, then, probably, patients can be cured completely. Early detection of such diseases is very important, and early-stage imaging can be done based on x-rays, mammography reports, or pathological reports. The purpose of this system is to provide predictions for the different major diseases like cancer and some general occurring diseases. Image processing along with machine learning techniques made it possible to find the chances of occurrence of cancer/tumor/lump in the human body. As per the predicted probability, a patient can make an early decision by discussing it with doctors. The system will predict the most possible disease based on the given symptoms and precautionary measures required to avoid the progression of disease. It will also help doctors analyze the pattern of presence of diseases in the society.

    Evaristus Didik Madyatmadja, Information Systems Department, School of Information
        Systems, Bina Nusantara University, Jakarta, Indonesia
    Astari Karina Rahmah, Information Systems Department, School of Information Systems,
        Bina Nusantara University, Jakarta, Indonesia
    Saphira Aretha Putri, Information Systems Department, School of Information Systems, Bina
        Nusantara University, Jakarta, Indonesia
    Yusdi Ari Pralambang, Information Systems Department, School of Information Systems,
        Bina Nusantara University, Jakarta, Indonesia
    Gede Prama Adhi Wicaksana, Information Systems Department, School of Information
        Systems, Bina Nusantara University, Jakarta, Indonesia
    Muhammad D. Raihan, Information Systems Department, School of Information Systems,
        Bina Nusantara University, Jakarta, Indonesia

The government's efforts in developing electronic-based government services by utilizing information technology are referred to as the concept of e-government. Tangerang City is one of the cities that applies e-government in an application called Tangerang LIVE. In the Tangerang LIVE application, a LAKSA feature is used as a place for complaints from the people of Tangerang. This research was conducted to classify complaint data and determine the priority of groups of complaints received from the LAKSA feature. The technique used to conduct this research is clustering using the unsupervised learning method and the k-means algorithm, which will classify and predict the class for each document. In addition, an analysis of the priority complaint data was carried out based on the group that was received the most. The analysis carried out is to find out the class predictions for each complaint received, and then labeling will be given so that the complaint belongs to a more specific group. The results of the predictions will be displayed in the browser using web services.

    Neelam Pramod Naik, SVKM's Usha Pravin Gandhi College of Arts, Science, and
        Commerce, India

The natural dialog system, Chatbot, plays an important role in business domains by properly answering customer queries. In the pattern matching approach of Chatbot development, the user input is matched with a predefined set of responses. The machine learning approach of Chatbot development uses the principles of natural language processing to learn from conversational content. This study focuses on the performance measurement of pattern-based and machine learning-based Chatbot systems. As per the user point of view, performance measurement parameters are the ability to answer quickly, accurately, and comprehensively; to understand questions clearly; user friendliness; personalization options; ethics followed; and ability to process user feedback. The comprehensiveness of the knowledge base, robustness to handle unexpected input, scalability, and interoperability are some of the parameters considered to evaluate the Chatbot system by expert point of view. In this study, the specially designed Chatbot Usability Questionnaire is used to measure the performance of the implemented Chatbot systems.

Abhijit Banubakode, MET Institute of Computer Science, India
Chhaya Gosavi, MKSSS's Cummins College of Engineering, India
Meghana Satpute, University of Texas at Dallas, USA

Social media has altered the way we interact with the world around us. Social media usage has taken the world by storm the previous couple of years, and the wide variety of users has grown manifold. The analysis of social networks has been given special attention in recent years, mainly because of the success of online social networks and media sharing sites. In intelligence management, social structures need to be revealed to see social behaviour and social change based on the interactions that have taken place between the social members. Social network mining is very important because of various reasons. For example, studying and analysing social networks allows us to understand social behaviours in different contexts. In addition, by analysing the roles of the people involved in the social network, we can understand how information and opinions spread within the network, and who are the most influential people. This chapter presents a methodical review of social media and mining by applying data mining algorithms to study social networks.

Reshma Nitin Pise, Vishwakarma University, India
Bharati Sanjay Ainapure, Vishwakarma University, India

User experience designers have to put in tremendous effort to convey complex information such that it can be easily understood and be visually appealing to the users. In today's world of big data, visualization techniques are essential to analyse massive amounts of complex data and make data-driven decisions. To support better decision making, visualization technologies enable users to uncover hidden patterns. During the COVID-19 pandemic, these techniques have been used as user interface in order to communicate the impact of the pandemic on the public. Considerable effort has been devoted to monitor the spread of the disease across the world and understand the various aspects of the pandemic. This chapter emphasizes the role of the data visualization technique as an effective user interface. Visualization of COVID-19 data is performed in the form of interactive dashboards, which can be beneficial to healthcare users and policy makers to plan the resource allocation and implement strategies to mitigate the effects of the pandemic.

Balasaheb Tarle, MVPS's KBT College of Engineering, India
M. Akkalakshmi, School of Technology, GITAM University, India

Improving classification performance is an essential task in medical data classification. In the current medical data classification technique, if data pre-processing is not performed, the approach is more time consuming and has less classification accuracy. Here, the authors proposed two pre-processing techniques for enhancing the classification performance on medical data. The first pre-processing technique is noise filtering to improve the data quality. The second pre-processing bag of words technique is used for better feature selection. Subsequently, the hybrid fuzzy neural network approach is used for classification to handle data imprecision during classification. This arrangement of data pre-processing and the fuzzy neural classifier method improve classification accuracy.

Chapter 13

Fetal heart rate (FHR) monitoring is done for accessing fetal wellbeing during antepartum and intrapartum phases. Although noninvasive fetal electrocardiogram (NIfECG) is a potential data acquisition method for FHR, extraction of fetal electrocardiogram (ECG) from the abdominal ECG (aECG) is one of the major challenging research areas. This chapter proposed and assessed a method suitable for single channel based on principal component analysis (PCA) for extracting fetal ECG. Maternal R peaks and fetal R peaks were detected using Pan Tomkins algorithm (PTA) and improved Pan Tomkins algorithm (IPTA), respectively. Performance of fetal QRS detection is assessed using two open-access databases available online. The method shows satisfactory performance when compared with similar methods and makes it suitable for using a single channel system.

Foreword

I congratulate all the editors, reviewers, and primarily, authors for successful publication of edited book by eminent International publisher with a year-long and persistent efforts.

This edited volume brings together thirteen chapters from six different countries (USA, Ireland, North Cyprus, Indonesia, Morocco, and India). These book chapters belong to various application domains such as health care, e-commerce, social networking, communication, and e-learning. This diversity makes the volume stand out from most books for its interdisciplinary approach in Human-Computer Interaction (HCI) and Data Science. The editors have made an effort to bring together research perspectives and voices from renowned Universities and Institutions across the globe. The edited book has the word 'handbook' in the title and it is a vital reference book based research experiments and experiences of international research community in the field of HCI and Data Science.

This edited book will be useful to a wide range of readers and researchers with different aspirations and requirements in the pursuit of knowledge. The faculty, research scholars, industry professionals, undergraduate and post-graduate students from Computer Science, Artificial Intelligence, Data Science, Information Systems, Social Sciences, and related disciplines, will be definitely interested in this book.

I hope, the lessons derived from these meticulously selected book chapters will be definitely useful to the researchers and the practitioners to percolate ICT knowledge through the life-changing everyday applications.

Rajiv Dharaskar
Indian Institute of Information Technology (IIIT), Kottayam, India
February 2022

Preface

This edited book is focused on major research initiatives from academic community as well as the industry involving faculty, researchers, professionals, research scholars, post-graduate, and undergraduate students. A broad range of industry professionals and technology users will also find this book useful, and so, will the enthusiastic graduate students, who are excited to study data science for interdisciplinary application development. From the last two decades, researchers are looking at the Human-Computer Interaction (HCI) as prominent research area with major real-world applications from various domains such as health care, e-commerce, social networking, communication, automobile, and e-learning. HCI is multidisciplinary field with an intrinsic relationship as a subfield to computer science. Most interactive computing systems have user-centred design and interact with users in their context of existence or the work.

Data science has been playing a vital role in almost all major fields such as finance, marketing, health care, social networking, automobile, e-learning, e-commerce and many more. Data Science, one of the most significant advances of this century, refers to an emerging area related to the collection, preparation, analysis, visualization, management, and preservation of both - structured and unstructured data. To discover, extract, compile, process, analyse, interpret, and visualize data, data science incorporates several technologies and academic disciplines. These include Statistics, Computer Science, Database Management, Computer Graphics, Artificial Intelligence, Machine Learning, Natural Language Processing, and others.

Thus, nowadays many of the researchers are interested in developing IT applications, which are user-driven with focus on issues, which can be addressed using Data Science. User-driven research and Data Science have gained much attention from many private, public sector, government organizations, and research institutes. This book covers a vast range of topics critical to the field of HCI and Data Science in an easy-to-understand language.

This edited book consists of chapters authored by researchers and academicians in the field of HCI, Data Science and interrelated disciplines from six different countries – USA, Ireland, North Cyprus, Indonesia, Morocco, and India. These chapters are reviewed by expert reviewers from 8 different countries – USA, Scotland (UK), Italy, Indonesia, Jordan, Uganda, Afghanistan and India. Each chapter has an abstract, keywords, introduction, background, main focus, methodology, results / recommendations, future research directions, references and additional reading. Readers can determine their interest level in any chapter quickly based on the abstract and keywords.

The first book chapter presents a real time video call-based crime reporting system, in which the crime victim or an eye witness, can start an end-to-end encrypted video call with the police present in the nearest police station. A data science approach is used to find the nearest police station. Once the police officer picks up the call, he/she will get the location of the crime and the nearest route to reach the crime spot. Police can even catch the criminals or handle the crime while it is happening. After the video call ends, a recording of that call will also be available to the police.

In the second chapter, authors have provided details about how six commercial products have sought to provide 3D spatial media solutions for the planning domain, and set out their own approach to developing an interactive, multi-platform City Information Model (CIM) for desktop / WebGL (on a PC), VR (HTC Vive) and MR (Microsoft HoloLens) for Dublin, informed by user requirements elicited through interviews with professional urban planners. They have demonstrated how a Unity game engine solution can be used to build and manage a multi-platform CIM project from initial stage to the final build. They have presented a core interactive simulations, including shadow analysis, flood resilience, visibility analysis, importing building models, and run-time modeling tool, which are crucial for City Information Modeling.

In the third chapter, authors have tried to link personalization and adaptation in e-learning. In a first step, they have defined adaptive e-learning after giving a historical overview of the different adaptive systems from open distance learning to e-learning as well as the components of adaptive systems. In the second part, they have discussed the notion of personalization in adaptive e-learning and the pedagogical scenario. Finally, in the last part of the chapter, they have proposed an approach to design a personalized and adaptive learning system based on the scenarios during the different types of pedagogical activities.

The fourth book chapter provides an interesting study based on contextual inquiry of Indian food ordering app users. The collected data, in interviews and other minute observations have been documented into five work models, which explain various facets of the food ordering and delivery process and related user experience of Indian users. The identified user types reveal insights into the unique mindset of Indian users when using and navigating these apps. The analysis of the work models and, various top food ordering apps has also highlighted several subtle, but important cultural implications in the process of ordering food.

The fifth chapter outlines an operational definition for a range of experiments that will examine a number of visual aesthetics to identify ways to influence mental models to test how well they will communicate to the user. Utilizing principles for semiotics and visual communication, the aim is to create a number of small interaction experiments that will be meaningful and resonating with the user, so that they will understand how users want to interact with objects without relying on conventional interaction paradigms. As these experiments will be a mixed method approach with equal emphasis on quantitive and qualitative data and will utilize a code book of visuals, the operational definition becomes the blueprint that will ensure a consistent procedure that will contain a full description of procedures and actions required to observe and measure the experiments, this will allow for a high level of transparency and replicable set of experiments.

The sixth book chapter gives a holistic review of the development of an android application titled Vaccination Management System (VMS) – 'Vacc-IT' as a comprehensive case study. Case studies make readers understand the concept in more impartial and tactile manner; one can make use of this experience in real-life circumstances for providing solutions to the complex problems. The significance of this case study is to represent authors' experience of developing software by using method of software engineering, understanding how to apply them to build an application.

The seventh chapter proposes a system which provides predictions for the different major diseases like cancer and some general occurring diseases. Image processing along with Machine Learning techniques made it possible to find the chances of occurrence of cancer / tumor / lump in the human body. As per the predicted probability, a patient can make an early decision by discussing it with doctors. The system will predict the most possible disease based on the given symptoms. The precautionary measures are also suggested to avoid the aggression of disease. It will also help doctors analyze the pattern of presence of diseases in the society.

The eighth chapter presents a research to classify complaint data and determine the priority of groups of complaints received from the LAKSA feature. The technique used to conduct the research is clustering using the Unsupervised Learning method and the K-Means algorithm, which will classify and predict the class for each document. In addition, an analysis of the priority complaint data was carried out based on the group that was received the most. The analysis carried out is to find out the class predictions for each complaint received, and then labeling will be given so that the complaint belongs to a more specific group. The results of the predictions will be displayed in the browser using web services.

The ninth chapter focuses on the performance measurement of pattern-based and machine learning-based chatbot systems. As per the user point of view, performance measurement parameters are: ability to answer quickly, accurately, and comprehensively, to understand question clearly, user friendliness, personalization options, ethics followed and ability to process user feedback. The comprehensiveness of the knowledge base, robustness to handle unexpected input, scalability and interoperability are some of the parameters considered to evaluate the chatbot system by expert point of view. In this study, specially designed chatbot usability questionnaire is used to measure the performance of the implemented chatbot systems.

The tenth chapter presents a methodical review of social media and mining by applying data mining algorithms to study social networks. Social media has altered the way we interact with the world around us. Social media usage has taken the world by storm and in the previous couple of years, the wide variety of users has grown manifold. The analysis of social networks has been given special attention in recent years, mainly because of the success of online social networks and media sharing sites. In Intelligence management, social structures need to be revealed to see social behavior and social change based on the interactions that have taken place between the social members. Social network mining is very important because of various reasons. For example, studying and analyzing social networks allows us to understand social behaviors in different contexts. In addition, by analyzing the roles of the people involved in the social network, we can understand how information and opinions spread within the network, and who the most influential people are. This paper presents a methodical review of social media and mining by applying data mining algorithms to study social networks.

The eleventh chapter emphasizes the role of data visualization technique in effective user interface design. Visualization of COVID19 data is performed in the form of interactive dashboards which can be beneficial to healthcare users and policy makers to plan the resource allocation and implement strategies to mitigate the effects of the pandemic. User experience designers have to put tremendous efforts to convey complex information such that it can be easily understood and visually appealing to the users. In today's world of Big Data, visualization techniques are essential to analyze massive amount of complex data and make data-driven decisions. During COVID 19 pandemic, these techniques are being used in user interface design in order to communicate the impact of pandemic to the public. Considerable effort has been devoted to monitor the spread of the disease across the world and understand the various aspects of the pandemic.

The twelfth chapter has proposed two pre-processing techniques for enhancing the classification performance on medical data. The first pre-processing technique is noise filtering to improve the data quality. The second pre-processing 'Bag of Words' technique is used for better feature selection. Subsequently, the hybrid Fuzzy-Neural Network approach is used for classification to handle data imprecision during classification. This arrangement of data pre-processing and the Fuzzy Neural Classifier method improve classification accuracy.

The thirteenth chapter has proposed and assessed a method suitable for single channel based on Principal Component Analysis (PCA) for extracting fetal ECG. Maternal R peaks and fetal R peaks detected using Pan Tomkins Algorithm (PTA) and Improved Pan Tomkins Algorithm (IPTA) respectively. Performance of fetal QRS detection is assessed using two open-access databases available online. The method has shown satisfactory performance when compared with similar method and make it suitable for using single channel system.

Acknowledgment

"On top of the world" that's our situation while editing this book, this is the only page where we have the opportunity to express our emotions and gratitude from the bottom of our hearts.

Someone had rightly said,
"Dreams comes only when put in Action"

Honestly speaking, we realized the same during the progress of our book editing. Behind every success, there is hidden resource, the power of which is beyond comparison. Timely reminders and keen interest of IGI Global publisher provided a constant guidance from time-to-time without which, this book project would have never completed on-time.

Being on the same line, we express deep sense of gratitude towards honorable members of the editorial advisory board and reviewer board for their timely guidance and support.

We specially thank all the authors, who proactively contributed to this book. Their patience about submitting multiple revisions from time-to-time motivated us to complete this quality work successfully.

We would also like to take this opportunity and thank all the enthusiastic users and experts involved in the research work presented in evocative book chapters. We extend our thanks to the funding agencies, which supported few selected research projects presented in this edited book.

We express our gratitude towards Bina Nusantara (BINUS) University, Jakarta; MET Institute of Computer Science, Mumbai; Vishwakarma Institute of Technology (VIT), Pune and MKSSS's Cummins College of Engineering for Women, Pune for motivating us to aim for such thought-provoking book project.

We thank Board of Studies (BOS): Computer Engineering and BOS: Information Technology, Savitribai Phule Pune University (SPPU), and BOS: Master of Computer Applications, Mumbai University.

We also thank members of Whatsapp groups - Doctoral Super Group – Computer Engineering of SPPU and PICT ME 2001 – 2003 group for helping us to reach out every corner of the teaching community.

We would like to express love and gratitude to our beloved family members and parents. Without their tremendous motivation and support, this book journey was impossible.

Finally, we are thankful to the heaven's almighty giving strength during this endeavor.

Yours Obediently,

Abhijit Narayanrao Banubakode
Ganesh Dattatray Bhutkar

Yohannes Kurniawan
Chhaya Santosh Gosavi

Section 1
Human–Computer Interaction and Applications

Chapter 1
Video Call–Based Real–Time Crime Reporting System

Priyadarshan Dhabe
Vishwakarma Institute of Technology, India

Ishwari Kulkarni
Vishwakarma Institute of Technology, India

Vedika Hatekar
Vishwakarma Institute of Technology, India

Rishabh Chaudhary
Vishwakarma Institute of Technology, India

Sagar Wankhade
Vishwakarma Institute of Technology, India

Divya Deepak Patwari
Vishwakarma Institute of Technology, India

ABSTRACT

Most of the crimes that happen these days don't reach the police either because nobody reports them or there is no real time proof. The citizens don't have the real-time images, videos related to the crime, and hence, it goes unreported. This chapter presents a real-time video call-based crime reporting system, where the crime victim or an eye witness can start an end-to-end encrypted video call with the police present in the nearest police station. A data science approach is used to find the nearest police station. Once the police officer picks up the call, he will get the location of the crime and nearest route to reach the crime spot. Police can even catch the criminals or handle the crime while it is happening. After the video call ends, a recording of that call will also be available to the police.

INTRODUCTION

There is a huge surge in the number of crimes which are taking place in India. Each new day, a different type of crime emerges. The main job of the police force is the identification and recognition of the criminals (Rasanayagam et al., 2018). But the cops face difficulties in finding the location of crime when it is happening and the correct evidences related to the crime. New advancements in technology are proving helpful to police to prevent the crime incidents and to enhance the overall performance of the police (Byrne & Marx, 2011). Most people don't find it convenient to go to the police station to re-

DOI: 10.4018/978-1-7998-9121-5.ch001

port the crime. In such cases, handheld devices like mobile phones and tablets can prove to be a helpful tool in the effective and online reporting of these varied crime incidents (Mcclees, 2019; Sekhri, 2020).

Table 1. Crimes not reported and their reasons

Type of Crime	Not Reported	Dealt with in Another Way/ Personal Matter	Not Important Enough to Report
All crimes	58	20	27
Rape	65	20	6
Robbery	41	20	13
Aggravated assault	44	31	16
Personal larceny	41	17	24
Theft	67	16	31

Source: *(https://www.nap.edu/read/18605/chapter/5#36)*

Our study, Table 1 shows that many crimes are not reported and their reasons in India. It shows the crime data between 2006 and 2010 in percentage. It shows the percentage of crime going unreported. Almost 58% of the total crimes had not been reported to the police. 20% of the cases were solved personally and 27% thought that it was not important enough to report the crime to the police. Our system makes it possible to report the crime in an easy manner using mobiles and thus can substantially increases reporting.

In most of the crime scenes, police find it difficult to get a real time proof of the crime and as a result the investigations keep on going for years and the criminals roam around freely, committing more crimes. This difficulty is also solved in our approach, since a complete video of the crime is instantly available to the police for investigation. Thus, it reduces investigation time also. As per our study, the authors felt a need of a system through which the police can see the crime incident in real time without even being present at the crime spot and even can handle the crime while it is going on. To solve the above problem, the authors of this chapter proposed a real time, video call based, crime reporting system. There would be two mobile application modules. A person passing nearby a crime incident (eye witness) can directly start an end-to-end encrypted video call with the police present in nearest police station and the location of the user will also be sent to the police. The police can see the crime going on with the help of this video call and they can reach the crime spot immediately and control the situation in a better way. There are two users of this system

1. Local public (common people) – who wants to report a crime incident.
2. Police officers – who will handle the crime. They would be provided with a User Identity (UserID) and Password by their respective police stations in which they are working.

BACKGROUND

The authors did some literature survey about the crime reporting system available till date and the pros and cons of these highly correlated systems are discussed below.

- **Mobile Solution for Metropolitan Crime Detection and Reporting:** This paper presents a solution for Crime Detection (Agangiba, 2013). There is a mobile application module which is used by the general public and the police. The information about the criminal activities is uploaded to the server by the police and some other information is uploaded by the general public remotely using the mobile application module. The police can upload information like wanted list of the criminals, list of missing items and latest arrests made by the police. The general public can upload data like found items information, data of the whereabouts of people who are in the police wanted list, information of criminal activities which are currently taking place. If the general public finds the missing item which present in the list, they can report the police about it. Or if they see the criminal who is mentioned in the wanted criminal list, they can immediately report the police.
- **Public Crime Reporting and Monitoring System Model Using GSM (Global System for Mobile Communication) and GIS (Geographic Information System) Technologies:** This paper presents a client-server architecture based system (Mwiya et al., 2015). The user reports the crime through a mobile application module and the nearest police station receives this notification as a pop-up on the screen. A two way Short Messaging Service kicks in. The police officer receives the phone number of the user and the user receives the phone number of the police station. The police can view reported crime incidents, assign reported crime incidents, analyze reported crime trends, call crime reporter. On the other hand, the citizens can create an account in the mobile application module, report a crime, view reported crime.
- **An Automatic Crime Reporting and Immediate Response System:** The proposed system uses a mobile application module that allows users to report crime anonymously or provide their personal information if they choose to (Mkhwanazi et al., 2020). When the user opens the app, he is asked to choose his location on Google maps and enter his personal details (if he wishes to). The user can send a photograph or video of the crime scene to the police along with some description of the crime scene. The crime reports will be received by a web interface hosted on a web server which will be present in the police stations. Case numbers will also be generated by this web interface. A device, developed using Raspberry Pi and Microsoft Internet of Things Asp.net will be present in the police vans (Smith, 2018). Whenever a crime is reported, the police officer will get an alert on their web server.
- **Ecops: An Online Crime Reporting and Management System for Riyadh City:** This paper presents an online crime reporting system in the form of an online application (Tabassum et al., 2018). This system allows the individuals from the city to log complaints and also helps the police in identifying the criminals. The citizens file an online complaint against the criminal and upload evidences and then the police officers start the investigation with the help of the information and evidences provided. The application is developed using Hypertext Preprocessor (PHP) and the database used is My Structured Query Language (MySQL). The different services available for the citizens are: missing person, stolen car/mobile phone, unidentified person/dead body and so on.

- **Robust Real-Time Violence Detection in Video Using CNN (Convolutional Neural Networks) and LSTM (Long short-term memory):** This system is used to detect violence in the video using deep learning (Abdali et al., 2019). The proposed system uses CNN as a spatial feature extractor. Adam optimizer is also used to increase the accuracy of the model. The output layer is a dense layer with sigmoid activation function that shows the probability of violence detection in the particular video. This system is highly robust and accurate. This system can also be used to detect crowd violence.

From the above literature survey, the following findings/conclusions can be drawn:

Finding 1: In the above papers, there is no real-time proof of the crime. Videos and images are used as crime proof. But they can be fake and thus, unreliable.

Finding 2: Most of the systems mentioned in the literature survey have used Short Messaging Service (SMS). But this SMS system cannot be used in emergency situations since it may happen that the police may check the SMS after some time when the crime has been completed. Thus, it makes impossible to handle the crime when it is going on using this SMS system. Hence, it may not prove beneficial in such scenarios. So, we felt a need for a system that can help the police to get real-time data of the crime incident.

Finding 3: The above literature survey shows the current location of the user but none of them have used the Location Tracking feature (tracking the location of the victim/user).

Finding 4: Call bouncing feature is not provided by any of the above systems, considered in the literature survey. Hence, we felt a need to include this feature in our system. This feature will ensure that the victim will be able to call any police officer present in a range of 30 kilometers from his current location and the call would not get disconnected just after making a single call. The user doesn't have to make a call to each and every police station separately, which saves his/her time.

Finding 5: None of the systems mentioned above have implemented the call recording feature. We felt the need to implement this feature because it proves helpful for investigating the case in future. Also, the recording serves as a proof of the crime incident.

As per our findings from the literature survey, we strongly believe that, a real-time end-to-end encrypted video call between a citizen reporter and the nearest police station can overcome the above drawbacks. Also a stored recording of the video call can be helpful to the police in further investigation of the case post the crime. If the police gets the exact location and the shortest path to reach the crime spot, it can be of huge benefit to them to reach the crime spot quickly. Location tracking is a useful and unique feature which is needed for better crime dealing. With this, the police officer can figure out the estimated time to reach the crime spot.

METHODOLOGY

The proposed system works as follows. Consider there is a crime going on somewhere and there is a person who is passing nearby who wants to report the crime to the police. The person will quickly open the application module and start an end-to-end-encrypted video call with the police officer present in the nearest police station. The nearest police station can be decided by using a data science algorithm.

If the call is not picked up by the police officer who is present in the nearest police station, it will be, automatically, transferred to the next nearest police station. In this way, the call will keep on bouncing till all the police stations within a range of 30 kilometers from the crime scene are covered. If anyone of the police officer, picks up the video call, video call would be started and police can see what is happening at the crime spot. For ex: who is the criminal, which type of weapons criminals are using (ex: in a murder, is it a gun or knife. If it a gun, then which type of gun it is and so on). The proposed system also has a feature of *Location Tracking* As soon as the police officer picks up the video call, the location of the person who started the video call that is the citizen reporter, will also be sent to the police along with the highlighted shortest route to reach the crime spot. It will keep a track of the location of the user.

Once the video call gets completed, a recording of that video call would also be available with the police. It would prove very helpful to them while doing investigation of the case in future. From the recording, they would get a clear idea about the number of people involved in the crime, what do they look like, time and spot of the crime and so on. The local public would be able to open the application module directly without having to register or login. The reason for not adding this feature is to keep the identity of the person making the video call anonymous.

The proposed system has 2 mobile application modules, one for the local public and one for the police officers. The intention behind creating two separate application modules was to increase security by allowing only the police to access the recording and other sensitive data. The video call is end-to-encrypted, which would not allow any third party to join the call or interfere with it, which makes the entire system more secure.

This system works properly even if the application module on the police officer's side is not running either in the foreground or in the background. In that case, the police officer will get a notification about the call in the notifications bar. As soon as the police officer taps on the notification, the video call would be started.

The Proposed System

Figure 1 depicts the working of the proposed system. The working is elaborated in the methodology section.

Figure 1. Working of the proposed system

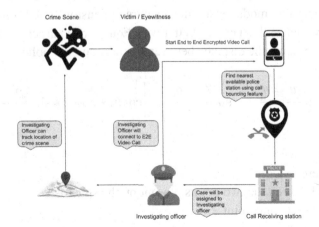

Features of the Proposed System

1. **Real time end-to-end encrypted video call**: The video call which the user would start with the police, would be end-to-end encrypted (Lewis et al., 2017). End-to-end encryption keeps the system entirely secure and free from external threats (Thakkar, 2021). Any third person, would not be able to interfere, even if he tries to. To implement this feature, Jitsi framework is used, which is an open source video conferencing software, which makes our video call fully encrypted and adds more security (*Jitsi meet security & privacy*, n.d.). The quality of this video call is MPEG-4 Part 14 (MP4). A unique feature of mp4 is that it has high video quality and requires less storage.

    The main reason why the citizens don't report the crime to the police is they feel that if they report the crime to the police their identity would be disclosed and then they would have to go to the court whenever the court calls them and act like an eye-witness of the crime. Even if a crime is going on, they would just ignore it and get busy with their own work. With the help of this feature, whenever the user starts a video call, his identity would be kept anonymous. So the user doesn't have to worry about disclosing his/her identity. In this way, the problem of crimes not getting reported to the police would be solved.

2. **Call bouncing functionality**: This is a unique feature which has not been implemented yet in any previous systems. The transferring of the video call from one police station to the next would prove to be a very essential feature in an emergency situation. For this feature, the current location of the user is stored in the Firebase Real-time Database. The location of the police stations (latitude and longitude) are also stored. To get the nearest police station, the Haversine distance formula is used.

    In the field of Data Science, most of the available datasets store the location related data in the form of latitude-longitude pair. Euclidean distance is useful to calculate distance between two points on a flat surface like the Cartesian plain. But it can't be used to find out the distance between two locations on the surface of a sphere (example: earth) since the Earth is not flat. Hence the authors have used Haversine formula. This formula is very useful to find places which are located within some radius from the current location. It is used to find the shortest distance between two points on the surface of a sphere (for ex: earth's surface) (Kettle, 2017). While working with raw location data in the field of Data Science, a basic requirement is to calculate distance between those locations. Calculating the distance provides an edge to the Machine learning model by adding an extra dimension called "distance" which improves the clarity and helps to visualize the data in a better way. Equation (1) describes the *Haversine formula*. This formula is used to compute the distance between the user and the police station.

$$d = 2r \arcsin \left\{ sqrt \left(\left[(\sin \frac{(\theta_2 - \theta_1)}{2}) * (\sin \frac{\theta_2 - \theta_1}{2}) \right] + \left[\cos \theta 1 * \cos \theta 2 * \sin \frac{a2 - a1}{2} * \sin \frac{a2 - a1}{2} \right] \right) \right\}$$

r - Radius of the sphere
d - Shortest distance between the two points present on the sphere
$\theta 1$, $\theta 2$ - Latitudes of point1 and point 2

α1, α2 - Longitudes of point1 and point 2

Table 2. Co-ordinates of various police stations

Police station location	Latitude	Longitude	Distance from the user's current location
Dabki Road,Akola	20.7002	77.0082	600 meters
Jawahar Nagar,Akola	20.69	77.08	3.4 kilometers
Jatharpeth,Akola	20.72	77.02	4.0 kilometers
Ganesh Nagar, Murtijapur	20.729	77.35	43 kilometers
Babhulgaon	20.85	77.19	12 kilometers

Table 2 consists of all the police stations which are present in the user's town (only 5 police stations are added just to keep it small. Any number of police stations can be added depending on the need). The authors collected the actual data of 5 police stations, in the town of one of the co-author. The current location of the user is latitude = 20.7099 and longitude = 76.9914.

Figure 2 shows a map, consisting of few blue dots which represent the police stations. The distance between the user and these 5 police stations (mentioned in Table 2) is calculated using *Haversine distance* formula (equation (1)). Using this formula, it becomes easy to find the nearest police station, next nearest police station and so on. Those police stations which are lying inside the circle are the ones within a range of 30 kilometers from the user's location. And those lying outside are beyond 30 kilometers. So a list of police stations, which are within a range of 30 kilometers from the user's location, would be displayed in ascending order on the user's application module. In this case, only Dabki Road Akola, Jawahar Nagar Akola, Jatharpeth Akola and Babhulgaon police stations would be visible to the user on his home screen. Once the user starts the video call, it would first be delivered to the nearest police station. It would keep on ringing for 45 seconds. If no one picks up the call, it is then transferred to the next nearest police station and so on till someone picks it up.

Figure 2. Calculation of distance using Haversine distance formula

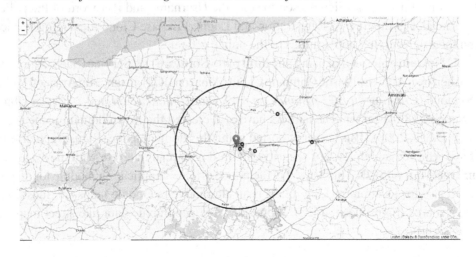

3. **Call Recording:** The recording of the video call would prove beneficial to the police in identifying and recognizing the criminals in future and also to figure out the weapons used by them and other necessary details. This recording would only be available on the police application module and not on the local public application module for security reasons. This recording is stored on Cloud Storage in compressed format. It has a good clarity and it is in the MP4 format. On clicking the *History tab*, the police can get a list of all the recordings and also the *timestamp* of the recording.

4. **Location Tracking**: Once the video call starts, the police will get the location of the person making the video call and the shortest path from the police station to the person would also be highlighted, so that they can reach the crime spot immediately and handle the situation there. There would be a continuous tracking of the user location. The police officer would be guided with the proper directions to reach the spot. The Firebase Cloud Firestore service is used to store the data of nearby police stations. Geolocator is a flutter plugin which is used to retrieve current location (latitude-longitude) of the victim. Open Source Routing Machine (OSRM) is used to help the police find the real time directions to track exact location of the user/victim.

Technologies Used

1. **Flutter:** It is used for mobile application development - both Android and iPhone Operating System (iOS) from a single codebase (*Flutter documentation*, n.d.). With flutter, there is no need to write a separate Swift code for iOS and Java code for Android. A single codebase, written in dart, is used for both. It has a rich and customizable user interface. The performance of the application modules which are built using flutter is good than other user interface development platforms for ex: React Native and Android. Everything is a widget in flutter. It also has a hot reload feature, which helps to fix bugs easily and also allows to do quick experimentation (Josephine, 2019). Hot reload saves the time by building only those files which have been modified.

2. **Firebase:** It is a real time database which uses Not Only SQL (NoSQL). There are different services provided by Firebase for example: Cloud Firestore, Cloud Storage, Real-time Database, Cloud Functions, Authentication and many more (*Accelerate and scale app development without managing infrastructure*, n.d.). For storing the recording of the video call, the Cloud Storage service is used. For storing the other details like the police stations locations, the Real-time Database is used. Firebase Authentication service is used to store the Username and Password of the police officer which is needed at the time of Registration and Login. Firebase Cloud messaging service is used to send the call receiving notifications to the police officer.

3. **AWS EC2 instance:** Instead of using any third party Software as a Service (SaaS), the authors have created their own Amazon Elastic Compute Cloud (Amazon EC2) instance on Amazon Web Services (AWS) cloud (*Creating an EC2 instance on AWS with Ubuntu 18.04*, n.d.). It is an Ubuntu Long Term Support 18.0.4 server. The authors have also created their own domain name ("cybercrew. online") (Doyle, 2008). This server is hosted using this domain name. By using their own server, they have achieved a high level of security. No third party can interfere with the system.

4. **OpenStreetMap (OSM):** This is used in the police officer's application module for displaying the maps and also for location tracking. OSM is an alternative to Google maps and most importantly it is open source (Samsudeen, 2020). It provides free geographic data like street maps and route planning services.

SOLUTIONS AND RECOMMENDATIONS

This section of the chapter consists of the user interface of the proposed system. The user interface has been designed keeping in mind the 'Golden Rules of User Interface Design' (*Shneiderman's Eight Golden Rules of Interface Design*, n.d.).

Figure 3 shows the Home Page of the user. It shows the list of all the police stations which are within a range of 30 kilometers from his current location. These police stations are arranged in ascending order, which means, the nearest police station is present at the first place, the second nearest at the second place and so on. Once the victim clicks on the video icon present at the bottom right corner, it will start an end-to-end encrypted video call with the nearest police station (the one listed at the first position). In the Figure 3, the authors have used one of the rules of the Golden Rules of User Interface Design – Reduce Short-Term Memory Load (Rule 8) which states that the user interface should be kept simple by making use of icons and visual elements instead of inserting huge information on the interface. There are multiple icons used here like the location icon, the video call icon, etc. which makes the interface user friendly.

Figure 3. User's home screen

Figure 4. Police officer login screen

Figure 4 shows the Police Officer Login screen. He will have to enter his User ID and Password, which would be provided by the police station to him. If the User ID and Password is valid, he would be displayed a success message – "Login Success". Once he logs in successfully, he can see the History and Find case tab along with the logout icon on the top right corner. In the Figure 4, the authors have used one of the rules of the Golden Rules of User Interface Design – Offer Simple Error Handling (Rule 5). If the user enters an invalid User ID or Password while logging in, he would be displayed a message saying "User ID or Password is incorrect".

Figure 5 shows the notification displayed to the user once he clicks on the video call icon. The notification contains the Report ID and the name of the police station to which the video call is sent. Important details of video call are mentioned on the pop up so that user is aware of everything. "End crime report" is highlighted in red so that the user can notice it quickly and end the crime report if he wants to. Every screen includes corresponding icons so that even if user is unable to read the information/guidelines present on the individual screens in emergency situation, he can still check the icons and take decisions quickly. In the Figure 5, the authors have used one of the rules of the Golden Rules of User Interface Design – Offer Informative Feedback (Rule 3). The user will get a feedback immediately in the form of this notification so that he will get an assurance that the video call has started.

Figure 6 shows the screen which appears on the police officer's application module through which he can either accept or reject the call. If he rejects the call, the call would be transferred to the next nearest police station. If he accepts the call, he would be asked to start the screen recording and then a video call would be started with the victim. After the video call gets started, the police officer can see the crime happening at the spot.

Figure 7 shows the video call between the police officer and the user. The clarity of the video call is good which can help the police officer in getting a clear view of the crime. For the video call feature, Jitsi framework is used. There are multiple features included for the video call. The features include mute oneself –if the victim doesn't want the voice to be heard, text message feature – if the victim/eyewitness is unable to speak due to some reason he can type his message in the chat box. The three dots present on the bottom right contains all the features.

Figure 5. Notification displayed to the user

Figure 6. Call receiving screen

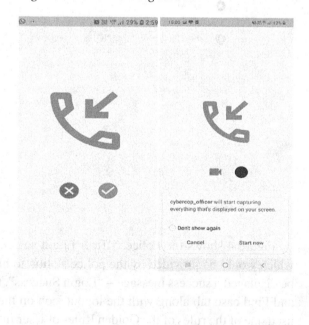

Figure 7. Video call started

Figure 8 displays the components of Find case tab and History tab. In the find case tab, the police officer will have to enter the Report ID in the search bar and the details of the report will be displayed. The details include Report ID, Police Station ID, Date and Time of the crime. In the History tab, all the reports under that particular police station would be displayed.

Figure 8. Find case and history tab components

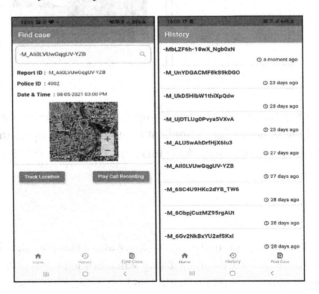

Figure 9(a) & 9(b) shows two important features. Figure 9(a) shows the real-time location tracking feature. After the user clicks on the Track Location button as shown in Figure 8, this screen would be displayed. The right tick mark on the map represents the location of the crime scene and the icon with car represents the location of the police officer. The shortest path to reach the crime spot is highlighted with a black line. With the help of this, the police officer would be able to track the location of the user (victim/eye-witness). Figure 9(b) shows the call recording feature. Once the video call is completed, this recording would be available only on the police officer application module under the History tab and not on the user application module. At first, the recording would be stored on the police officer's device in a compressed form and then after 3-4 minutes, this local copy would be deleted and the recording would be stored on the Firebase Cloud Storage. The format of the recording would be MP4.

Figure 9. Real-time location tracking and Call Recording

Figure 10 shows the notification received to pick up the call. The notification says 'Call Received. Tap to receive the call'. If the police officer's application module is not open, then he will get this type of notification in the notifications bar. On clicking this notification, the video call would get started.

USABILITY TESTING

Usability Testing is an important aspect in the field of software development. It is mostly done to check the friendliness of the software. It focuses on checking whether the user is able to understand the software, is he/she facing any issue while working with it and is the interface easy to understand. The most important aspect of usability testing is to find out the time required by the users to complete various tasks (Pawar & Bhutkar, 2021). The authors have computed the time required by various users while performing different tasks. The results are computed in tabular form below. There are total 5 tasks which are further divided into multiple sub-tasks. The participant users are 10 students from an Engineering college in India and they have not used this application module before.

Figure 10. Call received notification

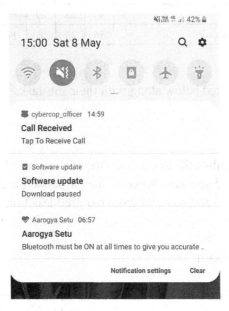

Table 3 shows the benchmark duration for various tasks. Task 1 is for the user application module and the remaining tasks (Task 2 to 5) are for the police officer application module. The results obtained from the participant users are tabulated below.

Table 3. Benchmark duration for various tasks

Task Number	Task	Benchmark Duration (In Seconds)
User Application		
1	Start a video call	5
Police Officer Application		
2	Login	15
3	Accept/Reject the call	5
4	Find a past report	30
5	Get recording and location of ongoing case	11

Table 4 shows the time required by the participant users for each task. Some participants took more time as compared to the benchmark time and others took less time.

Table 4. Task completion time for the selected tasks by each of the participant users

Task Number and Name	Completion time for participants (In Seconds)									
	A	B	C	D	E	F	G	H	I	J
Start a video call	10	8	12	7	4	15	6	11	20	16
Login	35	48	20	17	10	40	23	47	18	31
Accept/reject the call	4	10	6	3	8	11	2	5	6	3
Find a past report	45	38	29	35	40	56	21	26	33	37
Get Recording and Location of ongoing case	16	10	8	17	5	12	6	11	12	8

The five tasks involved are listed below along with their sub-tasks.

Task 1: Starting a video call

In this task, there is only one sub-task - Locate the video call icon and click on it. The benchmark time which is required for this task is 5 seconds. Some of the participant users required more time than the benchmark (example: 20 seconds) and some of them required less time than the benchmark (example: 4 seconds).

Task 2: Login (for the police officer)

There is only one sub-task for this task - Enter Username and Password in the required fields and click on the Login button. The benchmark time required for this task is 15 seconds although one of the participant users took 48 seconds to complete this task.

Task 3: Accept/reject the call

This task involves just one sub-task - locating accept and reject icon and then clicking the appropriate icon. The benchmark time is just 5 seconds, but some participant users also took a minimum of 2 seconds and a maximum of 11 seconds to complete this task.

Task 4: Find a past report

Followings are the steps/sub-tasks involved in this task:

Step 1: Locate and click on the History tab on the Home Screen
Step 2: Type the Case ID in the search box.
Step 3: Click on the required recording to play it.

Table 5 shows the completion time taken by the participant users for completion of the different sub-tasks/steps of task 4. Step 2 comparatively requires more time than Step 1 and Step 3. The maximum time required for Step 2 is 36 seconds.

Table 5. Completion time for the sub-tasks of task 4

Participant	Stepwise Completion Time (in Seconds)			Task Completion Time (In Seconds)
	Step 1	Step 2	Step 3	
A	18	22	5	45
B	12	20	6	38
C	7	17	5	29
D	8	24	3	35
E	12	21	7	40
F	15	36	5	56
G	8	11	2	21
H	9	13	4	26
I	10	17	6	33
J	8	25	4	37

Task 5: Get recording and location of ongoing case

Followings are the steps/sub-tasks involved in this task:

Step 1: Locate and click on the Find Case tab on the Home screen
Step 2: To get the victim's current location – click on the Track Location button
Step 3: To play the video call recording of the current case – click on the Play Call Recording button

Table 6 shows the time required for the completion of various sub-tasks of task 5. The minimum time required to complete task 5 is 5 seconds as opposed to the maximum time of 17 seconds.

Table 6. Completion time for the sub-tasks of task 5

Participant	Stepwise Completion Time (in Seconds)			Task Completion Time (In Seconds)
	Step 1	Step 2	Step 3	
A	5	6	5	16
B	6	2	2	10
C	3	3	2	8
D	9	5	3	17
E	2	1	2	5
F	7	2	3	12
G	3	1	2	6
H	5	3	3	11
I	3	5	4	12
J	3	2	3	8

Figure 11 shows the graphical representation of the time required (in seconds) for completion of various tasks by different participant users. From the figure, the following conclusion can be made - Participant I took the maximum time for task 1 completion, Participant B took the maximum time for completing task 2, Participant F took the maximum time for task 3 and task 4 completion, Participant D took the maximum time for completing task 5.

Figure 11. Time required for completion of various tasks

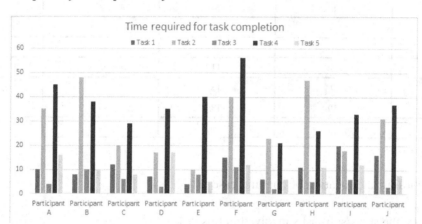

FEEDBACK AND SUGGESTIONS

The authors of this chapter took feedback from 15-20 Fourth Year Engineering students and faculties from various departments of their college regarding changes that need to be done to the User Interface. A Google Form was circulated to take the feedback and their responses were recorded in an Excel sheet. The questions which were asked in the form were of type - Is the user interface design good? On which screen can animations be added? What other changes can be made so that the user interface looks better and many more questions of this type. Most of them were comfortable with the existing design and the features which are currently implemented. The representatives of some positive responses that were received are listed below.

Response 1: Yes the user interface design is good. I don't think that there is any animation needed anywhere
Response 2: The user interface is very user friendly and everything looks fine
Response 3: The design is good. Blue and white is a good color combination
Response 4: Good initiative. This application can help lot of people. It's a win-win condition for both – local public and the police

Few suggestions that were received for the redesign are mentioned below.

Suggestion 1: In the Police application module - Background notification feature: Title of the notification is a bit confusing. Instead try to have an appealing title like "Incoming Call".

Suggestion 2: Police application module: List of all the recordings displayed to the police officer - the recordings can be named based on the date, time and location of crime instead of what is given currently. This would make it easier for police personnel to find a crime recording from history.

Suggestion 3: The home page for police application module seems quite empty. Something should be added to make it look better.

Suggestion 4: Add dynamic location fetching feature. Even if the victim/ eye-witness is moving, his/ her current location should be fetched accurately.

Suggestion 5: Currently the video call quality is very high. It's good, but what if the victim/eye-witness is present in an area where there is very less internet speed. So, try to keep the video call quality moderate –neither too high nor too low.

Suggestion 6: Add a feature to send audio, in case if the victim/eye-witness is not in a condition to start a video call.

From these suggestions, one can conclude that Graphical User Interface can still have scope of improvement.

FUTURE RESEARCH DIRECTIONS

This system can be modified by adding a new feature – checking the intensity of crime in the activity by using object detection. Object detection algorithm can be applied to the recordings of the video call which are stored in the database. Depending on the objects detected (For example: guns, knives, pistols or any other equipment), that particular crime scene can be categorized into multiple categories like low intensity crime, medium intensity crime and high intensity crime. If it is a high intensity crime, the police officer needs to pay more attention to it. This can also be helpful in this scenario: Imagine a situation where two crime activities are happening at the same time. The police officer receives a video call from both the victims. But he gets confused regarding which criminal activity he should investigate first. Now, at this point, if the algorithm classifies first crime activity as low intensity crime and the second crime activity as high intensity crime, his confusion would be cleared and he can quickly reach the crime spot corresponding to the second crime activity and start investigating the case. The Graphical User Interface can still have scope of improvement as per the collected feedback.

CONCLUSION

In this chapter, the authors have discussed about the real time crime reporting system, which can assist the local people to report crime to the nearby police stations without even visiting the police stations. It would be of huge benefit to the police in a way that the police can start investigating the crime while it is going on. The problem of crime going unreported by the local people would be solved with the help of this system. It is feasible because there is no use of any hardware and each and every software which is used is open source. The local people and the police officers just need to have an Android or iOS mobile phone along with an internet connection. This system can be very helpful to the people who cannot visit the police station due to some reason. It is a systematic and fast crime reporting system and hence it can help the police in investigating the cases in a much faster way.

Throughout the chapter, in all the figures (from Figure 1 to Figure 10), the authors have used the Strive for Consistency Rule (Rule 1) of the Golden Rules of User Interface Design. The layout, color code, icons and button size have been kept consistent throughout the chapter. Hence, this system focuses on the use of new and trending technologies to solve the issues and problems faced in the field of crime reporting and investigation.

REFERENCES

Abdali, A. R., & Al-Tuma, R. F. (2019, March 27-28). *Robust real-time violence detection in video using CNN and LSTM* [Paper presentation]. 2019 2nd Scientific Conference of Computer Sciences (SCCS), Baghdad, Iraq.

Accelerate and scale app development without managing infrastructure. (n.d.). *Firebase*. https://firebase.google.com/products-build

Agangiba, W. A., & Agangiba, M. A. (2013). Mobile solution for metropolitan crime detection and reporting. *Journal of Emerging Trends in Computing and Information Sciences*, *4*(12), 916–921.

Byrne, J., & Marx, G. (2011). Technological innovations in crime prevention and policing: A review of the research on implementation and impact. *Journal of Police Studies*, *3*(20), 17–40.

Creating an EC2 instance on AWS with Ubuntu 18.04. (n.d.). *CloudBooklet*. https://www.cloudbooklet.com/create-an-ec2-instance-on-aws-with-ubuntu-18-04/

Doyle, M. (2008). *How to setup your own domain name*. https://www.elated.com/set-up-your-own-domain-name/

Flutter documentation. (n.d.). *Flutter*. https://flutter.dev/docs

Jitsi meet security & privacy. (n.d.). *Jitsi*. https://jitsi.org/security/

Josephine, M. (2019). *Understanding hot reload in Flutter*. https://medium.com/podiihq/understanding-hotreload-in-flutter-2dc28b317036

Kettle, S. (2017). *Distance on a sphere: The Haversine formula*. https://community.esri.com/t5/coordinate-reference-systems/distance-on-a-sphere-the-haversine-formula/ba-p/902128

Lewis, J., Zheng, D., & Carter, W. (2017). *Effect of encryption on lawful access to communications and data*. Rowman & Littlefield.

Mcclees, E. (2019). *How the police use cell phone data in criminal investigation*. https://www.mctexaslaw.com/how-do-police-use-cell-phone-data-in-criminal-investigations

Mkhwanazi, K., Owolawi, P. A., Mapayi, T., & Aiyetoro, G. (2020, August 6-7). *An automatic crime reporting and immediate response system* [Paper presentation]. *2020 International Conference on Artificial Intelligence, Big Data, Computing and Data Communication Systems (ICABCD)*, Durban, South Africa.

Mwiya, M., Phiri, J., & Lyoko, G. (2015). Public crime reporting and monitoring system model using GSM and GIS technologies: A case of Zambia police service. *International Journal of Computer Science and Mobile Computing, 4*(11), 207–226.

Pawar, S., & Bhutkar, G. (2021). Usability Testing of Twitter App with Indian Users. *Human-Computer Interaction and Beyond, 1*, 35–73. doi:10.2174/9789814998819121010006

Rasanayagam, K., Kumarasiri, S., Tharuka, W., Samaranayake, N., Samarasinghe, P., & Siriwardana, S. (2018, December 21-22). *CIS: An automated criminal identification system* [Paper presentation]. *IEEE International Conference on Information and Automation for Sustainability (ICIAfS)*, Colombo, Sri Lanka.

Samsudeen, M. (2020). *Easily visualize OpenStreetMaps and Bing maps in Flutter*. https://www.syncfusion.com/blogs/post/easily-visualize-openstreetmaps-and-bing-maps-in-flutter.aspx

Sekhri, A. (2020). *The criminal law blog: Mobile phones and criminal investigations*. https://criminallawstudiesnluj.wordpress.com/2020/05/07/mobile-phones-and-criminal-investigations/

Shneiderman's Eight Golden Rules of Interface Design. (n.d.). *Capian*. https://capian.co/shneiderman-eight-golden-rules-interface-design

Smith, S. (2018). *Overview of ASP. NET Core MVC*. https://docs.microsoft.com/en-us/aspnet/core/mvc/overview?view=aspnetcore-5.0

Tabassum, K., Shaiba, H., Shamrani, S., & Otaibi, S. (2018, April 4-6). *E-cops: An online crime reporting and management system for Riyadh city* [Paper presentation]. 2018 1st International Conference on Computer Applications & Information Security (ICCAIS), Riyadh, Saudi Arabia.

Thakkar, J. (2021). *End-to-end-encryption: The good, the bad and the politics*. https://www.thesslstore.com/blog/end-to-end-encryption-the-good-the-bad-and-the-politics/

ADDITIONAL READING

Cloud Messaging. (n.d.). *FlutterFire*. https://firebase.flutter.dev/docs/messaging/usage/

Dubey, P. (2019). *Meet the journalist documenting India's unreported rape cases*. https://www.opendemocracy.net/en/5050/meet-the-journalist-documenting-indias-unreported-rape-cases/

KEY TERMS AND DEFINITIONS

Algorithm: An algorithm contains well-defined set of rules to be followed in order to solve a problem.

Data Science: A field related to extracting and analyzing of data to derive useful insights and inferences from it.

EC2 Instance: EC2 is nothing but Amazon Elastic Compute Cloud. It is a server which is virtual and it is used for running applications on AWS.

End-to-End Encryption: A system of communication where only the sender and the receiver can read the messages. Any third-party system cannot read the messages as they don't have any means to decrypt them.

Latitude: It is a coordinate that determines the north-south location of a particular place or point on the surface of the earth. The latitudinal lines run East-West parallel to the Equator.

Location Tracking: A system through which the current location of a person can be traced along with the directions to reach his location.

Longitude: It is a coordinate that determines the east-west location of a particular place or point on the surface of the earth. The longitudinal lines run North-South parallel to the Prime Meridian.

NoSQL Database: These Not Only SQL (NoSQL) databases store data in a document format instead of storing it in a tabular format consisting of rows and columns. It does not have a fixed schema and it can store very huge amount of data.

Real-Time Database: It is a database system that stores dynamic data. It syncs the user data in real-time.

Short Messaging Service (SMS): It is a communication system that allows the user to send and receive text messages through mobile devices.

Chapter 2
Building 3D and XR City Systems on Multi-Platform Devices

Tomasz Zawadzki

https://orcid.org/0000-0002-8780-1075

Arkin University of Creative Arts and Design, Cyprus

Rob Kitchin

Maynooth University, Ireland

ABSTRACT

In this chapter, the authors detail how six commercial products have sought to provide 3D spatial media solutions for the planning domain, and set out their own approach to developing an interactive, multi-platform city information model (CIM) for desktop/WebGL (on a PC), VR (HTC Vive), and MR (Microsoft HoloLens) for Dublin informed by user requirements elicited through interviews with professional urban planners. They demonstrate how a Unity game engine solution can be used to build and manage a multi-platform CIM project from initial stage to the final build. They discuss issues concerning the handling geographic data, data integration, UI development, multi-platform support, interaction types (controllers, gestures, etc.), and potential application. They present core interactive simulations, including shadow analysis, flood resilience, visibility analysis, importing building models, and run-time modeling tool, which are crucial for city information modeling.

INTRODUCTION

For three decades, the case has been made for utilizing a variety of 3D spatial media for understanding and modelling urban environments, including 3D GIS, virtual reality, and city information models. In the 1990s, several projects had started to develop nascent 3D virtual models of cities. For example, Kirby et al. (1996) created a 3D GIS model of Adelaide, Australia; Bourdakis (1997) used computer-aided design to create a geometric, textured model of Bath, England, which covered several square kilometers;

DOI: 10.4018/978-1-7998-9121-5.ch002

Chan et al. (1998) developed an urban simulation system for Los Angeles that combined GIS and VR; and Batty et al. (2000) produced a 3D model of Virtual London using CAD, GIS and VRML. Despite significant advances in 3D spatial technologies and the creation of 3D spatial datasets since the 1990s, as yet 3D spatial media have still not become mainstreamed in the planning profession. Moreover, there is little consensus as to how best develop such 3D spatial media in terms of approach and technologies, or their desired functionality Kitchin et al. (2021).

The objective of the chapter is to detail present approaches to 3D spatial media, assessing how six commercial products have sought to provide solutions for the planning domain and their functionality, and to set out our own approach to developing an interactive, multi-platform City Information Model (CIM), informed by user requirements elicited through interviews with professional urban planners. The development of our own CIM platform was to examine the potential to create a universal, multiplatform (for desktop/WebGL, VR (HTC Vive) and MR (Microsoft HoloLens), open-source solution using games engine approach (Unity) with extensive functionality that matches planners' expectations and needs, and to identify issues with such an approach and workable solutions. The platform needed to perform a number of tasks of interest to professional planners, such as placing new proposed buildings in the landscape, revealing viewsheds, sunlight/shadow analysis, run flooding simulations, and to display a variety of planning and property data (e.g., land zoning, development plans, planning permissions, property prices, architectural and heritage status) and some real-time data related to environment and transport.

BACKGROUND

Studies have utilized and assessed a series of increasingly sophisticated technologies for visualizing and simulation city landscapes, including: Computer-Aided Design (CAD) (Al-Kodmany, 2002), 3D modeling packages (Schreyer, 2013), 3D Geographic Information Systems (3D GIS) (Koninger & Bartel, 1998; Gu et al., 2011), Virtual Reality (VR) (Doyle et al., 1998; Salter et al., 2009; Portman et al., 2015), Mixed Reality (MR) (Guo et al. 2008; Ghadirian & Bishop 2008), and Building Information Modeling (BIM) (Crotty, 2011). Most recently, research has focused on developing nascent City Information Modelling (CIM) systems that utilize a number of these technologies such as 3D GIS, VR and MR, draw together and interlink at a city-scale a range of 3D landscape and building data, as well as other administrative and operational spatial data, and enable their exploration using a variety of query and simulation tools (Thompson et al., 2016; Stojanovski, 2018).

For those developing and promoting 3D spatial media the hope is that they will become an integral part of urban planning and development practice supporting better decision-making. They argue that 3D spatial media have the potential to improve significantly communication and comprehension by providing spatial representations that are closer to common perceptual experiences than maps, plans, and perspective drawings, and can be viewed from different perspectives and explored in an immersive way (Doyle et al., 1998; Pietsch, 2000; Paar, 2006; Shiratuddin & Thabet, 2011). As Gordon and Manosevitch (2010) note, immersed users potentially experience the streetscape, not the idea of the streetscape as conveyed by traditional maps and plans. This phenomenological experience increases with higher levels of detail and more photorealistic rendering of the architecture and terrain (Appleton & Lovett, 2005; Franklin et al., 2006). Consequently, a recurrent case has been made for the use of 3D spatial media to enrich public understanding of prospective urban design in public consultation, facilitate participatory planning, and help democratize the planning process (Doyle et al., 1998; Ghadirian & Bishop, 2008;

Wissen, 2011). From an urban design perspective, 3D spatial media offer opportunities to quickly and efficiently experiment, practice, simulate and assess design interventions, enabling rapid and iterative prototyping in a cost-effective way (Portman et al., 2015).

Yet, despite significant research and the development of numerous prototype and commercial systems, the applied use of technologies such as 3D GIS, VR/AR, and CIM have yet to be mainstreamed across the planning profession. In the 1990s and early 2000s, the technology was experimental, costly, bulky, underpowered, and provided a poor user experience: lacking realism, interactivity, and the required functionality (Drettakis et al., 2007). 3D data was difficult to source, suffered from poor spatial resolution, and was challenging to integrate with other spatial data from different formats and sources (Franklin et al., 2006). By the late 2010s, the performance and cost issues have been largely addressed. However, there are still issues with sourcing 3D data, integrating and linking data within systems, and providing a suite of interactive modelling and simulation tools that planners desire (Thompson et al., 2016). Generally, games engines used to underpin product development are not designed to act as 3D GISs, having a different coordinate system (x, z, y and true 0,0 origin, rather than x, y, z and latitude/longitude). 3D GISs do not possess the graphics rendering capabilities and developer tools of games engines.

XR (Extended Reality) is the combination of real and virtual environments where the interaction between human and machine is generated by wearables or computer technology. In other words, XR is an umbrella term that captures all AR, VR and MR together (Mann et al., 2018). In Virtual reality (VR) the user is immersed in a computer-generated interactive virtual world (Kim et al., 2000; Onyesolu, 2009a; Onyesolu & Akpado, 2009b). Augmented reality (AR) consists of overlaying computer-generated information on the real world, achieved by projection on clear glasses (Silva et al., 2003). In Mixed reality (MR) virtual objects are not just overlaid on the real world like a layer but can be placed behind real objects. This form of mixed reality can be considered as an advanced form of AR. Mixed reality is the next stage of holographic interaction in multi-mediated reality (Mann et al., 2018).

Our study sought to explore ways of over-coming the limitations of combining a games engine with 3D GIS to create a multi-platform CIM for Dublin that could handle and integrate a number of spatial data sources, including real-time data, and possessed a suite of tools that would have utility for the planning profession. To that end, our work was guided by an evaluation of the functionality of existing commercial systems and requirements interviews with 14 senior professional planners working in local government planning departments in Ireland (Kitchin et al., 2021). Our aim was not to produce a commercial product, however, but to use the process of building a functioning CIM as a means to examine viable solutions for imbuing games engines, in our case Unity, with some of the functionality of 3D GIS and addressing known issues in creating 3D spatial media.

CONTEXT FOR DEVELOPING A MULTI-PLATFORM 3D AND XR SOLUTION FOR CITY PLANNING

Existing 3D City Systems

A number of commercial 3D planning tools are presently available that claim to assist local authorities in advanced urban design, development, and managerial processes. Furthermore, there is a movement at present to augment these tools and present their functionalities via virtual (VR) and mixed reality (MR) technology. Many 3D city systems are focus on achieving high levels of 3D photorealism, whereas others are concentrating on city data visualization, integrating building information models (BIMs), or providing specific design interaction tools for city planners and urban management. We selected six 3D city systems to evaluate, each of which is relatively sophisticated and successful in displaying a 3D city model and associated spatial and temporal data: RealSim, Sitowise, VU.CITY, Skyline, Cityzenith and Virtual Singapore (see Figure 1). Our initial selection was made in 2017 at the start of our project and each of the systems has made big strides forwards in terms of the tools, functionality and user interface and experience in the intervening years. RealSim is an Irish company specializing in 3D real-time simulations that uses environment information models (that combine 3D mapping, architectural and engineering information) to create detailed (LOD 2 or 3 with some texturing or photorealism) virtual reality landscapes in which planning related simulations can be performed. Sitowise is a Nordic company specializing in smart city solutions. One of its products is Aura, a virtual 3D environment for creating and managing an urban digital twin (including GIS and BIM data), and visualizing and simulating built environment data, including material textures. VU.CITY, a UK-based company, produces 3D models at 15cm accuracy of city landscapes that allows collaborative exploration and the running of various planning-related simulations. Skyline Software Systems is a US-based company that specializes in 3D earth visualization and services. Its TerraExplorer application is a 3D GIS digital twin that enables the management, visualization and analysis of various 3D data, imagery and other spatial data. Smart World Pro by Cityzenith is likewise a 3D platform for visualizing and analyzing digital twin data. Unlike the other approaches examined, Virtual Singapore is a government initiative to produce a dynamic, collaborative 3D city model of the nation that enables asset management, modelling and simulation, and planning and decision-making, and research and development.

We categorised the functionalities and tools currently provided by these six 3D city systems in relation to city planning and urban data visualization as available in 2017 (see Table 1). What is clear is that no system provided a full suite of potential useful functionality, as discussed by our interviewees (see next section) or provides a comprehensive multiplatform solution. In part, this is because systems are targeting different aspects of the planning system rather than the full suite of planning tasks, are concentrating on particular platform solutions, or the functionality is difficult to produce either technically or because of limitations in data supply and quality.

Figure 1. Existing city systems: (a) RealSim, (b) Aura by Sitowise, (c) VU.CITY, (d) TerraExplorer by Skyline, (e) Cityzenith, (f) Virtual Singapore

Table 1. Core feature comparison of six commercial city 3D spatial media

		Building City Dashboards	RealSim	Virtual Singapore	VU.CITY	Smart World Pro	Skyline	Sitowise
Platform	Desktop	Y	Y	Y	Y	Y	Y	Y
	VR	Y	Y	N	Y	N	N	Y
	MR	Y	N	N	N	N	N	Y
View	First person view	Y	Y	Y	Y	N	Y	Y
	Bird's eye view	Y	Y	Y	Y	Y	Y	Y
	Inside building examination	N	Y	Y	N	Y	Y	N
3D Environment	Show/hide elements	Y	Y	Y	Y	N	N	Y
	Sunlight	Y	Y	N	Y	Y	N	N
	Water physics	Y	Y	Y	Y	N	N	N
	Animated trees	N	Y	N	N	N	N	Y
	Crowd	N	N	N	N	N	N	Y
	Traffic	N	Y	N	N	N	N	Y
	Underground city infrastructure	N	N	N	Y	N	Y	Y
Simulations	Flood resilience	Y	N	N	N	N	N	Y
	Visibility analysis	Y	N	N	N	N	Y	N
	Shadow analysis	Y	Y	Y	Y	Y	Y	Y
	Lighting simulation	Y	N	N	N	N	N	Y
	Managing noise pollution	N	N	N	N	N	Y	Y
Data	GIS/Spatial	Y	Y	Y	Y	Y	Y	Y
	Real-time	Y	Y	Y	Y	Y	N	N
	Traffic cameras	N	N	N	Y	Y	N	Y
	Lidar	N	N	N	N	N	Y	N
Model information	BIM	N	Y	Y	N	Y	N	Y
	CIM	Y	N	Y	Y	Y	Y	N
	Zoning info	Y	Y	Y	Y	N	N	N
	Semantic information	N	N	Y	N	N	Y	Y
	Point and click height information	N	Y	Y	N	N	N	N
	Highlighting buildings	Y	Y	Y	Y	Y	Y	Y
Planning tools	Building markers	N	Y	N	N	N	Y	Y
	3D manipulation	Y	Y	N	N	Y	N	Y
	Import 3D models	Y	Y	N	Y	Y	N	Y
	City planning timeline	Y (CONCEPT)	N	N	Y	N	N	Y
	TOTAL	20	20	15	19	13	14	23

Information that is attributed to a 3D model is a representation of key concepts and their relationships, constraints, rules, and operations regarding specific data semantics of a chosen discourse. In this context, we specified six types of information models including building information models (BIMs), city information models (CIMs), city zoning information, point and click height information, highlighting specific buildings, and semantic information. While some 3D tools choose to focus on either Building Information Modeling (BIM) (RealSim, Sitowise) or City Information Modeling (CIM) oriented (VU. CITY, Skyline), others attempt to do both (Virtual Singapore, Smart World Pro).

Navigation in a virtual environment is important for users to explore simulated space. We therefore investigated the most used navigation modes; including first person, bird's eye view, and internal building structure explorations (a first-person view for inspecting BIM models). A bird's eye view is currently supported by all 3D systems. Internal building examination was accessible in 4 of 7 solutions. 3D cities are often built for larger-scale observations, where the camera is located to enable whole city perspectives, or for exploration specific buildings in the model. 3D navigation was crucial to reach the street level and one solution did not support this at all (Smart World Pro).

Interactive virtual environments can be enhanced by adding static ecological elements. When building 3D urban models, 3D environments can be supplemented with animated milieu, including trees and parks, pedestrians and crowds, traffic, and so on. Having the option to switch ecological elements on and off is crucial for data visualization purposes, where they may obscure GIS data layers. Furthermore, hiding ecological elements – as a feature – was only absent in Smart World Pro and Skyline. This feature also helped the user to view underground infrastructures, which were provided for VU.CITY, Skyline, and Sitowise. Other ecological features included sunlight, water physics, and animated trees. Making 3D cities come alive is not an easy task and some 3D tools did not offer these features, such as simulated traffic and crowds.

3D planning tools should facilitate planners in making informed decisions based on the available data. 3D tools should, therefore, improve the decision-making process by including the relevant tools for various urban planning applications. Our research localized four main features and tools that were implemented in each of the 3D tool analyzed. The first feature was based on using markers to constrain the building outline and generate a mesh between those points (starting from flat polygon). This approach was used in RealSim, Sitowise and Skyline. The second feature was interacting with 3D objects, and manipulating their position, rotation and scale. The third feature was the ability to add 3D objects with or without textures created in external 3D software packages; such those created in CAD and other modelling software. This feature allows city planners to use their own 3D models. This model importing tool was available in Virtual Singapore and Skyline. By combining multiple proposed building models a timeline slider could be manipulated for visualizing future planning and development scenarios. This was based upon assigning each scenario to one point in time and scrubbing through the timeline. By viewing different timeline development simulations, planners can potentially foresee any future problematic construction interactions. Interacting with these features was done so with advanced user interface modules. This feature was provided by two of the systems, VU.CITY and Sitowise.

Displaying and accessing data is a key feature for local authority planners. Data in this context relates to distinct pieces of information, usually formatted in a specific way. Generally, each 3D tool supported GIS data standards. However, real-time city data was not supported by Sitowise and Skyline. Platform relates to the basic hardware or software on which a 3D tool runs. In this study, desktop PC, VR, and MR fall into this category; where each of the evaluated systems can be presented on platforms that facilitate different modalities of interaction. Through the analysis of current marketing materials and open-source demo versions of their software, it was observed that of the 3D urban planning systems assessed, the standard application platform was desktop PC (available for all solutions). The use of VR was supported by RealSim, VU.CITY and Sitowise only. MR experiences was limited to Sitowise. Access to multiplatform solutions (PC, VR, MR) by planners may be a key feature in the future, as emergent immersive solutions may help to reach wider audiences. Therefore, there is potentially a market for applications to be more flexible with regards to the platform. In this way, immersive and engaging experiences can be harnessed to facilitate preplanning and co-design planning processes.

User Requirements

In addition to evaluating existing systems, to guide our own development and research we interviewed 14 experienced planners (Senior Executive Planner (n = 5), Senior Planner (n = 4), Executive Planner (n = 3), a Senior Architect (n = 1), and a technical staff member (n = 1)) who had worked across all aspects of local government planning (e.g., strategic planning, development management, compliance, and enforcement). Their knowledge of 3D approaches to planning and the various products available was broad. However, their applied experience of using 3D spatial media was constrained and the cohort admitted having very little hands-on experience of using such tools in their day-to-day work. They noted that a small number of colleagues might produce bespoke 3D models as part of their work, but this depended on the project and skills of particular team members. The use of 3D spatial media was not generally seen as a constituent part of mainstream practice for LA planners and their current use largely focused on the visual aspects of communication and assessment of design plans. However, while the use of 3D spatial media in planning departments was relatively limited, all the interviewees recognized their potential to contribute to the planning system and to their day-to-day work with respect to strategic visioning, public consultation, pre-planning processes, development management, application assessment, compliance, and enforcement.

When consulted as to what specific features they would desire in 3D spatial media for planning our interviewees were rather hesitant and speculative. In the main, they anticipated using any system as a visualization and scenario planning tool to test different scenarios and assess proposed developments and its potential effects upon the existing landscape prior to any significant investment. Or they imagined using a system as a 3D GIS that would enable different data layers – existing plans, development, housing and heritage information, utility infrastructure, social/economic variables, environmental factors – to be visualized and queried. They were most interested in a desktop platform to fit their existing working arrangements and technical competences, rather than a headset-based solution, but would welcome the opportunity to test the affordances of an immersive experience. Across the 14 interviewees the suite of functionality and features detailed (in Table 1) were discussed. Using the interviews as a guide we then designed our own multiplatform system to examine the viability and issues in creating a working CIM and the affordances created through different platforms (desktop, VR, MR). To provide additional context we also explored the approach and functionality of existing 3D city systems.

The BCD Project

Initial Stage – Feedback from City Planners and Development Direction

Based on the evaluation of existing systems and the feedback from our interviews with planners, the Building City Dashboards (BCD) project mapped out a potential multiplatform solution (Figure 2) using the Unity game engine as the core development environment.

Unity3D software can run on multiple platforms with online and offline modes. In our case, we focused on the Windows platform only where the development process was performed. Unity3D also allows users to publish the developed games on other platforms (especially XR platforms with full support) and provides a variety of functions and module libraries for multi specifications of gaming development (Bae & Kim, 2014). For the BCD project, we had created each system from scratch. The initial stages involved 3D data integration with corresponding attributes, multiplatform UI development – including interaction design and developing other useful features (especially real-time simulations). Most 3D modeling software packages cannot cope with spatial data because of the mapping projection systems used. Unity likewise does not support a real-world coordinate system and there are no transformation tools or libraries for coordinate conversions. We thus had to devise a process for successfully transforming and importing spatial data using ESRI CityEngine, a 3D GIS platform. In addition, the Unity 3D game engine supports very limited input formats (e.g., fbx, sbx and .obj) which focuses on geometry, vertex and faces ordered. Thus, it creates limited interoperability during the conversion process such as loss of semantic and attributes (usually provided in external CSV file) (Buyuksalih et al., 2017).

The project was split up into three categories: BCD Desktop/WebGL, BCD VR and BCD MR to be accessible on different devices (desktop - PC unit; VR – HTC Vive glasses; MR – Microsoft HoloLens glasses). An AR version was not developed because BCD MR is more advanced. Core modules were created in Unity grouped into categories including: UI elements, 3D environment, planning tools, scene components and explorability (navigation modes).

Figure 2. Multi-platform support in Unity with dedicated output file extensions
Sourcing Input Data - Dublin 3D City Model (D3D) and City Layers

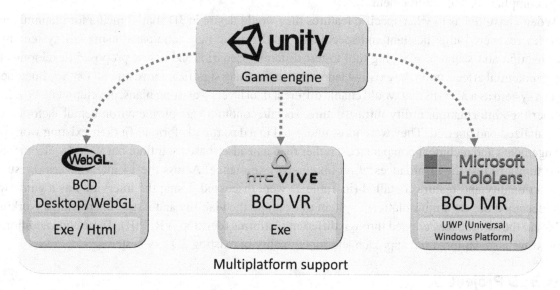

The Dublin city model was obtained for research from a Dublin-based private surveying company D3D. The city model compromised two square kilometers of a central area of the city. The model was created in 3D Studio Max. The main buildings were fully 3D models while the rest of the city was created using satellite photos and photogrammetry. The main buildings had real-world textures superimposed in the form of photos previously prepared in Photoshop. Additional data layers were sourced from myplan. ie (a government planning portal), along with other data providers such as the Central Statistics Office and Dublin City Council. These data layers were grouped into five categories: Planning history (architectural heritage, national monuments); development land use (development plan, planning applications); environmental (noise levels, air quality); property prices (price paid register); and Census data (various demographic and housing data).

BCD – Coordinate System for 3D Model and City Layers

The Unity games engine utilizes a different coordinate system to traditional geographic data systems. Whereas geographic data is anchored around a latitude and longitude coordinate system, Unity employs a fixed 0,0 origin, a localized scale, and the main plane of movement is forward/backwards (horizontal) rather than up/down (vertical) as with mapping systems. Consequently, geographic data imported into Unity needs to be rotated and realigned to gain the correct plain of movement, and data layers need to be fused to ensure they share the same local scale and origin point. The initial step then was to establish common coordinates for the 3D model and data layers for use in Unity. This was achieved by importing the model and layers into City Engine, a 3D GIS package, to marry them together, saving as a .fbx file. The next stage of the project was loading the city model into the Unity engine and assign missing textures. Not all textures were imported correctly so they had to be fixed by using shaders in Unity. The peelings with a partially transparent structure, like trees, required the use of additional shaders that were able to render the alpha channel. In addition, to improve the realism of the virtual scene, a realistic animation model of water, sky and sun has been added, which introduces the time of day and night.

BCD - Interactive City Maps

The idea behind city model was to combine the 3D terrain and building model with 3D layers and create the possibility of interacting with the data. After fusing the model and data layers, the next step was to combine the city layers with text data. The city layers contained two types of files - shape files (* .shp) and text data files (* .csv). A CSV reader script was used to read the content of the CSV files. It was necessary to create a class for each layer in order to directly reference a CSV file, with reading the table contents and displaying individual values enabling interactive queries. In the case of adding interaction to the layers that with areal data, no pinpoints were needed. In cases where the data objects were relatively small, for instance the markers for the paid property register, it was necessary to attach the pinpoint in the form of a 3D external object. The last stage in creating interaction was adding a map click detector using the MouseSelectHighlight function. The base interaction created for the BCD VR used Map Click Detector as Vive Input Utility was able to process all standard elements from Unity if they were attached to Canvas with Raycast Target added. In the case of the BCD MR, the Map Click Detector from the standard BCD 3D version could not be used. In this case the IMixedRealityFocusHandler components were used.

BCD - Cross-Platform Interfaces, Interaction Modes and Navigation

It was necessary to develop the UI interface for each BCD project separately. We decided to have three independent projects where the base content was the same (3D model with city layers). Other used UI components had to be dedicated to each platform to ensure optimal operation. For BCD Desktop we used all standard Unity UI elements with some extra packages imported to the project like GILES, real-time clouds, Ciconia Double Shader (for tree transparency), etc. The BCD VR project used the Vive Input Utility package which did not require many changes from our BCD initial desktop version, except from a design perspective. The menu had to be rebuilt and assigned to the left controller but there was one Canvas script to recognize all the previous desktop tools in VR. Based on that, most of the functionalities from BCD Desktop could be transferred directly to VR. It was especially important to transfer simulations.

The situation changed with the BCD MR project. All the features of the BCD Desktop did not work in MR and it was necessary to import the Mixed Reality toolkit with all predefined UI components. We replaced all standard UI components by Mixed Reality UI components from the toolkit to make a new interface for BCD MR. The result was we had the same project running across platforms with three user interfaces (Figure 3) and different interaction modes (Figure 4).

Figure 3. Cross platform BCD project UI interfaces, menus and display windows for: (a) desktop version; (b) VR version; (c) MR version

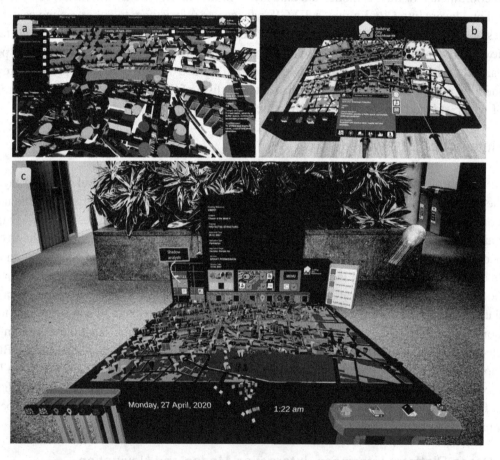

BCD Desktop was designed to meet user requirements in a traditional way. There are no extra haptic devices required to interact with the project. Specific information about data layers such as land-use zones, property price data, monuments service data, planning applications, etc. can be requested through mouse interaction in the PC version. PC screen is the output window where the user can see the results of their own actions. Interaction in VR is very different to a standard PC. In our case, we used HTC Vive rig with two controllers. The main menu was assigned to the left controller while the right controller contained a pointer to perform actions. The BCD VR project contained two scenes – one for a street view where the user had a normal scale and a bird's eye view for a larger city overview. All interactive content from the menu (checkboxes, sliders, etc.) could be activated or deactivated by pressing triggers in the right controller. Before performing any action, a pointer from the right controller had to face the desired tool from the menu. On the top of the right controller, a function to teleport was assigned. There are no interaction controllers for BCD MR. The user can use their own fingers to perform predefined gestures (Air Tap, Tap and Hold, Bloom) and interact with interactable elements from the project like checkboxes, sliders or other elements. On every platform the BCD project lets the user navigate in a different way. In BCD Desktop there is no physical movement and exploration is performed on the PC screen. While BCD VR allowed exploring the Dublin city by physical movement or by virtual teleport BCD MR allows full physical movement and there is no option to teleport.

Figure 4. Cross-platform interaction modes

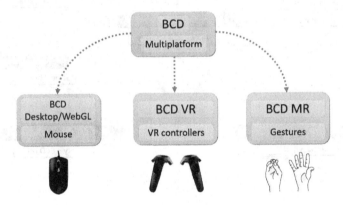

Each of the three platforms were built in parallel using the Unity editor. Development passed through a number of stages (see Figure 5). The next stage included creating simulations, features and tools for public users and city planners. The last stage was to build a UI interface for desktop, VR and MR and adjust all features to be utilized on each platform. The result was suite of modules and components (see Figure 6). BCD Desktop/VR required one build from Unity and can be launched directly afterwards from an .exe file. BCD MR required one build to UWP (Universal Windows Platform) and the second deployment stage from Visual Studio to Microsoft HoloLens device. To perform deployment to the device-specific settings were applied including: solution configuration, solution platform and attachment.

BCD - Features and Tools for City Planning

The BCD project included a number of core features to facilitate city planning actions: interactive layers, shadow analysis, flood resilience, visibility analysis, and adding buildings (see Table 2).

Visualization in 3D urban planning provides an interactive platform for communicating with the public and utilizing different data layers. The traditional approach in visualization is to demonstrate information and data within a 2D framework (Figure 7a). The 2D layers are complex and only planning professionals can fully manipulate information. Consequently, the potential use of 3D, VR and MR systems in the BCD project has been explored in depth to overcome the limitations of 2D systems.

Figure 5. The BCD project development stages

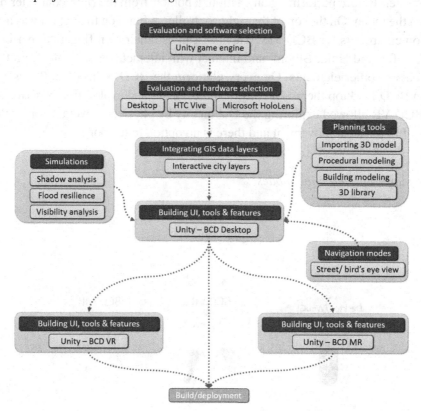

Figure 6. An overview of the BCD project modules and components

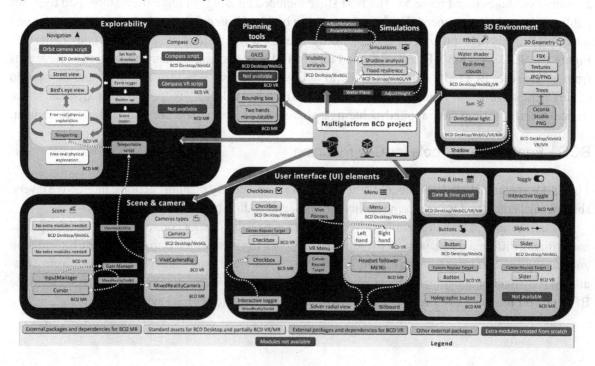

Table 2. Features and tools for city planners available on every platform

Features	BCD Desktop	BCD VR	BCD MR
Shadow analysis	YES	YES	YES
Flood resilience	YES	YES	YES
Visibility analysis	YES	Under development	Under development
Runtime 3D tool – basic shapes	YES	-	-
Procedural 3D modeling tool	YES	YES	-
Importing 3D objects	YES	Under development	Under development
Building library	-	-	YES
Interactive city layers	YES	YES	YES

Figure 7. BCD desktop app: (a) interactive city layers; (b) shadow analysis; (c) flood resilience; (d) visibility analysis

Shadow analysis is a 3D analysis of the shadow cast by a building or landscape object based on solar position. The effect of proposed large and tall buildings on the surrounding environment is a key aspect of planning appeals as it materially affects the quality of life for residents and workers. BCD Desktop/ VR and MR include shadow simulation for a single day with soft and hard shadows simulations which are rendered together to increase photorealism (Figure 7b). The tool enabled an assessment of shadow impact and its length of time in an area.

Flood resilience is an acceptable level of flooding that the urban system can tolerate (Batica, et al., 2016). Flood risk management is important for urban areas as it may prevent or reduce the impacts of flooding and decrease the level of damage (Tucci, 2006). This feature is fully supported by the BCD project on all platforms including desktop using a toggle slider to raise and lower water levels (Figure 7c).

Visibility analysis provides an assessment of vistas and the impact of new developments on views and sightlines. They are used mainly for planning purposes, from new infrastructure implementation to the development of new buildings, routes, or other city landscape components. The tool creates an output raster that displays the terrain (Mat et. al., 2014) that can be seen from a specific point of view. Currently, this feature is available for the BCD Desktop version (Figure 7d) and is under development for VR and MR.

A key feature for planning 3D spatial media is the ability to add buildings to an existing landscape to assess their potential impact on the environment. We implemented three solutions to perform this task. The first was to enable 3D models of proposed buildings to be placed directly into the model, to move them about and to rotate and scale them to create unique building compositions and proposals. Currently, this feature was included in the BCD Desktop version of the project (Figure 8 a-d.). This feature is under development for VR/MR. A second option is to add a building from a predefined library, and to transform, rotate, scale, duplicate or remove it. Each object from the library contain their own texture, which is fixed. Using this tool, we can construct new buildings, green spaces or other landscape components (Figure 9a). We created a library of buildings for BCD MR to support city planning in mixed reality instead using simple planning feature (Figure 9d). A third tool enables the user to create and adapt a new building using a simple toolkit that specifies shape, size, number of floors, and roof shape and to alter these parameters in real-time for desktop (Figure 9b) and VR (Figure 9c).

Figure 8. BCD Desktop app: a run-time 3D building importer: (a) translation; (b) rotation; (c) scaling features; (d) multiple objects composition

Figure 9. Runtime 3D modeling tool, interactive buildings library: (a+b) desktop; (c) VR; (d) MR

FUTURE RESEARCH DIRECTIONS

Our research has highlighted that despite a couple of decades of research and development, 3D spatial media still lack maturity and there are many questions and technical challenges that require further fundamental and applied research. In particular, while games engines provide high quality graphics and user experience, they are poorly suited to handling spatial data and to act like a GIS. Fundamentally, the games engine has a different coordinate system with a fixed 0,0 origin and localized scale, and the main plane of movement is horizontal rather than vertical as with mapping systems. Importing and aligning spatial data is therefore not at all straightforward involving the rotation, centering and realignment of data, and constitutes a specialist task with no established procedure. Research is needed to make this process simpler and effective, to the point where a professional planner with moderate technical skills can achieve it quickly and effectively (at present this is not the case; indeed, it took us quite some time to solve this issue).

In addition, there is a need to investigate what the affordances and limitations of tools and tasks across platforms and to establish what works well for particular tasks, any shortcomings and potential solutions. This needs to involve user-testing by planners in planning environments on real planning tasks. It is clear to us that many commercial solutions have been driven by the technology and the ideas and aspirations of developers who may have little planning domain knowledge, rather than user requirements set out by practicing planners (Kitchin et al., 2021). Consequently, the use cases and tools of some systems do not align well with the work requirements and practices of the planning system. As a result, despite a fact that there is a noticeable growth in the development and commercial interest in 3D, BIM, CIM, and GIS software, there is still a lack of universal, multiplatform, and open-source solution with extensive functionality that matches planners' expectations, and this is likely to remain the case for some time without stakeholder-led research and development.

In our own case, the BCD project sought to provide an open-source CIM solution that works across desktop, VR and MR platforms. Using mixed reality technologies that combine GIS and CIM advances current research in the field. MR despite quite popular in entertainment industry it has not been well utilized for GIS and CIM related research, despite its obvious potential benefits. This technology in the future may be a help for planners who are considering the use of 3D spatial media for assessing planning options and making planning decisions. Our research is likely then to further investigate the development of a MR approach. This will include examining the desired functionality and how best to implement solutions, and HCI aspects concerning how users experience and utilize the system. Future project development may also include more features for multiuser MR solutions where more than a single user will be able to interact and explore the 3D planning environment using Microsoft HoloLens device.

CONCLUSION

Despite 30 years of research and development relating to 3D spatial media, and the creation of a number of functioning and affordable systems, such media have yet to become mainstream tools in professional planning. Indeed, while planners can see the potential benefits of using 3D spatial media, they remain somewhat skeptical of their adoption in the short-term due to data access and quality issues, technical capacity in planning departments, and the limited functionality and match-up to critical tasks in the planning process. Their perception is that even with further refinement and enhancements the technology will mostly prevail in the pre-planning process, rather than the processes of planning assessment, compliance and enforcement. Our project sought to evaluate the specifications and functionality of existing systems, and to use user requirement information and feedback from planners, to consider the design and production of a CIM that would address planner concerns and have utility for the everyday work of planning departments. Our aim was to design and develop an open source, multiplatform 3D spatial media solution that utilized games engine technology and included the functionality outlined in Table 1. The project combined GIS, CIM and XR, producing three platform applications (desktop/VR/MR) with five navigation modes: two for desktop (BCD desktop street view and bird's eye view, two for VR (street view and bird's eye view) and one for MR (bird's eye view). Developing three platforms enabled us to investigate the issues of building a CIM for different platforms, to explore their various affordances, and to examine the different types of experience and their possible consequences with respect to use. The resulting system provided a workable solution that planners felt was interesting and had potential utility, though they remained somewhat skeptical that such a system will be mainstreamed in the short-term due to institutional and cultural factors. Our research highlighted that involving planners in the design, build and testing will be important to help ensure that the systems developed are fit-for-purpose and to foster stakeholder buy-in.

ACKNOWLEDGMENT

This study was funded by Science Foundation Ireland (SFI) (grant number 15/IA/3090).

REFERENCES

Al-Kodmany, K. (2002). Visualization Tools and Methods in Community Planning: From Freehand Sketches to Virtual Reality. *Journal of Planning Literature, 17*(2), 189–211. doi:10.1177/088541202762475946

Appleton, K., & Lovett, A. (2005). GIS-based visualization of development proposals: Reactions from planning and related professionals. *Computers, Environment and Urban Systems, 29*(3), 321–339. doi:10.1016/j.compenvurbsys.2004.05.005

Bae, J. H., & Kim, A. H. (2014). Design and Development of Unity 3D Game Engine-Based Smart SNG (Social Network Game). *International Journal of Multimedia and Ubiquitous Engineering, 9*(8), 261–266. doi:10.14257/ijmue.2014.9.8.23

Batica, J., & Gourbesville, P. (2016). Resilience in Flood Risk Management-A New Communication Tool. *Procedia Engineering, 154*, 811–817. doi:10.1016/j.proeng.2016.07.411

Batty, M., Dodge, M., Jiang, B., & Hudson-Smith, A. (2000). *New technologies for urban designers: the VENUE project.* Centre for Advanced Spatial Analysis Working Paper Series 21, University College London.

Bourdakis, V. (1996). From CAAD to VRML: London Case Study. In *The 3rd UK VRSIG Conference Full Paper Proceedings*. De Montfort University.

Buyuksalih I. Bayburt S. Buyuksalih G. Baskaraca A. Karim H. Rahman A. (2017). 3D modelling and visualization based on the Unity game engine – advantages and challenges. *ISPRS Annals of Photogrammetry, Remote Sensing and Spatial Information Sciences.* doi:10.5194/isprs-annals-IV-4-W4-161-2017

Chan, R., Jepson, W., & Friedman, S. (1998). Urban Simulation: An Innovative Tool for Interactive Planning and Consensus Building. *Proceedings of the 1998 American Planning Association National Conference*, 43-50.

CityZenith. (2021, December 5). *SmartWorldOS.* https://cityzenith.com/smartworldos-tm

Crotty, R. (2011). *The Impact of Building Information Modelling: Transforming Construction.* Routledge. doi:10.1016/j.compenvurbsys.2004.05.005

Doyle, S., Dodge, M., & Smith, A. (1998). The potential of web-based mapping and virtual reality technologies for modelling urban environments. *Computers, Environment and Urban Systems, 22*(2), 137–155. doi:10.1016/S0198-9715(98)00014-3

Drettakis, G., Roussou, M., Reche, A., & Tsingos, N. (2007). Design and Evaluation of a Real-World Virtual Environment for Architecture and Urban Planning. *Presence: Teleoperators and Virtual Environments, 16*(3), 318–332. doi:10.1162/pres.16.3.318

Franklin, R., Heesom, D., & Felton, A. (2006). A Critical Review of Virtual Reality and Geographical Information Systems for Management of the Built Environment. *Proceedings of Information Visualization*, 1-6. doi:10.1109/IV.2006.6

Ghadirian, P., & Bishop, I. D. (2008). Integration of augmented reality and GIS: A new approach to realistic landscape visualisation. *Landscape and Urban Planning*, *86*(3-4), 226–232. doi:10.1016/j.landurbplan.2008.03.004

Gordon, E., & Manosevitch, E. (2010). Augmented deliberation: Merging physical and virtual interaction to engage communities in urban planning. *New Media & Society*, *13*(1), 75–95. doi:10.1177/1461444810365315

Gu, N., Kim, M. J., & Maher, M. L. (2011). Technological advancements in synchronous collaboration: The effect of 3D virtual worlds and tangible user interfaces on architectural design. *Automation in Construction*, *20*(3), 270–278. doi:10.1016/j.autcon.2010.10.004

Guo, Y., Du, Q., Luo, Y., Zhang, W., & Xu, L. (2008). Application of augmented reality GIS in architecture. International Archives of the Photogrammetry, Remote Sensing and Spatial Information Sciences XXXVII, 331-336.

Kim, J., Park, S., Yuk, K., Lee, H., & Lee, H. (2000). Virtual reality simulations in physics education. *Interactive Multimedia Electronic Journal of Computer-Enhanced Learning*. http://imej.wfu.edu/articles/2001/2/02/index.asp

Kirby, S. D., Flint, R., Murakami, H., & Bamford, E. (1997). The Changing Role of GIS in Urban Planning: The Adelaide Model Case Study. *International Journal for Geomatics*, *11*(8), 6–8.

Kitchin, R., Young, G., & Dawkins, O. (2021, online first) Planning and 3D spatial media: Progress, prospects, and the knowledge and experiences of local government planners. *Planning Theory & Practice*. Advance online publication. doi:10.1080/14649357.2021.1921832

Koninger, A., & Bartel, S. (1998). 3D-GIS for Urban Purposes. *GeoInformatica*, *2*(1), 79–103. doi:10.1023/A:1009797106866

Mann, S., Furness, T., Yuan, Y., Iorio, J., & Wang, Z. (2018). *All Reality: Virtual, Augmented, Mixed (X), Mediated (X,Y), and Multimediated Reality*. CoRR. abs/1804.08386.

Mat, R. C., Shariff, A., Zulkifli, A., Rahim, M., & Mahayudin, M. (2014). Using game engine for 3D terrain visualisation of GIS data: A review. *7th IGRSM International Remote Sensing and GIS Conference and Exhibition*. 10.1088/1755-1315/20/1/012037

Onyesolu, M. O. (2009a). Virtual reality laboratories: The pedagogical effectiveness and use in obtaining cheap laboratories using the computer laboratory. *Journal of Science Engineering and Technology*, *16*(1), 8679-8689.

Onyesolu, M. O., & Akpado, K. A. (2009b). Virtual reality simulations in computer engineering education. *International Journal of Electrical and Telecommunication Systems Research*, *3*(3), 56-61.

Paar, P. (2006). Landscape visualizations: Applications and requirements of 3D visualization software for environmental planning. *Computers, Environment and Urban Systems*, *30*(6), 815–839. doi:10.1016/j.compenvurbsys.2005.07.002

Pietsch, S. M. (2000). Computer visualisation in the de- sign control of urban environments: A literature review. *Environment and Planning. B, Planning & Design*, *27*(4), 521–536. doi:10.1068/b2634

Portman, M. E., Natapov, A., & Fisher-Gewirtzman, D. (2015). To go where no man has gone before: Virtual reality in architecture, landscape architecture and environmental planning. *Computers, Environment and Urban Systems*, *54*, 376–384. doi:10.1016/j.compenvurbsys.2015.05.001

RealSim. (2021). *Jersey 3D*. https://realsim.ie/realsim-city/

Salter, J. D., Campbell, C., Journeay, M., & Sheppard, S. (2009). The digital workshop: Exploring the use of interactive and immersive visualisation tools in participatory planning. *Journal of Environmental Management*, *90*(6), 2090–2101. doi:10.1016/j.jenvman.2007.08.023 PMID:18558460

Schreyer, A. C. (2013). *Architectural Design with SketchUp: Component-Based Modelling, Plugins, Rendering and Scripting*. John Wiley & Sons.

Shiratuddin, M. F., & Thabet, W. (2011). Utilizing a 3D game engine to develop a virtual design review system. *Journal of Information Technology in Construction*, *16*, 39–68.

Silva, R., Oliveira, J. C., & Giraldi, G. A. (2003). *Introduction to augmented reality*. National Laboratory for Scientific Computation.

Singapore, V. (2021). *National research foundation*. https://www.nrf.gov.sg/programmes/virtual-singapore

Sitowise. (2021). *AURA*. https://www.sitowise.com/references/aura-user-interface

Skyline. (2021). *TerraExplorer for desktop*. https://www.skylinesoft.com/terraexplorer-for-desktop/

Stojanovski, T. (2018). City Information Modelling (CIM) and Urban Design: Morphological Structure. Design Elements and Programming Classes in CIM. *City Modelling & GIS, 1*(36), 507-516.

Thompson, E. M., Greenhalgh, P., Muldoon-Smith, K., Charlton, J., & Dolník, M. (2016). Planners in the Future City: Using City Information Modelling to Support Planners as Market Actors. *Urban Planning*, *1*(1), 79–94. doi:10.17645/up.v1i1.556

Tucci, C. E. (2007). *Urban Flood Management*. World Meteorological Organization. http://www.apfm.info/pdf/Urban_Flood_Management_En_high.pdf

VU City. (2021). *London*. https://www.vu.city/cities/london

Wissen, U. (2011). Which is the appropriate 3D visualization type for participatory landscape planning workshops? A portfolio of their effectiveness. *Environment and Planning. B, Planning & Design*, *38*(5), 921–939. doi:10.1068/b36113

Chapter 3
Personalization in Adaptive E-Learning

Lamya Anoir
https://orcid.org/0000-0003-4787-5974
Abdelmalek Essaâdi University, Morocco

Mohamed Khaldi
https://orcid.org/0000-0002-1593-1073
Abdelmalek Essaâdi University, Morocco

Mohamed Erradi
Abdelmalek Essaâdi University, Morocco

ABSTRACT

In the face of technological innovation, the field of education has undergone a progressive evolution through the use of technology. Among the techno-pedagogical trend, the authors find the adaptive E-learning which is a new reform. This trend consists in providing personalized learning adapted to individual and collective needs, both in terms of learning pace and content. Through this chapter, they try to link personalization and adaptation. In a first step, they define adaptive e-learning after giving a historical overview of the different adaptive systems from open distance learning to e-learning as well as the components of adaptive systems. In the second part, they define the notion of personalization in adaptive e-learning and the pedagogical scenario. Finally, in the last part of the chapter, they propose an approach to design a personalized and adaptive learning system based on the pedagogical scenarios during the different types of pedagogical activities.

INTRODUCTION

Trends come and go and the best of the reforms or innovations in teaching and learning are always lost. The personalization of teaching and learning cannot be understood without a reflection and propositions on the training of people and teams involved in the educational project and especially in the new reform of e-learning.

DOI: 10.4018/978-1-7998-9121-5.ch003

Nowadays, there are many solutions to realize an adaptive and personalized learning platform. On the one hand, most of these platforms focus on adapting learning paths. By pre-testing the learners and on the basis of the results obtained, the system proposes a personalized learning path so that the content can be adapted to their individual needs. On the other hand, there is a solution that focuses on adapting the learning rhythm and style (Anoir et al., 2020).

With the emergence of new learning technologies personalization refers to a pedagogical approach that takes place in an intermediate space where teaching and learning come together in the form of personalized training devices, adapted and intended for different learner profiles in a social learning context (Tadlaoui & Khaldi, 2020).

Indeed, adaptive learning is a new method that combines technology and pedagogy to meet the challenges of the educational field. It includes adjustments according to the needs of each learner and personalized learning according to the specific skills and needs of each learner. These adaptive educational systems promise to take into account the learner's personal information (knowledge, preferences, capacities, objectives...). The main idea of adaptive learning is to meet the individual needs of each learner in the learning process. Therefore, the role of the teacher is to understand the situation of each learner and to adjust the program. This is why technology can be an effective solution. Adaptive learning does not impose a single plan on all learners, whatever their individual abilities and needs, but it allows them to develop personalized learning and to have the motivation to keep acquiring knowledge.

Our proposed work is based on a scientific context through which, in the first part, we evoke a general context that proposes an overview of adaptive e-learning, personalization, scenarios of the learning activity and in the second part the architectures of personalized scenarios of different learning situations.

ADAPTIVE E-LEARNING BETWEEN PAST, PRESENT AND FUTURE

From Open Distance Learning to e-Learning

Distance learning was developed long before the Internet was deployed. It originated in the Anglo-Saxon world, notably through the open university, which was inaugurated in 1969, based on a project of the university of all knowledge, this project offered the possibility of accessing professional and university qualifications by capitalizable units and with a great deal of distance communication with the use of cassettes, television and radio broadcasts, telephone tutoring, etc (Batime, Weber, 2007).

In the end of the 1980s to 1990s, Distance Learning (DL) originated in correspondence education in London in 1840. The emergence of technological tools such as the telephone, radio, television, CD-ROM, and the Internet, have helped to expand the means of access to distance learning. The intention of the creators of the media consists in the transmission of knowledge, as well as the modality used to deliver the courses. In terms of possible course modalities, we could make a distinction between face-to-face, hybrid and distance learning modes. The first one is the traditional and classical model of the course (courses offered in amphitheatre, tutorials or practical work,)... (d'Ortun & Jézégou, 2005).

According to Chasseneuil, 2000, Open Distance Learning is an organized learning system that takes into consideration the individual and collective dimensions of the learners, and presents complementary learning situations in terms of time, place, pedagogical approaches, technological and resource mediations. It includes individualized learning and access to local or distance resources and skills. Thinking about the opening learning means thinking about the rhythms and sequences to be presented, whether in modules or in courses. Distance then becomes an integral part, not only is it perceived as an obstacle, but accompaniment, tutoring and group work must be introduced (Chasseneuil, 2000).

The term distance education has been alternately applied to various projects, providers, audiences and media by many different researchers, its characteristics are that teachers and learners are separated in space and/or time, learning is voluntarily controlled by learners rather than by distance teachers, and non-continuous communication between learners and everyone else is intermediated (Keegan, 1986; Garrison & Shale, 1987).

Perraton in 1988 defined the role of teacher in distance learning by choosing the most effective media instrument, the teacher becomes a facilitator of learning rather than a communicator of a fixed set of information (Perraton, 1988).

The term Distance education has subsequently evolved to describe other forms of learning, e.g. online learning, e-Learning, technology, mediated learning, online collaborative learning, virtual learning,). Thus, the commonalities found in all definitions is that some form of instruction occurs between two parties (a learner and an instructor), it is held at different times and/or places, and uses different forms of instructional materials (Moore et al., 2011).

Since the 1960s, E-Learning has evolved in different areas such as: in business, education, training sector and military, In school, "E-Learning" refers to the use of software to enhance online learning, while in business, higher education, military and training sectors, it refers only to a range of online practices (Nicholson, 2007) .

Indeed, e-learning is an English term that means learning by electronic means. It refers to the use of technological learning instruments to enhance the process of acquiring new knowledge or updating existing knowledge.

E-Learning could also be considered as an evolution of distance learning, which has exploited the latest technological tools to emerge in the context of education and especially Teaching-Learning. E-Learning refers to the use of multimedia technologies and the Internet, in the educational environment to improve the quality of learning by facilitating access to resources and services, as well as exchanges and collaboration at a distance.

ADAPTIVE E-LEARNING

Adaptive learning, sometimes referred to as intelligent teaching, is a pedagogical method that uses technology as a teaching tool and is responsible for organizing human resources and learning materials according to the unique needs of each learner.

The term "adaptive" is associated with a broad range of system features and functions in the e-learning industry, so the quality attributable to the system must be limited when using this term.

Adaptive learning has been described as a concept ready to redesign education. Its appeal to educators comes primarily from the potential promise of personalized learning (Kerr, 2015). Its attraction to policy decision makers its promises of accountability, increased productivity, and cost savings (Webley, 2013). Though the initial investment cost is very high, online adaptive learning is less expensive than traditional alternatives such as classroom instruction (Spring, 2012).

Adaptive learning is an educational technology, rather than a method. In addition, it is important that the web-based instructional medium be adaptive since it is going to be used by a much larger range of learners, a web instructional medium that is designed with a particular class of users in mind may not be suitable for other users (Boticario et al., 2005).

An adaptive learning environment is a renamed environment that has the ability to monitor learners' activities, interpret them according to the domain-specific model, and deduce learners' requirements and preferences from the explained activities. Finally, take actions based on the learner's available knowledge and the subject matter to dynamically support the learning process. The previous informal definition site should differentiate the concept of adaptability from those of adaptability/configurability, flexibility/ extensibility, or the simple support for intelligent mapping between available/available media and formats and the characteristics of access devices (Paramythis & Loidl-Reisinger, 2003).

An adaptive system must be capable of:

- Managing learning paths adapted to each learner
- Monitoring learner activities
- Interpreting activities using specific models
- Detecting user needs and preferences
- Exploiting the knowledge of learners in the domain to dynamically facilitate the learning process.

A hypermedia system developed in the context of information retrieval in the 1990s. The objective is to use the functions of the hypermedia framework to personalize the system. These systems take into account the objectives, preferences and knowledge of each learner to present fragments of information on hypermedia pages and propose different links to navigate between these pages. On the one hand, research in this area has produced learner models that incorporate different forms of knowledge, and on the other hand, it has produced adaptation technologies that allow the use of annotations to specify the document content or adapt to the navigation structure (Zniber, 2010).

Indeed, adaptive hypermedia systems (AHS) allow learners to progress independently at their own pace, while teachers can simultaneously capture the big picture and individual learners in learning situations. Teachers play the role of knowledge experts. They can get precise statistics on their monitor to understand how the learner as a whole is progressing in a particular subject, which parts of the course are well assimilated. In addition to this global situation, the adaptive learning system also allows teachers to track individual learners.

Adaptive systems are more specialized and focus on adapting the learning content and the presentation of that content.

User information is needed to modify the behavior of the system to satisfy the user's needs at every step and all the time. In adaptive systems, this information is stored in a profile or model of the user. Therefore, this profile allows the adaptability of the system. In the context of e-Learning, and in particular adaptation in the Teaching-Learning domain is assigned, the form of the instructions and the way the learner is educated.

There are several possibilities for adapting teaching. In this chapter, we will present the four main ones: theoretical approaches; the macro-adaptive approach; the micro-adaptive approach; the treatment/ interaction of aptitudes and the collective constructivist approach (Table 1).

Table 1. Theoretical approaches to adaptation of teaching

The collective constructivist approach	The collective constructivist approach insists on how an e-learning system can be integrated into the learning process. The learner takes an active role in the learning process, where knowledge is constructed through experiences in the specific knowledge domain, according to the constructivist learning theory. This approach is based on the use of collaborative technologies, where the pedagogical approach of collaborative learning activities.
The macro-adaptive approach	The first experiment in personalized learner instruction was at the macro level. Learners are grouped or categorized. This grouping results in consistent assessments of and had little effect on adaptation because the groups were very rarely given different instructions
The micro-adaptive approach	The micro-adaptive approach is characterized by the exploration of learning needs during instruction to adapt them. These needs are examined and an appropriate prescription is generated. The micro-adaptive approach is separated into two main processes, the diagnostic process and the prescriptive process. The diagnostic process is used to characterize the learner by identifying the aptitude or prior knowledge and to formulate the task. The normative process, the interaction between the learner and the task is optimized by adapting the learning content for the learners.
The treatment/interaction of aptitudes approach	Strategies for adapting instruction to learners' aptitudes recommend different types of instruction for learners with different profiles. This approach also offers the learner full or partial control over the learning process. The learner is able to control the style of instruction or the process. Three levels of control are defined in this approach, complete independence, partial control within a given task scenario and fixed tasks with rhythm control

Types of Adaptive System

In this section, we will present the different types of adaptive systems using the theoretical approaches previously introduced:

- **Computer Managed Instruction (CMI)** Systems offer many macro-adaptive instructional features that allow the teacher (tutor) to monitor and control the student's learning activities. In addition, CMI systems incorporate features of micro-adaptive models (e.g., prediction of learners' learning needs).
- **Macro adaptive educational systems**: The macro-adaptive approach is considered the oldest approach where learners were simply tracked by aptitude test qualities. This type of system was developed to adapt the operation of the system to the abilities of the learner.
- **Intelligent Tutoring Systems (ITS):** Are adaptive teaching systems applying Artificial Intelligence (AI) techniques. The goal of ITS is to provide the benefits of instruction automatically and in a profitable way (Shute & Psotka, 1994). ITS consists of components representing learning content, instruction and teaching strategies as well as mechanisms for understanding a learner's learning state in consideration. ITS is a true example of personalized learning. Two large families of ITS designs for personalization can be identified. The first, personalization, implies that all learners follow the same learning path, but at different rhythms. The second, identifies a specific pattern that allows each learner to follow a specific learning path based on their responses. In ITS, these components are placed in the expertise module, the learner module, the tutoring module and a user interface module as shown in Figure 1 (Brusilovsky, 1994):

The expertise module evaluates the learner's performance and generates the instructional content.

Figure 1. The components of an ITS (Brusilovsky, 1994)

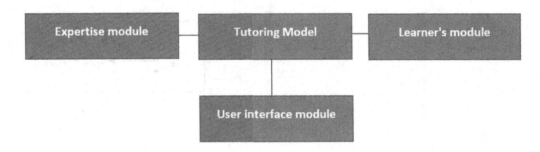

The learner module represents the user's current knowledge and evaluates his or her reasoning strategies and conceptions, which allows ITS to determine the appropriate teaching process to proceed.

The tutoring module contains information for the selection of teaching materials.

The user interface module is the communication component that controls the interaction between the learner and the system. STI applies the micro-adaptive model from the decision to learn in the diagnosis and the teaching prescriptions are generated during the task. In addition, a combination with aptitude variables allows the expertise module to generate conditions for obtaining instructions based on the learner's characteristics (Mödritscher et al., 2004).

Adaptive hypermedia systems (AHS) can be traced back to the beginning of the 1990s. The hypermedia model has been extended using user models. AHS are inspired by ITS and try to combine educational systems and hypermedia systems based on adaptation. Therefore, three criteria are satisfied by "AHS". The first criterion is that the system is based on hypertext or hypermedia, the second criterion is that a user model must be applied and thirdly, the system is able to adapt the hypermedia using this user model. Now, AHS have been used in educational systems, e-commerce applications, information systems and help systems.

The Learner Model in Adaptive Hypermedia System

The learner model is an essential element in adaptive e-Learning systems. The adaptation of an e-Learning system mainly involves the selection and presentation of each learning activity taking into consideration the learner's knowledge of the subject matter and other relevant learner characteristics. Therefore, the learner model is used to modify the interaction between the system and the learner to meet the individual needs of learners.

According to Kay, there are three main ways that a learner model can assist in adaptation. These are represented in Figure 2, indicated by arrows. Between the small rectangles the interaction between the user and the system is delineated (Kay, 2000).

The arrows interpret the actions of the learners in front of the interface. It covers all possible actions, which are available through the user interface, such as (mouse actions, typing on the keyboard,). In this case the user model can support the system to interpret this information. In addition, the learner model can help the system to interpret incorrect learner actions

Figure 2. The role of the user model in adaptation

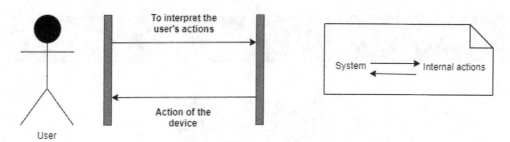

The arrows interpreting the interface actions represent the actions initiated by the system. A learner model can be used to control and modify these actions to the learner's preferences. This process consists of adapting the behavior of the system and turns to the learner or the adaptation of the content as well as the presentation of the content. Adaptive hypermedia systems focus on adapting navigation and content by considering the preferences and domain knowledge stored in the user model. The learner's model supports the system during internal actions. Often, the internal actions are filtering processes where the received information is sifted. These internal actions are influenced by the learner's model, especially by the knowledge and learning of the learner's preferences. After this internal process, the system generates an action at the interface. The form of the presentation of this action is also affected by the learner's model

Learner models can be used in very different ways, depending on the actions and characteristics of the learner in the system. As there are different types of adaptive e-learning systems, the learner models applied are different. To describe models of the learner in educational adaptive hypermedia systems, the possible adaptations must be introduced first.

According to Brusilovsky, mainly the presentation of hypermedia and navigation through hyperspace can be adapted as illustrated in Figure 3. These two aspects are subdivided into several adaptive hypermedia technologies (Brusilovsky, 2001).

To be able to adapt the presentation of learning content and navigation for the needs of the learner, a model of the learner is needed, including objectives or tasks, knowledge, pre-requisites and learner preferences.

Brusilovsky describes a new type of adaptation for web-based systems. The nature of web-based systems allows the user to change their learning environment. Thus, several, different hardware, software and platforms can be used by the same user which requires adaptation to the user's environment (Brusilovsky, 2001).

An adaptive hypermedia system should contain a domain model, a learner model, an adaptation model, also known as a pedagogical model, and an adaptation engine.

The domain model describes how information is structured and linked together. The learner model represents a set of learner characteristics and preferences for navigating the hypermedia space and the adaptation model consists of pedagogical rules, which define how the domain model relates to the learner model in order to provide adaptation. The adaptive engine is responsible for processing the adaptation by manipulating the navigation fragments or the page content before the adapted page is sent to the user interface (De Bra et al., 1999)

Figure 3. Adaptive hypermedia technologies (Brusilovsky, 2001)

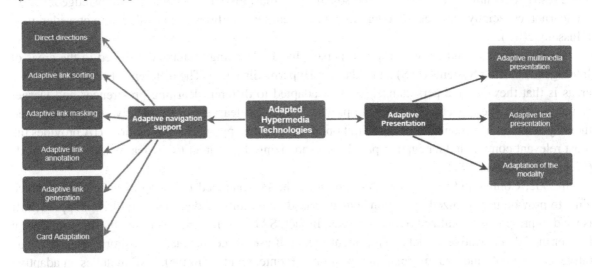

The models proposed in the work of De Bra et al. and the learner model in ITS are similar. The domain model serves the same purpose as the expert model in ITS. The learner models provide insight into the models applied in different types of systems. Preferences and characteristics are essentially modeled in a student or learner model by all systems.

An adaptive system needs information about the user's object adaptation to the system, a user model is needed, this model can be used in these three different types of system actions. The system can interpret the user's actions according to the characteristics stored in the user's model, which allows the instruction to be adapted. Adaptive macro systems employ a simple model of the user. The instruction is adapted for the forward mode and no adaptation is processed during the learning activity. The user models used in ITS and AHS are more sophisticated and store more information about the learners. The focus is on user and system interactions during instruction and on domain knowledge. This allows the system to be adapted to the learner's preferences and current state of knowledge.

EVOLUTION OF PERSONALIZED EDUCATIONAL HYPERMEDIA SYSTEMS

In recent years, the evolution of the Web and especially the emergence of the news have encouraged the development of personalized educational hypermedia systems to support and facilitate teaching and learning based on the needs of learners in the context of the implementation of adaptive E-Learning reform.

Adaptive educational hypermedia systems create a model for learners' needs, characteristics and knowledge, it identifies and adapts the needs based on the learner's interaction with the system (Brusilovsky, 2003). Adaptive teaching approaches and techniques allow for personalized learning environments adapted to different individual needs (İnan & Grant, 2011). Adaptive learning environments also allow learners to identify their own learning methods, as well as personalized learning opportunities based on their needs (Aydogdu, 2020).

This while most adaptive, personalized systems focus firstly on learners' preferences, interests, and behaviors, neglecting the importance of the learner's abilities. Indeed, according to Hussain in 2012, some researchers have pointed out that personalization must take into account the knowledge levels of the learner, especially with regard to learning where learners' abilities can be taken into consideration. (Hussain, 2012).

In 1982, Sleeman and Brown proposed personalized e-learning systems developed in the areas of Intelligent Tutoring Systems (ITS) and Adaptive Hypermedia (AH). The difference between these two areas is that they provide personalized content adapted to different learning preferences and learner characteristics. The objective of ITS is to provide content to learners in an adaptive mode. However, these systems set limits on learners and limit opportunities to support free exploration. HA provides the most relevant content and navigation path by personalizing the content to the learners' learning needs (Sleeman & Brown, 1982).

In 2002, Conlan and his collaborators provided the Personalized Learning Service (PLS), which aims to provide personalized education courses based on a multi-model, metadata-driven approach. It is used to provide personalized online services. In fact, SAP's architecture is based on three models: a learner model, a narrative model and a content model. It uses three metadata repositories (learner, narrative and content) and two information repositories (content and narrative). SAP includes an adaptive engine that uses Java System Shell (JSS) wizards with personalized functions as the basis for its rules engine. The role of the rules engine is to generate a personalized curriculum model based on the narrative and learner models. The personalized curriculum model based on extensible markup language (XML) encapsulates the learner's curriculum structure and generates content based on the learner's learning needs (Conlan et al., 2002).

In 2005, Chen et al. demonstrated their personalization of e-learning systems using item response theory, which provides personalized learning based on the difficulty of the course material and the learners' responses (Chen et al., 2005). Therefore, by considering the impact of learners' abilities on personalization, taking these abilities into account can improve learning performance (Chen, 2008).

In 2009, according to Hendler, many researchers used technology and principles of the Semantic Web to find new ways to design a personalized adaptive online learning system based on the use of ontology to describe knowledge (Hendler, 2009).

In 2013, Yarandi and colleagues proposed a system that provides adaptability based on the learner's learning style based on the Felder-Solomon method. This education method is a hybrid method that combines ITS and AH methods. These are adaptive technologies that can be personalized to the learner's needs (Yarandi, et al., 2013).

The Personalized Learning Object Recommender System (PLORS) was proposed by Canadian and Chinese researchers such as Imran in 2016. PLAORS provides object-based learning recommendations in the course. The purpose of the system is to enable the learning management system (LMS) to provide recommendations to learners, taking into account the learning objects they visit and the learning objects visited by other learners with similar profiles. PLORS uses information about learners by accessing log data tracked by LMS, such as their learning styles, behaviors, preferences... objects. The overall objective of PLORS is to provide learners with recommendations for learning objects when the learning objects that learner's access are different from those accessed by other similar learners (Imran et al., 2016).

In 2018, Zhou et al. proposed a new comprehensive model for personalized learning recommendation. The model is based on clustering and machine learning technology. It is based on the similarity measurement features of learners. Learners are clustered to form an LSTM Long Short-Term memory to predict the student's learning path and sufficient performance. Then select a personalized learning path based on the results of the predicted path, and finally recommend a comprehensive adaptive learning path specifically to test learners (Zhou et al., 2018).

In 2019, Mwambe and Kamioka proposed an approach based on Brain Computer Interface (BCI) which is an e-learning system for prior knowledge assessment, the e-learning Prior Knowledge Assessment System (ePKAS) which can detect the learner's knowledge level history and multimedia content. The ePKAS algorithm's matching score is based on information about learning activities using collaborative tools. The model is categorized by learning philosophy and learning content, and personalized through the adaptation model. The model is associated with three related concepts to generate personalization. These concepts are: domain model, user model and personalize package. The latter is associated with a learning session and provides personalized learning content relevant to a learning concept (Al Abri et al., 2020).

All of the initiatives described in this section show that the research in the area of personalized learning is rich and its evolution and implementation differs depending on the context and situation. Personalized learning systems generally use technology to enhance adaptive and personalized learning opportunities for all learners

PERSONALIZATION IN ADAPTIVE E-LEARNING AND THE PEDAGOGICAL SCENARIO

Personalization between Individualization and Differentiation

The term personalization is often encountered in the literature and refers to providing information specifically adapted to the needs of an individual or group of individuals. According to Weibelzahl, personalization can be provided by adapting the content or visualization of the system to the learners' preferences (Weibelzahl, 2003).

Personalized learning is a systematic learning design that focuses on adapting the learning to the learners.

Personalized learning provides flexibility and support for learners to learn what, how, when, and where to learn and to demonstrate knowledge proficiency. Specifically, this flexibility and support is designed around instructional methods, content, activities, objectives, and learning results (Walkington & Bernacki, 2020).

Personalization is different from differentiation and individualization, personalization requires a major shift in focus from a teacher-centered approach to an authentic, learner-centered approach. Personalized forms of learning offer an approach adapted to the diverse abilities, preferences, interests, and other needs of each learner. Thus, it gives students more autonomy to develop their own learning paths and with more opportunity for creativity, collaboration, content creation (Song et al., 2012).

The notion of personalization of learning includes the individualization of teaching, where the learner can progress at his or her own rhythm, and can choose different learning methods according to their preferences or profile (Bejaoui et al., 2017).

Personalizing is not individualizing. Individualizing is about one-on-one instruction, while personalizing is about the collective and cooperative dimension of learning. Personalizing one's teaching is above all trying to respond to the identified needs of groups of learners. The diagram in Figure 4 shows us the difference between individualizing and personalizing (Connac, 2018; Tadlaoui & Khaldi, 2020).

According to Sylvain Connac defines the individualization of learning as a new organization on the part of the teacher, in order to respond to the needs of learners and also adaptations of his teaching practice (Connac, 2012).

Individualization of learning can be achieved in three ways:

- **Individual work**: each learner is required to perform alone without interaction, adapted to each or the same for all.
- **Isolated work:** learners with specific profiles who are removed from the class to complete a task
- **Individualized work:** each learner is given or chooses an assignment that corresponds to him/her and has several ways to do it without any interaction

Figure 4. Personalization and individualization

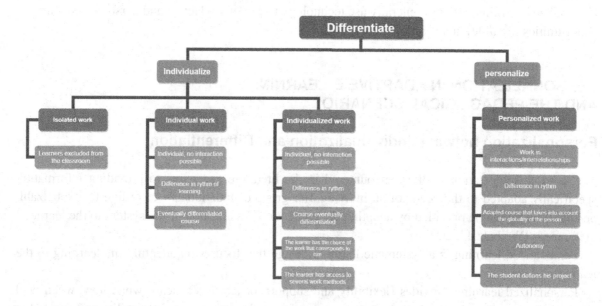

Pedagogical differentiation in schools is therefore not synonymous with individualization of teaching: even if there is no differentiation without more individualized management of learning processes, this does not mean that learners work alone or with only one teacher (Perrenoud, 1995).

Differentiation and individualization are modes of pedagogical organization that allow the implementation of the personalization process. The differentiation of pedagogy, or differentiated pedagogy, implements a flexible framework in which learning is sufficiently explicit and diversified so that learners can work according to their own appropriation paths while remaining within a collective approach to teaching the common knowledge and skills required.

Consequently, in pedagogy, individualization is not personalization. The individualization of learning consists in creating paths adapted to the profile of each learner. In particular, it would mean that learners coexist in the same class, each performing activities that correspond to them, but without any interaction. In personalization, it is the learner who chooses the resources that seem relevant to him or her after having conducted a reflective activity on him or herself and on his or her learning (Lefevre et al., 2012; Avanzini, 1992).

In conclusion, the personalization of learning corresponds to the set of pedagogical organizations that considers the learner as a person, i.e., that recognizes both his or her individual dimension and the political nature of the human condition. Personalization therefore consists in assembling three pedagogical approaches: the didactic approach, individualized work and cooperative interactions.

The Didactic Approach: construction of knowledge through the social confrontation of representations.

Individualized work: each learner carries out work with a certain degree of autonomy, solicits the help of a classmate or provides assistance.

Cooperative Interaction: allows learners to work together, to ask for help from a classmate or to provide their own.

Personalization promotes the development of the learner's personality by helping him/her to determine his/her learning in an autonomous way that is adapted to his/her needs and abilities.

Personalized Learning and Cooperative Learning

Cooperative learning presents the best practical example of contemporary teaching, and corresponds to a socio-centered learning mode, where personal success is subordinated to the success of the group. However, two main principles are recognized from the outset by the main researchers in the domain: individual responsibility and positive interdependence (Blondin, 2020).

Individual responsibility refers to the learner's personal management of learning, and involves the learner in achieving a goal and contributing to the improvement of individual academic performance by promoting positive work behaviors and learner autonomy (Johnson & Johnson, 1994).

Cooperative learning is based on groups with very diverse profiles, heterogeneous groups. Figure 5 supposed to energize exchanges and promote interactivity.

Figure 5. The cooperative approach according to Henri & Lundgren-Cayrol, 1997

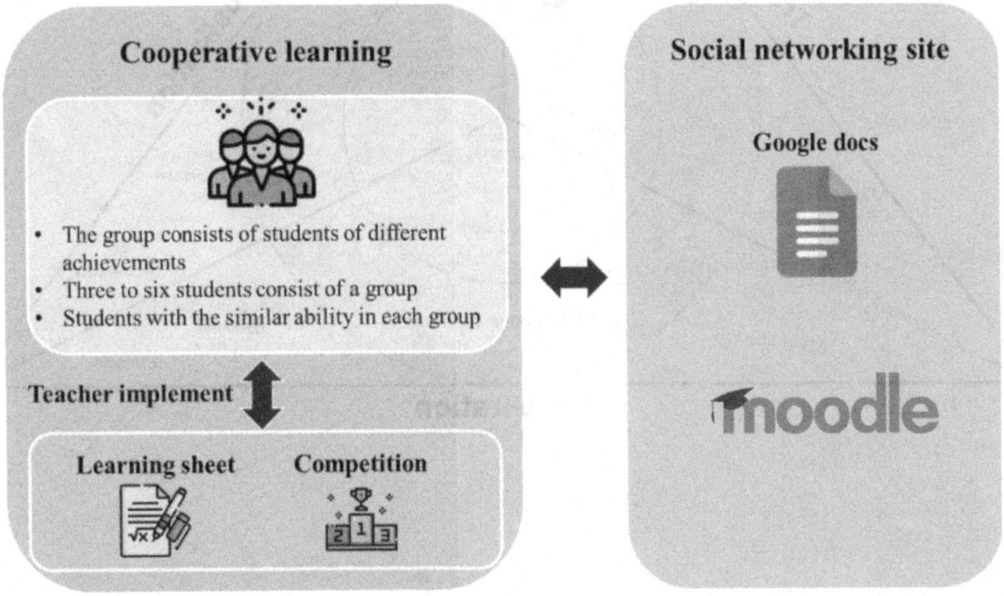

Collaborative learning is designed to progress and cooperative learning to fix learning (Baudrit, 2007). Indeed, cooperative learning corresponds to a division of tasks between learners, where each one can autonomously and responsibly accomplish his or her part of the work that cooperative learning teaching methods, models, and procedures organize learners so that they:

- Work in groups toward a common objective or result.
- Share problem situations
- Conduct work through interdependent behavior
- Take into account individual contributions and efforts

Cooperative groups generally work toward a common or shared objective. The way to achieve the objective through cooperation relies on the distribution of tasks and responsibilities within the group.

In the journal Education and socialisation, Sylvain Connac proposes an article in which he questions these different terms (Figure 6). He provides a clarification for a better understanding of pedagogical action and, more precisely, a matrix of three reference points for thinking about forms of personalization, presenting personalization as a closer organization than differentiation

Figure 6. The target of educational differentiation (Connac, 2021)

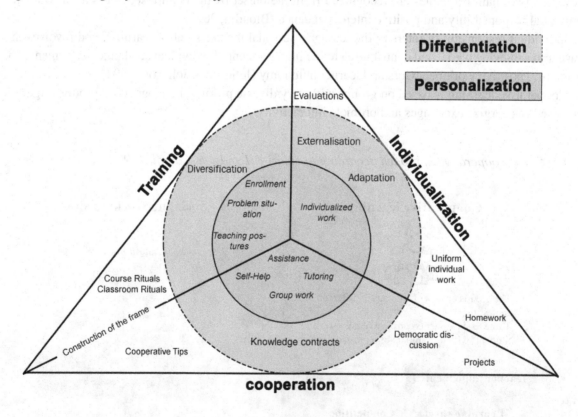

In conclusion, personalization is linked to cooperation and to a conception of the person, where the person is an individual. Personalization is not based on group work, where the important thing is the instructions and activities given by the teacher, with cooperation we are not in close control of the learners' activities.

The Pedagogical Scenario

The personalization of learning activities is a fundamental issue in the research of personalized adaptive hypermedia systems, pedagogical practices are the source of the implementation of personalized learning activities or more precisely the personalization of pedagogical scenarios based on different types of pedagogical approaches. Generally, a pedagogical scenario describes the course of a learning activity, its objectives, the planning of tasks, the description of the learners' tasks and the modalities of evaluation, it is the result of a process of design of a learning activity that has resulted in the implementation of the scenario

The scenario has a triple role: it defines precisely the activities proposed to the learners on IEP (Interactive Education Objects), it also specifies the control of the learner's progress during a pedagogical activity; finally, it determines the pedagogical assistance according to his progress (Anoir et al., 2020).

In the process of educational engineering, the interest in educational situations is expressed, where the situation is the central element of the educational treatment that intervenes in the stages of knowledge modeling, media processing and communication (Paquette, 2002). The pedagogical scenario includes two other scenarios: the learning scenario and the assistance scenario, including descriptions of specific activities for learning, we are talking about the set of activities intended for learners and organized in a coherent whole, and the assistance scenario, specifies the modalities of intervention of the tutor teachers as designed to support the learning scenario (Quintin et al., 2005; Villiot-Leclercq, 2007; Paquette et al., 1997).

The process of pedagogical scenarization is described in the form of a theater metaphor, which we reproduce by using the version that is expressed in the development of a learning unit is described by an element called method, which organizes the different deployments in the form of pieces. A piece is composed of acts performed in sequence. The acts are made up of scores that associate a role with an activity performed in an environment (Pernin, 2005).

Scenarization is understood as the process of developing educational scenarios designed to be used and operated in a learning environment. It is implemented by teachers, trainers or educational engineers to align complex learning situations and interact between different objects (resources, activities, instruments, tools) (Lamya et al., 2021).

Indeed, the pedagogical scenario is the result of the design process of learning activities. It represents an a priori or posterior description of the learning situation or of the unfolding of a learning unit, and aims at assigning a specific set of knowledge, roles, activities and resources for handling knowledge, tools and services necessary for the implementation of the activity. In our case our objective is to propose a general approach to the personalization of the pedagogical scenarios during the different types of pedagogical activities by taking into consideration the learning styles of the learners, their preferences and their profile. In the following part we propose the personalization of the architecture of a pedagogical scenario in an adaptive Hypermedia System during the different types of learning activities.

PERSONALIZATION OF THE ARCHITECTURE OF AN PEDAGOGICAL SCENARIO IN AN ADAPTIVE HYPERMEDIA SYSTEM

Pedagogical scenarios according to the socioconstructivist method, the design of learning paths and personalized pedagogical scenarios must take into account the fact that learners are not only independent individuals, but also individuals who actively participate during the learning situation, as well as individuals who belong to the collective where learning occurs through social links and relationships.

As Koper points out, a pedagogical modeling language must allow for the adaptation of content and activities to each learner, in terms of preferences, prerequisites, and especially their pedagogical needs in learning (Koper, 2001).

Scenarios are composed of one or more activities that can belong to one or more of the following classes:

- **Learning activity**: Actions performed by learners.
- **Assisting activity:** Actions performed by a trainer or another type of facilitator, person or software.

The scenario aims at building a comprehensive, supported and mediated learning process. Scenario building is primarily a work of content design, resource organization, event planning and implementation to support learning, i.e., integrating the contributions of different experts in the field to design and implement scenarios.

The open scenario can be modified or personalized to better meet the needs of learners and their learning, which we refer to as adaptive or adaptive scenes (Pernin & Lejeune, 2004; Law & Sun, 2012).

Adaptation is generally done to the learner's profile, which refers to a set of information about a learner or a group of learners, captured, collected or deducted at the end of one or more educational activities (Pernin & Lejeune, 2004).

On the one hand, the adaptation can be done in advance of the adaptive hypermedia system, and different scenarios of the system will be modeled in advance, but according to different types of learners' profiles

On the other hand, it can be done in an adaptive hypermedia system, which allows learners to dynamically adapt the learning scenario according to their performance and their learning rhythm.

In the work carried out in the design of educational scenarios, it is accepted that their description is part of a life cycle taken from the software development domain. A representation of this life cycle inspired by the work conducted by (Laforcade, 2004; Vantroys, 2003; El-Kechai, 2008), which is presented in figure 6 which describes the iterative and incremental process for designing a scenario based on 6 steps

Initial expression of requirements.

- Analysis and design.
- Implementation or set-up.
- Deployment.
- Testing.
- Evaluation.

According to Maha et al. 2021, the design of a scenario must follow a number of essential steps, including five (Khaldi et al., 2021):

Figure 7. Iterative process for designing a pedagogical scenario

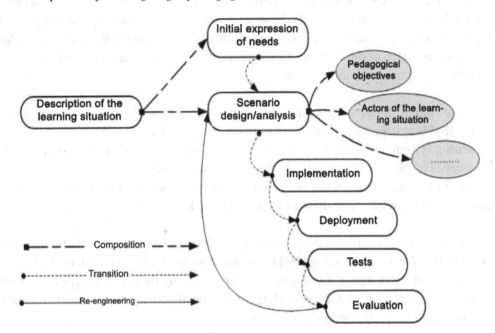

Definition of the objective(s), Sequencing, Development of the scenario, Implementation, Evaluation

The design and implementation of the courses is based on the principle of incremental design, which defines a working mode in which the products that are developed will be progressively refined. There are two main tools for online scenario teaching. These tools are effective to the extent that they help to approach the scenario process in an organized and rational methodology.

- **The Activity Diagram (AD):** The role of each of the actors (teacher, learner and class group) in the scenario is clarified in an activity diagram (AD) inspired by the UML (Unified Modeling Language) diagrams used for IT project management. The AD must highlight the scenario flow in the context of personalization by locating the intervention of the two categories of actors in the sequence of activities.
- **The Specification Table (TS):** this table corresponds to a description of each of the tasks proposed to the learner by reference to a series of dimensions of which we quote
    - Nature, origin and purpose of the material submitted to the learners and the results expected from them; Sequencing of the proposed tasks and the criteria for this sequencing; Structuring and regulation tools; Monitoring and interaction procedures.

In order to produce and maintain a personalized and adaptive scripting within the framework of an adaptive e-Learning system, it is necessary to propose adapted activities and a gradation of complexity in accordance with the learner's level, learning style, preferences,... To do this, it is necessary to know the learner's state of knowledge in relation to the task in order to alter it according to the learner's profile (for example, increase the difficulty or propose assistance), we then speak of personalization (Lamya et al., 2021).

Open Distance Learning (ODL) is considered today as the most reliable way to widen access to education while improving the quality of education, promoting peer collaboration and giving learners a greater sense of autonomy and responsibility in learning (Calvert, 2006). It refers to modular teaching where the modularization of the content of each module is made up of learning situations.

The module is composed of three systems:

- **An entry system:** It takes care of the management of the flow of students entering the module, it is through this system the learner accesses the training module.
- **A learning system:** also called the body of the module, it is the training itself that must be adapted to the needs of the learner according to the activities to be carried out.
- **An output system:** manages the end of the module and the orientation that is necessary on the acquisition of knowledge and mastery of skills by the learner.

Based on the work carried out by Burgos (Burgos, 2008), depover and his collaborators (Depover et al., 2014) as well as the work carried out by khaldi and other researchers (Khaldi et al., 2021), concerning the adaptation of the design of a pedagogical scenario during the different types of activity as well as the personalization of each scenario according to the type of activity, the following Figure 8 presents the 4 types of scenario during a learning situation.

Figure 8. Example of a life cycle of a pedagogical scenario of a learning situation

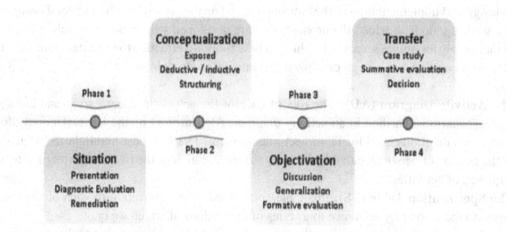

At this stage and based on the proposals of our theoretical framework, we propose architectures of scenarios showing the stakes of personalization of pedagogical activities in the teaching-learning practices in the different learning situations without taking into account the discipline, or the concept created.

After identifying the learner's preferred learning styles, our work consists in designing pedagogical scenarios that correspond to their styles during a learning activity.

SITUATIONAL SCENARIO

In the situational activity, we propose a situational scenario in which the teacher's role is to set up the learning situation, the scenario in this activity is a tool for the presentation of the learning situation and also diagnostic to situate the state of knowledge of the learner before the beginning of the situation. The teacher can then know the strengths and weaknesses of the learner and adapt afterwards by proposing a remediation activity with resources adapted to the learner's needs.

Figure 9. Personalized situational scenario

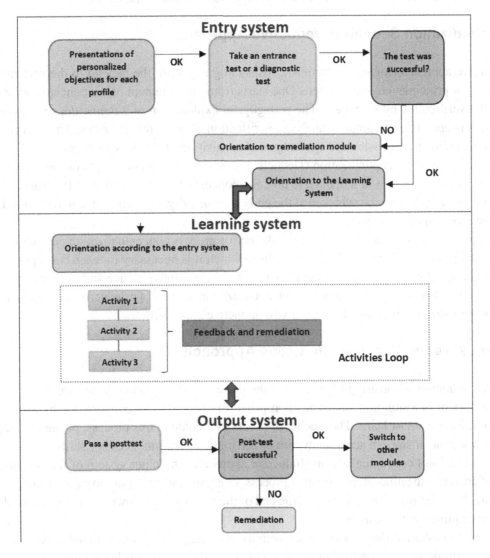

In the situational scenario, the entry system consists of presenting personalized objectives according to each learner profile in order to ensure a learning orientation. In this phase, we propose a pre-test in order to diagnose the learner's deficiencies in order to position his or her course. The learning system includes content, activities, learning support elements as well as elements that facilitate the structuring of knowledge and the output system consists of orienting the learner at the end of the training based on the results of the post-test to verify that the learner has correctly understood the concepts in this activity.

CONCEPTUALIZATION SCENARIO

In the structuring activity, we propose a structuring scenario that links the structuring / conceptualization activities (inductive approach, deductive approach), the objective in these activities is to favor the construction of knowledge and its use in the development of skills in the learner

Conceptualization Scenario: Deductive Approach

The deductive approach (logical deduction) consists in going from the general to the particular, from the abstract (or principles) to the concrete. One starts from the statement of the concept and/or the rule to go to the verification by examples. The pedagogical exploitation of a theme does not exclude this approach: concepts, rules, examples, analysis, verification of concepts and rules. This is a conception of explicit teaching: transmission of knowledge and acquisition of skills by the learner.

In the Scenario of conceptualization (Deductive approach), the input system of the scenario of the activity of conceptualization of a deductive process, concerns the presentation of the learning activity by defining the objectives to be achieved at the end of the activity, the knowledge to be learned and the skills to be acquired by the learner.

The learning system of the scenario of the deductive process conceptualization activity consists of activating the prior knowledge of the learners, from which it is necessary to teach concepts, target notions, provide examples and contrast examples, put the learners into practice and evaluate the learning.

The output system of the scenario of the conceptualization activity of a deductive approach is a review of the conceptualization activity of the proposed deductive approach.

Conceptualization Scenario: Inductive Approach

The inductive approach consists of going from the particular to the general, this approach is one that places the student in a situation where he appropriates by herself or in cooperation, by exploration or observation, what he must learn. The teacher then acts as a guide in this process, placing the learner in situations where he or she can accompany him or her in the development of her skills.

In the Scenario of conceptualization (Inductive approach), the input system of the scenario of the activity of conceptualization of an inductive process, concerns the presentation of the learning activity by defining the objectives to be achieved at the end of the activity, the knowledge to be acquired and the skills to be acquired by the learner.

The learning system of the scenario of the activity of conceptualization of an inductive process consists of an illustration of a theoretical process and testing the relationships between two or more events, it serves to evaluate the learning, and consolidate them to make the learners produce the definition, provide examples and counter-examples of the concepts or notions to be learned, and finally to activate the prior knowledge of the learners. Indeed, Inquiry, Induction, Problem Solving, Decision Making and Discovery are terms that are used interchangeably to describe indirect instruction. The first phase in this system involves the completion of the task by each learner and then the discussion of the learners' results followed by the interpretation of the results obtained to justify the empirical results obtained and to confront them with theoretical laws and rules.

The output system of the scenario of the conceptualization activity of an inductive approach is a review of the conceptualization activity of the proposed inductive approach.

Figure 10. Personalized conceptualization scenario (Deductive Approach)

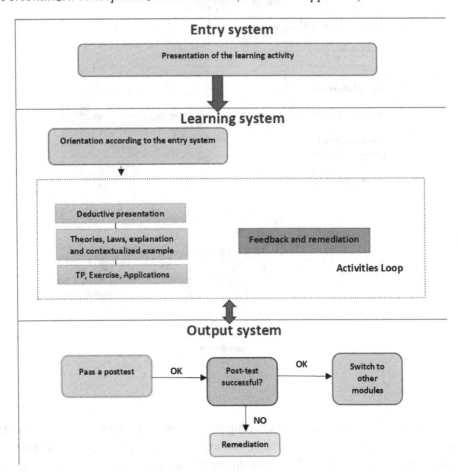

EVALUATION SCENARIO

Formative Evaluation

Pedagogical evaluation in the general sense is a systematic approach to determining how well a learner has learned in relation to a standard, such as course objectives or average learner performance. To make the evaluation process valid, it is necessary to know what to evaluate, how to evaluate it, and what instruments to use. Two forms of evaluation can be used, depending on the objectives to be achieved: formative evaluation and summative evaluation.

Figure 11. Personalized conceptualization scenario (Inductive Approach)

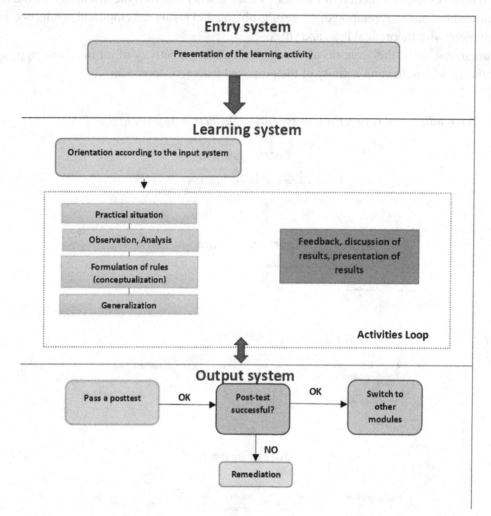

Formative evaluation is designed to favor learning progress and to inform the learner and the teacher about what has been learned or what needs to be improved. It is aimed at specific learning objectives and involves one or more interventions. It is done during the activity and aims to report on the learners' progress and enable them to understand the nature of their mistakes and difficulties encountered. It can be facilitated by the teacher, but can also take the form of self-evaluation or peer feedback.

The scenario of the input system for the formative evaluation activity concerns the presentation of the evaluation activity by declaring the learning situations/activities to be evaluated by identifying the knowledge and skills to be tested in the learner.

The scenario-based learning system for formative evaluation of a learning situation. It starts with a presentation of the tasks to be performed and their instructions according to the proposed formative evaluation (exercises, questions, etc.). The next step concerns the learner's performance of the proposed tasks by trying to test by himself the levels of knowledge acquisition and skills to be acquired and his ability to apply them in the given situations on the one hand and by analyzing his involvement and engagement in the construction of his knowledge on the other hand. The last step of this learning system is the remediation of difficulties encountered by the learner and adapting his learning according to the context and the situation.

The output system of the scenario of a formative evaluation of a learning situation concerns a review of the evaluation activity taking into account the results of the remediation and adaptation already treated in the learning system.

Figure 12. Personalized evaluation scenario (formative evaluation)

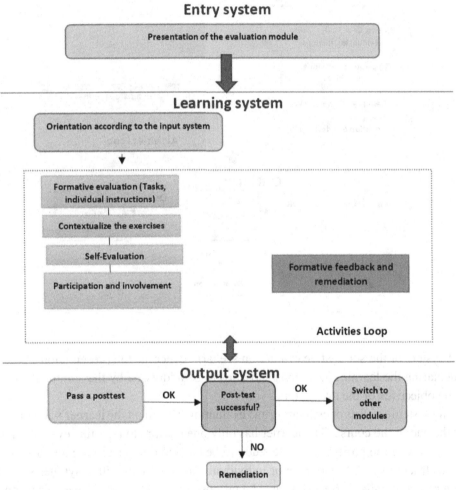

Summative Evaluation

Summative or certificate evaluation is used to attest or recognize learning. It occurs at the end of a teaching process and serves to sanction or certify the degree of mastery of student learning. It is the responsibility of the teacher and must be carried out in a way that is fair and equitable and reflects the students' achievements.

Figure 13. Personalized evaluation scenario (summative evaluation)

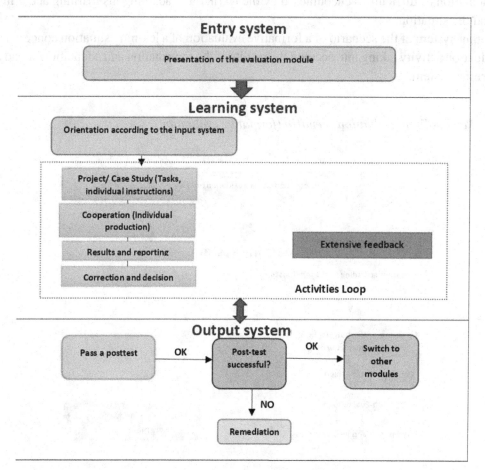

The input system of the summative evaluation scenario concerns the presentation of the evaluation activity by declaring the learning situations/activities to be addressed by the summative evaluation by identifying the objectives of the evaluation.

The learning system consists of estimating and evaluating the sum of the learner's acquired knowledge and skills at the end of the course. The learner has only one attempt to pass this evaluation, he/she first offers a presentation of the project or a case study to be carried out, specifying the tasks to be carried out and their instructions in a cooperative or individual way to end up with a synthesis and the results presented in a report. Finally, corrections must be proposed by the teacher to make decisions.

The output system of a summative evaluation scenario concerns an evaluation of the evaluation activity taking into account the results obtained for an adaptation and an improvement of the learning for a future training.

CONCLUSION

Personalization in adaptive e-Learning has become a very important topic in scientific research in recent years.

Adaptive learning is about providing personalized instruction to fit the needs of each individual in terms of learning speed and content. Due to the digital transformation of education, the pedagogy is particularly possible. Therefore, in addition to the possibilities offered by digital technology, it seems necessary to study the meaning of learning and teaching in this ever-changing world and that technology is experiencing exponential progress.

Personalization aims to develop individualized learning programs for each learner with the intention of involving them in the learning process.

Adaptation is usually performed on learner profiles, which specify a set of information about the learner or a group of learners that is captured, collected or inferred after one or more learning activities. The adaptation can also be realized in advance of the adaptive hypermedia system where different scenarios of the system will be modeled previously, but according to different types of learners' profiles.

On the other hand, it can be done in an adaptive hypermedia system, which allows learners to dynamically adjust the learning scenarios according to their performance and learning speed. The initial design of the scenario allows to define a priori the organization and the process of the learning situation, and to define more precisely the learning activities.

The proposed approach is based on a pedagogical framework that consists in personalizing the different learning scenarios according to the different types of activities.

FUTURE DIRECTIONS

We see mainly directions in which to continue this work, our proposal presents an approach that allows personalization in adaptive e-Learning in order to develop a compliant training device. The notion of personalization of learning includes the individualization of teaching, where the learner can progress at his own pace, and the differentiation of learning, where he can choose between different learning methods according to his own preferences or characteristics in order to develop a personalized and adaptive system in the results that we can publish in future articles.

ACKNOWLEDGMENT

I wish to express my sincere appreciation to my supervisors, Professor Khaldi Mohamed and Erradi Mohamed, and all members of our team Computer Science and University Pedagogical Engineering who have the substance of a genius, they convincingly guided and encouraged me, we thank also Higher Normal School, Abdelmalek Essaadi University, for their support in our works and scientific researches.

REFERENCES

Al Abri, A., Jamoussi, Y., AlKhanjari, Z., & Kraiem, N. (2020). PerLCol: A Framework for Personalized e-Learning with Social Collaboration Support. *International Journal of Computing and Digital Systems*, 9(03).

Avanzini, G. (1992). Pourquoi l'individualisation? AECSE, Individualiser les parcours de formation. Actes du colloque des 6 et 7 décembre 1991, Lyon.

Aydogdu, Ö. (2020). A Web Based System Design for Creating Content in Adaptive Educational Hypermedia and Its Usability. *Malaysian Online Journal of Educational Technology*, 8(3), 1–24. doi:10.17220/mojet.2020.03.001

Batime, C. & Weber, E. (2007). La formation ouverte et/ou à distance, un levier pour des dispositifs de formation en mutation. *Vie sociale, 4*(4), 127-150.

Baudrit, A. (2007). Apprentissage coopératif/Apprentissage collaboratif: D'un comparatisme conventionnel à un comparatisme critique. *Les Sciences de l'Education pour l'Ere Nouvelle, 40*(1), 115–136. doi:10.3917/lsdle.401.0115

Bejaoui, R., Paquette, G., Basque, J., & Henri, F. (2017). Cadre d'analyse de la personnalisation de l'apprentissage dans les cours en ligne ouverts et massifs (CLOM). *Revue STICEF (Sciences et Technologies de l'Information et de la Communication pour l'Éducation et la Formation), 24*(2).

Boticario, J. G., Santos, O. C., & van Rosmalen, P. (2005). Issues in Developing Standard based Adaptive LearningManagement Systems. *EADTU 2005 Working Conference: Towards Lisbon 2010: Collaboration for Innovative Content in Lifelong Openand Flexible Learning.*

Brusilovskiy, P. L. (1994). The construction and application of student models in intelligent tutoring systems. *Journal of Computer and Systems Sciences International, 32*(1), 70–89.

Brusilovsky, P. (2003). Developing adaptive educational hypermedia systems: From design models to authoring tools. In *Authoring tools for advanced technology Learning Environments* (pp. 377–409). Springer. doi:10.1007/978-94-017-0819-7_13

Burgos Solans, D. (2008). *Extension of the IMS Learnin Design specification based on adaptation and integration of units of learning*. Academic Press.

Calvert, J. (2006). *Achieving Development Goals - Foundations: Open and Distance Learning*. Lessons and Issues.

Chasseneuil. (2000). *Formations ouvertes et à distance l'accompagnement pédagogique et organisationnel*. Collectif de Chasseneuil.

Chen, C. M. (2008). Intelligent web-based learning system with personalized learning path guidance. *Computers & Education, 51*(2), 787–814. doi:10.1016/j.compedu.2007.08.004

Chen, C. M., Lee, H. M., & Chen, Y. H. (2005). Personalized e-learning system using item response theory. *Computers & Education, 44*(3), 237–255. doi:10.1016/j.compedu.2004.01.006

Conlan, O., Wade, V., Bruen, C., & Gargan, M. (2002, May). Multi-model, metadata driven approach to adaptive hypermedia services for personalized elearning. In *International Conference on Adaptive Hypermedia and Adaptive Web-Based Systems* (pp. 100-111). Springer. 10.1007/3-540-47952-X_12

Connac, S. (2012). Analyse de contenu de plans de travail: Vers la responsabilisation des élèves? *Revue des Sciences de l'Education*, *38*(2), 323–349. doi:10.7202/1019609ar

Connac, S. (2018). *La personnalisation des apprentissages: agir face à l'hétérogénéité, à l'école et au collège*. ESF Sciences Humaines.

Connac, S. (2021). Pour différencier: individualiser ou personnaliser?. Éducation et socialisation. *Les Cahiers du CERFEE*, (59).

d'Ortun, F., & Jézégou, A. (2005). Formations ouvertes. Libertés de choix et autodirection de l'apprenant. Paris, France: L'Harmattan. doi:10.7202/018979ar

De Bra, P., Houben, G. J., & Wu, H. (1999, February). AHAM: A Dexter-based reference model for adaptive hypermedia. In *Proceedings of the tenth ACM Conference on Hypertext and hypermedia: returning to our diverse roots: returning to our diverse roots* (pp. 147-156). 10.1145/294469.294508

Depover, C., De Lievre, B., Decamps, S., & Porco, F. (2014). *Analyse et conception des scénarios d'apprentissage*. Le Département des Sciences et de la Technologie de l'Education Université de Mons.

El-Kechai, H. (2008). *Conception collective de scénarios pédagogiques dans un contexte de réingénierie: Une approche par la métamodélisation située* (Doctoral dissertation). Université du Maine.

Garrison, D. R., & Shale, D. (1987). Mapping the boundaries of distance education: Problems in defining the field. *American Journal of Distance Education*, *1*(1), 7–13. doi:10.1080/08923648709526567

Hendler, J. (2009). Web 3.0 Emerging. *Computer*, *42*(1), 111–113. doi:10.1109/MC.2009.30

Henri, F., & Lundgren-Cayrol, K. (1997). *Apprentissage collaboratif à distance, téléconférence et télédiscussion. Rapport interne no 3* (version 1.7). Montréal: LICEF. http://www.licef.teluq.uquebec.ca/Bac/fiches/f48.htm

Hussain, F. (2012). *E-Learning 3.0= E-Learning 2.0+ Web 3.0?* International Association for Development of the Information Society.

Imran, H., Belghis-Zadeh, M., Chang, T. W., & Graf, S. (2016). PLORS: A personalized learning object recommender system. *Vietnam Journal of Computer Science*, *3*(1), 3–13. doi:10.100740595-015-0049-6

Inan, F., & Grant, M. (2011). Individualized web-based instructional design. In *Instructional Design* (pp. 375–388). Concepts, Methodologies, Tools and Applications. doi:10.4018/978-1-60960-503-2.ch212

Johnson, D. W., & Johnson, R. T. (1994). *Learning Together and Alone (ouvrage original publié en 1975)*. Allyn and Bacon.

Kay, J. (2000). User modeling for adaptation. *User Interfaces for All, Human Factors Series*, 271-294.

Keegan, D. (1986). *The foundations of distance education*. Croom Helm.

Kerr, P. (2015). Adaptive learning. *ELT Journal*, *70*(1), 88–93. doi:10.1093/elt/ccv055

Koper, R. (2001). *Modeling units of study from a pedagogical perspective-the pedagogical meta-model behind EML.* http://eml. ou.nl/introduction/docs/ped-metamodel. pdf

Laforcade, P. (2004). Modélisation et méta-modélisation UML pour la conception et la mise en oeuvre de situations problèmes coopératives. Doctorat de l'Université de Pau et des Pays de l'Adour. *International Journal of Computer Trends and Technology, 69*(6), 28–35. doi:10.14445/22312803/IJCTT-V69I6P105

Lamya, Kawtar, Mohamed, & Mohamed. (2020). Personalization of an educational scenario of a learning activity according to the learning styles model David Kolb. *Global Journal of Engineering and Technology Advances, 5*(3), 99-108. doi:10.30574/gjeta.2020.5.3.0114

Law, E. L. C., & Sun, X. (2012). Evaluating user experience of adaptive digital educational games with Activity The01·y. *International Journal of Human-Computer Studies, 70*(7), 478–497. doi:10.1016/j.ijhcs.2012.01.007

Lefevre, M., Broisin, J., Butoianu, V., Daubias, P., Daubigney, L., Greffier, F., ... Terrat, H. (2012). *Personnalisation de l'apprentissage: comparaison des besoins et approches à travers l'étude de quelques dispositifs.* Academic Press.

Maha, K., Omar, E., Mohamed, E., & Mohamed, K. (2021). Design of educational scenarios of activities in a learning situation for online teaching. *GSC Advanced Engineering and Technology, 1*(1), 49-64.

Mödritscher, F., Garcia-Barrios, V. M., & Gütl, C. (2004). The Past, the Present and the Future of adaptive E-Learning. *Proceedings of ICL 2004.*

Moore, J. L., Dickson-Deane, C., & Galyen, K. (2011). e-Learning, online learning, and distance learning environments: Are they the same? *The Internet and Higher Education, 14*(2), 129–135. doi:10.1016/j.iheduc.2010.10.001

Nicholson, P. (2007). A history of e-learning. In *Computers and education* (pp. 1–11). Springer. doi:10.1007/978-1-4020-4914-9_1

Paquette, G. (2002). *L'ingénierie du téléapprentissage: pour construire l'apprentissage en réseaux.* Sainte-Foy: Presses de l'Université du Québec.

Paquette, G., Aubin, C., & Crevier, F. (1997). Design and Implementation of Interactive TeleLearning Scenarios. *Proceedings of ICDE'97 (International Council for Distance Education).*

Paramythis, A., & Loidl-Reisinger, S. (2003). Adaptive learning environments and e-learning standards. In *Second European conference on e-learning* (*Vol. 1,* No. 2003, pp. 369-379). Academic Press.

Pemin, J.-P. (2005). Langages de modélisation de situations d'apprentissage: l'approche Leaming Design. Séminaire du Groupe Rhône Alpes d'Initiative sur les Normes et Standards dans les Technologies d'Information et de Communication pour l'Education, Lyon, France.

Pernin, J.-P., & Lejeune, A. (2004). Dispositifs d'apprentissage instrumentés par les technologies: vers une ingénierie centrée sur les scénarios. Dans Actes du colloque TICE, 407-414.

Perraton, H. (1988). A theory for distance education. In D. Sewart, D. Keegan, & B. Holmberg (Eds.), *Distance education: International perspectives* (pp. 34–45). Routledge.

Perrenoud, P. (1995). *La pédagogie à l'école des différences*. ESF.

Quintin, J. J., Depover, C., & Degache, C. (2005, May). Le rôle du scénario pédagogique dans l'analyse d'une formation à distance. In Analyse d'un scénario pédagogique à partir d'éléments de caractérisation définis, actes du colloque EIAH, Montpellier.

Shute, V. J., & Psotka, J. (1994). *Intelligent Tutoring Systems: Past, Present, and Future (No. AL/HR-TP-1994-0005)*. Armstrong Lab Brooks AFB TX Human Resources Directorate.

Sleeman, D., & Brown, J. S. (1982). *Intelligent tutoring systems*. Academic Press.

Song, Y., Wong, L. H., & Looi, C. K. (2012). Fostering personalized learning in science inquiry supported by mobile technologies. *Educational Technology Research and Development*, *60*(4), 679–701. doi:10.100711423-012-9245-6

Spring, J. (2012). *Education networks: Power, wealth, cyberspace, and the digital mind*. Routledge. doi:10.4324/9780203156803

Tadlaoui, M. A., & Khaldi, M. (2020). Concepts and Interactions of Personalization, Collaboration, and Adaptation in Digital Learning. In M. Tadlaoui & M. Khaldi (Eds.), *Personalization and Collaboration in Adaptive E-Learning* (pp. 1–33). IGI Global. doi:10.4018/978-1-7998-1492-4.ch001

Vantroys T. (2003). *Du langage métier au Langage technique, une plateforme flexible d'exécution de scénarios pédagogiques*. Doctorat de l'université Lille.

Villiot-Leclercq, E. (2007). *Modèle de soutien à l'élaboration et à la réutilisation de scénarios pédagogiques*. Academic Press.

Walkington, C., & Bernacki, M. L. (2020). *Appraising research on personalized learning: Definitions, theoretical alignment, advancements, and future directions*. Academic Press.

Webley, K. (2013). The adaptive learning revolution. *Time Magazine*, 6.

Weibelzahl, S. (2003). Evaluation of adaptive systems. *User Modeling*, *2003*, 292–294.

Yarandi, M., Jahankhani, H., &Tawil, A. (2013). A personalized adaptive e-learning approach based on semantic web technology. *Webology*, *10*(2).

Zhou, Y., Huang, C., Hu, Q., Zhu, J., & Tang, Y. (2018). Personalized learning full-path recommendation model based on LSTM neural networks. *Information Sciences*, *444*, 135–152. doi:10.1016/j.ins.2018.02.053

Zniber, N. (2010). *Service-Oriented Model for Personalized Learning Process Design* (Doctoral dissertation). Université Paul Cézanne-Aix-Marseille III.

Chapter 4
Contextual Inquiry of Food Ordering Apps:
An Indian Perspective

Ganesh D. Bhutkar
Vishwakarma Institute of Technology, India

Mishail Shailendra Singh
Vishwakarma Institute of Technology, India

Yohannes Kurniawan
Bina Nusantara University, Indonesia

ABSTRACT

Due to rapid digitization in India, a large section of the Indian population has gained access to fast and affordable internet services such as online food ordering. It offers a fascinating opportunity to research the way Indian people utilize food ordering apps. This chapter provides an interesting study based on contextual inquiry of Indian food ordering app users. The collected data, in interviews and other minute observations, have been documented into five work models, which explain various facets of the food ordering and delivery process and related user experience of Indian users. The identified user-types reveal insights into the unique mindset of Indian users when using and navigating these apps. The analysis of the work models and various top food ordering apps have also highlighted various subtle but important cultural implications of ordering food.

INTRODUCTION

In the recent years, there has been rapid digitization and growth of internet services in developing countries, including India. The internet penetration has also increased at a rapid rate in India, with over 250 million new internet users added in the last 5 years (statista.com, 2020). As a result, there has been a surge in the number of people accessing internet-based and app-based services over traditional services.

DOI: 10.4018/978-1-7998-9121-5.ch004

One such important service is provided through food ordering or delivery applications. Though the concept of food ordering is not new, and the more traditional way of ordering by calling a restaurant has existed for a long time, the advent of Food Ordering Apps (FDAs) has significantly improved the ease and convenience of ordering the desired food from a restaurant. While earlier a customer had to keep note of all the restaurants providing food delivery, their phone numbers, and timings too, now most food ordering applications do all the book-keeping for the user. These apps remove all the hassles in ordering food, making it a simple and easy process. This has resulted in a massive growth of the food delivery market and has also resulted in an increase in the business profits. Consequently, there is an emergence of several food ordering mobile app brands, in the highly competitive food ordering business. Figure 1 shows two leading food ordering apps.

Figure 1. Screenshots of leading food delivery apps - (a) Zomato and (b) Swiggy

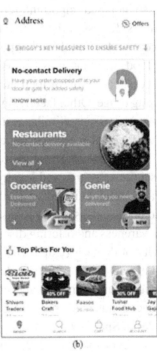

(a)   (b)

The rise of food ordering apps has led to a change in the mindset and perception of Indian customers towards ordering of food, which creates an interesting avenue for research about Indian users. Since the Indian diaspora is very culturally, religiously as well as ethnically diverse, the food habits of customer groups and families also vary significantly among different user groups. Another dimension of diversity in India, is the economic split between customers or users. Food ordering apps are used by the rich, middle class, lower-middle class as well as the poor users of India. All these aspects lead to starkly different food ordering preferences and app usage trends among Indian users. Understanding these differentiating dimensions and related user categories can significantly help in improving the design of future food ordering apps. The main objective of this research paper is to perform a contextual inquiry with the Indian users of food ordering apps and build 'work models' from the data obtained, to derive related vital aspects, which would be useful for the design of future food-ordering apps. In the process, an extensive literature review related with food ordering apps and a peer app review of leading food ordering apps is also performed to support the contextual inquiry and to find the design trends available in the related apps and suggest room for improvement.

LITERATURE REVIEW

A literature review of the currently existing research papers on food ordering or delivery apps has been completed to better understand the domain of food ordering and delivery. For this, research papers in the domain of food ordering / delivery were studied. Initially, Google Scholar was searched for research papers with the keywords - food delivery, India, Zomato and Swiggy. Papers which were relevant to Indian users and which also included important trends in food ordering, were selected and studied further.

Several research papers discussed the factors that affect the usage of a food ordering apps. A study on the customer's perception to digital food app services analyzed the factors that affected the attitude of customers towards food ordering apps (Parashar et al. 2017). This study revealed that comfort in ordering, followed by good condition of food and the availability of nearby restaurants were the most important factors affecting usage. Other factors, in order of importance were, good discounts, availability of reward points and payment issues. Similar results were found in another study that aimed to analyze the benefits and disadvantages of food ordering apps from the point of view of restaurants and as well as customers or users (Saxena 2019). The study found that customers were the most motivated to order when they received discounts, rewards and loyalty points which resulted in the increase in the ordering volume from a restaurant. Mitali Gupta discussed the marketing strategies which have been successful in garnering a huge audience such as highly focused marketing via conventional media and using social media to create brand awareness and offering discounts, rewards and loyalty points that are personalized depending on the activity of the user (Gupta 2019).

Another aspect that affects usage of food ordering apps is habituation. Habitual decisions are decisions that require no conscious effort; the decisions do not depend on a selection among the options provided. Instead, the decision is made because it has become a routine process to use the same service for the same function. Jelita Sparta et al. proposed that getting a user habituated into using an app, can increase user app engagement (Sparta et al. 2019).

Nur Fazri Ilham et al. suggested that pictures, reviews credibility and personalization features on the apps may have positive effect on user's satisfaction on accessing the apps. The study found that pictures of the food items provided by a restaurant and pictures of restaurants' ambience helped a customer decide whether they will eat at the restaurant or not. If pictures were present on the menu with unfamiliar dishes, the chance that a customer would transact increased. The study also found that credible reviews by experts increased customer satisfaction (Ilham et al. 2017). Another study found that flexible payment options along with efficient customer support played an important role in the ordering behavior of a user (Zomato, 2020). Allowing payment through multiple online portals, wallets, or cash on delivery resulted in an increase in ordering volume. A user is more likely to trust an app and order, if efficient customer support is present, so that the user can rightfully give proper feedback or have their issues resolved.

Many research papers that were analyzed have highlighted some common aspects of food ordering apps. These trends are summarized as follows:

- **Personalization of discounts** to suit the user based on his activity, as well as **offering loyalty rewards** is a significant factor affecting order frequency.
- Users are more likely to order if the app provides **flexible payment options** along with multiple gateways.
- **Expert reviews on dishes and restaurants** increase the chances that a user will transact with the restaurant. **Credible reviews from experts** along with **pictures of unfamiliar dishes** increase the likelihood of user ordering.
- Notifying the user based on the time of day and his location via a **personalized push notification** can help increase user interaction with the app.
- Complete profiles of restaurants along with pictures of restaurant's ambiance and the restaurant's dishes encourages the user to order from that restaurant.
- Providing **schedulable orders** can help get users habituated to using a specific app for ordering. This can get users to order food more consistently from a particular app.

ANDROID APP REVIEW

A systematic review of selected food ordering apps on Google Play Store, has been conducted. The most used apps as per app downloads and the highest rated apps were selected. These selected five apps can be mainly divided into two categories: general-purpose food ordering apps, which allow users to order food items from available restaurants, and single-franchise apps, which allow ordering from a single parent organization's in-house restaurants or franchises. The selected general-purpose apps include Zomato (Zomato, 2020), Swiggy (Swiggy, 2020), and FoodPanda (FoodPanda, 2020). And selected single-franchise apps include Faasos (Faasos, 2020) and Domino's (Domino's, 2020). The peer app review has been conducted in two phases – first, based on app features and functionalities and then, based on user feedback, user experience and app usability.

Review of User Feedback, User Experience and App Usability

A thorough peer review of the different aspects of food ordering apps related with user feedback, user experience and app usability of the selected apps was performed. These were then related to the app performance in the marketplace for comparison. The following insights have been drawn after reviewing all the selected apps in terms of their usability aspects.

- Most of the apps (3/5) provide **easy navigation** between screens using buttons that are present on every screen.
- General-purpose ordering apps (Zomato, Swiggy, FoodPanda) **focus more on details** rather than images whereas single franchise apps (Domino's and Faasos) **focus more on large images** instead of details. General purpose apps also include **more advertisements** when compared to single franchise apps.
- Single franchise apps (Faasos and Domino's) have more **customizable menus and options** than General-purpose ordering apps (Zomato and Swiggy).

- Not much correlation exists between rating of app and number of advertisements. Zomato includes the greatest number of advertisements and promotions followed by Swiggy. Domino's and Faasos have comparatively less of advertisement.
- Most downloaded apps (Zomato and Swiggy) branch off beyond just food ordering and includes various other functionalities like table booking, delivery of groceries and others.

Review of App Features and Functionalities

Initially, a review of five selected apps, has been conducted based on app features and functionalities, and the related comparative details are depicted in Table 1.

Table 1. Comparison of selected food ordering apps based on features and functionalities

Features and Functionalities	Food Ordering Apps				
	Zomato	**Swiggy**	**FoodPanda**	**Faasos**	**Domino's**
Order self-pickup	Yes	No	No	No	Yes
Table reservation	Yes	No	No	NA	No
Delivery of groceries	Yes	Yes	No	No	No
Restaurant profiles	Yes (detailed)	Select restaurants, (less detailed)	No	No	NA
Personalize discounts	Yes	Yes	No	Yes	No
Schedulable orders	Yes	Yes	No	Yes	No
Expert Reviews	Yes	No	No	No	NA
Flexible payments	Yes	Yes	Yes	Yes	Yes
Push notifications	Yes	Yes	Yes	Yes	Yes
Multiple restaurants ordering	No	No	No	Yes	No
Personalized recommendations	No	Yes	No	No	No
Coupon / Discount application	User needs to select the coupon / discount	User needs to select the coupon / discount	User needs to select the coupon / discount	User needs to remember and type the code	User needs to remember and type the code
Guaranteed delivery in certain time	On certain orders. With extra fee.	No	No	On certain orders	On each order

The following observations have been made after carefully reviewing the selected apps as seen in Table 1, based on the app features and functionalities:

- All apps include push notification service and flexible payment options.
- Most of the apps (3/5) include **personalized discounts** for user (Tandon et al. 2021) and other reward systems like loyalty points.
- Most of the apps (3/5) allow **schedulable orders** for users.
- Most of the apps (3/5) allow **guaranteed delivery in a definite time** on certain orders.

- Most of the apps (3/5) allow users to **select coupon codes** instead of remembering them.
- Few apps (2/5) include restaurant profiles to give users a sense of actual ambiance of the restaurant.
- Few apps (2/5) allow order self-pickup.
- **Zomato is also the most multi-purpose app** with features like table reservation and delivery of groceries.

RESEARCH METHODOLOGY

The research method used for evaluating and analyzing the design of food delivery apps, is contextual inquiry. When ordering a meal using food delivery apps, the users must make quite a few selections - from choosing a restaurant, ordering a dish, to making a payment. The UI design of these apps is required to be quite user-friendly to encourage users to order the food items. This is only possible, if the app design approach is user-centered, conforming to the user's cultural and religious aspirations. Therefore, a contextual inquiry is ideal for investigating into user requirements and related usability issues with respect to design of food ordering apps. A similar approach of using contextual inquiry for the design of a food carrier has been conducted by Kale et.al. (Kale et.al. 2015).

Contextual inquiry of food ordering apps with the users, is conducted primarily in three stages, viz. conducting the contextual inquiry interviews, developing work models from the obtained data, and analyzing and deriving key aspects from the obtained work models (Wikipedia, 2020). The usefulness of contextual inquiry for studying ethno-graphic factors is well demonstrated in the work by Wani et.al, where it was used to analyze factors that influenced work engagement by using twitter (Wani et al. 2020).

Participant Users and Their Interviews

A total of ten participant users were selected for the contextual inquiry interviews. The number of users for interviews were restricted in pandemic times due to local covid 19 guidelines. These participant users were college students in the age group of 19 - 22 years. These students were easily available around and food ordering apps are quite popular among them. Four of these participant users belonged to upper-middle class and rich households, while the remaining six belonged to lower-middle class households. These participants were asked about their food ordering app usage frequency prior to the interviews to get an idea about the users' familiarity with the food ordering apps. Out of these, three participants were heavy users, who usually ordered at least once a day, four participants were moderate users who ordered multiple times a week, and three participants were light users, who only ordered occasionally when there was a need for it. Multiple sessions of interviews ranging between one to four rounds were conducted with each of the participating users over a period of a couple of weeks. Occasionally, participants would order together in conjunction with someone else, usually their roommate or friend, with whom they shared a hostel or apartment. In that case, the partner was also interviewed and observed. A few of the participant users were also acquainted with each other and would occasionally order together, which resulted in an overlap of the interview sessions.

Since the food ordering process is a casual task, a casual interview environment was created. The participants were visited in their own hostel room or residential flat, where they normally used the food ordering app. This was done because it is essential to instill a sense of partnership among the participants

(Wikipedia, 2020). These participants were made to feel comfortable while ordering food items, so that they would not do things differently in presence of an observing interviewer.

While the participants used the apps, they were interviewed and observed. They were asked broad and open-ended questions, so that the users could provide appropriate and true feedback (Amaresan 2020). The questions were aimed at understanding the food ordering behavior of the participants, while observations made during the food ordering process helped to identify their inconveniences and difficulties. The questions asked were along the lines of - "Why did you choose ...... over ....?". These kinds of questions elicited a subjective response, which was analyzed in a greater depth. Since most food ordering apps also keep track of users' orders, these past orders were also analyzed with their consent.

Over the course of the contextual interview, participant users were made aware about the research objectives, researchers' observations, and their interpretations. For example, if the researcher interpreted from his observation that the user had made an order due to its short arrival time, then the researcher questioned the user to verify whether that was really the case. The researchers were also responsible for steering the focus of the interview towards the ordering of food and the assessing the usability issues of the food ordering apps. Due to the casual nature of the interviews, if the participants deviated from the main task of ordering food, or if the conversation tended in a direction which was not useful for the purpose of the interview, the researchers brought the focus back to the main task in hand.

WORK MODELS

The observations and results of the Contextual Inquiry have been encoded into five different work models. These work models have the purpose of quantifying and structuring the data into different models which help in the interpretation of the data, which is a necessary step to derive useful facets about the application domain of food ordering apps. The work models that have been developed are discussed below.

Flow Model

The purpose of the flow model is to identify user types and capture how the different user types communicate and interact with each other. During contextual inquiry, several distinct user types were identified. A mapping of the interaction among these user types is an important aspect of the flow model. In this case, there is generally only one end user, though sometimes a couple of users cooperatively order in conjunction. It is crucial to focus on interaction between the different user types and apps features or functionalities and identifying user types based on their interaction with the app, rather than establishing the interactions between different user types.

User Types

The purpose of the flow model is to identify user types and capture how the different user types communicate and interact with each other. During contextual inquiry, a few distinct user types were identified, during interviews of the users and based on authors' own past experiences, several other user types were proposed. A mapping of the interaction among these user types is an important aspect of the flow model. In this case, there is generally only one end user, though sometimes a couple of users cooperatively order in conjunction. It is crucial to focus on interaction between the different user types and apps features or functionalities and identifying user types based on their interaction with the app, rather than establishing the interactions between different user types.

Deal Seekers: These are the users who usually order heavily discounted meals using the food ordering app (Tandon et al. 2021). They are more motivated to order when a good deal is present, rather than when they have an urge to eat good food. If any decent offers or discounts are not present, they tend to get their meals from their regular sources. One of the major observations used to characterize this user-type was fact that some user participants would abandon the process of ordering a food dish after spending a significant amount of time browsing through various dishes from different restaurants. **The rationale for abandoning the process of ordering would often be the unavailability of discounted meals**, even though the users could easily the dish. Participants in this user-type **would browse through multiple ordering apps before placing an order**, to ensure that they could get the meal at the lowest price. Another commonly observed behavior was that these **users would club multiple orders of different users together**, so that delivery charges of multiple orders could be avoided.

Gourmet Foodies: These are the users who like to explore different dishes frequently. **They like to try out different dishes, they have not had before, without much regard to the cost of the dish.** They are more open to eating foods of different cultures. Once of the behavioral characteristics of participants in this user type was that **these users were more likely to eat outside in the actual restaurant itself, instead of ordering the dish from the app. The primary purpose of using the app was to review price and dishes of a restaurant.** Once the users decided to try a dish, they would go to the restaurant to eat the dish. The ambience of the restaurant also played an important part in trying out the dish.

Fitness Enthusiasts: These are the users that usually only order healthy food and follow a fixed diet plan. **They prefer detailed nutritional information about the food they order**. The calorific value of different food items is a deciding factor for ordering a dish. **Many user participants only used food ordering apps to order healthy meals, when such options were not available nearby.**

Pure Locavore: These are the users, **who only prefer to eat local cuisine and foods**, and rarely try new dishes from different cultures. They are less open to trying new dishes, and they prefer to only eat the dishes they are familiar with. The defining behavior of this user-type was that **they would only order from a few local restaurants. They would spend relatively less time browsing the app and try dishes only from familiar restaurants**. They would usually repeat order from the recent orders section of the app. The users that belonged to this type had usually visited the restaurant before ordering from there or had heard a positive review of the restaurant from a friend.

Routine Orderers: These are the people regularly order from restaurants. They do not usually cook food for themselves, but instead depend on online ordering for getting their meal as they generally lack cooking facilities at their residence. Participants who fall in this user type tend to show some overlap with other user types such as deal seekers, locavore, and fitness enthusiast. **These users would usually order from budget restaurants and try to apply as many discounts as possible**, however they are not put off from ordering if no deals were available. **They also order from only a few specific restaurants, and do not spend much time browsing the app.**

Late Night Orderers: These are the users, who usually stay awake at night, and **order food late at night, usually after 12 pm**. They usually stay up at night due to professional or personal commitments and they are usually willing to pay extra for a late-night meal. **Such orders were rare, and the participants did not mind the hiked-up prices** for the restaurant as no other options were present.

Summary of User Types Based on Ordering Behavior

The contextual inquiry results have been used to characterize the different user types that were identified based on their actions and ordering behavior. A detailed summary of the characteristics of different user types has been presented in Table 2, which relates different ordering behaviors to the user types.

Table 2. User categorization related with food ordering apps

Aspect of Comparison	User Types					
	Deal Seeker	**Gourmet Foodie**	**Fitness Enthusiast**	**Pure Locavore**	**Routine Orderers**	**Late Night Orderers**
Heavy use of deals / discounts	Yes	No	No	No	Yes	No
Time spent browsing apps	More	More	Not much	Not much	Not much	Not much
Clubbing of multiple orders together	Frequently	Rarely	Rarely	Sometimes	Sometimes	Rarely
Open to trying new dishes	Somewhat open	Very open	Somewhat open	Not open	Somewhat open	Somewhat open
Preference to restaurant booking than ordering	No	Frequently	No	Sometimes	No	No
Use of nutritional information	No	No	Yes	No	Sometimes	No
Preference to local cuisine	No	No	No	Yes	No	No
Repetition of orders of food items or from specific restaurants	No	No	No	Yes	Yes	No
Time of Ordering	Normal Mealtime	Normal Mealtime	Normal Mealtime	Normal mealtime	Normal mealtime	Late Night
Frequency of Ordering	High	Low	Normal	Normal	Very High	Low

Derived Flow Model

The analysis of identified user types has revealed insights into the app usage behavior of different users of food ordering apps. This analysis is used to derive the flow model, which focuses on mapping the interaction of different user types with a set of features that will be most helpful to the users and allow them to use the app optimally, as depicted in Figure 2. The suggested features are - **Intelligent recommendations** of dishes and restaurants, **dynamic filtering and sorting** of restaurant and dishes throughout the app instead of a single screen, **displaying additional information** about selected dishes, showing **suggested alternatives** to dishes, timely notifications for ordering, and a **cumulative payment feature**. The importance of these suggested features varies for different user types.

Figure 2. Derived flow model depicting interaction between user types and app functionalities

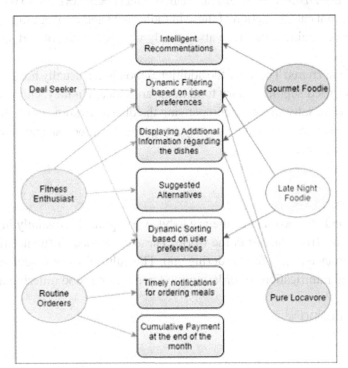

Artifact Model

There are many different artifacts or things with which a user interacts during food ordering and delivery process. The artifact model deals with identifying the different artifacts generated or used in the work process and studying how these artifacts are used. It is used to explain the necessity of the different artifacts for the functioning of the work process. In case of a food ordering app, there are many different artifacts that are used, apart from the app itself. These artifacts affect the food ordering and delivery process and may even prevent a user from food ordering. These artifacts are listed here.

Utensils: Utensils are important artifacts to consider, as the user of a food ordering app will often require some utensils to eat their dish if the packaging of the dish does not allow user to eat their dish directly. A consequence of this is that if a user lacks utensil, the user may not order, or order a dish which does not require the use of utensils. It was observed that ordering pizza was a common choice when there was an absence of utensils, as eating a pizza did not require any utensils apart from the container of the pizza.

Newspaper / Papers: Sometimes, due to unavailability of proper utensils, newspapers were often substituted for plates. Newspapers were also commonly spread under food items to prevent the food items from staining the surface it was kept on.

Food Containers: Food containers are used to transport the ordered food. These container's quality depends on restaurant from which the order is placed. Few restaurants offer food in high quality containers, which can be used to eat food directly, without needing any utensils. Sometimes, the availability of these containers is a deciding factor for selecting the restaurant to order food. It was also observed that occasionally users would not discard high quality containers but would retain them for storing other items.

Ordered Food Items / Dishes: These are the main products being offered to the users of food ordering apps. The most relevant categorization of these in India are vegetarian, egg-based, or non-vegetarian food and the containers containing them are also usually wrapped with colored stickers to identify the category of the meal.

Supplementary Food Items: These are the additional food items usually present with the main dish. Some of the commonly used supplementary food items are sauce, chutney, chilly, chopped onions and farsan - a traditional Indian salty snacks accompanying the dishes. In some cases, the importance given to the quality of the supplementary food items may supersede the importance given to the quality of the main dish when choosing a meal.

Cultural Model

The Indian food diets and their associated dietary habits vary quite significantly in different regions of the country as well as that from the rest of the world. These differences influence the way people order and it is of great importance to any food ordering app. The cultural work model serves to encapsulate the cultural impacts and ramifications of ordering food items using food ordering apps.

Taboos in Food Ordering

Figure 3. Similar looking meat-based dishes (a) beef and (b) mutton

(a)　　　　　　　　(b)

Although the Indian mindset has become more open and receptive to the dietary practices of other subcultures existing in India as well as other regions across the world, the situation is far from ideal (Natrajan et al. 2018). Natrajan et al. in their work - Provincializing' Vegetarianism, have found that the **overall extent of vegetarianism is much less than the common perception and overall extent of beef-eating is more than the double of what is commonly claimed.** These are important facts because they suggest that food ordering apps must cater to multiple demographics as they are all prevalent in the Indian culture. Therefore, there are taboos associated with eating food that is prohibited in one's culture. **One** of the most obvious taboo is eating beef, especially for Hindu community- the majority population of India. While none of the interviewed participants ate beef, their food ordering decisions were impacted by it. **It was observed that few participant users would not order any mutton-based dishes from areas with predominantly Muslim population, in fear of being served beef instead of the ordered mutton**. Figure 3 depicts similar-looking beef and mutton dishes. **While all the participants were comfortable ordering vegetarian dishes from restaurants in Muslim populated areas**, one of the participants would did not order any meat-based dish from the same, whereas one other participant user was open to ordering chicken-based dishes but not any other meat-based dish.

Impact of Choice of Staple

The choice of staple consumed by people plays an important part in the way people use food ordering apps. Rice and wheat in form of flat bread (of many types such as Roti, Chapati, and Naan) forms the bulk of the Indian diet. **A diet without Rice and/or Roti / Chapati was considered as incomplete by many users**. A consequence this is that users would often order together in conjugation with other users, such as their roommate. This is because **most of the traditional meals require two or three different dishes or accompaniments to be ordered, namely, the main dish (cooked vegetable or meat dish), flat breads such as roti, chapati or naan, and rice**. Generally, the **portion size served by restaurants for each of these dishes or accompaniments, is in excess for a single person**. Therefore, a more traditional meal was usually only be ordered when the user could share the dish with someone else. **It was observed that the dishes consisting of only a single portion, were preferred by users who ordered alone**. These commonly included rice-based dishes such as biryani and pulao, south-Indian dishes like idli and wada, and international dishes such as noodles, pizza, and burgers.

Feasibility of Cheaper Food Items in Food Ordering

Cheaper food items that are not consumed as the one of the three main meals of the day viz. breakfast, lunch, and dinner are termed as fast foods in this study. Even though fast food was consumed by all the participant users in the study on a regular basis, it was observed that fast foods along with breakfast meals were rarely ordered. This observation suggests that **light meals like fast food snacks and breakfast are rarely ordered using food ordering apps**. One of the reasons for this was cheaper prices of fast foods compared to regular meals. As the prices of fast foods were comparable to the delivery costs itself, users were hesitant to order. It provides evidence for anchoring bias in food ordering, where a user's mind is anchored to the price of original item, affecting their judgment to make an order (Brewer et al. 2002).

Effect of Time of Ordering on User Decisions

Something as trivial as the time of food ordering can give us important insights into the mindset of a user. An interesting observation was that users belonging to the user type - **deal seeker, would often start the ordering process much earlier than other users. The important factor affecting this decision was the hiked-up delivery prices during prime-time**. On the other hand, users ordering late at night did not mind the heavily marked up prices of the dishes.

Effect of Spending Habits on Food Ordering App Usage

The spending habits of users was heavily influenced by their user-type. The users categorized in the user type **of deal seekers, were more regular users of food ordering apps,** and were more aware about the different offers and discounts available, along with vital features of food ordering apps. In fact, **Indian users of deal seeker type, could be considered as 'power users' of food ordering apps.** This contrasts with users belonging to user type of **gourmet foodie, who ordered less frequently, but ordered relatively expensive food dishes.** Another factor that affected the spending habits of users is the payment system. Availability of online payment options was essential as many users did not wish to deal with the hassle of getting the exact bill amount in cash, whereas few users preferred to pay only by cash.

Implications on Design Resulting from the Cultural Model

From studying the cultural model, a few design improvements to the current food ordering apps are apparent. One such design improvement would be to incorporate different visual themes for non-vegetarian, vegetarian, egg-based, and beef-based dishes. From the cultural model, it is obvious that dishes containing beef are important to consider separately from other dishes, especially in India. However, most apps do not contain a separate indication of beef-based dishes, and non-vegetarian dishes are clubbed in the same category and identified with a common red color. This makes it hard to differentiate regular non-vegetarian dishes with beef-based dishes, as many Indian dishes have ambiguous names, and it is not easy to identify the contents of the dish by name alone. For example, the names of many Indian non-vegetarian dishes include the word *gohst*, which is used to refer to both mutton as well as beef. For this visual theme to be effective, it should be prominent in the cart section of the app, so that users can know if there are any non-vegetarian or beef-based items in cart, as demonstrated in figure 4.

Figure 4. Cart visual theme for (a) beef (b) non-vegetarian (c) egg (d) vegetarian dishes

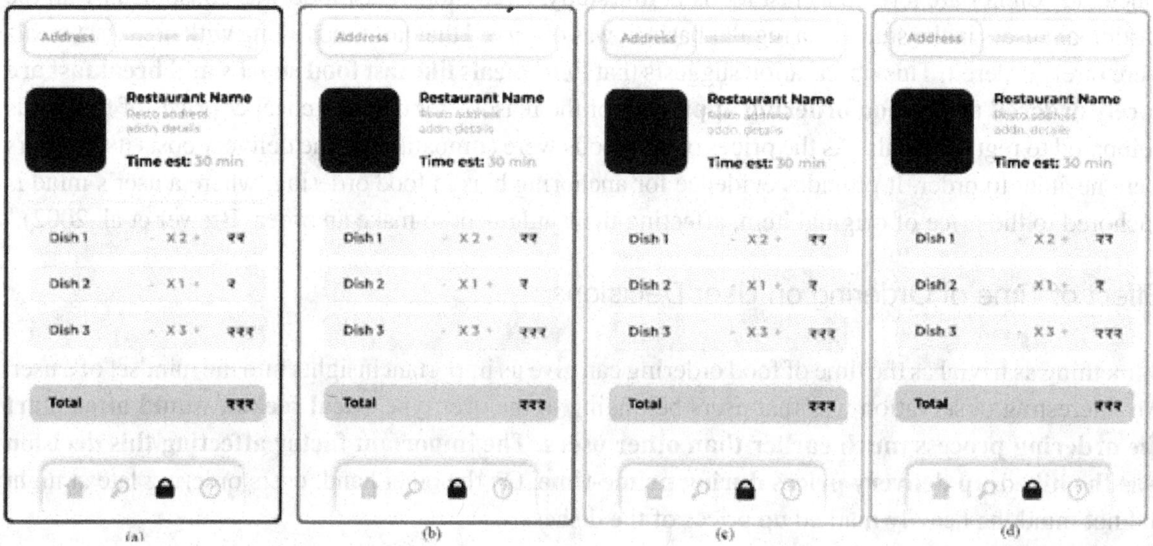

Physical Model

The physical model encapsulates the physical environment where the work is done. In case of a food ordering app, the physical model is used to capture the different physical aspects of food ordering which are discussed below.

Delivery Location

This is the location where the ordered food is supposed to be delivered. The most common delivery locations were **residential apartments** and **college hostels**. The **college campuses** were also observed to be delivery locations rarely. The orders were sometimes also done at a friend's residential apartment. The orders were not always placed from the delivery location; sometimes the orders were also placed on the way to the apartment to save time on delivery.

Location of Receiving

The location of receiving the food parcel, was not necessarily the same as the delivery location. The reasons for this, were – inability of the delivery executive to locate the exact address of delivery and the exact location being unreachable by a vehicle due to some obstruction, usually construction work. This was usually counteracted by the user by meeting the delivery executive at some common well-known landmark near the delivery location and by the user walking the distance. **If the user had opted for Cash on Delivery (COD), then one of the issues arising from this situation, was the lack of spare change by the delivery executive**. This required the user to walk back to his residential apartment to get the spare change.

Route of Delivery

The delivery of the food parcel is usually done along an optimal route calculated by a path finding algorithm. This allows the app to estimate the time taken for delivery, which an essential factor for selecting a restaurant to order and must be accounted for when ordering. **It was noted that if the delivery time was too high over a particular route, then ordering from some restaurants was not feasible due to some prior engagement of the users.**

Physical Identification of Delivery Executive

The primary method used by users to identify delivery executives was through contacting the delivery executive using their mobile phones. The food ordering apps also included information of the delivery executive as well as their vehicles. **The delivery executives of certain food delivery apps like Zomato were also required to wear a uniform, which could be used to identify the delivery executive.**

Sensory Model

The sensory model incorporates the ways in which a user senses or perceives the events that are occurring. In case of food ordering apps, these events can be selections made by the user, such as food dish and/or delivery address of the order, and the completion of an action such as making a bank transaction for a payment. The different ways in which sensory information was understood by the user is discussed below:

Visual Feedback: Many food ordering apps made use of visual feedback to convey food order-related information to the user. Some of the observed visual feedbacks were – enclosing the total price discount inside a **blue box** in Zomato, **red dot and green box denoting the delivery address** in Zomato and Swiggy respectively, and count badges on different icons such as cart icon indicating the number of items in cart.

SMS Alerts (Vibration Feedback): These alerts inform the user of completion of certain events. These events include SMS text messages for **completion of bank transaction** and status of food delivery including **notification for successful order, preparation of dish, and dish out for delivery.** It was observed that many of these alerts, were not read, but were only sensed through vibrations for completion of event.

Push Notifications (Vibration Feedback): These alerts are generated by the app to convey status messages as well as promotional messages. These are usually communicated with targeted users frequently. **The push notifications were usually observed at regular time of meals.** They were also observed with during seasonal promotions.

Auditory Feedback: One of the more prominent auditory feedback was a **payment completion sound**. Apps like Swiggy and Zomato played a distinct short but identifiable sound for completion of payment and successful order. Another distinct sound feedback was played **when the delivery executive was about to reach the location.** These sound feedbacks are different from the regular notification sound of the participant users' mobile devices, which allowed them to easily recognize the occurrence of some event. The call by the delivery executive on arrival was another auditory feedback that informed the users to receive the food parcel.

VITAL ASPECTS OBSERVED AND RELATED DESIGN CONCERNS

The work models obtained from contextual inquiry was used to derive different aspects about the usage of food ordering apps and its users. These aspects can be used to improve the user experience and ease of using the app. The various important aspects observed from the contextual inquiry are presented here.

- **Some people would only order a dish using a food ordering app if a good deal were present** (Tandon et al. 2021). They would also employ various methods to reduce the price of order, specifically, they would club different orders together to avoid multiple delivery charges, browse through multiple food ordering apps to get the dish at its lowest price, keep track of all the available offers and their validity, and start ordering early before prime ordering time to avoid the price hikes deployed by many apps.
- **Some people would only prefer to order local cuisines and they restricted their ordering only to certain restaurants they had visited before.** This sharply reduced the number of choices they had, but also made ordering food more efficient. This was clearly contrasted with some other people who were more open to trying different dishes and were more likely to explore dishes they had not had previously.
- **Some users of food ordering app ordered regularly, and they had replaced cooking food with ordering from restaurants for their daily nutritional needs.** They were more dependent on us-

ing a food ordering app for their meals, and certain situations such as closing of restaurants and unavailability of food delivery agents usually posed a problem for them.

- Apart from the intended use of food ordering apps to order food, people also used food ordering apps for other purposes. **These users were to use the food ordering apps as a recommendation system to find new restaurants and dishes, check out the ambience of new restaurants they had not visited before, and for checking whether a restaurant that had a certain dish.**
- **The religious beliefs of the users also impacted the ordering behavior of the users.** Some Hindu users were hesitant on ordering mutton-based dishes from restaurants with Muslim sounding names and restaurants located in predominantly Muslim populated areas.
- Things unrelated to the actual dish also influenced the decision to order food for users of the food ordering app. **Things such as the availability of utensils or ability to eat the dish without utensils, the quality of the food containers offered, and the quality of the supplementary food items provided were sometimes more important to consider than the actual dish.**
- **Rice and flat breads like as chapati, roti, and naan were the primary staple of most user participants, and meals without it were considered as incomplete.** It was also observed that the portion size of an ordered dish was usually more than required for a single person. This compelled users to order together and share meals when eating a traditional Indian dish.

An important insight derived by characterizing user-types in the flow model was that a user's user-type defined his app usage behavior. Segregating users based on their user-type was helpful in analyzing how a user used the food ordering app and was useful in pinpointing the features and design aspects that would be the most helpful to the users. For example, a user belonging to the user-type routine orderer would place the most importance on ordering quickly and reducing the time spent browsing, which can be achieved by reducing the choice complexity (Rainer et al. 2010). Similarly, users belonging to the user-type of deal seeker user-type would be more interested in a visual layout which focuses on the deals, compared to a user of the fitness-enthusiast user-type, who would be more interested in the calorific-values of the dishes and prefer the focus to be on it.

CONCLUSION AND FUTURE WORK

The contextual inquiry of food ordering app users has uncovered many useful insights regarding the ordering behavior and usage behavior of the food ordering app users. An important finding was that the intent of using a food ordering app was an important factor to consider in optimizing the user experience of the app. This led to an interesting and extensive categorization of users based on their ordering behavior, and how the users of different categories depended on food ordering apps. This categorization of users was vital to optimize the user experience of the app according to the user behavior, from a functional design perspective. The contextual inquiry also highlighted several ethnic challenges and inconveniences of using a food ordering app, from an Indian point of view.

A future prospect of this study is to use it to construct design solutions for problems identified in this study and build that into a functional food ordering app prototype. The app design can be then be evaluated during production using formative evaluations such as heuristic evaluation and cognitive walkthrough, which will help refine the final product design of the app.

REFERENCES

Amaresan, S. (n.d.). *The Expert's Guide to Contextual Inquiry Interviews.* https://blog.hubspot.com/service/contextual-inquiry

Brewer, N., & Chapman, G. (2002). The Fragile Basic Anchoring Effect. *Journal of Behavioral Decision Making, 15*(1), 65–77. doi:10.1002/bdm.403

Contextual Design. (n.d.). https://en.wikipedia.org/wiki/Contextual_design

Contextual Inquiry. (n.d.). https://en.wikipedia.org/wiki/Contextual_inquiry

Domino's Pizza. (n.d.). https://play.google.com/store/apps/details?id=com.Dominos&hl=en_IN

Faasos. (n.d.). https://play.google.com/store/apps/details?id=com.done.faasos&hl=en_IN

FoodPanda. (n.d.). https://play.google.com/store/apps/details?id=com.india.foodpanda.android&hl=en_IN

Gupta, M. (2019). A Study on Impact of Online Food Delivery App on Restaurant Business Special Reference to Zomato and Swiggy. *International Journal of Research and Analytical Reviews, 6*(1).

Ilham, N., WuriHandayani, P., & Azzahro, F. (2017). The Effects of Pictures, Review Credibility and Personalization on Users Satisfaction of Using Restaurant Recommender Apps. *2nd International Conference on Informatics and Computing (ICIC).*

Internet Usage in India. (n.d.). https://www.statista.com/topics/2157/internet-usage-in-india

Kale, P., Bhutkar, G., Pawar, V., & Jathar, N. (2015). Contextual Design of Intelligent Food Carrier in Refrigerator: An Indian Perspective. In *IFIP Working Conference on Human Work Interaction Design.* Springer. 10.1007/978-3-319-27048-7_15

Natrajan, B., & Jacob, S. (2018). Provincialising Vegetarianism putting Indian Food Habits in Their Place. *Economic and Political Weekly, 53*(9), 54–64.

Parashar, N., & Ghadiyali, S. (2017). *A Study on Customer's Attitude and Perception towards Digital Food App Services. Amity Journal of Management.*

Pimplapure, M. (2019). Consumer Behavior towards Food Delivery App. *Indian Journal of Applied Research, 9*(7).

Rainer, G., Scheibehenne, B., & Kleber, N. (2010). Less may be More When Choosing is Difficult: Choice Complexity and Too Much Choice. *Acta Psychologica, 133*(1), 45–50. doi:10.1016/j.actpsy.2009.08.005 PMID:19766972

Saxena, A. (2019). An Analysis of Online Food Ordering Applications in India: Zomato and Swiggy. *4th National Conference on Recent Trends in Humanities, Technology, Management & Social Development (RTHTMS).*

Sparta, J., Alsumait, S., & Joshi, A. (2019). Marketing Habituation and Process Study of Online Food Industry (A Study Case: Zomato). *Journal of Community Development in Asia.*

Swiggy. (n.d.). https://play.google.com/store/apps/details?id=in.swiggy.android&hl=en_IN

Tandon, A., Kaur, P., Bhatt, Y., Mantymaki, M., & Dhir, A. (2021). Why do People Purchase from Food Delivery Apps? A Consumer Value Perspective. *Journal of Retailing and Consumer Services, 63,* 63. doi:10.1016/j.jretconser.2021.102667

Wani, N., Bhutkar, G., & Ekal, S. (2017). Conducting Contextual Inquiry of Twitter for Work Engagement: An Indian Perspective. *International Journal of Computer Applications, 168*(9), 27-36.

Zomato - Restaurant Finder and Food Delivery App. (n.d.). https://play.google.com/store/apps/details?id=com.application.zomato&hl=en_IN

Chapter 5
Removing the Screen:
Measuring the Effectiveness of Aesthetically Relevant UI Design for New Technologies

Nina Lyons
Technological University Dublin, Ireland

Matt Smith
Technological University Dublin, Ireland

ABSTRACT

This chapter outlines an operational definition for a range of experiments that will examine a number of visual aesthetics to identify ways to influence mental models to test how well they will communicate to the user. Utilising principles for semiotics and visual communication, the aim is to create a number of small interaction experiments that will be meaningful and resonate with the user so that they will understand how users want to interact with objects without relying on conventional interaction paradigms. As these experiments will be a mixed methods approach with equal emphasis on quantitative and qualitative data and will utilise a code book of visuals, the operational definition becomes the blueprint that will ensure a consistent procedure that will contain a full description of procedures and actions required to observe and measure the experiments. This will allow for a high level of transparency and replicable set of experiments.

INTRODUCTION

The *elements* of a *User Interface* (UI[1]) both communicate to the user and provide a means for the user to communicate with the computer. When we wish to evaluate or improve an existing UI, or design a novel UI from scratch, it is desirable to be able to measure how effective it is. One opportunity offered by computing devices is that large volumes of quantitative data can be automatically collected during user interactions. Such datasets may contain both specific data relating to hypotheses being evaluated,

DOI: 10.4018/978-1-7998-9121-5.ch005

such as successful task completion and time taken, but may also offer further insights into understanding patterns and relationships neither anticipated nor obvious in the raw data. In this chapter we argue that the combination of a visual communication theory principled approach to experimental design, with quantitative data sets and modern data analytical tools, offer UI researchers opportunities to rigorously investigate both traditional and novel UIs and human-computer interactions. In this introduction we provide an overview of the concepts and aims of the chapter, followed by sections defining and reviewing important theoretical concepts, and we conclude with a detailed description of an operation definition and a sample UI experiment, its data analysis, and present preliminary findings from data collected to date.

User Interfaces are a visual communication medium that have enabled the use of computers and computing devices to move beyond the domain of experts. These graphical UIs have utilised visual communication principles to create visual languages for users so that they can understand how to use, interact with, and complete tasks on a computer. The visual languages have been based on concepts that users understand, and relate their computer tasks to real world tasks such as working on a desktop, typing on a typewriter, and putting files in folders or trash bins. These metaphor-based UIs are a common-sense approach to a complex problem, and have been very successful.

Augmented Reality (AR) has been around for decades, across an ever-increasing range of hardware devices. As a result, users of AR have become unconsciously reliant on the design patterns of the devices rather than the technology to interact with the AR. The *mental models* that drive these interactions require investigation to identify whether better user experiences can be achieved; for example AR interactions that facilitate the user by offering interaction cues related to the *real-world view or real-world environment*, rather than limited and unnatural device-based controls. This chapter lays the foundation for a mixed-methods research methodology to investigate users' perceptions when interacting with UIs in their environment through AR. The proposed methodology in this chapter is part of a larger research project that frames UIs as being shaped by the users' environment rather than the device, and examines how visual UI elements can cause a cognitive change in the user that will affect their mental model. The changed mental model then alters the user's behaviour, so that they instinctively interact with the real-time view rather than the device.

Our approach is not a straightforward quantitative or qualitative study that investigates the effectiveness of a single visual with users. Instead, our research examines a range of different visuals, and their combination across multiple contexts. While there is an emphasis on understanding, the research requires quantitative data to evaluate whether the understanding of a few relates to the interactional behaviours of the many. If we can demonstrate how several visual communication principles can influence user mental models and behaviour, it provides a foundation for much future work on creative and novel UI design, for many different media.

In this chapter we present the design and preliminary results for a piece of qualitative research that needs to be validated through quantitative data and which will inform future speculative work. Due to the complexity of the proposed research an *operational definition* will be defined. The operational definition is a structured way of consistently recording the individual elements of an experiment. For instance, the operation definition proposed here will include:

- A description of procedures and actions of the experiments
- The conceptual definitions of the dependent variables being observed and measured
- And independent variables being observed and measured.

This operational definition will set out the steps for a procedure that will combine a quantitative approach with a hermeneutic phenomenological method, to understand and interpret the data in light of the user's point of view. In terms of this study, the operational definition will define:

- The conceptual definitions of perception
- Mental models in terms of the study
- Perception and mental models as their roles as dependent variables.
- Visuals as independent variables and set out categories in a *code book* to ensure accurate measurement of effects.

In doing so, we aim to demonstrate how semiotics and Gestalt perception principles add value and analysis of the visuals utilised in the study and their effect on users. This categorisation should help understand the quantitative data and support the understanding gained from interviews with a small set of users, since a broader understanding of the many will be achieved through large data sets. It is hoped that the interviews will highlight specific details that cause cognitive change in the user and affect behaviour, while also directing further investigation of variables.

BACKGROUND

Augmented Reality

Augmented Reality (AR) is commonly described as, "an experience that supplements the real world with a virtual layer of information" (Lowry, 2015). AR is meant to enhance our experience of the real world through integration of digital content (McCoy, 2018). Current applications in training (Little, 2018; MacPheadran, 2018), health care (Ingram, 2017) and retail (Sandler, 2018) all use AR to enhance the users' experience. The use of the word "layer" in most descriptions of AR can sometimes be detrimental, to our way of conceptualising AR and separating it from its device. The usage of this word suggests that one creates a 2D visual for this medium and then simply adds a virtual layer. 'Layer' is not adequate descriptor of the different types of digital information that can be added, including 2D graphics, 3D graphics, audio (e,g. music, effects, speech) or haptic (e.g. device vibration/movement). 'Layer' also presupposes that the distinction between 2D and 3D is not well-defined, and that the visual assets can be used either in 2D or 3D interchangeably. Additionally, the use of the word 'layer' brings with it a set of connotations which can limit one's way of thinking. Changing the wording from 'layer' to 'virtual overlay' can help remove the connotations and expand thinking on how to use the virtual overlay as a visual communication medium, not just a static digital layer. When presenting content, AR has the unique advantage of being able to use two channels of presentation within the user's environment. Ultimately, the presentation style of AR could be a nuanced form of visual communication whereby the user is presented with relevant information in their environment in a way that the presentation of the virtual overlay becomes visually realistic in the real-time view. In such a situation the virtual overlay seamlessly becomes part of the real-time view. By real-time view we mean the view seen by the user via the AR device in real time. In order to create effective UIs and presentation layers for this medium and understanding of the user perception of their environment and the devices they use becomes of the utmost importance.

SEFAR Research Project

Semiotic Evaluation Framework for Augmented Reality (SEFAR) is a research project currently being undertaken by the authors exploring visual communication theory, namely semiotics and Gestalt perception principles to create a framework that would help content creators and digital designers to design and build contextually engaging content for AR experiences. It is hoped that by doing so users' experience of AR will be enhanced. Visual communication theory that would help pave a path forward for the virtual overlay of AR relies heavily on how users perceive their environment. Visual communication theory is fundamental to the process because it will enable designers to know how best to present the virtual overlay of AR to users within different environments. To do this effectively, it is important to understand how users interact with, and move through their environment, but also how they interact with and read user interfaces (UIs) in general, and when these become part of their environment. This approach defines user interfaces and the virtual overlay of AR as phenomenal objects, and as such requires a phenomenological study to truly understand how the user perceives that with which they are interacting. This involves measuring many variables that need to be consistent to ensure the validity of the study. As such, a rigorous, well-structured methodology is required to ensure consistency and accuracy in what is being observed and measured across multiple variables. Therefore an operational definition[2] is required to define what exactly is meant by a number of terms, what is being observed and measured and what change in results will direct the qualitative investigation.

Understanding behaviour generally requires a phenomenological study to interpret users' behaviour as they interact with a phenomenon. In the case of the research described in this chapter, the user interface within the context of the real-time view of an AR device is the phenomenon. The larger research project will endeavour to load the real-time view with visual cues to measure their effect on the users' perception within their environment. Due to the variety and number of visuals that could potentially be employed to highlight different levels of effect on behaviour, a full phenomenological study might be unwieldy and unnecessary. This could be approached more easily if a comprehensive baseline was first established. This could be achieved by running a smaller experiment using a combination of qualitative and quantitative approaches. This smaller experiment would yield a set of results that would then serve as a baseline comparison for the same experiment with a much larger set of participants. In order to have clarity around what is being measured, how it is being measured and how an understanding is being established and interpreted it is important to have all variables and methods outlined in an operational definition. This operational definition will provide the structure for all the visual experiments developed for the SEFAR research project to ensure clarity and transparency for all the results presented at future milestones.

VISUAL THEORY OF UI DESIGN

When computers started to move out into other industries with a more diverse cohort of users, they needed a communication system closer to human language (Callahan, 1994). Callaghan explains,

"User interfaces for computer programs took a large step forward when they began to incorporate more indexical and iconic elements in their design. User-interface elements were developed, chiefly at Xerox PARC, which enabled users to point at objects on a bit-mapped display (indexical signing), manipulate them by dragging them with a mouse (again, indexical), and which represented the underlying logical entities by things that "looked like them" on screen (iconism). Because of the fact that indices and icons are understood before symbols — babies recognize the touch of their mother and her face, long before they understand the concept of "mothers" — these novel elements of user interface design proved a boon to new computer users, casual users, and those entering an unfamiliar computing domain. And by adding to text such elements as color, font, and visual setting (e.g., a stop sign next to a warning message in a dialog box), they can enhance an experienced user's interactions with the computer as well" (Callahan, 1994).

The terms indexical, indices and icons and how they are utilised here, is part of the field of semiotics. These terms are part of the typology that Pierce (1883) offered to classify "types of signs", or to be more clear, "modes of relationships" between the sign and the signified (Chandler, 2007). The following three modes arose from Pierce's triadic model of the sign (Chandler, 2007).

1 Symbol/symbolic: a mode in which the signifier does not resemble the signified but which is fundamentally arbitrary or purely conventional - so that his relationship must be agreed upon and learned: e.g. language in general (plus specific languages, alphabetical letters, punctuation marks, words, phrases and sentences), numbers morse code, traffic lights, national flags.

2 Icon/iconic: a mode in which the signifier is perceived as resembling or imitating the signified (recognizable looking, sounding, feeling, tasting or smelling like it) - being similar in possessing some of it qualities: e.g. a portrait, a cartoon, a scale-model, onomatopoeia, metaphors, realistic sounds in 'programme music', sound effects in radio drama, a dubbed film soundtrack, imitative gestures.

3 Index/indexical: a mode in which the signifier is not arbitrary but is directly connected in some way (physically or causally) to the signified (regardless of intention) - this link can be observed or inferred: e.g. 'natural signs' (smoke, thunder, footprints, echoes, non-synthetic odours and flavours), medical symptoms (pain, a rash, pulse-rate), measuring instruments (weathercock, thermometer, clock, spirit-level), 'signals' (a knock on a door, a phone ringing), recordings (a photograph, a film, video or television shot, an audio-recored voice), personal 'trademarks' (handwriting, catch-phrases) (Chandler, 2007, pp. 36-37).

Chandler (2007) goes further to point out that these three modes of relationship are listed "in decreasing order of conventionality" (Chandler, 2007, p.37), by which he means symbol/symbolic are conventional where as icon/iconic and index/indexical are less conventional and more referential (Chandler, 2007). This concept of referential has been further expanded by Hodge and Kress (1988) who suggested that the mode of index/indexical is an act of judgement or inference whereas the mode of icon/iconic is closer aligned to perception (Hodge and Kress, 1988).

This theory is embedded in visual communication and so are the visual principles and theory that have shaped UIs. The early work as described by Callahan (1994) became the benchmark for UI design, with design patterns and guidelines developing from this point. They evolved over the following decades enabling a more commonplace understanding of these complex machines. UIs provided the computer and its user with a common language, that facilitated communication and, in turn enabled the user to complete tasks using the computer. This focus on enabling the user to understand how to use the technology makes up a large part of the Human Computer Interaction (HCI) principles. HCI frames the communication between the user and the computer as the UI creator designs an interface that allows the computer to communicate with its user (De Souza, 2005). There are ideas that challenge this such as semiotic engineering (De Souza, 2005) that suggests the alternative, whereby the designer is speaking to the user through the medium of the interface. While this approach is different, the same visual language is utilised.

With the variety of devices now available the established guidelines and patterns within the field of HCI, and more recently UX, have evolved to allow an easy transition from desktop to laptop to tablet and smartphone for software applications, web-based applications and websites. While not everything quite fits, and some transfer of meaning is lost between different devices, the majority of the meaning is inferred by users and can be understood which has allowed for large user uptake of technology and devices.

As the established guidelines and patterns were developed for desktop screen, and then adapted for different screens, it was a small leap from what was working to what needed to work, and the guidelines, patterns and conventions were adapted, tweaked and shoe-horned into place. However, what happens when the screen is removed? Do the screen conventions still have a role to play? Augmented Reality relies on a device but not necessarily a screen. It has a real-time view, either viewed through a smartphone, or headset or smart glasses. Depending on the device, interactions consist of tapping on the smartphone screen, using hand gestures or a remote control, and in the case of some smart glasses, tapping on a pad at the side of the glasses, all in an effort to interact with a virtual overlay that creates a digital interface within the real-time view. Instead of a singular screen that attempts to communicate to the user, the environment of the real-time view and everything in that environment are all potential communicators. This makes AR UIs increasingly complex. Can a single common UI effectively communicate successfully when each object, surface, location and sensor could potentially have a virtual overlay with digital information? It would be similar to looking at multiple screens each trying to communicate with the user all at the same time. Add to this the possibility that each screen would have the same visual patterns to communicate with the user, potentially meaning that nothing is communicated successfully as all the information starts to blend into one and nothing stands out. This would suggest that established patterns that work for desktop applications, mobile apps and websites will not necessarily make sense for the UI of AR. If we take the example of an AR art gallery experience, users are unlikely to expect to interact with a painting in the same way that they would interact with an image on their smartphone. Equally, users do not want a full website of information in this new visual space. We believe that users expect more from the medium and as such they should be offered more than a mere replication of existing content and current presentation style in this new medium. To sustain long-term interest in an AR-based presentation of information, the design of interfaces needs rethinking. Developing for AR using existing screen patterns and conventions is less likely to create engaging experiences for this medium. However, that is not to say that the original benchmark work and the theories that helped to develop the established guidelines and pattern cannot help again.

VISUAL COMMUNICATION AND THE ROLE OF SEMIOTICS AND GESTALT

Visual communication is the process of interpreting different signs to have meaning. As Hollis (1994) explains; "Visual communication in its widest sense has a long history. When early man hunted for food, spotted the imprint of an animal in the mud, he was looking at a graphic sign. His mind's eye saw the animal itself" (Hollis, 1994, p.7). As mentioned previously, some signs we have learned from being taught at a young age (symbol/symbolic) or from experience (index/indexical and icon/iconic) and we now intuitively understand without consciously thinking about them.

The study of signs has developed a great deal in the 100 years since the terms semiotics and semiology were first coined to describe this area of study (Pierce, 1883). Many people have taken up the mantle from those early semiologists, including Barthes (1966) who expanded on the original theories of Saussure & Pierce (Chandler, 2007) on how different signs interact with each other to create new meaning. Barthes' analysis and evaluation of cultural signs and symbols and how they interact expanded the subject from linguistics to include visuals and people, society and body language. Further work by Hodge & Kress (1988) and van Leeuwen & Kress (1996) looked at the visual combination of signs and symbols to such an extent that they have departed from the original landscape of linguistics and now focus solely on visual elements. Kress and van Leeuwen evaluate how a sign or symbol is structured and the elements that make a sign or symbol communicate. They have identified different elements in the construction of meaning, which are: text, image, illustration, and colour; these are referred to as "modes of communication" (1996, p.35). They recognise these graphical elements individually and together, how they can be used to create and communicate meaning, as well as how each mode can affect the overall meaning of a composition.

The complexities of visual communication and graphic design go beyond identifying and assigning meaning to individual objects, signs, and symbols. Barthes' evaluation of the front cover of the Paris Match edition no. 326 in July 1955 (Barthes, 1972), is a deconstruction and explanation of the different signs and signifiers at work to communicate a message through every aspect of its composition. His analysis delves into the construction of interaction between the multiple signs and symbols. Moreover, this evaluation identifies how a sign and/or symbol can be anything once it has a cultural context and is understood by society. Then it can be used to communicate and make meaning.

With this in mind, the construction of graphic images, as well as the images themselves "are more than descriptive illustration of things seen or imagined. They are signs whose context gives them a unique meaning, and whose position can lead to a new signification" (Hollis, 1994, p. 7). This description by Hollis illustrates the depth of semiotics within graphic design or any design within the realm of visual communication. Graphic designers and digital designers actively use semiotics and Gestalt principles to create meaning every day. The graphic elements also referred to as modes of communication by Kress and van Leeuwen (1996) are manipulated and arranged by designers to create meaning. The format in which a composition is realised vastly influences the construction of the message being communicated.

Previously user interfaces existed to allow users to interact with a computing device; when the context was the device. However, now the context is the environment accessed through the real-time view of the AR enabled device. While to some, even many, this sounds the same, for those who are tasked with communication and creating meaning it changes everything. A well-constructed user interface is a powerful communicator that has clear messaging and intention that allows users to complete complex tasks with a few simple interactions. However, for the UI to communicate as succinctly as possible within the user's environment, it is first important to understand how users perceive their environment and the objects within it.

PERCEPTION

Human perception has been observed, researched, discussed and debated for centuries. How it is described, studied, rationalised and defined vary depending on the different schools of thought. Marleau-Ponty describes perception as follows;"the spontaneous method of normal perception, that kind of living system of meanings which makes the concrete essence of the object immediately recognizable ... the subject's intentions are immediately reflected in the perceptual field" (Marleau-Ponty, 1945, p.151).

He goes further and argues that consciousness is not merely a representative function or power of signification. Consciousness is a projective activity, which develops sensory data beyond its own specific signification (Marleau-Ponty, 1945). Over the decades, two distinct approaches to understanding perception and how humans perceive have developed. While both have some similarities and are even utilised together at times, they very much stand in opposition to each other. These are:

- Bottom up processing as defined by Gibson (1966). This is also know as the data-driven process, since Gibson believed that perception starts with a stimulus. He maintained that processing is carried out in one direction from the retina to the visual cortex (Gibson, 1966).
- Top down processing as defined by Gregory (1970). This approach utilises contextual information in pattern recognition. Gregory argued that perception is a constructive process, which relies on prior knowledge to help interpret frequently ambiguous stimuli. As such Gregory presents perceptions as a hypothesis based on prior knowledge which actively constructs our perception of reality based on the environment and the individual's prior knowledge (Gregory, 1970).

In his seminal book "The Perception of the Visual World" Gibson stated that:

The visual world can be described in many ways, but its most fundamental properties seem to be these: it is extended in distance and modelled in depth; it is upright ...

(Gibson 1974, p.3).

This analysis of what we see and perceive is important for AR, because essentially we are not designing for AR nor the environment where the virtual overlay will exist, instead we are designing UIs from the point of view of how users perceive their environment and how they understand what is presented in front of them in this new way. Screen-less technologies will essentially exist around user's needs to work at a different level. For UIs to be successful, an understanding of how users perceive their environments, UIs in general and UIs within their environments needs to be established. Once such a baseline understanding has been established then more appropriate and effective UIs that suit the users can be designed.

Users are no longer sitting at a screen trying to complete tasks with a UI that was designed so that the computer makes sense to the user. The user already has an understanding of their environment, there are *anchors* and *sense-making tools* in their perception that allow them to understand their environment. The virtual overlay of AR should then utilise the user's knowledge and perception of their environment to build UIs based on that perception of their environment. Ittelson & Kilpatrick's study (1951) is referred to as an example of a classical study of perception (Izard, 1977). In that study they stated; "Some remarkable optical illusions show that what we perceive does not directly correspond to reality, it is a subtle blend of the external world and the many sessions of our experience" (Ittelson & Kilpartick 1951, p.50).

In their study they surmise that, "the world that each of us knows is a world created in large measure from our experience in dealing with the environment" (p.50). That when encountering phenomena they cannot be explained by referring to reality, because reality and perception do not correspond simply because any given retinal pattern there are an infinite number brightness-size-distance combinations to which that pattern might relate to (p.50). From this standpoint they concluded that, "when faced with such a situation, in which an unlimited number of possibilities can be related to a given retinal pattern the organism that what has been most probable in the past is the most probable in the immediate occasion" (Ittelson & Kilpartick 1951, p.50). Izard (1977) references this and builds on it by surmising that the perceptual process is not just a simple transformation of sensory input and instead "the observer tends to add something to the sensation resulting from the stimulus pattern" (Izard, 1977 p.143). This addition from previous experience or knowledge aligns with Gregory (1970) and his top-down processing theory. This in turn aligns itself with how visual design utilises semiotics. Taking associated cultural visuals to make meaning and using their context or out-of-context to either further the meaning or subvert the meaning. Where perception is about making sense, semiotics is about making meaning. This distinction helps to frame how users perceive their environment and how that visuals can make sense, resonate with meaning and influence mental models.

MENTAL MODELS AND COGNITIVE CHANGE

As outlined by Payne in the book HCI Models, Theories and Frameworks (as cited in Carroll, 2003), "The user mental model of the device is one of the most tantalising ideas in the psychology of human-computer interaction (HCI). Certainly, it is one of the most widely discussed theoretical approaches to HCI that progresses cognitive science at the same time as having a genuine practical input" (Carroll, 2003, p.135). Payne's use of the word "tantalising" is significant. Payne later explains; "yet mental models remain a tantalising - rather than fulfilling - theoretical concept because even a casual inspection of the HCI and cognitive science literature reveals that the term is used in so many different ways as to be almost void of any force beyond the general idea of users' knowledge about the system they use" (as cited in Carroll, 2003, p.135).

Unfortunately, this is true. The situation is further exacerbated when the concept can be manipulated to rationalise any argument concerning the user's need for a working understanding of a device (as cited in Carroll, 2003). That said, mental models are a useful theoretical approach when investigating behaviour as it allows us to bridge the gap between how a user perceives something and the ensuing impact on behaviour. Payne (as cited in Carroll, 2003) describes how "mental models are constructed by processing language, but the same models might also, in principle have been constructed through interaction with and perception of the world" (p.146). Taking this view, we can define mental models for this study as follows: mental models allow us to frame a user's understanding, and their particular behaviour, within the context of their environment. In this way, mental models can be considered benchmarks, so that when a cognitive change occurs as described by Johnson-Laird (2013), whether by intrinsic or extrinsic cause, that change may have lasting effects on mental processes. If a cognitive change occurs that follows through to a change of behaviour then this can be measured and reflected upon in order to gain an understanding of the user, the cognitive change, the cause and the effect on behaviour. This gives a framework for studying the causes and effect of a change of behaviour.

METHODOLOGY RATIONALE

As we have seen, much of the early UI design foundations have their roots in semiotics, and while the term has fallen out of the day-to-day vocabulary of UI design, the practices and principles are still part of the concept formation and work of UI designers. This is evidenced in how users interact with evolving UIs; when a user does something automatically that is because they instinctively understood what was being communicated, it made sense to them, it had meaning.

In a future of ubiquitous computing with a myriad of smart devices, what does removing the screen mean? In terms of design, it is an opportunity to pave the way for a new visually communicative medium, that is open for experimentation and interpretation. In terms of the virtual overlay of AR, there is an opportunity to create new user interfaces that allow data to be consumed from our environment. As humans, we already consume visually from our environments with our brains constantly taking sensory input from our surroundings. The virtual overlay of AR adds to this contextual data by adding digital data to it. The purpose or aim of the data will originate with its creator, but what is common to a future virtual overlay will be that it will sit within a highly visual space and needs to be welcomed there by the user if it is to be interacted with.

How users see and perceive relationships between visuals, icons and text in user interfaces is hugely important. Designers are already familiar with the process of constructing highly communicative UIs for software applications, mobile applications, websites and more - essentially all screen-dependent devices.

However, the virtual overlay of AR is different in that it has the potential to inform, add meaning, define objects, deflect meaning and even subvert the meaning of objects within the immediate environment of the user. Consequently, insight into the limits of understanding, patience, willingness of the user and how they perceive and understand UIs and visuals in this new environment, along with how they interact with them becomes hugely important for those creating for this space. As with every communication design project, designers must know their audience and the context of the communication. However, AR adds another layer to this. Previously designers had to know their audience and their specific context, but now they must also understand how the audience perceive AR and how that specific audience, the users perceive and interact with their immediate environments. When we understand this, then we can start to design for screen-less technology that is device independent.

When studying perception in this context, that is, understanding how users comprehend and navigate their environment and/or interactions, a base understanding needs to be achieved in order to make comparisons with a set of variables. This baseline set of data of how humans achieve and complete different tasks is required so that designers understand their motivations around interactions, choices, decisions, frustrations and ultimately users' behaviour as they interact with a phenomenal object such as their environment. As previously mentioned, since the virtual overlay of AR will be part of their environment real-world environment or view, it means that it too is a phenomenal object and can be studied in two ways:

1. A phenomenal object as it interacts and augments an existing phenomenal object or
2. As part of, indistinguishable from the original phenomenal object of the environment.

Both lines of investigation require a baseline understanding of how users interact with their environment. We shall design and run experiments around this baseline in order to interpret meaning and understanding.

The aim of the larger research project includes developing an interaction design theory that utilises visual communication theories to describe the user's mental model as being influenced by the virtual overlay of AR, rather than the physical device. We hope to answer questions such as:

- Can we better explain and predict how users perceive and interact with AR systems?
- Can this lead to improved AR system designs? Such as: better notification and interactions systems to enhance user experience overall.
- Can this lead to improved user experiences? Such as: better communications of intended narratives via AR-enhance systems

Our research is tasked with investigating how visuals and visual cues can affect perception when interacting with different types of AR user interfaces. It is hoped to find the types, themes and thresholds of the visuals, to create communicative interfaces within the context of the user's environment rather than relying on established device patterns. It is hoped that by having an understanding of the users' perception as they interact with different interfaces utilising different visual types that new theory and guidelines can be established to help anchor the SEFAR framework that will aid digital designers in the visual medium of AR.

The research aims to investigate how different visual theories, such as semiotics and Gestalt, can be utilised to help further understand users' perception when interacting with AR and to help develop rules around the conceptual model when creating different narratives for AR artefacts. In order to successfully investigate what is being proposed and utilise the theory across various applications, while also testing a range of visuals for their communicative value and potential to influence, many experiments need to be conducted. These experiments will contain a wide variety of variables and variable combinations.

The aim is to observe and reveal insights into the effectiveness of the application of theory and effectiveness of the images that will in turn give an underlying blueprint to the SEFAR framework. To achieve a consistent procedure the proposed operation definition will contain a full description of procedures and actions required to observe and measure the experiments, this will allow for a high level of transparently and replicable set of experiments.

PROPOSED METHODOLOGY

While this study will be made up of a series of experiments, it is planned that a single operational definition can be used to define the overall procedures for all. Essentially it will be a blueprint for all experiments within the study.

Our initial experiments will investigate the effectiveness of different visuals in terms of influencing users' perception of how to interact with simple screen-based user interactions and interfaces. This initial experiment is testing the communication value and threshold of meaning without being corrupted by being on a new medium. This is essential for a benchmark. The experiments will explore the effectiveness of different visuals and their thresholds of meaning and sense-making, and when communication breaks down in the standard medium of a screen-based website. To establish an accurate account and find common baselines and benchmarks several different experiments with a variety of images and interactions will be required in order to first establish effective visuals across a number of categories. The aims of these initial experiments are:

1. Understanding a range of effective visuals that effect change in a user's behaviour with an interface
2. Understanding the visual thresholds that affect users' perception and effect change in their behaviour with an interface
3. Understanding the change in the user that caused or did not cause a change in behaviour

Aims 1 and 2 above are quantitative data sets where we want to know broadly which images are effective and how effective they are across a large number of users. Aim 3 is more nuanced. We want to know how a user felt when interacting with a number of images. Aim 3 would require a phenomenological study to gain a deep understanding through observation, interview and reflection in order to interpret the person's lived experience with the particular phenomena within the study. These proposed experiments will investigate the effectiveness of different visuals on user behaviour when interacting with the virtual overlay of AR. These experiments are not focussed on one particular or singular image, instead a range of image categories each with a set of characteristics will be utilised. Each image from each category will be tested to gauge the threshold of meaning that affect how people interact with systems. The visuals will vary in content, style, colour, brightness, position, context and composition. Due to the volume of visuals a standard traditional, standalone phenomenological study is not feasible. While the information and data from a phenomenological study is required it will not be fully attainable with the number of visuals, environments, devices and interaction types involved. For instance, Figure 1 presents a set of sketches that shows the desired mouse cursor paths we wish the user to take in the initial experiment. Users are aware that a mouse drag from A to B is a straight line movement. This initial experiment is looking at what visual cues can be used to change their behaviour and take a non-linear path.

Reducing any of these variables to set up a standard phenomenological study would not satisfy the requirements of this research which will rely on conclusions drawn from the user data as they interact with a variety of images in these experiments. The aim is that these experiments will allow a new understanding of the effectiveness of visuals, of the different aspects of the visuals and their thresholds of communicability as meaningful communicators to a wide set of users. This approach we have proposed will be a true combination of qualitative and quantitative methods whereby an initial results from users' perception with a certain set of visuals will establish a baseline understanding of users' behaviour as influenced by the visuals. These images and interactions will be used with a wider user sample to see if similar results are achieved. Any changes to the original set will direct the further phenomenological study. From this baseline set of images and results the images will be changed to see how they affect communication. These will be gauged against a set of assumptions and again, any deviation from the expected results will be the focus of a phenomenological study before introducing a larger data set. This iterative, branching process will continue across a full set of images. It is important to mention that these images are not random. We are utilising quantitative content analysis which is an established method for systematic analysis of well defined media (Krippendorff, 2004). This method requires principled decisions on what will be analysed, whether the experiment elements comprise all the available content or a representative sample or simply a sample and from that compiling a code book (Bock, Isermann & Knieper, 2011). However, for the purposes of this research the methodology will be used for the creation of images rather than the analysis of the images, focussing on the image composition to create meaning and effect behaviour in the user. The code book will contain specific information and criteria to inform the image creation. This is an important part of the operational definition as it allows consistent creation and analysis of imagery and graphics.

Figure 1. Sketches of the expected and desired paths of interaction

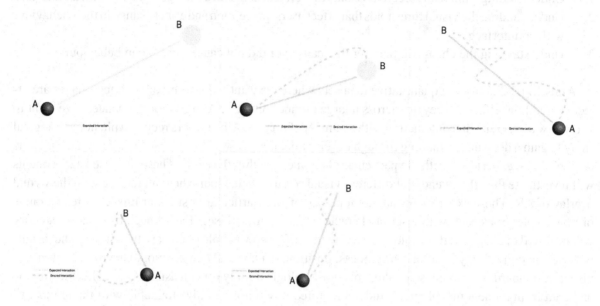

As previously outlined a code book of visuals will be included in the operational definition along with the aims, research questions, hypothesis, and method consisting of independent and dependant variables, apparatus and participants. This structure will ensure consistency and reliable results across visuals, contexts and computing devices and different AR enabled devices.

OPERATIONAL DEFINITION

The operational definition has a number of criteria that need to be satisfied when running each experiment. Table 1 below presents the elements for a generic operations definition.

The structure of the operational definition aims to give as much detailed and consistent information so that all experiments across the research project are carried out consistently. As a result any of the experiments in this research can be confidently replicated regardless of medium whether it is web or AR.

INITIAL EXPERIMENT TO TEST THE OPERATION DEFINITION

This initial experiment is the first of the benchmark experiments while also testing the viability of the operational definition.

Table 1. The structural outline of the different sections of the operational definition

Research Question	This outlines the area or subject under investigation and how it will help the overall research project.
Aim	This states the aim of the particular test and how it relates to the overall research project.
Characteristics of Interest/Hypothesis	This specifically states what is being observed and what is being measured.
Measurement Instruments	This will outline the equipment & methods that will be used to take measurements during the tasks.
Data Recording/Classification Method	This will outline what data will be recorded and how it will be classified.
Decision Criteria	The decision criteria will determine if the experiments were a success or not.
Method	This outlines the procedure used for setting up the experiments and taking measurements. It will outline the participants, the task, how it will be measured and observed.
Apparatus	This specifically states what devices will be used in the experiment.
Code Book	The code book is the catalog of images that will be used throughout the research project. It is a record of the visuals that will be used. These have been created specifically to influence behaviour in specific interactions.
Dependant & Independent Variables	While many of the tasks will be similar, the independent variable will change. In each case the independent variable will be stated alongside its dependant variable.
Experiment Description	This outlines the procedure for the experiment. And gives specifics on: 1. Task Description 2. Expected Interaction 3. Desired Interaction 4. Sample 5. Observation 6. Measurement

INITIAL EXPERIMENT TO TEST OPERATIONAL DEFINITION RESULTS AND DISCUSSION

A trial run of experiment 1 was performed in Q4 2021 on 6 participants (3 male, 3 female). The results from this trial run are summarised in Figure 2.

The automated tool collects the x,y coordinates of the mouse movement. These data points can be collected and visualised in a graph, displaying how each participant interacted with each screen, see Figure 3. This gives us a very accurate and visual way to analyse a large set of data from a large sample.

With this initial test sample of 6, all 6 were interviewed. In a larger sample only a small percentage would be interviewed to confirm the data collected and establish the influence the visuals had on the collective mental model of the sample. However, when anomalies occur, those users would be identified and asked to take the questionnaire. This deep dive into the data would seek to understand why these users interacted differently to the majority and establish why their mental models were not influenced by the visuals in the same way. These deep dives should provide strong qualitative data on the specifics of visuals and the influence they have. In cases where the majority of users have interacted adversely to what was expected, the regular questionnaire sample will catch that data.

This use of a combined methods approach with a code of book of visuals will allow for a vast amount of testing to be conducted quickly and efficiently, ideally yielding a large set of quality data into visuals that influence users' mental models. The data will hopefully create a composite of what visuals have the potential to influence users mental models even in the most basic of interactions.

Table 2. Uses the operational definition to organise the experiment

Research Question	To what extent can the introduction of some simple visual cues affect the user's interaction. It is hoped that this experiment will become a benchmark for further research into the visuals that can affect the user's conventional mental models.
Aim	The aim of this experiment is to examine the effect a set of visuals can have on user behaviour. This will lay the foundation as to whether simple visuals can be effective in changing user behaviour.
Characteristics of Interest/Hypothesis	Can simple visual cues change the user's interaction behaviour with a system. If so, is there a threshold between the communication value of the cues, where no behavioural change can be identified
Measurement Instruments	Computer, with a web-based artefact, will record (x,y) paths of points on the screen where the mouse was moved & human observation of the path (when recorded movement is replayed on screen).
Data Recording/Classification Method	The path shape will be calculated using line and curve fitting functions (straight line/curved line avoiding some visual elements) - along with a measurement of confidence. There will also be human opinion as to the path shape. Calculated and human opinion on shapes will be compared for correlation.
Decision Criteria	Does the data indicate a change in behaviour due to the visual cues presented? Did the user move the mouse cursor around the visual cues and follow the path presented rather than interacting as they normally would?
Method	The tasks will be run through a web browser. The participants will be presented with 5 visuals. Each visual will have a task instruction. As they complete the task the web based artefact will record the x,y, coordinates of the mouse movement. This web-based task can be shared with a number of participants, who will then be asked to send it on to another 3 candidates in order to establish a random set of participants using the snowball sampling technique. A sample set will be observed during the task and asked to take part in a post task questionnaire to get an understanding of their interaction behaviour during the task. This will be done in person and remotely.
Apparatus	Web-based artefact that will measure the x,y coordinates of the mouse movement, and mouse button press-and-release actions as the user drags the objects from the different points.
Code Book	The code book visuals are those that have a range of visual cues introduced. It is hoped that these cues will influence the behaviour of the user. The visuals are created in a web page that will allow the user to interact and move an object from one point to another.
Dependant & Independent Variables	While many of the tasks will be similar, the independent variable will change. In each case the independent variable will be stated alongside its dependant variable.

continues on following page

Table 2. *Continued*

	Experiment Description The procedure for this experiment is as follows: 1. **Setup** 2. The web-based artefact that can track the mouse movement will be presented to the participant. It will display the 5 different interactions. 3. **Task** 4. Participants will be asked to follow the on-screen instructions. 5. Expected interaction 6. We expect that the interactions will be the straight line drag-and-drop from the starting points to the end points. 7. **Desired Interaction** 8. We have introduced a number of visual cues to disrupt the expected interaction. The desired interaction is for the user to avoid the visual cues such as the grass, rocks and cliff edge that are "blocking" the route of the expected interaction. 9. **Sample**
Experiment Description	10. For this initial test, 6 participants were recruited: 11. - 3 were observed as they completed the tasks and had exit interviews 12. - 3 were not observed as they completed the tasks 13. **Observation** 14. There are two methods of observation: 15. - the physical observation of some of the participants as they complete the tasks and the automated recording of the interactions of all of the participants. 16. **Measurement** 17. There are three main aspects that are being measured in this experiment. 18. 1 - firstly, how far, if at all, did the participants deviate from the expected interaction 19. 2 - how close was their actual interaction to that of the desired interaction 20. 3 - the effectiveness of the visuals in their respective tasks to disrupt the expected interaction. 21. Exit interviews with those that were observed were undertaken.

continues on following page

101

Table 2. Continued

Experiment Outline for each visual	
	While these tasks are very similar, the visuals are very different. Due to the different visuals there are no dependant variables. However, these tasks are consistent in their set up. The visuals are the independent variables where by different visual cues are introduced. The visual cues are placed along the anticipated path in order to disrupt the visual line that the user might take. Also, the visual cues are of different kinds, from grass, to rock to a cliff edge with water. Each image is a variable in that it is introducing a visual cue along the anticipated path.

Artifact 1

1. Task Description

Figure 2. has been recreated in an interactive web based artefact. It has two points, A & B. The points are set diagonally from each other with A in the lower left hand corner of the screen and B in the upper right hand corner of the screen. There is a ball at point A. There is a circular area at point B. The instructions state, "Please move the ball from A to B".

2. Expected Interaction & 3. Desired Interaction

The expected interaction is that the user will use a straight line drag, moving the ball from A to B. This first interaction should give a baseline benchmark of the user and their motivation based on the visual that is presented to them.

4. Sample

Image/Screen 1

Sketch of expected interaction for experiment benchmark   Screenshot of screen 1 from artefact.

Sketches of the expected and desired paths of interaction and sample of screen 1 of web-based artefact

5. Observation

Notes from observation of experiment

6. Measurement

Notes of measurement

continues on following page

Table 2. Continued

Experiment Outline for each visual (Continued)	**Artifact 2**
	1. Task Description
	Image 2 has been recreated in an interactive web based artefact. It has two points, these are not labelled. A ball is located near the bottom left-hand corner of the screen and a box that is visibly open on top, is located near the top right hand corner. The instructions state, "Please put the ball into the box."
	2. Expected Interaction
	The expected interaction is that the user will use a straight line drag, dragging the ball towards the box and placing it on the box graphic.
	3. Desired Interaction
	The visual cue being utilised is the open box. The box flaps are open showing the inside of the box. It is hoped that this will suggest to the user that the ball can only be put into the box from the open top. Will the visibly open box affect the user's anticipated behaviour?
	4. Sample
	Image/Screen 2
	Sketches of the expected and desired paths of interaction and sample of screen 1 of web-based artefact
	5. Observation
	Notes from observation of experiment
	6. Measurement
	Notes of measurement

continues on following page

Table 2. Continued

Experiment Outline for each visual (Continued)	**Artifact 3** **1. Task Description** Image 3 has been recreated in an interactive web based artefact. It has two points, these are not labelled. A dog is located near the bottom right-hand corner of the screen and a dog house located near the top-left hand corner. A curving path is provided to show the route from where the dog is to the dog house. Grass and some trees line the path. The instructions state, "Please take the dog home." **2. Expected Interaction** The expected interaction is that the user will use a straight line drag, taking the dog from its point of origin to the dog house. **3. Desired Interaction** The visual cues such as the grass, trees and bushes have been introduced with the aim of disrupting the user's normal interaction. The curving path with grass areas visually interfere with the expected path. Trees and bushes have also been added to hopefully deflect the user from just moving the dog with a straight line drag. Does the simple cue of a winding path, edged with grass and bushes disrupt the user's mental model? **4. Sample** Image/Screen 3 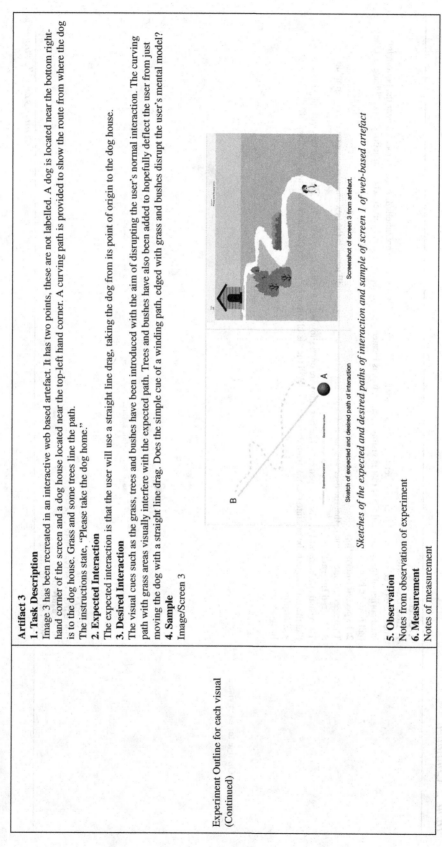 Sketch of expected and desired path of interaction Screenshot of screen 3 from artefact. *Sketches of the expected and desired paths of interaction and sample of screen 1 of web-based artefact* **5. Observation** Notes from observation of experiment **6. Measurement** Notes of measurement

continues on following page

Table 2. Continued

| Experiment Outline for each visual (Continued) | **Artifact 4**
1. Task Description
Image 4 has been recreated in an interactive web based artefact. It has two points, these are not labelled. A boat is located in the bottom, just right of screen centre. An island with a tree is located in the centre of the screen. There is a number of protruding rocks between the boat and the island. There is a stretch of open water that is unimpeded by large protruding rocks.
The instructions state, "Take the boat to the island with the tree."
2. Expected Interaction
The expected interaction is that the user will use a straight line drag, taking the boat from its position and place it by the island.
3. Desired Interaction
The protruding rocks are the visual cues that are being utilised. They are placed along the line of the expected interaction to visually block the anticipated interaction. Ideally, it is hoped the user will move the boat around the initial rock and up to the island through the open water. Does the simple cue of a stretch of unobstructed waterway disrupt the user's mental model?
4. Sample
Image/Screen 4

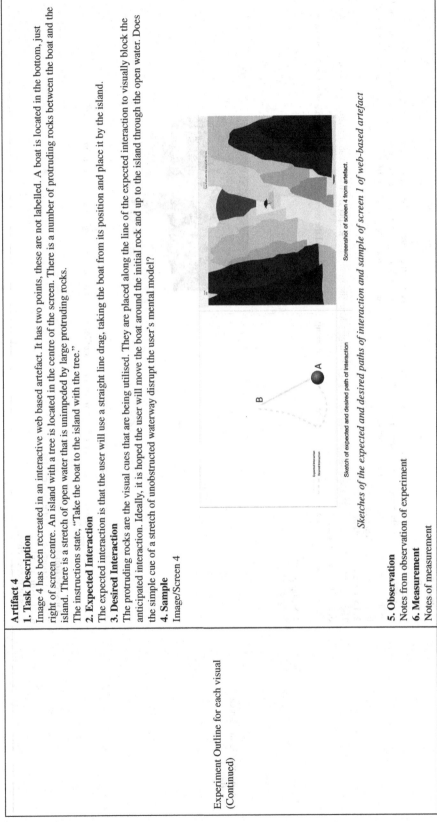

Sketches of the expected and desired paths of interaction and sample of screen 1 of web-based artefact

5. Observation
Notes from observation of experiment
6. Measurement
Notes of measurement |

continues on following page

Table 2. Continued

| Experiment Outline for each visual (Continued) | **Artifact 5**
1. Task Description
Image 5 has been recreated in an interactive web based artefact. It has two points, these are not labelled. A figure (lighthouse keeper) is located just left of centre near the bottom of the screen and a lighthouse is located just right of centre near the top of the screen. A jagged path is provided to show the route from the lighthouse keeper's position to the location of the lighthouse. The path is part of a cliff path surrounded by water. The instructions state, "Take the lighthouse keeper to the lighthouse."
2. Expected Interaction
The expected interaction is that the user will use a straight line drag, taking the lighthouse keeper from its point of origin to the lighthouse.
3. Desired Interaction
The visual cues of the jagged cliff path, surrounded by water are being utilised. It is hoped the user will stick to the path and not move out over the water.
4. Sample
Image/Screen 5

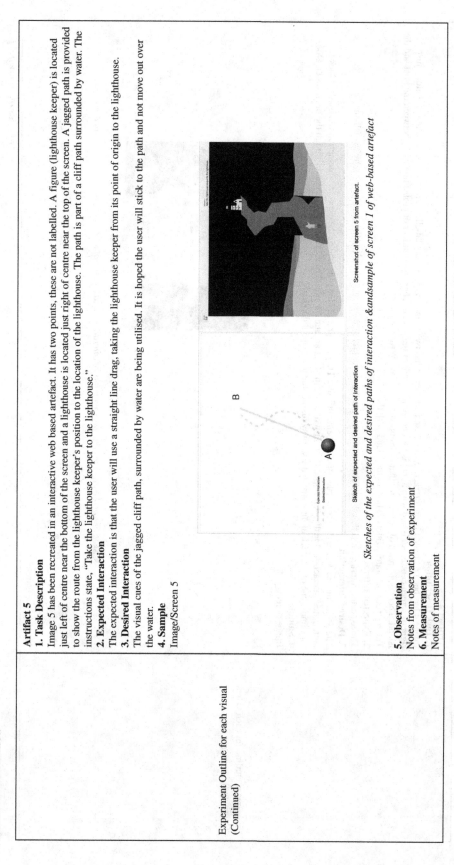

Sketches of the expected and desired paths of interaction &andsample of screen 1 of web-based artefact

5. Observation
Notes from observation of experiment
6. Measurement
Notes of measurement |

The data from the initial sample of 6, shows some anomalies with screen 3, where the visual cues did not fully disrupt the expected interaction path and it was found through the interviews that grass really doesn't inhibit as they walk on grass all the time, whereas rocks and cliff edges were perceived as actual disrupters to the users.

As a bench mark experiment, it is an encouraging result, and motivates us to conduct the experiment, using this operation definition to ensure consistency with a larger number of users in the near future.

Figure 2. Results from initial test

	Participant 1			Participant 2			Participant 3			Participant 4			Participant 5			Participant 6		
	Expected	Desired	Interviewed	Expected	Desired	Interviewed	Expected	Desired	Interviewed	Expected	Desired	Interviewed	Expected	Desired	Interviewed	Expected	Desired	Interviewed
Task1	X	X		X	X		X	X		X	X		X			X	X	
Task2		X			X		X				X		X				X	
Task3		X			X		X				X		X				X	
Task4		X			X			X			X			X			X	
Task5		X			X			X			X			X			X	

Figure 3. Mouse movement data points visualised in graph

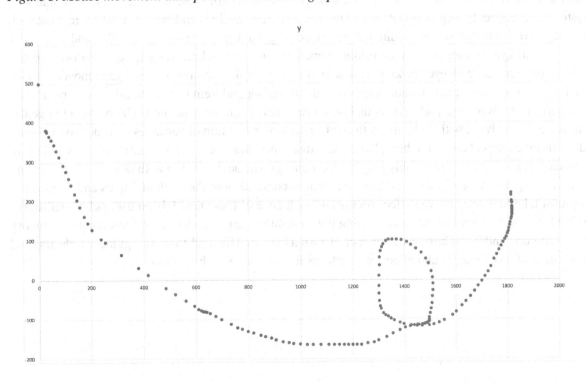

FUTURE DIRECTION

This is a preliminary blueprint for an operational definition for a mixed methods approach that will be the basis of a number of comprehensive screen based and AR based UI experiments. Having outlined the operational definition in detail, it aims to be clear and instructive while ensuring consistency and allowing for replicability. While this area of research is becoming an increasingly more qualitative space, having a strong structured mixed methods approach in place will help collect quantitative data alongside qualitative findings. While this operational definition is quite specific to the experiment outlined here and those that will make up the larger research project that was mentioned earlier, it can be refined for future research projects of different kinds.

Due to the consistency that the operational definition creates, the output of data from the different experiments will allow for a greater analysis of results across the different UI combinations and allow for more in-depth finding and insights in a structured way to help with the publishing of results. Also, with greater more integrated insights, it potential gives UI designers more visual tools to create new UIs for new mediums.

CONCLUSION

Organising this type of experiment in this way gives structure to the variables, the data collection, analysis & deeper investigations. It also allows for replication by other researchers but also forms a blueprint for further study in this vein of research.

In this chapter we have provided an overview of a research approach to UI involving visual communication theories driving a highly quantitative experimental methodology. During user interactions, computing devices allow automatic recording of large quantities of quantitative data; for example web systems can collect timing information and user actions such as links and buttons clicked, text entered, mouse movements and so on. Additional hardware (e.g. built-in to headsets) can also add additional data, such as eye tracking, and in the future biometrics such as EEG, heart-rate, skin conductance and so on. For example, with eye-tracking data, it would be possible to compare users' gaze movements, to analyse whether they "plan" a path before actually dragging and item to a destination on screen - and comparisons between eye paths and actual item drag paths could be generated. The resulting large datasets can be analysed both deductively through statistical evaluation of variables recorded to explicitly allow us to test hypotheses, and through inductive discovery data science analytical techniques. Different interface technologies, most notably Augmented Reality (AR) devices, offer both new opportunities and new challenges to UI designers, and these challenges continue onto the methodologies and approaches we must take to investigate the effectiveness and influence of these new UIs on user behaviour. In the SEFAR research project we are investigating how a semiotic approach to visual communication theory can guide our understanding of the impact of visuals in AR UIs, and therefore guide the design and evaluation of more natural and effective interfaces for the use of such systems.

REFERENCES

APA. (2021). *Operation Definition entry in APA Dictionary of Psychology*. American Psychological Association. Retrieved from: https://dictionary.apa.org/operational-definition

Barthes, R. (1966). Introduction à l'analyse structurale des récits. Communications, 8(1), 1–27. doi:10.3406/comm.1966.1113

Barthes, R. (1972). *Mythologies*. Jonathon Cape.

Bock, A., Isermann, H., & Knieper, T. (2011). Quantitative content analysis of the visual. In *The SAGE handbook of visual research methods* (pp. 265–282). SAGE Publications Ltd. doi:10.4135/9781446268278. n14

Callahan, G. (1994). Excessive realism in GUI design: Helpful or harmful? Software Development.

Chandler, D. (2007). *Semiotics - the Basics* (2nd ed.). Routledge. doi:10.4324/9780203014936

De Souza, C. (2005). *The Semiotic Engineering of Human-Computer Interaction* (1st ed.). The MIT Press. doi:10.7551/mitpress/6175.001.0001

Gibson, J. (1974). *The Perception of the Visual World*. Greenwood Press.

Gibson, J. (1978). *The Ecological Approach to the Visual Perception of Pictures*. MIT Press. doi:10.2307/1574154

Gregory, R. (1970). *The Intelligent Eye*. Weidenfeld and Nicolson.

Hodge, R., & Kress, G. (1988). *Social Semiotics*. Polity.

Hollis, R. (1994). *Graphic design - A concise history* (1st ed.). Thames and Hudson.

Ingram, M. (2017). *Medical Students are using Augmented Reality to Study Patients in 3D*. Retrieved from: https://fortune.com/2017/05/03/medical-augmented-reality/

Ittelson, W. H., & Kilpatrick, F. P. (1951). Experiments in Perception. *Scientific American, 185*(2), 50-56.

Izard, C. (1977). *Human Emotions*. Springer Science+Business Media, LLC.

Johnson-Laird, P. N. (2013). Mental models and cognitive change. *Journal of Cognitive Psychology, 25*(2), 131–138. doi:10.1080/20445911.2012.759935

Kress, G. (2010). *Multimodality A social semiotic approach to contemporary communication* (1st ed.). Routledge.

Kress, G., & van Leeuwen, T. (1996). *Reading images - The grammar of visual design*. Routledge.

Krippendorff, K. (2004). Reliability in Content Analysis. *Human Communication Research, 30*, 411–433.

Lowry, J. (2015). *Augmented reality is the future of design*. Retrieved from https://thenextweb.com/augmented-reality/2015/08/31/augmented-reality-is-the-future-of-design/

MacPhedran, S. (2018). *Augmented Manufacturing: The Big Six Hololens Use Cases for Manufacturers*. Retrieved from https://blog.smith.co/2018/Augmented-Manufacturing

McCoy, E. (2018) *Storytelling Strategies for Augmented and Virtual Reality*. Retrieved from https://killervisualstrategies.com/blog/storytelling-strategies-for-augmented-and-virtual-reality.html

Merleau-Ponty, M. (1945). *Phenomenology of Perception* (C. Smith, Trans.). Éditions Gallimard, Routledge & Kegan Paul.

Payne, S. (2003). Users' Mental Model: The Very Ideas. In J. Carroll (Ed.), *HCI Models, Theories, and Frameworks - Toward a Multidisciplinary Science* (pp. 135–156). Morgan Kaufmann. doi:10.1016/B978-155860808-5/50006-X

Peirce, C. S. (Ed.). (1883). *Studies in Logic, by Members of The Johns Hopkins University*. Little Brown. doi:10.1037/12811-000

Sandler, E. (2018). *Zara Stores Target Millennials with Augmented Reality Displays*. Retrieved from https://www.forbes.com/sites/emmasandler/2018/04/16/zara-stores-targets-millennials-with-augmented-reality-displays/#7ec8a40c2315

ENDNOTES

[1] Almost all non-technical computer users use a Graphical User Interface (GUI), although some technical IT professionals use "terminal" applications, which offer text-only Command Line Interfaces (CLI). In this chapter we will only be referring to graphical user interfaces, so UI should be interpreted as GUI in all instances.

[2] "A description of something in terms of the operations (procedures, actions, or processes) by which it could be observed and measured." (APA 2021). Operational definitions described precisely what is to be measured, what instrument is to be used, and the method of data collection/classification.

Chapter 6
Significance of Software Engineering Phases in the Development of a Software Application:
Case Study

Sushama A. Deshmukh

https://orcid.org/0000-0002-0569-7121

Maharashtra Institute of Technology, India

Smita L. Kasar

Maharashtra Institute of Technology, India

ABSTRACT

Software engineering is the extensive study of how to build a software product using software development life cycle stages, beginning with requirement analysis phase to the last phase of testing and maintenance. This approach in the development of software application ensures completion of the project within the stipulated period without compromising quality of the software with effective utilization of resources. The most important is to develop a quality product. Case studies make readers understand the concept in a more impartial and tactile manner; one can make use of this experience in real-life circumstances for providing solutions to the complex problems. The significance of this case study is to represent the authors' experience of developing software by using method of software engineering, understanding how to apply them to build an application. This chapter gives a holistic review of the development of an Android application titled Vaccination Management System (VMS) "Vacc-IT" as a comprehensive case study.

DOI: 10.4018/978-1-7998-9121-5.ch006

INTRODUCTION

Software is the collection of code modules, and engineering is the application of principles in building something qualitative. Hence, Software Engineering (SE) is the application of principles, methods, strategies to develop a quality solution in the form of the software application (Pressman, a). The quality of the software is measured in terms of its characteristics, which may be characterized as operational, transitional, and maintenance (Pressman b). Institute of Electrical and Electronics Engineers (IEEE) definition of SE is defined as the "The application of a systematic, disciplined, quantifiable approach to the development, operation, and maintenance of software; that is, the application of engineering to software" Roger Pressman. SE comprises some phases, from its very initial stage of requirement collection and analysis to the last stage of testing and maintenance, where each phase has its own deliverables (Jalote). In the beginning of 1960s, the development of SE was considered as an challenging task to execute. The development of SE cause difficulty in maintaining when accompanied with hardware, which generated several difficulties, such as surpassed deadlines, over-budget software, need large maintenance and de-bugging, incomplete needs of customers, and so on for software engineers.

The aim of the Software Development Life Cycle (SDLC) is to produce an efficient and peculiar software product, in given timeline, within the budget and the most important to fulfil the client requirement to achieve customer satisfaction (Jalote). SE suggests few fundamental process models for developing software, which ensures the quality of the software. The objectives of the industry could be smoothly established by analysing and resolving the actual problems. To fulfil the objectives the software engineer or the entire team of engineers should embrace diverse strategies that circumscribes the tool layers, process and methods. Relying upon the nature of the project and application the model for engineering software should be processed

All software process models are based on the common approach of SDLC with a slight difference in their execution process. Basic software process models are Linear Sequential Model (LSM)/Waterfall Model, Rapid Application Development Model (RAD), Prototyping Model, Evolutionary/Incremental Process Models. Each process model has its own specialty (Shylesh, 2017). Including usability task in to basic SDLC model is capable of building usable applications (Velmourougan, et al., 2014). Study on few fundamental process models in detail with SDLC (Navita, 2017) is summarized as, LSM/Waterfall life cycle model is easy to understand and implement, it is ideal for small projects and the projects whose duration, requirements and budget are fixed, while Prototyping model is used in situations where requirements are not complete and fixed, developers may not sure about technical aspects of the application to be built, and client can provide its input during development. In the waterfall model, process development cannot proceed to the next phase unless and until the previous phase is fully completed. It executes all the phases in sequential manner from beginning to end (Barnett &Raja, 1995). RAD/Incremental model is an incremental software development model that focuses on a short development cycle e.g. 90-60 days and reusability of components [9]. The evolutionary software development approach is suitable for large problems to develop software in versions, they are iterative. E.g. is Spiral model. It is used when experimenting on technology, new skills and requirements are incomplete (Boehm, 1988). Iterative and incremental development improves the features and functionalities of the software (Larman, & Basili, 2003). Software is designed by inputting requirement analysis results and constructed by the component-based method (Yu, 2018). The gaining of knowledge from the practical campaign, benefit the evolvement of user-centred applications with preferable communication between team, resulting into focusing on the software quality in users satisfaction (Lopes, et al., 2018). The comparative analysis based on the software development methodologies shows the use of two methods: heavyweight as well as lightweight. Software development methodology should be chosen based on project owner profile, project details, complexity of project, cost, development time, developer's technical skill etc. In some cases, the experienced team and project, manager together give a best methodology (Saranya, et al., 2017).

The primary intention of this case study is to showcase, how the entire SDLC is applied to develop a Vaccine Management System application. In this case study, the application described is developed using the approach of LSM, as the requirements and time duration are fixed. Project scope stays static, full design documentation minimizes the changes. It is a structured way of developing of project. Detailed documentation helps for completing the work when any one of the key member loses a project

https://developer.ibm.com/technologies/devops/articles/waterfall-model-advantages-disadvantages/ accessed on 25.05.2021. Study says that, successfully fulfilling the requirements and avoiding overflow of budget or time produce quality software products (Paulson, 2001). The way used for the management of development of a project is a software development methodology, which faces the problem at the time of development. It is important to note that project development process may vary depending on the situation and the organization. The combination of the different methods enhances the quality of the software (Young, 2013). Requirement engineering is the first step of software project development. It is one of the most significant parameters to assess the standardization of the software (Mushtaq, 2016). Requirements for the project case described in this paper are collected through a Google survey form, to identify the functional and non-functional requirements of the developed project.

Significance of case study: Case study is one of the assessment tools in the teaching and learning process for helping readers to make understand complex things/issues or objects. Case study-based approach can be used as a part of problem-based learning in the development of student (Honest, 2017), (Bonney, 2015). In academics as well as in industry, consequence of the case study approach is to effectively learn and train the software designers and software engineers https://essaymin.com/blog/ importance-of-a-case-study/ accessed on 25.05.2021. The case study can be used to educate diverse courses, topics and modules in academic as well as in any profession (Hilburn, et al., 2006). Complex cases are realistic and congenital; replicating formats through cases strengthens the understanding of the topic in an easy way in line with the teaching and learning objective (Bolinger, et al., 2011). Theoretical aspects of software engineering can be effectively delivered by discussing cases to provide end to end perspective of the curriculum (Herold, et al., 2011). Teaching students through case studies make them understand and master the theories better by enhancing practical ability (Zhang & Li, 2010).

Application of case study approach always helps in answering questions that begin with "why" and "how". The case study described in this manuscript gives you an in-depth understanding of the topic. It serves you with detailed investigation of a subject of the topic as well as can help you to enhance experience or affix strength to the existing knowledge. Case study is one of the qualitative approaches of performing the analysis of real –life scenarios and confers a basis of putting ideas and development of methods.

BACKGROUND

The SDLC is simply not a methodology, but rather the SDLC provides an enlarged information about the various phases in the lifecycle of a software application. SDLC is a process of generating software with the lowest cost and highest quality in the shortest time as much as possible. It offers a clear flow of phases, which assist an organization to hurriedly generating high-quality software that is well-tested and ready for production utilization. The SDLC framework consists of the set of instruction to be followed by the system designers and developers. It consists of the steps involved in each phase in which each phase users the results of the previous phase. These phases are planning, Requirement Analysis (RA), design, coding, testing, deployment, and maintenance. Figure 1 illustrates SDLC phases, where each phase has its own deliverables.

Figure 1. SDLC Phases and deliverables at each stage

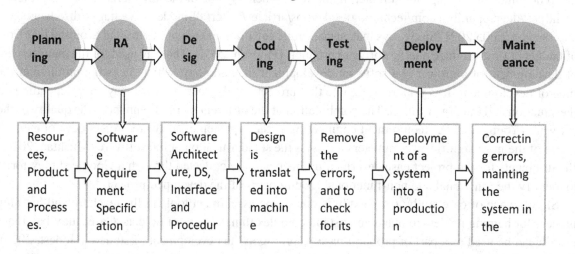

Planning: In this stage, requirements like the resource and cost are analyzed for implementing the SDLC. This helps to identify the risks involved, and it can be further analyzed to soften the risks by sub-planning. Besides, the implementation of the project with the lowest risk and feasibility is obtained using the planning process.

RA: This stage tries to fix the system by identifying the problem as the analysis's aim. Here, the system is broken down into several pieces, and then the situation is analyzed to obtain the goal of the project. Hence, the definite requirement is obtained in this stage by breaking down the system.

Design: The detailed design of the system is described in this stage. The details, like the process diagrams, business rules, screen layouts, design functions, and operations are provided. However, the collection of the modules or collection of the new system is the output of this stage. The approved requirement document gets its initial requirement by this design stage. By considering the workshops, prototype efforts, and interviews, the design elements for each requirement are identified. The entity-relationship diagram with the full data dictionary, pseudo-code, business rule tables, screen layout diagrams, and functional hierarchy diagrams are the elements of the design elements. Based on the design elements, the engineers and the developers develop the system with minimal additional inputs.

Coding: The programming language is chosen, and then the developer builds the system based on the design. The task is subdivided into several modules or units, and the subdivided task is assigned to various programmers. The coding stage is the longest process in the SDLC process.

Testing: The developed code is tested in various stages and is termed the software testing stage. Here, the testing stages, the number of iterations are analyzed, and the different opinions exist in this grey area. The defect rectification and the validations are deployed in this phase.

Deployment: The goal of the production stage is to use the product by the user. The product is moved to production through various deployment stages like the staging or testing environments, which helps the stakeholders to use the product safely before releasing the product in the market.

Maintenance: The essential aspect of the SDLC is the maintenance stage. Here, the new changes will be implemented as key position changes. The object-oriented and the traditional approaches are the two different approaches in the development of the system. The design technique and the structured analysis are called the traditional method. The information system is called as the object-oriented approach, in which the object collection are combined together to form the entire system of information.

This case study project represents few specific goals as follows: The purpose of the case scenario explored in the chapter concentrate on different modules designed as a part of a case for which software product is developed. A case module could be considered a mini case study. Design and development of each component of the case is described under product development by using scenario including actors, appearance and occurrence of it which is related to the processes such as forming project development team, problem identification, management of scope, time, cost and quality in the software process model. The Case Study Project is intended to cover the complete SDLC project management, RA and specification, design, implementation, testing, and maintenance.

Case Study Elements: Project Charter, Scope Statement, Software Requirement Specification, Data Flow Diagram, UML Diagrams, Project Schedule Management, Cost Management, Quality Policy, Quality Management Plan, Quality Review, Test Plan, Test Case, Test Result, Data Dictionary.

COMPREHENSIVE CASE STUDY FOR THE DEVELOPED PROJECT

Every year lot of children in India risks their lives due to lack of timely vaccinations. These vaccinations are free for all children under the age of 5 in India (In government hospitals). Large numbers of kids miss their vaccinations because of parents forgetting the vaccination scheduled dates or from lack of awareness on immunization and required vaccinations. Thus, we provide a solution for children by giving timely immunization reminders to parents and increasing immunization awareness, also bridging up the gap between patient and doctor by providing an Android App. Vaccination is the administration of a vaccine to help the immune system develop protection from disease. Vaccinations are generally given at particular intervals considering the age of a patient. It is difficult to remember a particular date on which the patient should be vaccinated. To address this issue the "VACCINATION MANAGEMENT SYSTEM (VMS)" is developed.

This project is an android based application, where the Patients can be notified via doctor using SMS, E-mail regarding their Vaccination. The patient can also book an appointment if required for their vaccination. This is useful for Doctors, parents, or patients. The facility to view the national vaccination schedule is availed in the application.

Several benefits of the developed systems include a notification that helps in avoiding any missed vaccination, which might result in various dysfunctions in Babies; Doctor will view the appointment request for the patient, to turn down the usage of paper and help digitize the process, to remind patients with upcoming vaccinations. To create awareness about the importance of vaccination to sustain a healthy life, to provide a medium/portal of communication between the patients and the doctors, patients will receive SMS, emails, and in-app notifications with upcoming vaccinations. The present application is developed strictly adhering to the SDLC phases by using LSM to enhance the quality of the application.

PROJECT CHARTER/PROJECT BRIEF (GOALS, ROLES AND RESPONSIBILITIES)

Project Charter Attributes

- Project Title: "Vacc-IT"
- Project Start Date: 1 July, 2019
- Project Finish Date: 25 November, 2019
- Budget Information: An initial estimate provides a total 16 hours per week including lab work.

Software Development using LSM Approach

- Develop a survey about various existing System Websites/Software/Applications to determine the important features of Vacc-IT.
- Review the documents of other similar systems relating to the Vacc-IT.

SCOPE STATEMENT

This project was aimed to develop an application. Patients can be notified via doctor using SMS, E-mail regarding their Vaccination. The patient can also book an appointment if required for their vaccination. This is useful for Doctors, parents and patients. Facility to view the national vaccination schedule is availed in the application. Vaccination is the administration of a vaccine to help the immune system develop protection from a disease. Being such an important factor of our life, it's hard for the parents to keep track of vaccination according to its schedule. As we know giving vaccination to infants cannot be missed under any circumstances. To give solution to this problem, we provide with a solution of VMS, which help to maintain a record of everyone with every minute detail of When, Where, Which vaccination are given to the individual. Also, user will be timely notified about their next dose of vaccination via email/SMS/in app notification.

DEVELOPMENT TEAM

Table 1 shows the roles and responsibilities of the software development team members.

Table 1. Roles and responsibilities

Name	Role	Position
Dr. Smita L. Kasar Ms. Sushama A. Deshmukh	Instructor Instructor and Supervisor	Project Manager
Tejas Devda	Team Leader	Developer
Ninad Dere	Team member	Developer

SCOPE MANAGEMENT SOFTWARE REQUIREMENT SPECIFICATION

Software Requirement Specification (SRS) is the foundation for developing a software application. A good SRS should be Correct, Complete, Consistent, Unambiguous, Verifiable, Modifiable, Traceable, design independent, Testable, Understandable by the customer.

RA is the process of gathering and interpreting facts, diagnosing problems, and using the information to recommend improvements on the system. System analysis is the problem-solving activity that requires intensive communication between the system users and system developers.

For the Requirement gathering, we have taken a survey from various people including Doctors. The survey included the entire requirement for this application and gave us some information about on which platform the application should be developed. Also, the facilities which users need in order to have a user-friendly environment was a part of the survey. Table 2 gives details about survey analysis.

Users' cognition analysis regarding importance of vaccine scheduler and management system application. We conducted a survey that brought in the following facts. The survey has been filled by 200 participants. They gave their opinion in the form of selecting yes/no and selecting an option from the list of options for a few questions that have multiple options. Then requirements were classified into functional and non-functional requirements.

Table 2. Survey analysis

	Have you ever missed a Vaccination or someone you know missed their vaccination?	Are you aware of the National Vaccination Schedule?	Do you have the medical history of your Vaccination record?	Do you think digitalized way of maintaining a Vaccination record is preferable?	Do you think Vaccination scheduling notifications are important?
Yes	60	60	36.5	95.9	97.3
No	40	40	63.5	34.1	23.7
Parameters	Which platform do you think will be user friendly? (%)	Parameters	Which medium you prefer for vaccinations reminders? (%)		
Android Application	71.6	Email	3.6		
Desktop Application	3	Notification	6.4		
Website	21.6	SMS	40.5		
SMS	3.8	All of the above	40.5		

As can be seen, based on the responses received from each participant, it was indeed necessary to develop a system that could remind the users about their vaccine schedule.

PROJECT PLANNING

Gantt Chart

A Gantt chart is a horizontal bar chart showing the start and end dates of each task within a project. It shows the tasks on the vertical axis and time on the horizontal axis. The tasks are shown sequentially. The figure below represents the order in which "Vacc-IT" was made into reality.

The time periods in which various tasks like literature survey, requirement collection, analysis, design and implementation, etc. were brought into action. Planned vs. Actual executed timeline for the development of the project is shown in Table 3 and Table 4.

Planned Time Line:

Table 3. Task organization and project planning

Task #	Task	Start date	# Working days	End date
1	Literature Survey	7/15/2019	44	8/24/2019
2	Requirement Collection	8/13/2019	11	8/24/2019
3	Requirement Analysis	8/26/2019	6	8/31/2019
4	Requirement Validation	9/2/2019	6	9/7/2019
5	Planning	9/9/2019	6	9/14/2019
6	Design	9/16/2019	6	9/21/2019
7	Implementation	9/23/2019	34	10/31/2019
8	Testing	10/4/2019	5	10/8/2019

Actual Time Line Executed:

Table 4. Task organization and actual software development time line

Task #	Task	Start date	# Working days	End date
1	Literature Survey	7/15/2019	40	8/24/2019
2	Requirement Collection	8/13/2019	13	8/27/2019
3	Requirement Analysis	8/28/2019	10	9/7/2019
4	Requirement Validation	9/9/2019	6	9/14/2019
5	Planning	9/16/2019	6	9/21/2019
6	Design	9/23/2019	6	9/28/2019
7	Implementation	9/30/2019	40	11/9/2019
8	Testing	11/11/2019	6	11/16/2019

Gantt chart for planned Schedule of VMS shown in figure 2.

Figure 2. Gantt chart for planned schedule of VMS

	# Working days	6/24	7/14	8/3	8/23	9/12	10/2	10/22	11/11
Literature Survey	44								
Requirement Collection	11								
Requirement Analysis	6								
Requirement Validation	6								
Planning	6								
Design	6								
Implementation	34								
Testing	5								

Figure 3 illustrates the Gantt chart for the actual schedule required for the development of the application.

Figure 3. Gantt chart for Actual Schedule of VMS

Task List	# Working days	6/24	7/14	8/3	8/23	9/12	10/2	10/22	11/11	12/1
Literature Survey	40									
Requirement Collection	13									
Requirement Analysis	10									
Requirement Validation	6									
Planning	6									
Design	6									
Implementation	40									
Testing	6									

In reference with codementor blog (https://www.codementor.io/blog/app-development-costs-6gd-nah10b7), to know/understand how much an app might cost, the most popular mobile apps were referred for studying the cost. Blogging says that even though there isn't a Kelley's Blue Book for the costs of developing apps, estimating the costs of developing an app similar to the app that you want to build can help you. The following simple formula is used to estimate VMS app cost:

(Features * Time) * Hourly_Rate = Approximate Cost   (1)
288Hrs *100$ = 28800$.

21,142 INR by considering 1\$ = 73.3 INR as on date 30th December 2020. Considered 100\$ hourly rate, considering weekly 14 hrs on an average and 2 developers.

As an hourly rate is needed to calculate the total app development cost, it's important to know the variations in hourly rates for app developers. For calculating project cost, we have divided each feature implementation process into tasks and subtasks, time required for designing UI and functions part of these tasks. Each screen has API integrations and validations. Generally, a development charge varies from \$50 to \$250 per hour depending on many factors. Here we have roughly calculated the cost by assuming rate 100\$ per hour. Total days required for development are 127 and considering per day 1.5-2 hrs, total 288 hrs utilized to develop VMS application, including 100 hrs needed for literature analysis and requirement collections. The table shows VMS software application feature list with the required development time. Table 5 illustrates the feature development task list and actual development time required.

Table 5. Feature development with task list and actual software development time required in hours

Sr. No.	Sections	Feature/Functionalities List	Required Time (Hrs)
1	Patient Dashboard	• Registration	6
		• Login	4
		• Adding Child,	6
		• My Child-Check child progress	10
		• Date Picker	2
		• Appointment Booking	10
		• Appointment Canceling	6
		• Warning/confirmation of canceling	8
		• Appointment History/Verification	10
2	Doctor Dashboard	• Registration,	6
		• Login	4
		• Check Patients	5
		• See the booked/scheduled appointment	10
		• Notify patients for appointments	5
		• NVS	2
		• Setting (password change, account delete)	6
		• Calendar	4
		• Appointment Reminder Notification	6
		• SMS	5
		• Email	5
		• Appointment Booking	8
		• Appointment Rescheduling	84
		• Confirmation	3
		• Account delete	2
		• Password Reset	
3	Firebase Firestore Database	• Firebase user authentication	5
		• User Collection	6
		• User Profile collection	6
		• Patient Collection	5
		• Patient Profile collection	5
		• Doctor Profile collection	5
		• Doctor Patient collection	5
		• Doctor Appointment Collection	6
Total Development Time Required in Hrs			**188**
(Features * Time) * Hourly_Rate = 288Hrs *100\$			**= Approximate Cost 28800\$**

Average Hourly Rate: $61-80 and Median Hourly Rate: $61-80. These values are referred from https://www.codementor.io/freelance-rates/mobile-app-developers. Rates are also varies depending on the experience of the developer and his working geographical locations (country wise different hourly rates).

LITERATURE SURVEY

Negandhi, et al., (2016) developed a mobile-based Effective Vaccine Management (EVM) appliaction for effectively managing the vaccination system. Here, the data collected using dashboards and factsheets for representing the vaccine supply. It offered the guidance to the human resource for the effective vaccination. This method offered enhanced cold chain space with 87%. Akshita, et al., (2021) implemented a VMS using the block chain, which effectively managing the logistics, distribution, and vaccine stocks. This method improved the transparency and integrity of the overall process and ensured the equitable and fair distribution. This method diagnosed the User's Health conditions and offered the vaccine appointment. HAN Zongmei, et al., (2020) modelled SWOT analysis, which was used to enhance the standardization and normalization for vaccine management. This method mainly overcomes the problem in the insufficient human resource allocation and the latest issues in the cold chain management. This method offered efficient and better information system for vaccine management. Keraj, (2020) developed a web application, named e-Vacc for enhancing the organization and management of vaccination process data. This method was used to identify each person, who received the vaccination. Also, it minimized the workload of the vaccination providers and overcome the issues like, data efficiency, labor force, and flexibility. Anyhow, this method had the drawback of poor data operation. Nie, et al., (2021) developed a blockchain technology to a vaccination management system. It provided the historical injection information about the vaccination and traceability information. Also, digital signature mechanism enhanced the data confidentiality. It offered true vaccines traceability information. Table 6 portrays the review on existing methods in the VMS.

Table 6. Review on existing methods

Author	Method	Application
Negandhi, et al., (2016)	mobile-based EVM	• It offered the guidance to the human resource for the effective vaccination • This method offered enhanced cold chain space with 87%.
Akshita, et al., (2021)	block chain-based VMS	• This method improved the transparency and integrity of the overall process and ensured the equitable and fair distribution. • This method diagnosed the User's Health conditions and offered the vaccine appointment.
Zongmei, et al., (2020)	SWOT analysis	• This method mainly overcomes the problem in the insufficient human resource allocation and the latest issues in the cold chain management. • This method offered efficient and better information system for vaccine management.
Keraj, (2020)	e-Vacc	• It minimzed the workload of the vaccination providers. • It overcomes the issues like, data efficiency, labor force, and flexibility.
Nie, et al., (2021)	blockchain technology	• It provided the historical injection information about the vaccination and traceability information. Also, digital signature mechanism enahanced the data confidentiality. • It offered true vaccines traceability information.
Proposed method	Vacc-IT	• It allows patients to book appointments and requests e-consults. This software sends SMSs and e-mails to patients on a time-to-time basis based on the vaccination profile so that they don't miss a date. • Effective vaccination scheduling is allotted to the patients.

PROJECT DESIGN PHASE

Design Phase: The software requirement specification document is the foundation of the design and implementation phase. Once the requirements has analyzed and classified into its functional and non-functional requirement, now the turn is to translate them into different design diagrams. These diagrams are used to describe internal as well as external behaviour of the system, data flow from beginning up to the end, communication of each module with internal and external entities. The design phase gives details about 4 aspects of the software those are, software architecture, data structure, interface and process or algorithmic details. These visual representations give blueprint of the application which is to be developed and helps to better understand the working of the software and its components. The requirement model is expressed by scenario-based elements, class-based elements, flow-oriented and behavioural elements. Figure 4 shows the block diagram of the VMS. The VMS for mobile application has been implemented to safeguard vaccine potency, increase the vaccine availability, and to improve the supply chain. Both doctors and patients login to the system through the mobile application. The VMS allows patients to book appointments and requests e-consults. Doctors can remind patients about vaccination updates with the VMS. This software sends SMSs and e-mails to patients on a time-to-time basis based on the vaccination profile so that they don't miss a date. Also, the system maintains the previous health records and vaccination details of patients. Based on these details, the vaccination scheduling is allotted to the patients.

Figure 4. Block diagram of the VMS

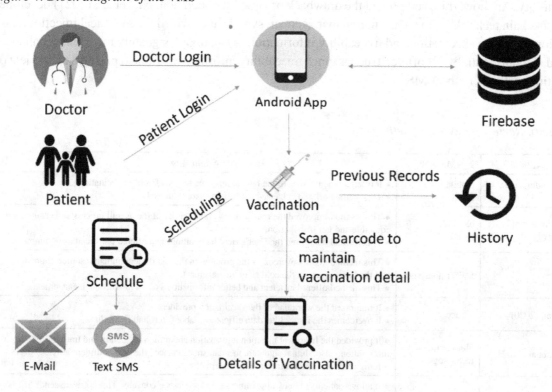

USE CASE

Figure 5 shows use case diagram of VMS that captures the system's functionality and requirements. A Use Case consists of actions and actors. Actors perform action in order to achieve a task. In the below use case diagram, there are three actors named Doctor, Patient and Firebase. Doctor and Patient inherits Vacc-IT user, which has common functionality in between them. There is a total of sixteen actions that represent the specific functionality of the vaccination system. Each actor interacts with a particular action.

Figure 5. Use case diagram of VMS

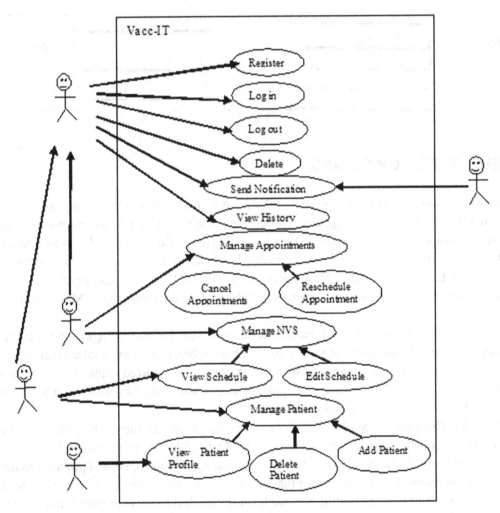

DATA FLOW DIAGRAM

A context diagram (figure 6) is a data flow diagram that only shows the top level, otherwise known as Level 0. At this level, there is only one visible process node that represents the functions of a complete system regarding how it interacts with external entities. The figure below shows a context Data Flow

123

Diagram that is drawn for a Vaccination system "Vacc-IT". It contains a process (shape) that represents the system to model, in this case, the "Vacc-IT". It also shows the participants who will interact with the system, called the external entities. In this example, the Doctor and patient are the entities who will interact with the system. In between the process and the external entities, there is data flow (connectors) that indicate the existence of information exchange between the entities and the system. Figure 6 shows the context level DFD for VMS.

Figure 6. Context level data flow diagram of VMS

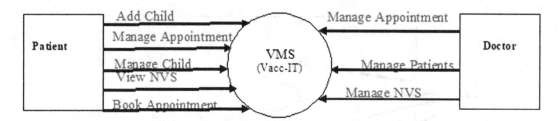

IMPLEMENTATION OR CODING

Documentation about structural and behavioural aspects of the software designs are transferred into a machine-readable form that is coding. Here, the actual software building process begins. Software is the collection of modules, and each module is developed by group of developers. Tasks and functions are divided into units or module and are assigned to the developers to start development of the application by using coding standards/guidelines. Developers use suitable tools for writing compiling and debugging the code. This is the longest phase of software development. For developing VMS system following technology stack is used.

Firebase*:* Firebase gives you functionality like analytics, databases, messaging and crash reporting so you can move quickly and focus on your users. Firebase is based on Google infrastructure and scales automatically, for even the largest apps hence make it easy for an android application to be dependent on firebase. Since "Vacc-IT" is an android application, firebase came to a good help for maintaining records and the database for the doctors and the users.

Android Studio: Android Studio is the official integrated development environment for Google's android operating system and is designed specifically for Android development. Android studio consists of various tools which could be found by the developers in making the application. It provides an integrated development environment for the developer that makes the creation of the application a less hectic task.

GIT: *GitHub* is a web-based hosting Service for software development project that use the Git revision control system. GIT comes into handy when there is a problem in combining the work of a team working on the same subject but are individually working on different topics. GIT played a major role in helping the developers of VMS, "Vacc-IT".

Adobe XD: Adobe XD is a vector-based user experience design tool for mobile applications and web pages. It is used for the interface design so that the application can provide the user with a great experience and it comes in handy when there is a need of vector art in the application. Adobe XD was used in designing various aspects of "Vacc-IT" such as the logo and some internal vectors for the application.

TESTING AND QUALITY MANAGEMENT

Quality is a feature that cannot be incorporated once the software is developed; it is essential to take care of quality from very first stage of the development life cycle of software. The goal of Quality Management (QM) is to manage the quality of software and of its development process. Quality attributes are understandability, portability, testability, usability, reliability, adaptability, efficiency, modularity, robustness, etc. A SQA plan is created to define SQA strategy for a development team. It may include an inspection process, which has stages as, planning, overview meeting, preparation, meeting, rework and follow-up. The process of quality management is presented in figure 7.

QUALITY PROCESS

Linear Sequential Model (LMS) or Waterfall Life Cycle software process model is used for software development because of fixed time duration and requirements. This method is very simple and easy to use. In this method, every phase is completed before starting the next phase, which avoids the overlapping of various phases. The project scope was fixed early before the start of the project.

QUALITY REVIEW

QR is a process of examining the software by conducting review meetings. During the review process software is examined by project workforces, administrators, consumers, customers, user senates, or other interested parties for comment or approval. As this is the academic project quality review taken by the panel of four members which includes technical domain expert as well as the associate professors who have experience of working on this type of projects. Following Table 7 describes quality reviews conducted by the team.

Figure 7. Quality management process

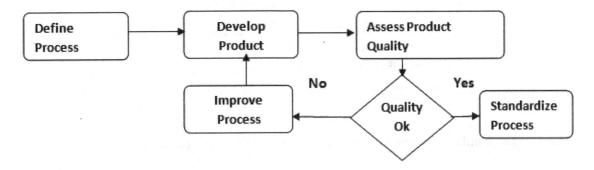

Reports of reviews have been made by one of the reviewers, he also recorded all the issues that have been raised by the members, documented, and conveyed to the developers to serve as an action item checklist to do the necessary corrections and updates.

Table 7. Quality review

Name	Purpose
SRS Review	SRS is the foundation of any application development. A good SRS has characteristics such as concise, unambiguous, consistent, complete, implementable, testable and traceable. A review of the Software Requirements Specification of VMS is conducted by both the software developer and the review panel which has 4 members.
Peer Review	Peer review is performed for all the documents and code of all the modules or functionalities of VMS by the respective authors and developers respectively during different software development activities. It helped in performing disciplined engineering practice for detecting and correcting the defects in software artifacts. Developers worked on the suggestions given by the members about adding more functionalities and incorporated those in the development of the application.
Formal Technical Review (FTR)	FTR is a software quality assurance activity performed by software engineers. The objectives of the formal technical review are to find out errors in function, logic, or execution for any demonstration of the software, to authenticate that the software under analysis meets its requirements, to ensure that the VMS has been represented according to predefined standards, to achieve that is developed in an identical fashion, to make projects more controllable. Each FTR will be successful only if it is properly planned, controlled, and attended.

USER INTERFACE DESIGN STEPS

Figure 8 depicts the steps involved in GUI interface design

Figure 8. Steps involved in user interface design

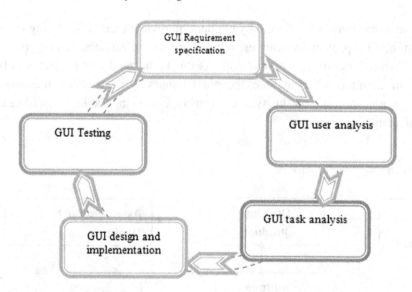

The framework utilized for designing the GUI needs to follow the specific steps of GUI

- GUI Requirement specification: The GUI designers have to create the list of all the functional and the non-functional GUI requirement for developing the VMS android application.
- User analysis: The designer has to analyze the requirements of the patient and doctors for VMS application according to the preference and knowledge of the user.

- Task analysis: The designer need to evaluate the task to be performed by the developed VMS software, which is listed in the hierarchical form.
- Design and Implementation: The VMS application software should be designed according to the requirements, user preference and the task and it should be implemented into the codes.
- Testing: The VMS software is now tested by evaluating the user acceptance, compatibility and usability.

SOFTWARE METRICS

Software metrics assist in planning, tracking, monitoring, and controlling the software project indirectly assessing the quality of the software. Generally most of the software quality assurance systems use the common metrics those are Lines of Code (LOC) in a program, Function Point Analysis, Cyclical Complexity of the code, no. of classes and interfaces, cohesion and coupling between modules, etc.

TEST PLAN AND TEST CASE

Here three types of testing are used, Unit testing, Black Box Testing and White Box Testing. Testing is the process of thorough study of a program with the intention of finding bugs and errors before the product is delivered to the client.

Unit testing is performed by module developer individually to uncover errors, by testing the graphical user interface, local data structures, boundary value analysis, independent and error handling paths by designing test cases. Each functional component is unit tested.

Emphasis of Black Box Testing (BBT) is on the functional requirements and the information domain of the software. BBT is used after White Box Testing (WBT) is performed. BBT discovers incorrect or missing functions, interface errors, errors in data structures, behaviour or performance errors, initialization, and termination errors.BBT uses the SRS as basis for building tests. The objective of WBT is to provide execution assurance of control and looping structures, about all statements and conditions executed at least once. Internal working of the software is verified; also logical paths are tested by creating test cases for checking specific sets of condition and /or loops.

TEST CASE AND TEST RESULTS

Test case designs uncover errors in a complete manner with a minimum effort and time. The test case is one of the quality assessment tools to investigate working functionality of the software. We have created a test case document maintained with the remark of the pass or fail as a test result using manual testing which is referred to as the test log. Table 8 shows one of the sample test cases for the scenario of rescheduling appointments with different test case parameters. Test case helped us in improving the quality of VMS.

Table 8. Test case for rescheduling appointment

TC ID	Test case Title / Test Objective	Test Priority	Feature/ Module	Test Steps	Expected Result	Test Result
TC001	To verify authorization for my appointment	M	Reschedule Appointment	Open My Appointments & check appointments displayed	My appointments should show only appointments scheduled by logged in user	Pass
TC002	To verify appointment reschedule when valid date value is provided & user confirms reschedule	H	Reschedule Appointment	1. Open a valid appointment. 2. Provide valid date value & click Reschedule button. 3. Select Ok button on confirmation message popup.	Confirmation message indicating appointment reschedule should be displayed to the user. If user confirms reschedule then appointment should get rescheduled.	Pass
TC003	To verify appointment reschedule when valid date value is provided & user cancels reschedule	H	Reschedule Appointment	1. Open a valid appointment. 2. Provide valid date value & click Reschedule button. 3. Select Cancel button on confirmation message popup.	Confirmation message indicating appointment reschedule should be displayed to the user. If user confirms reschedule then appointment should get rescheduled.	Pass
TC004	To verify appointment reschedule when invalid values are provided	H	Reschedule Appointment	1. Open a valid appointment. 2. Provide invalid date value (past date) & click Reschedule button.	Appointment should not get rescheduled. User should be shown appropriate error message.	Pass
TC005	To verify if Reschedule option is available only for valid appointments	H	Reschedule Appointment	1. Open My Appointments & check appointments displayed 2. Select any past appointment & check Reschedule button. 3. Reflect any future appointment & check Reschedule button	Reschedule button should be enabled only if a future appointment is selected.	Pass

SCREENSHOTS FOR REFERENCE

Figure 9 shows the screenshots of different activities performed for rescheduling an appointment, such as Rescheduling appointment, confirmation for rescheduling, Rescheduling SMS send, Rescheduling mail send, Notification sent, Appointment booked notification, Appointment reminder notification.

Figure 9. Screenshots of app

DATA DICTIONARY

A data dictionary, or metadata warehouse, is a compacted depository of information about data such as denotation, relationships to other data, origin, usage, and format. The data dictionary (Databases) of VMS is described in table 9.

Table 9. Data dictionary table

Data store name	Description	Inbound data flow	Outbound data flow
FireStore Database	All the information related to doctors and patients profiles are stored in the fire database also appointments related data. Patients' history. When the doctor/patient login then in compare the user detail with data store in user database.	Login/ Signup	Login/logout/signup
Fire database	All the information of doctors, patients, appointment, and history of records is stored in the fire database in an appropriate form.	Send notifications, Scheduling and reschedule Appointments Search, Alter/view site info, Upload file and Reminders.	Send notifications, Scheduling Appointments Search, Alter/view site info, Upload file and Reminders

CONCLUSION

Software engineering life cycle is used successfully to develop complete VMS (Vacc-IT) software application approximately near to the planned schedule. Effective planning enabled the utilization of the resources effectively. Application of engineering principles, SE methods or processes emphatically to develop software maintains the quality of the application. This complete example will help readers, especially students, to understand how to apply SDLC and LSM processes in the development of and management of software products. In addition, the project enumerates the case modules (mini case studies), that will be helpful to understand and apply various software engineering phases, methods to design and develop a quality software application during the project development. The reader will also get basic knowledge of designing test case with results and role of it in persuading the quality of the software.

Future Directions: In the future, we will further extend the study by analyzing various complexities faced during the software development process. Importantly, we will facilitate an effective testing standard that renders maximal coverage during the software testing phase in the software development process. Furthermore, the deep evaluation of software development risks, such as Scheduling and timing risk, functionality risk, subcontracting risk, requirement management risk, resource usage risks, performance risk and the personal management risk will be done. Furthermore, we have to evaluate the factors associated with the risks management and how the factors influence the successful management. The future research further concentrates on the components involved in the software management risk, and what are the practices involved in the risk management tasks. Due to the lack of well-established research framework this study concentrates on the generation rather than testing hypothesis. Hence, in future more consideration will be given to the testing of hypothesis. Further, the relation between the environmental contingencies and the software risk management will be evaluated in the future research.

REFERENCES

Akshita, V., Dhanush, J. S., Varman, A. D., & Kumar, V. K. (2021). Blockchain Based Covid Vaccine Booking and Vaccine Management System. In *Proceeding of 2nd International Conference on Smart Electronics and Communication (ICOSEC)*. IEEE.

Barnett, W. D., & Raja, M. K. (1995). Application of QFD to the Software development process. *International Journal of Quality & Reliability Management*, *12*(6), 24–42. doi:10.1108/02656719510089902

Boehm, B. W. (1988). A spiral model of software development and enhancement. *Computer*, *21*(5), 61–72. doi:10.1109/2.59

Bolinger, J., Herold, M., Ramnath, R., & Ramanathan, J. (2011). Connecting reality with theory — An approach for creating integrative industry case studies in the software engineering curriculum. *Frontiers in Education Conference (FIE)*, T4G-1-T4G-6.

Bonney, K.M. (2015). Case Study Teaching Method Improves Student Performance and Perceptions of Learning Gains. *Journal of Microbiology and Biology Education*. doi:10.1128/jmbe.v16i1.846

Herold, M., Bolinger, J., Ramnath, R., Bihari, T., & Ramanathan, J. (2011). Providing end-to-end perspectives in software engineering. *Frontiers in Education Conference (FIE)*, S4B-1-S4B-7.

Hilburn, T. B., Towhidnejad, M., Nangia, S., & Shen, L. (2006). A Case Study Project for Software Engineering Education, *Proceedings, Frontiers in Education. 36th Annual Conference*, 1-5. 10.1109/FIE.2006.322302

Honest, N. (2017). Applying case study based approach as part of problem based learning student development. *International Journal of Advanced Research in Computer Science*, *8*(9). doi:10.26483/ijarcs.v8i9.4962

Jalote, P. (n.d.). *Software Engineering: A Precise Approach*. Wiley India.

Keraj, B. (2020). *Analysis, design and implementation of the Albanian Vaccination Managemnet Syatem*. Epoka University.

Larman, C., & Basili, V. R. (2003). Iterative and Incremental Development: A Brief History. *Computer*, *36*(6), 47–56. doi:10.1109/MC.2003.1204375

Lopes, A., Valentim, N., & Moraes, B. (2018). Applying user-centered techniques to analyze and design a mobile application. *J Softw Eng Res Dev*, 6. doi:10.1186/s40411-018-0049-1

Martin, J. (1991). Rapid application development. Macmillan Publishing.

Mushtaq, J. (2016). Different Requirements Gathering Techniques and Issues. *International Journal of Scientific & Engineering Research*, *7*(9).

Navita. (2017). A Study on Software Development Life Cycle & its Model. *IJERCSE*, *4*(9).

Negandhi, P., Chauhan, M., Das, A. M., Neogi, S. B., Sharma, J., & Sethy, G. (2016). Mobile based Effective Vaccine Management Tool: An m health Initiative Implemented by UNICEF in Bihar. *Indian Journal of Public Health*, *60*(4), 334–340.

Nie, P., Zhou, X., Wang, C., Zheng, H., & Zeng, Y. (2021). Design and Implementation of Coronavirus Vaccines Information Traceability System based on Blockchain. *Proceeding of International Symposium on Artificial Intelligence and its Application on Media (ISAIAM)*.

Paulson, L. D. (2001). Adapting methodologies for doing software right. *IT Professional, 3*(4), 13–15.

Pressman, R. S. (n.d.a). *Software Engineering: A practitioners approach* (5th ed.). Mc-Graw Hill Publication.

Pressman, R. S. (n.d.b). *Software Engineering: A Practitioner's Approach* (7th ed.). Mc-Graw-Hill.

Saranya, P., Monica, V., & Priyadarshini, J. (2017). Comparative Study of Software Development Methodologies. *International Research Journal of Engineering and Technology*.

Shylesh, S. (2017). *A Study of Software Development Life Cycle Process Models*. SSRN: https://ssrn.com/abstract=2988291

Velmourougan, S., Dhavachelvan, P., Baskaran, R., & Ravikumar, B. (2014). Software development Life cycle model to build software applications with usability. *International Conference on Advances in Computing, Communications and Informatics (ICACCI)*, 271-276. doi: 10.1109/ICACCI.2014.6968610

Young, D. (2013). *Software Development Methodologies*. https://www.researchgate.net/publication/255710396

Yu, J. (2018). Research Process on Software Development Model. *IOP Conf. Ser.: Mater. Sci. Eng, 394*, 032045. doi:10.1088/1757-899X/394/3/032045

Zhang, J., & Li, J. (2010). Teaching Software Engineering Using Case Study. *International Conference on Biomedical Engineering and Computer Science*, 1-4.

Zongmei, H., Xiaoping, X. U., Lihua, G. U., Aizhen, P., & Minhong, L. (2020). A SWOT analysis of vaccine management in Zhejiang Province. *Journal of Preventive Medicine, 12*, 655–658.

Section 2
Human–Computer Interaction and Data Science

Chapter 7
Disease Prediction System Using Image Processing and Machine Learning in COVID-19

Sonal Raju Shilimkar

MKSSS's Cummins College of Engineering, India

Varsha Pimprale

MKSSS's Cummins College of Engineering, India

Chhaya R. Gosavi

iD https://orcid.org/0000-0002-2348-0698

MKSSS's Cummins College of Engineering, India

ABSTRACT

Diseases such as cancers, pneumonia, and COVID really need to be detected at the right time. If early detection and treatment of such diseases get started as soon as possible, then, probably, patients can be cured completely. Early detection of such diseases is very important, and early-stage imaging can be done based on x-rays, mammography reports, or pathological reports. The purpose of this system is to provide predictions for the different major diseases like cancer and some general occurring diseases. Image processing along with machine learning techniques made it possible to find the chances of occurrence of cancer/tumor/lump in the human body. As per the predicted probability, a patient can make an early decision by discussing it with doctors. The system will predict the most possible disease based on the given symptoms and precautionary measures required to avoid the progression of disease. It will also help doctors analyze the pattern of presence of diseases in the society.

DOI: 10.4018/978-1-7998-9121-5.ch007

INTRODUCTION

Evaluation of technology in the healthcare system makes life more convenient in detecting and treating disease. Nowadays, data or medical records are easier to collect and store. Using this data technology, one can easily detect some critical health issues at an early stage. Machine Learning algorithms and image processing techniques show fundamental potential in detecting multiple major diseases like cancer, pneumonia, diabetes and many others. Image processing plays an important role in visualising disease which makes it convenient to doctors and patients to view internal diseases.

Prediction of major and minor diseases is vital for the early detection of health threats. Such diseases can affect health majorly. Early identification of diseases like cancer, pneumonia is important so that patients and doctors can make early decisions about treatment. Using the latest technology trends including image processing and machine learning makes this task easier. Using this technology one can easily identify disease. Machine learning and Image processing gives more accurate results than naked eye and predicts within fraction of seconds.

This proposed system is web application which will predict disease:

- Based on symptoms.
- Based on image reports (like x-ray, mammography, MRI, etc)
- Based on given diagnosis report parameter values.
- Suggest nearby specialists based on predicted disease.

OBJECTIVE

Human Computer Interaction (HCI) is used to detect multiple diseases with minimal time and with easy steps. The objective of the system is to develop a web application where users can detect disease by selecting symptoms, by uploading image report, by providing extracted parameter values from diagnosis report and by suggesting specialist for specific disease with contact information of doctors. This system also predicts minor diseases from symptoms and major diseases like cancer and pneumonia. In Cancer, very specific to - Brain Tumour, Breast Cancer and Skin cancer. The main objective of the project is to provide a system which will provide a time saving and more safe system to predict diseases in this pandemic situation.

For detecting minor diseases from symptoms, users need to select symptoms from a given list and then after clicking on detect disease the detected disease will be displayed. For detecting cancer and pneumonia user have 2 options:

1] Detect from image reports which is early-stage prediction for this user need to upload a specified image report for ex. MRI image to detect brain tumour, mammography image for detecting breast cancer and so on. Users can upload images using the browse option after clicking on the tumour/disease detected result will be shown. Another option is to view tumour regions for displaying tumour/cancer regions in image reports provided. By clicking on 'View Tumour Region' option users will be able to view the tumour region in highlighted colour.

2] Detecting if cancer/disease is present or not by providing extracted parameter values from the diagnosis report if any value is not available, the user can enter 0 values for that field and then after clicking on detect tumour/disease final prediction will be shown.

BACKGROUND

It is estimated that more than 70% of people are prone to body diseases like cancer, viral infections and many other general/major diseases. Around 30% of the population succumbs to death because of ignoring the early general body symptoms. Hence it is important to identify and predict disease at the earliest stage to avoid any unwanted casualties.

The authors did some literature review about the prediction of disease and observed the pros and cons of these highly correlated systems are discussed below.

- **Detection of Brain Tumour Using Image Classification:** This paper presents a solution for Detecting brain tumour by performing the classification of tumour based on the image features using SVM classification, the 80% of the dataset is trained on the SVM algorithm and the 20% of the data is tested for the kind of tumour (Vaishnavi & Girarddi, 2019). They have used a Support Vector Machine (SVM) technique which has given more clear predictions. Also, Image classification techniques are used to give appropriate results (Smitha, Shaji & Mini.MG, 2011). But in this case, 80% of the dataset was trained and accuracy was only 60-70%. Use of very complex formulas was there (Patel, Gandhi, Shetty & Tekwani, 2017).
- **Leveraging Deep Learning Techniques for Malaria Parasite Detection Using Mobile Application:** In this paper, authors had used Convolution Neural Network (CNN) -based end-to-end deep learning model to improve malaria detection on thin blood smear images (Mehedi, 2020). The advantages of using this system are 97.3% accurate results. They worked on Feature Extraction and then fully connected networks (CNN) to detect Malaria. This system was much more user friendly as mobile based. Also, they have used the National Institute of Health (NIH) dataset which is publicly available malaria dataset. While the limitations are Images may not be cleared from mobile and Mobile Application based not so efficient for detection of cells from images.
- **Melanoma Skin Cancer Detection using Image Processing and Machine Learning:** In this paper, the author analysed the accurate prediction of skin cancer and also to classify the skin cancer as malignant or non-malignant melanoma. Some pre-processing steps were carried out which followed Hair removal, shadow removal, glare removal and also segmentation (Maheshvari & Sankarie, 2020). Pre-processing techniques are used to give more detailed results. Also, the classifiers are used which are trained such that it will learn new features. But in this paper the models work on complete dataset and not for a given report-image. Use of dividing and Processing images from all steps may lead to creating a huge dataset (Ansari & Sarode, 2017).
- **Brain Cancer Detection from MRI: A Machine Learning Approach (Tensorflow):** In this paper, the author has used Machine learning with image classifiers to detect the presence of cancer cells efficiently in the brain using MRI. It results in saving lots of time for radiologists and surgeons. For this TensorFlow is used for the detection of brain cancer using MRI. In Tensor flow they have used a convolutional neural network with 5 layers. Results are good but the system can be used by surgeons and radiologists to detect brain tumours more easily and efficiently. Very basic image classification method of lenet architecture is used but more powerful approaches can be used for more accurate results. The more sophisticated system should be used to take MRI images in dicom format directly and operate on them (Sawant, Bhandari, Yadav, Yele, & Bendale, 2018).

Following are some of the results concluded from research papers for such kind of diseases:

1. **Breast Cancer:**
   a. Deep Neural Network in breast cancer screening: Accuracy- 97%, Year-2019 (Gupta, & Chawla, 2019)
   b. 2. Deep learning to improve breast cancer early: Accuracy- 92% year-2017. (Han, Zhongyi, Wei, Zheng, Yin, Li & S. Li, 2017)
   c. Detecting and classifying lesions in mammography with deep learning technology- CAD, Accuracy-86%, Year-2018 (Giri & Kumar, 2017)
2. **Lung cancer:**
   a. Pathologist-level classification of histologic patterns on resected lung adenocarcinoma slides with deep neural networks, Accuracy-90% Year-2019.
   b. Lung Cancer Detection and Classification Using Deep CNN: Accuracy: 96% year-2018.
   c. Classification and mutation prediction from non-small cell lung cancer histopathology images using deep learning, Accuracy-82% Year-2018.
   d. Knowledge-based analysis for Mortality Prediction from CT Images: Accuracy-95% Year-2018.
3. **Brain Tumour:**
   a. Segmentation and Detection of Tumour in MRI images Using CNN and SVM Classification: Accuracy -91% year-2018.
   b. BRAIN TUMOR DIAGNOSIS USING IMAGE PROCESSING: A SURVEY: Year-2017.
   c. Automatic Tumour Segmentation Using Convolutional Neural Networks: Year-2018 Accuracy-90%.
4. **Skin Cancer:**
   a. An artificial neural network approach for detecting skin cancer: Year-2019 Accuracy-80%.
   b. Deep Learning Can Improve Early Skin Cancer Detection: Year-2019 Accuracy-97.78% (Vijayalakshmi, 2019).

Generative Adversarial Neural Networks for Pigmented and Non-Pigmented Skin Lesions Detection in Clinical Images: Year-2018 Accuracy-92%. (Sagar & Saini, 2016)

5. **COVID:**
   a. Automated deep transfer learning-based approach for detection of COVID-19 infection in chest X-rays: Year-2020.
   b. Review of artificial intelligence techniques in imaging data acquisition, segmentation and diagnosis for covid-19- IEEE: Year-2020.
   c. Finding covid-19 from chest x-rays using deep learning on a dataset: year-2020.
6. **Malaria Detection:**
   a. Image analysis and machine learning for detecting malaria: year-2018.
   b. Identifying Malaria Infection in Red Blood Cells using Optimized Step-Increase Convolutional Neural Network Model: Year -2019.
   c. Malaria Disease Identification and Analysis Using Image Processing: year-2018.
7. **Disease Prediction from Symptoms:**
   a. Prediction of Diseases in Smart Health Care System using Machine Learning – Year-2020.
   b. Intelligent heart disease prediction system using data mining techniques (IEEE) -Year-2018.

c.   Disease Prediction Using Machine Learning: Year -2019.

As per our findings from the literature survey, we strongly believe that, there is a strong need of a system during this time of pandemic for prediction of major diseases such as Cancer, Pneumonia, diabetes etc. which will not only detect the disease in its early stage but also the chances of curing will also be more (Frunza, 2011). The treatment of these kinds of diseases should start at its early stage to decrease its mortality rate (Shinde & Jadhav, 2014).

METHODOLOGY

The proposed system works at different steps which are as follows:

Step 1: Dataset Preparation

This step involves the collection of different report dataset for different diseases. Dataset is csv format containing symptoms and disease associated to it; csv dataset containing tumour parameters from extracted diagnosis report and status of tumour present or not; image report dataset for specific disease like MRI dataset for brain tumour, Mammography image dataset for breast cancer, x-ray image dataset for pneumonia and skin spot image dataset for skin related dataset. This dataset is collected from UCI repository. Dataset is available at Kaggle and UCI.

Step 2: Developing machine learning model for disease prediction

In this step machine learning model for predicting disease; Decision tree, Random Forest and Naïve Byes machine learning algorithms are prepaid to detect disease based on symptoms and parameter values of extracted diagnosis report. And a Pretrained machine learning model for predicting disease based on image reports.

Step 3: Training and testing dataset

The disease prediction machine learning model will be trained on the given dataset; the 3-machine learning model mentioned in the below section will be trained for the csv dataset. And pre-trained machine learning models will be trained for image report dataset.

Step 4: Deployment

In this step trained machine learning models and other techniques will be combined together for final deployment to make the system more interactive and convenient to use for normal users.

The above diagram is a detailed flow of data between different system modules including both internal as well as external entities.

Figure 1. Data flow diagram of the system

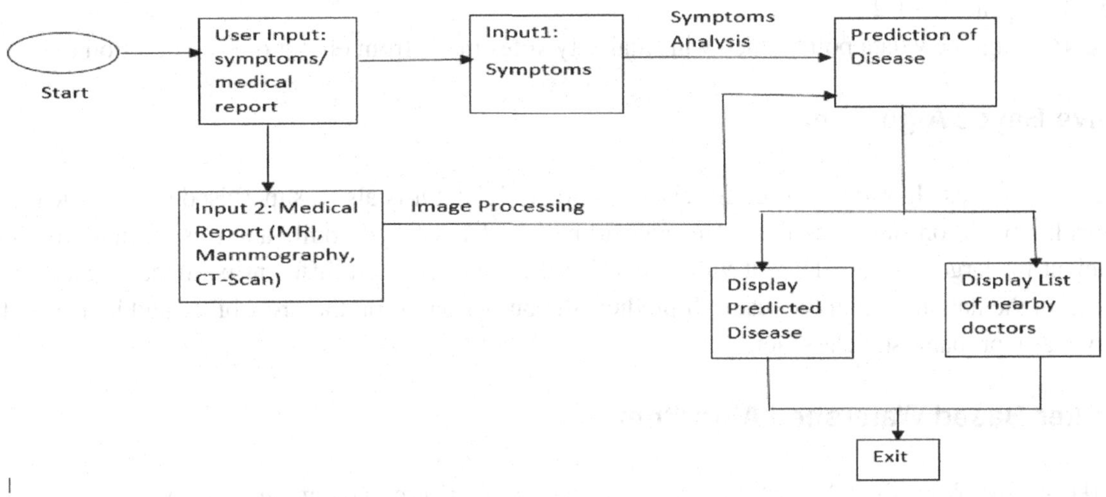

ALGORITHMS USED

Decision Tree Algorithm

Decision Tree is used for both regression and classification techniques. It is a tree-structured supervised machine learning algorithm. Its design is like a tree-structured where "Decision Nodes" are for making decisions and have branches which represent decision rule/condition and "Leaf Node" does not have any branches representing the final outcome. For decision making it asks questions in Yes/No fashion and further makes decisions by adding branches and creating subtrees. For understanding complete process, it follows following steps:

Step 1: The tree starts with the root node- contains a complete dataset.
Step 2: Using Attribute selection measure it finds the best suitable attribute in a given dataset.
Step 3: It further divides these best possible attributes into subsets.
Step 4: It creates a new decision tree node containing the best suitable attribute.
Step 5: Repeat steps from step 2 until it does not find any suitable attributes and then final attributes are represented as leaf nodes which is a final output.

Random Forest Tree Algorithm

Random Forest Tree is also used for regression and classification techniques and also it is a supervised machine learning algorithm. Except it is based on ensemble learning. Random forest is used to solve complex problems. It contains a various subset of a given dataset which are decision trees. It takes the prediction from each decision tree and based on the most common output; the final decision is made as the final output. The working process is as follows:

Step 1: Select any random point from the given dataset.

Step 2: With the selected subsets build the decision trees.

Step 3: Repeat step 1-2.

Step 4: Assign new data point which wins majority votes made from output of each decision tree.

Naïve Bayes Algorithm

The Naïve Bayes algorithm is used for classification only and it is also a supervised machine learning algorithm based on Bayes theorem. This algorithm's model is easy to build and it is particularly more efficient for large datasets. Here it will categorize the data based on different parameters and then it will train the data to obtain the result. It predicts the output based on the probability and hence is also known as a probabilistic classifier.

Marker-Based Watershed Algorithm

Marker-Based Watershed Algorithm is a segmentation algorithm and can be used to display affected regions by disease; like tumours present in MRI images. Using marker-based segmentation can be used in a better way to display such regions. This algorithm marks foreground objects and background areas. This algorithm follows following steps:

1. Scan colour image and convert it into grayscale.
2. Calculate gradient magnitude- borders of objects are high gradient and body of object is low gradient.
3. Mark foreground area- use erosion and dilation to clean the image.
4. Mark background area- using thresholding technique mark background area and colour it in dark colour pixels.
5. Display the result- display final binary foreground, background area and border of object. Foreground area is coloured in rainbow colour style.

Figure 2. Architecture of the system

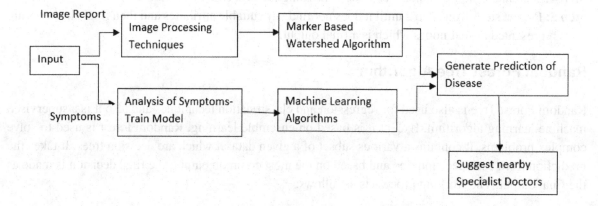

Finally, these techniques are combined together to predict multiple major and minor diseases mentioned earlier.

1. **Module 1: Predict disease based on symptoms:**

Users are asked to select symptoms from a given list; users can select these symptoms accordingly. To predict disease based on symptoms 3 machine learning algorithms mentioned above are used. CSV dataset is provided for training and testing as an input to these algorithms. The CSV data provided contains symptoms and disease associated with it. Combination of symptoms is included in this CSV file by 1 if symptom is present and 0 if not present.

The 3 Machine Learning algorithms used, namely Decision Tree, Random Forest and Naïve Bayes will predict disease individually using their own techniques and then the result given by these 3 algorithms is compared; the best predicted or suitable result is displayed as the final detected disease.

Figure 3. Symptoms based prediction data flow diagram

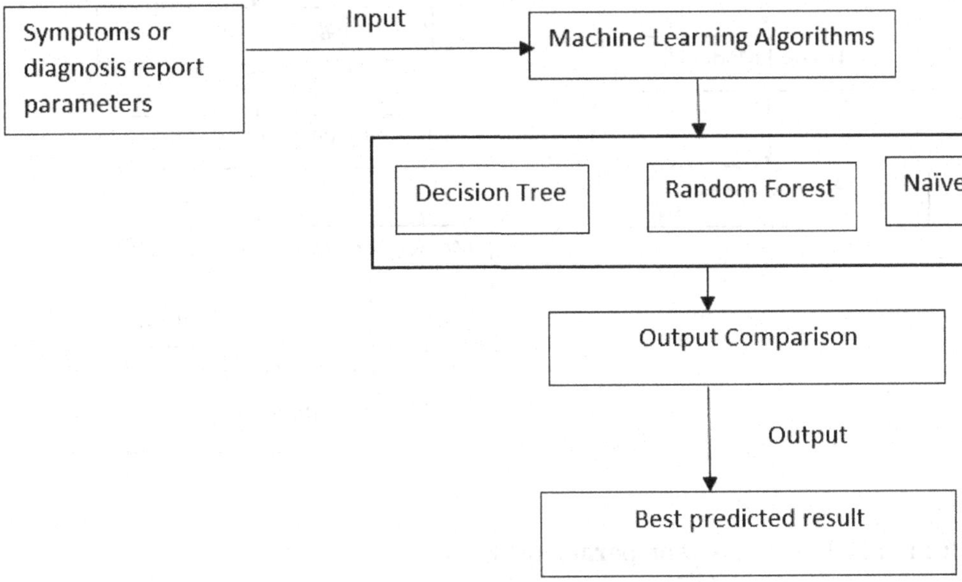

2. **Module 2: Predict disease based on image reports:**

For predicting disease based on image report user need to select image from 'Browse' option based on selected disease for example, to predict brain tumour user will be asked for brain MRI image, for predicting breast cancer user will be asked to upload mammography image and so on based on selected disease image report will be specified (Hamad,simonov & Naeem,2018).

After uploading an image- some image processing techniques will be applied to that image. Image will be converted to grayscale image first, then a series of erosion and dilation techniques will be applied to remove noise. After following these steps, the image will be given to a pre-trained machine learning model; this machine learning model is trained by providing a large image dataset. Pretrained machine learning model will predict if a selected disease is detected or not. After that user can view the affected region in the provided image report by clicking on 'View Region' option- Marker based watershed algorithm is used to display this region.

Figure 4. Image based prediction data flow diagram

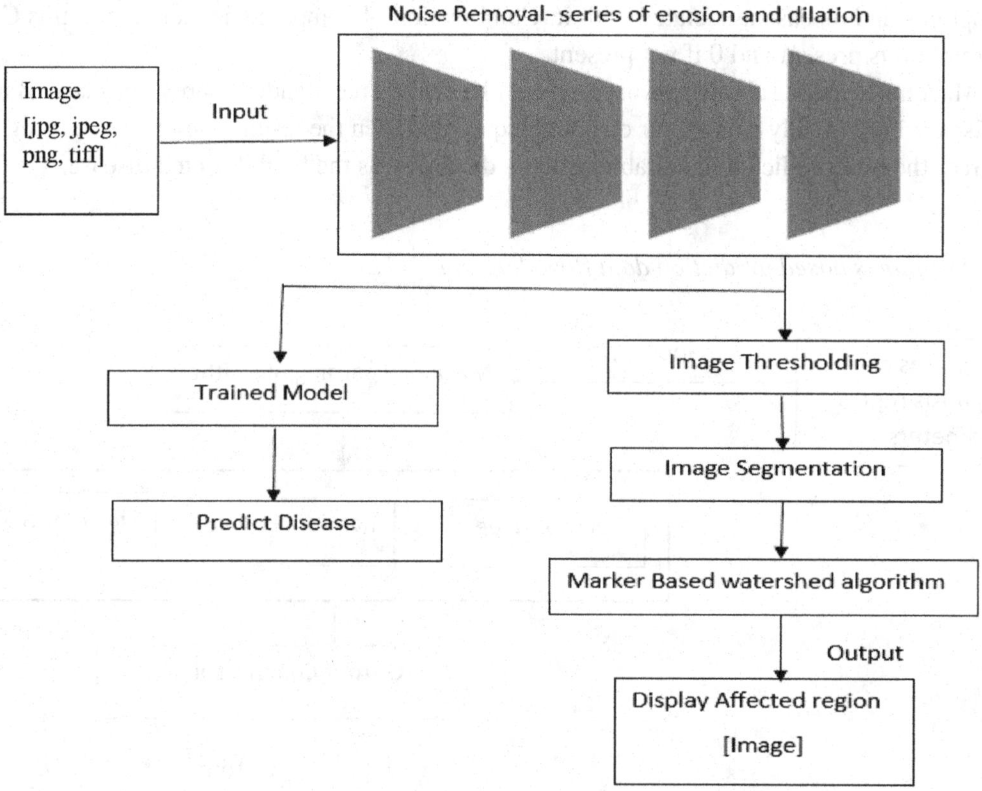

3. Module 3: Predict disease based on parameter values:

For predicting disease, users need to enter extracted parameter values from the diagnosis report; for example, brain tumour extracted diagnosis report values like radius, diameter, skewness etc. in a given field. These values will be analysed by the three machine learning algorithms mentioned above. CSV dataset containing parameter values is provided for training and testing purposes for the same. Machine Learning algorithms will predict if disease is present or not individually, then the final result given by the mentioned algorithm will be compared and the best suitable result will be displayed as a prediction.

4. Module 4: Suggest Nearby specialist:

Based on the user's given location at the time of registration and disease predicted user can view nearby specialists for the specific disease and their contact information which will save user's time and they can get diagnosed as soon as possible.

OVERVIEW OF MODULES

There are various modules in which this system is developed. They are mentioned as follows:

User Input Module

In User input module user is responsible to enter input for following:

- Register: Users need to create an account to use the system. User is responsible for entering registration details. After registration the user will get a unique ID called patient id. Users need to save this id for future login.
- Login: To use the system user needs to login. For login users need to enter patient id-generated at registration process. And password. After successful credentials users will be able to login else errors will be displayed.
- Upload Report: For predicting disease based on image report users need to select image report. Image reports like MRI for detecting brain tumor, mammography for detecting breast cancer, spot/mole image for detecting skin cancer, chest x-ray for detecting pneumonia.
- Enter Parameters: For predicting disease from histology/pathology report details users need to enter parameter values for given fields.

Parameter Based Prediction

- This module is responsible for predicting disease-based on symptoms or diagnosis report parameters. For predicting disease from symptoms, the system will ask users to select symptoms from a given list. For detecting disease based on pathology report values, users will be asked for entering values into given fields.
- Based on given symptoms or pathology report values the 3 machine learning algorithms used (i.e.Decision Tree, Random Forest, Naïve byes) will predict disease individually. For training and testing of this algorithm's csv data is provided.
- The result given by each algorithm will be compared to give a more accurate result.
- The more suitable result will be displayed as predicted disease.

Image Based Prediction

- This module is responsible for detecting disease based on image reports like MRI, mammography, x-ray and so on. After selecting a specific disease, the user will be able to select the image file from the browse option. Users need to select an image report for which he wants to detect disease.
- The input image will proceed through image processing techniques. Series of erosion and dilation techniques to remove noise. Thresholding and segmentation to separate foreground and background area and to get target region.
- Marker-Based Watershed Classification algorithm used to display affected regions in colour format.

Suggest Nearby Specialists

- This module is responsible for suggesting nearby specialist based on-
- User's given location Detected Disease
- Based on the above two features the nearby specialist list will be displayed. The specialist's name along with address and contact information and speciality will be displayed which will save the user's time.

TOOLS AND TECHNOLOGIES USED

Below are the tools and technologies used to build this system:

- **Python**
  - ◦ Python is an interpreted and also a high-level programming language. It is a general-purpose programming language and is also dynamically typed which supports multiple programming paradigms.
  - ◦ It consists of powerful scientific packages and modules which are perfect for doing Big Data Operations. Some libraries are-

Pandas: It helps in data analysis. It provides data structure and operations for data manipulation on tables.

Xlrd: This module is used to extract data from a spreadsheet for reading, writing and modifying the data in python.

NumPy: NumPy is an array-processing package provided by Python. It provides an array object which is multidimensional and high performance. It also provides various tools for working with these arrays and is a fundamental package for scientific computing with Python used in many applications.

- **TensorFlow**

Tensorflow is an open-source python library used for deep learning and machine learning applications. Initially it was not an open-source library but later due to its diverse use google made it a open source library. It works as it accepts multi/high dimensional data called tensors then by using multi-dimensional arrays it performs data handling operations. Tensorflow supports both Python and C++ APIs. It also has integration with Java and R. Tensorflow saves the computation time and memory as if you perform these computational operations normally on CPU it will take much more time and require large space whereas TensorFlow saves it. Compared to other deep learning libraries like Keras and torch, Tensorflow has a faster compilation time.

- **Flask**

Flask is a micro-framework, its type of python module which can be written in python that allows you to progress web applications very easily. flask produces tools, libraries, and technologies that permit the building of web applications. It's called a micro framework because it only gives the necessary modules for web development, such as routing, request handling, sessions, and so on. With more functionalities such as data handling, the developer could also use an extension. This model was integrated into the web using a flask, it takes inputs from the user so that it can make predictions. It's an Application Programming Interface (API) that loads this trained model and gets inputs from the users to fill in their test results. Here, Tree models are also deployed on the web through an API that is a flask.

- **Human Computer Interface (HCI):**

Computer users are confident enough and self-assured with their successful experiences about how they should deal and get work done with computers. Every small success with the computer software allows its user to explore more and gain more and more knowledge. This interface with the computer leads the programmer and its user to expand their knowledge in different domains as well. Using the golden rules of interface as guidelines the designing of this web application is prepared.

The three user interface design principles are: 1. Place users in control of the interface 2. Reduce users' memory load 3. Make the user interface consistent. These principles are generally thought to be common across all computer hardware and software environments. They also apply across all interface types and styles. These principles should even endure as new user interface technologies emerge.

Following are the screenshots of the website developed for our work. Using HCI concepts and Golder rules, the interface is much more user friendly and convenient to use.

With reference to the Golden Rule- 1 that is Place Users in Control -The home page of the web applications is a customized design placing patient/s in control of the interface. The home page is meant for a patient to enter his/her id and password. For the first time, patients have to register for the profile so that he/she will get his/her id and password respectively to enter into the system.

1. Home page of the web application.

Figure 5. Home page of web application

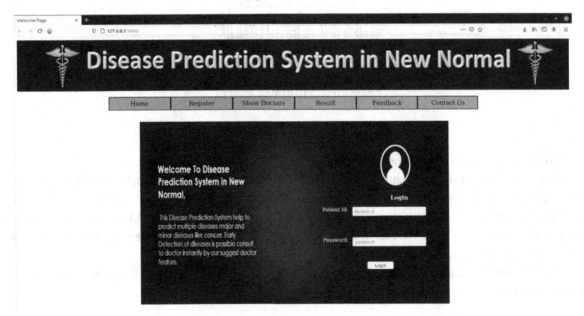

The prediction can be done based on the patient's inputs or based-on images of X-rays or some reports.

Module 1: User Input Modules

Figure 6. User registration page

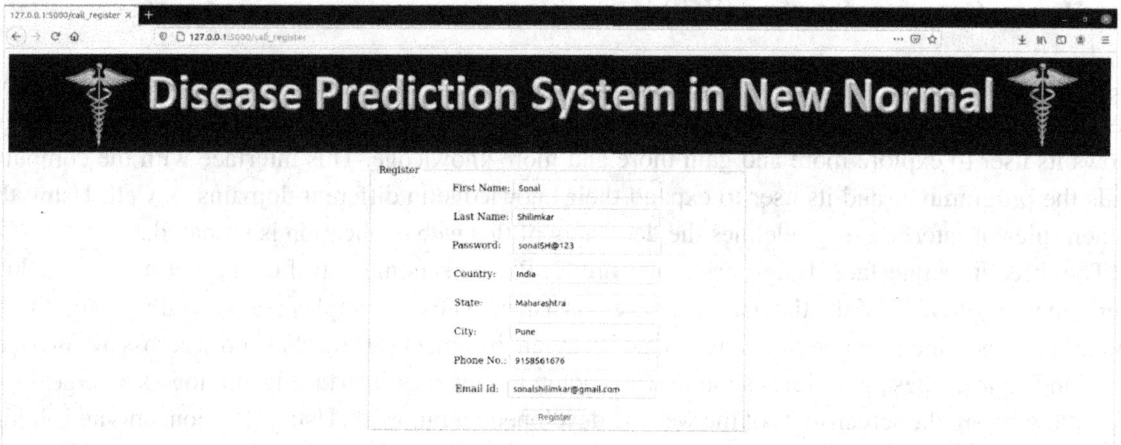

After filling the basic information, the patient's registration is completed and his/her ID is generated by the system

Figure 7. Patient Id generated

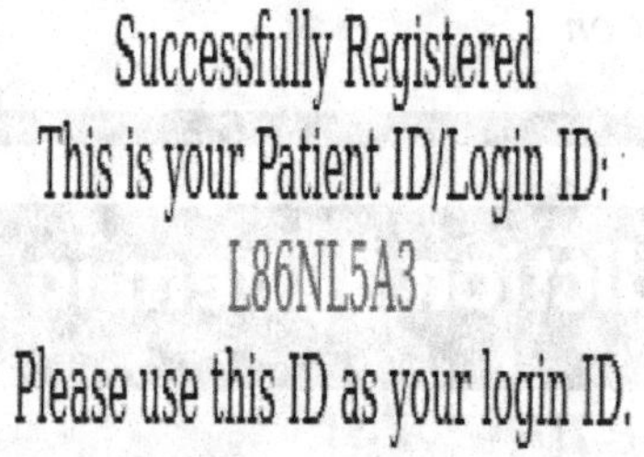

Successfully Registered
This is your Patient ID/Login ID:
L86NL5A3
Please use this ID as your login ID.

Patients can login by using those credentials.

Using the Golden Rule - 2: that is Reduce Users' Memory Load - The human brain is having limitations of storing limited information. On our website, the Icon menu is used to reduce the memory load. The computer interface of our system can help patients remember information while using our website. Drop down list is used in the GUI so that the patient can select the value of the parameter or its range rather than remembering it.

After that the Selection of Disease Page will appear. This page is consistent throughout the application to select the type of disease.

Figure 8. Login page

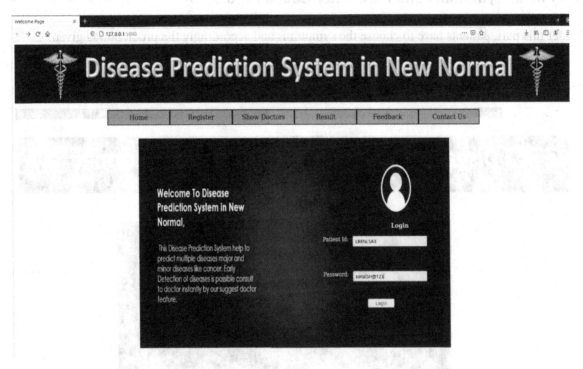

In the below figure 9, a patient can easily find the specific icon for that particular disease. So patients do not have to remember the information.

Figure 9. Selection of disease page

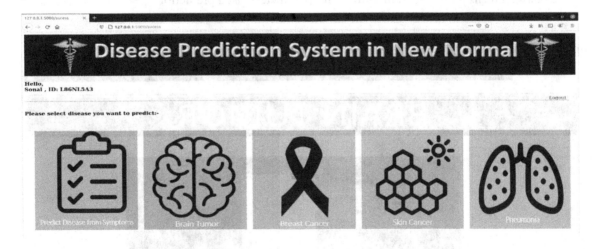

Module 2: Symptoms and Parameter Based Prediction

Under this part, patients have to choose the symptoms and accordingly the prediction is given.

Figure 10. Symptoms based prediction symptoms selection

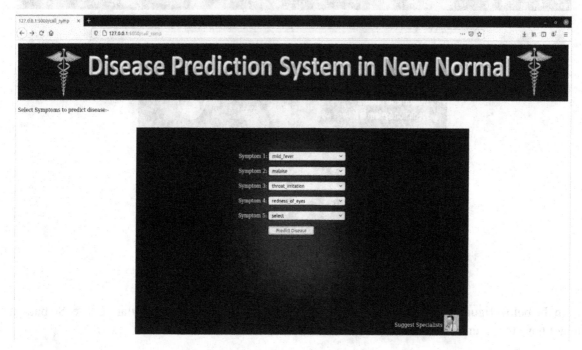

The below screenshot is for Brain Tumour for parameter-based prediction.

Figure 11. Brain tumour prediction from parameter based values

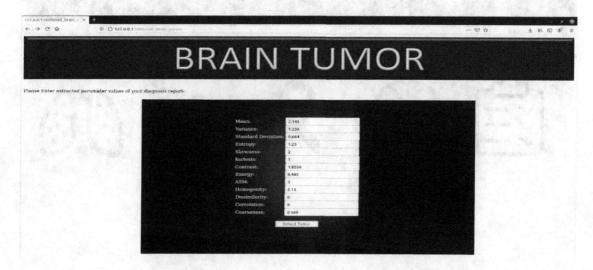

Figure 12. Skin cancer prediction from parameter based values

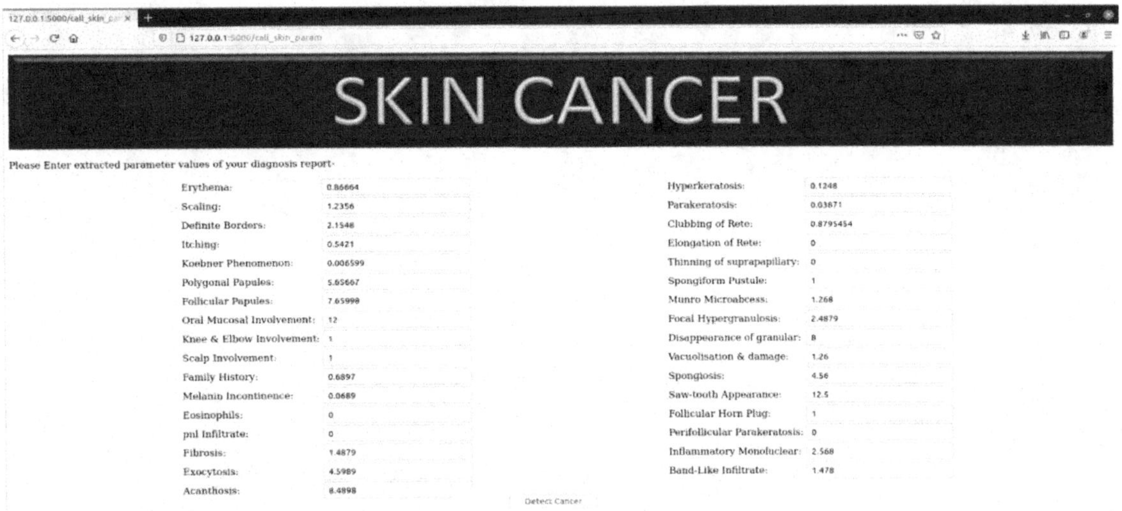

The above screenshot is for skin cancer for parameter-based prediction.

With reference to Golden Rule -3 that is to make the Interface Consistent – In our system Consistency refers to the Colour, font, the instruction to proceed further, step by step guidelines are consistent with respect to all types of diseases. User interface consistency is a key aspect of usable interfaces which make the interface more convenient and easier to use. Almost all the web pages colour, font, size is kept the same to make our GUI more consistent for the patient.

Module 3: Image Based Prediction

The below screenshot is for Image Based Prediction Brain Tumour:

Figure 13. Image based prediction brain tumour

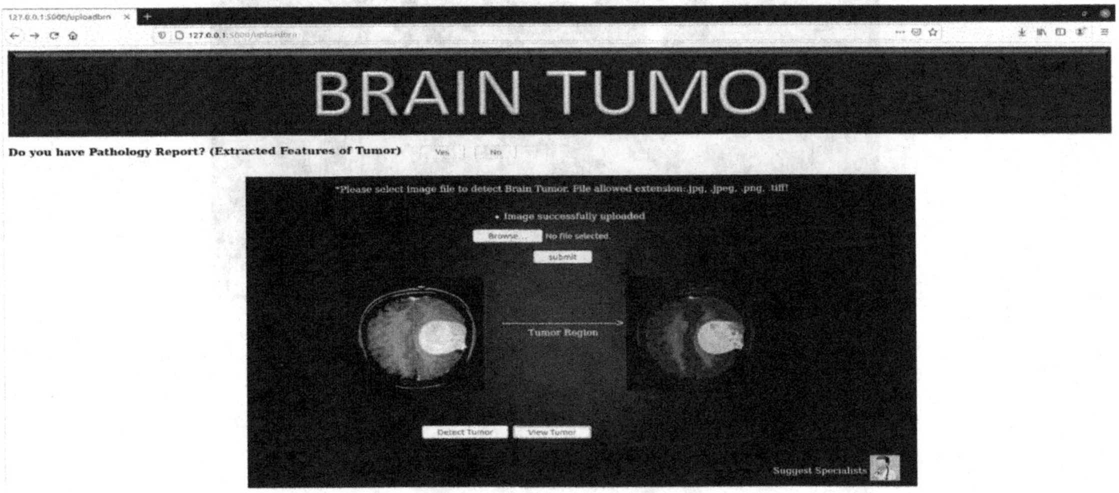

Figure 14. Brain tumour prediction

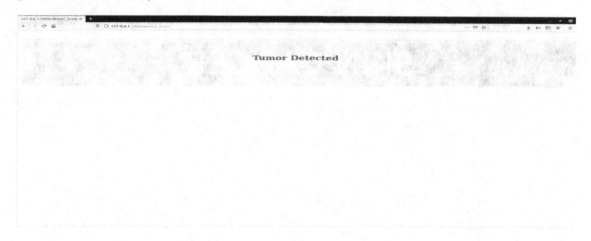

The above figure shows that the brain tumour exists. These types of web pages are kept consistent for better understanding for the patient.

The below screenshot is for Image Based Prediction for Breast Cancer.

Figure 15. Breast cancer prediction

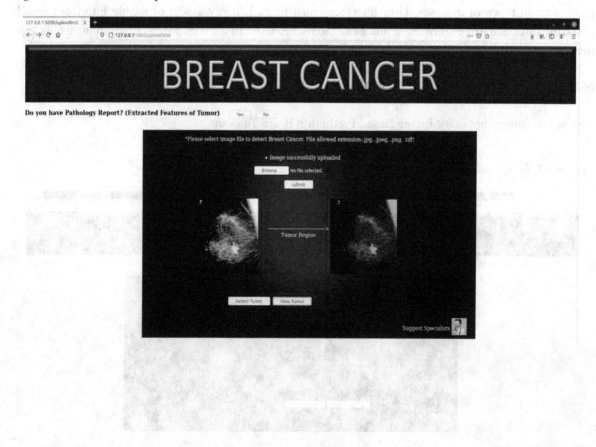

Figure 16. Skin cancer prediction

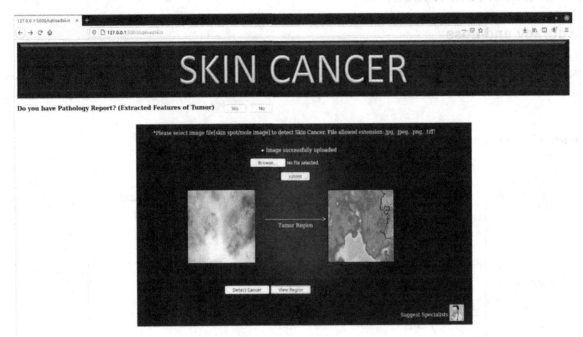

The above screenshot is for Image Based Prediction for skin Cancer. So instead of storing the parameter-based information, patients can upload the image of X-ray, report etc and can predict the disease. The below screenshot is for Image Based Prediction for pneumonia.

Figure 17. Pneumonia prediction

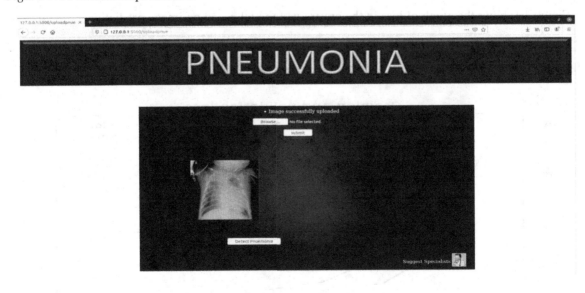

EXPERIMENT AND RESULT

Accuracy and Loss

Accuracy and Loss of pretrained models for image-based prediction is calculated by metrics using Keras libraries. Figure 18 shows the graph of accuracy for the pre-trained model based on image prediction.

Figure 18. Accuracy of pretrained model for image based prediction

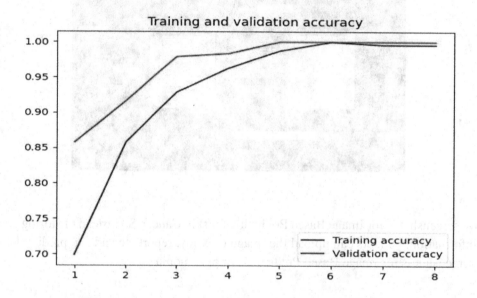

Figure 19 shows the graph of loss in the pre-trained model based on image prediction.

Figure 19. Loss of pretrained model for image based prediction

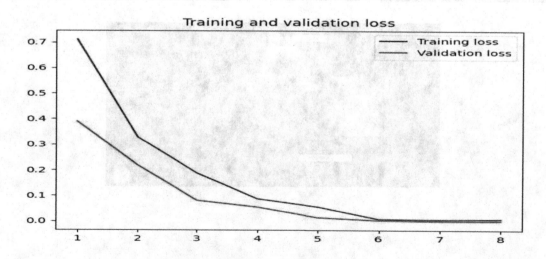

Results

For Image based report disease prediction the dataset for training and testing is given. The dataset contains different images including affected by disease and normal ones, dataset images contain images from different sides, blurred ones, different sizes and different affected region sizes. This proposed system processed the given input image to remove noise, sharpening, and segmentation for better result. The following diagram shows the input image given, disease predicted and affected region

Figure 20. Overall results showing images of affected area by disease

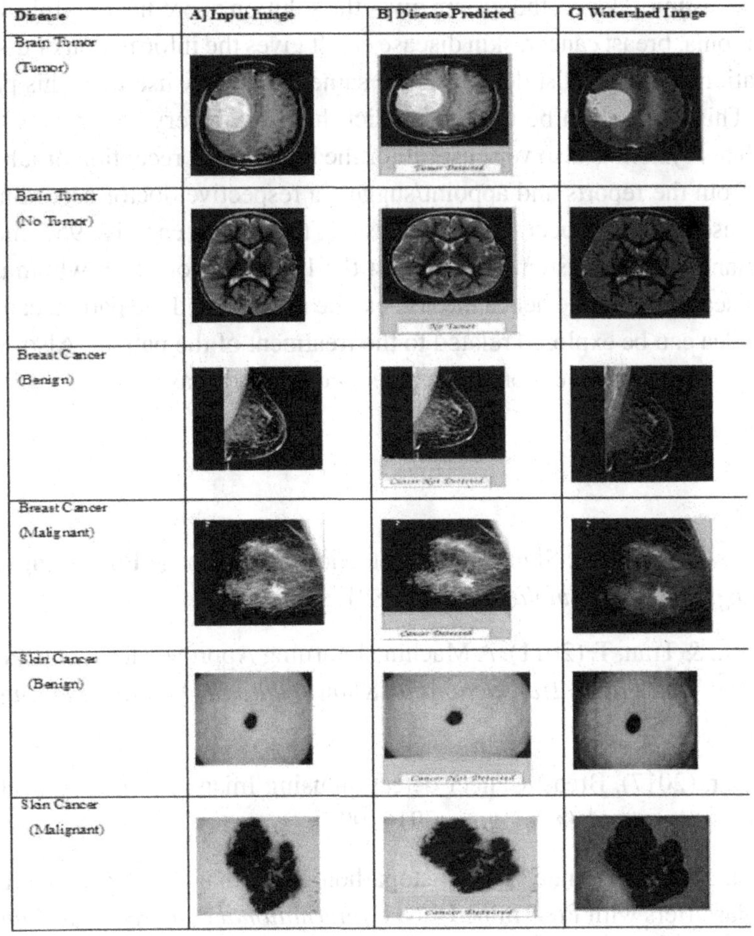

FUTURE RESEARCH DIRECTIONS

With the improvement in HCI technologies, the same system using the same techniques can be applied to detect multiple other diseases. Adding new diseases and training the machine learning model instantly is possible. Detecting disease through video dataset and 3d images can be done using the same techniques. Furthermore, users and doctors or hospitals can add their role which will make communication within patients and doctors more convenient and adding roles will make it a better system for prediction. In future, System can be extended to the proposed system such that there can be a client-server or cloud-based model which will help to keep updating the system for adding new diseases and update specialist doctors and there will be no need for users to install the system on their machine; it will be available for everyone.

CONCLUSION

The system gives a reliable solution to predict the diseases. With this system, the prediction of the severe diseases can be done on-time. Hence, the system gives the solution to predict multiple diseases and useful currently for- pneumonia, breast cancer, skin disease etc. It gives the information of disease detected and the contact information of a specialist doctor for the same. It's highly useful in this pandemic situation for safety reasons. This system can be used to predict the disease very shortly and to take corrective treatment on time. This system is also very useful for the hospitals at reception or laboratories to check a patient's disease from the reports and appoint/suggest a respective doctor accordingly. It seems that for detecting major diseases like cancer, image processing techniques can give 95% more correct results than the naked human eye. This system will suggest the list of doctors with whom users can consult. Early detection of disease is possible hence the risk can be reduced and the patient can be treated well in time. In future, the idea can be explored related to the treatment of the patient. Also, it can be extended to build a system to predict for some more general and complex diseases.

REFERENCES

Ansari, U. B., & Sarode, T. (2017). Skin Cancer Detection Using Image Processing. *International Research Journal of Engineering Technology*, 2875–2881.

Frunza, O., Inkpen, D., & Tran, T. (2011). A Machine Learning Approach for Identifying Disease Treatment Relations in Short Texts. *IEEE Transactions on Knowledge and Data Engineering*, *23*(6), 801–814. doi:10.1109/TKDE.2010.152

Giri & Saravanakumar. (2017). Breast Cancer detection using Image processing Techniques *Oriental. Journal of Computer Science and Technology*, 391–399.

Gupta, K., & Chawla, N. (2019). Analysis of Histopathological Images for Prediction of Breast Cancer Using Traditional Classifiers with Pre-Trained CNN. *International conference on Computational Intelligence and Data science(ICCIDS 2019)*, 878-889.

Hamad, Y. A., Simonov, K., & Naeem, M. B. (2018). Breast Cancer Detection and Classification using Artificial Neural Networks. *1st Annual International conference on Information and Sciences (AICIS)*, 51-57. 10.1109/AiCIS.2018.00022

Han, Z., Wei, B. Z., Zheng, Y., Yin, Y., Li, K., & Li, S. (2017). Breast Cancer Multi-classification from Histopathological Images with Structured Deep Learning Model. *Scientific Reports*, *7*(1), 1–10. doi:10.103841598-017-04075-z PMID:28646155

Masud, M., Alhumyani, H., Alshamrani, S. S., Cheikhrouhou, O., Ibrahim, S., Muhammad, G., Hossain, M. S., & Shorfuzzaman, M. (2020). Leveraging Deep Learning Techniques for Malaria Parasite Detection Using Mobile Application. Wireless Communications and Mobile Computing, 1-15.

Patel, Gandhi, & Shetty, & Tekwani. (2017). Heart Disease Prediction Using Data Mining. *International Research Journal of Engineering and Technology, 04*, 1705–1707.

Sagar & Saini. (2016). Color Channel Based Segmentation of Skin Lesion from Clinical Images for the Detection of Melanoma. *2016 IEEE 1st International Conference on Power Electronics, Intelligent Control and Energy Systems (ICPEICES)*, 1-5.

Sawant, Bhandari, Yadav, & Yele, & Bendale. (2018). Brain Cancer Detection from Mri: A Machine Learning Approach (Tensorflow). *International Research Journal of Engineering and Technology, 5*, 2089–2094.

Shanthi, D., Maheshvari, P. N., & Sankarie, S. (2020). Survey on Detection of Melanoma Skin Cancer Using Image Processing and Machine Learning. *International Journal of Research and Analytical Reviews*, 237-248.

Shinde, P., & Jadhav, S. (2014). Health Analysis System Using Machine Learning. *International Journal of Computer Science and Information Technologies*, 3928–3933.

Smitha, P., Shaji, L., & Mini, M.G. (2011). A Review of Medical Image Classification Techniques. *IJCA Proceedings on International Conference on VLSI, Communications and Instrumentation (ICVCI)*, 34–38.

Vaishnavi & Girarddi. (2019). *Detection of Brain Tumour Using Image Classification*. https://www.researchgate.net/publication/327497285_Detection_of_Brain_Tumor_using_Image_Classification

Vijayalakshmi, M. (2019), Melanoma Skin Cancer Detection using Image Processing and Machine Learning. *International Journal of Trend in Scientific Research and Development (IJTSRD)*, 780-784.

Chapter 8
Grouping Public Complaints in the City of Tangerang Using K–Means Clustering Method:
Contextual Text Analytics

Evaristus Didik Madyatmadja

Information Systems Department, School of Information Systems, Bina Nusantara University, Jakarta, Indonesia

Yusdi Ari Pralambang

Information Systems Department, School of Information Systems, Bina Nusantara University, Jakarta, Indonesia

Astari Karina Rahmah

Information Systems Department, School of Information Systems, Bina Nusantara University, Jakarta, Indonesia

Gede Prama Adhi Wicaksana

Information Systems Department, School of Information Systems, Bina Nusantara University, Jakarta, Indonesia

Saphira Aretha Putri

Information Systems Department, School of Information Systems, Bina Nusantara University, Jakarta, Indonesia

Muhammad D. Raihan

Information Systems Department, School of Information Systems, Bina Nusantara University, Jakarta, Indonesia

ABSTRACT

The government's efforts in developing electronic-based government services by utilizing information technology are referred to as the concept of e-government. Tangerang City is one of the cities that applies e-government in an application called Tangerang LIVE. In the Tangerang LIVE application, a LAKSA feature is used as a place for complaints from the people of Tangerang. This research was conducted to classify complaint data and determine the priority of groups of complaints received from the LAKSA feature. The technique used to conduct this research is clustering using the unsupervised learning method and the k-means algorithm, which will classify and predict the class for each document. In addition, an analysis of the priority complaint data was carried out based on the group that was received the most. The analysis carried out is to find out the class predictions for each complaint received, and then labeling will be given so that the complaint belongs to a more specific group. The results of the predictions will be displayed in the browser using web services.

DOI: 10.4018/978-1-7998-9121-5.ch008

INTRODUCTION

Digital transformation is a new challenge for every country in the era of Industrial Revolution 4.0. Implementation of Smart City in Indonesia that creates the concept of smart governance be a challenge. Smart Governance is one of the dimensions of Smart Cities, which includes all aspects of political involvement and community service, as well as local government operations (Lopes, 2017). In implementing the smart city concept, the government is required to be able to provide governance that is transparent, accountable, collaborative (involving all stakeholders), and participatory (i.e., citizen participation) (Lopes, 2017). One example is providing a digital platform for the public to submit complaints to the government regarding the problems they are experiencing in their respective regions.

The Tangerang City Government has launched the Tangerang LIVE application. This application can help people to find information about Tangerang City. In the application, there is a feature to make a complaint called LAKSA or "Layanan Aspirasi Kotak Saran Anda". The public can submit complaints about education, health, infrastructure, security, and social affairs in Tangerang City.

However, with the complaints, aspirations and complaints received, the Government must determine the complaints and complaints that must be followed up first. Therefore, from the amount of data received by the Government, it must be sorted according to the priority of complaints so that the problems with the most complaints will be immediately followed up by the stored parties. The amount of data on complaints and complaints received by the Government can be defined as Big Data. The term "big data" refers to data that is so large, fast or complex that it is difficult or impossible to use traditional methods. Big Data is a combination of structured, semi-structured, and unstructured data collected by an organization that can be used to obtain information and be used in machine learning projects, predictive modeling, and other analytical applications (Rouse, 2014).

The data used to perform the analysis is text, then the Data Mining method that will be used is Text Mining. Text Mining can also be referred to as Text Data Mining. Text mining refers to the process of extracting interesting and inappropriate patterns or knowledge from unstructured data. According to (Tan, 1999), Text Mining is believed to have more potential than Data Mining. Recent research has shown that 80% of company information is contained in text documents. *Text Mining* is a multidisciplinary field that involves information search, text analysis, grouping information, grouping, categorization, visualization, database technology, machine learning, and data mining. Text Mining aims to extract information from unstructured data and semi-structured data and find new patterns and information that is difficult to obtain without doing in-depth analysis.

With a large number of incoming complaint data, data processing will become more complicated and time-consuming. Therefore, an approach is needed to group the data to trigger follow-up or decision-making from the data.

The analytical method used is clustering, by identifying subgroups in the data so that the data points in the same subgroup (cluster) are very similar, while the data points in different groups are very different. Or it can be concluded to find homogeneous subgroups in the data so that the data points in each cluster are as similar as possible based on similarity measurements such as Euclidean-based distance or correlation-based distance. Each of the clusters formed will be a complaint category to assist the Tangerang City Government in dealing with problems.

Unlike supervised learning, the clustering method is considered an unsupervised learning method because there is no basic truth to compare the output of the clustering algorithm with the actual label to evaluate performance.

Here we use the k-means algorithm in processing clustering analysis. K-Means clustering is one of the most popular clustering algorithms and is usually the first thing that practitioners apply when solving clustering tasks to get an idea of the structure of the dataset. The purpose of k-means clustering is to group data points into subgroups that do not overlap or overlap.

By using K-Means Clustering in this analysis, it is to divide the complaints and complaints obtained in the Tangerang LIVE application on the LAKSA feature into several groups to find out what complaints should take precedence for handling or priority complaints.

BACKGROUND

Smart City

A relatively new venue for the governance system is the smart city paradigm. The role of big data on people, the community and intelligent development is being debated more and more. The purpose of this study is to investigate the impact of big data in sustainable urban development on smart city governance. This study also employed case-study procedures for three well-known intelligent cities in the U.S., Europe and Asia, as well also produced a conceptual framework to describe the application of big data to the many dimensions of a sustainable intelligent city. The paper (Ismail, 2016) suggested that the use of big data in public sector smart city government, by using the citizen-centered approach, may enhance the governance capability of people, economies, the environment and infrastructure. The paper provides thorough explanations on the Smart City based upon critical assessment of existing practices and their relevance to smart city administration (Sarker et al., 2020).

Study done by (Lopes, 2017) attempts to answer the question: "What governance models are being implemented in smart cities?" The interviews' empirical analysis reveals that Smart Cities and e-Government have followed a similar evolutionary path, both leading to smart government. According to the study, all of the efforts are primarily reliant on technology and follow a similar smart governance approach, which combines collaborative, open, and participatory governance. We argue that the development of smart, creative, inventive and sustainable municipalities requires modern technology, innovation and smart governance.

The Government of Jakarta, Indonesia, begins to adopt intelligent city principles via a mobile application to react to citizens' complaints named QLUE. However, in comparison to the number of people, QLUE consumption and adoption levels remain low. Therefore, the study studied the drivers of the behavioral intention of citizens to utilize the Smart City System (QLUE) based on the S&C model. The results reveal that the intention of behavior to use QLUE is impacted by social impact and impacts (Fitriani et al., 2017).

However, some key difficulties have to be handled immediately with regard to the deployment of smart cities, including an ineffective human resources component, inefficient governance and ICT policy, lack of government commitment and poor stakeholder and society engagement. The key elements impacting the growth of intelligent urban development in Indonesia are explored in this research. The findings of this study reveal that the features of the E-GEEF model are significantly linked to the Smart Sustainable City. This research helps to develop a model of link between essential elements in Smart Sustainable City that affect technology adoption and suggests policymakers and local authorities to provide more focus to concerns which impact Smart Sustainable City successfully (Darmawan et al., 2020).

The paper proves that the dominant methods to urban governance are based on the legacy of reductionist philosophy and tools for public administrations not completely compatible with the complexity of urban infrastructures. However, new technical developments linked to the concept of intelligent cities and developing socio-political trends bring up new potential to build methods to governance that can overcome these incompatibilities in urban systems. On the other hand, the effective implementation of urban infrastructure improvements, which are known to us as complex social systems, calls for smarter governance approaches compatible with the paradigm of systems. The rate of social and technological development in the city landscapes is rapid. This Conceptual paper provides information on how the municipal governments should closely watch such development and adjust the governance approach, or governance could become a significant obstacle to the use of technological advantages in addressing more complex municipal concerns (Razaghi & Finger, 2018).

E-Government

Citizens and businesses communicate electronically with public agencies in the e-government transaction. Government, public, private, and NGO stakeholders are the participants in projects of e-government (Meiyanti et al., 2018)

The research done by (Lytras & Şerban, 2020) looks at e-government as one of the main applications of smart cities in our modern society. They discovered that e-services, especially e-government services, are not as readily available to residents with poor digital abilities and to those with little access to the internet, as is technically normal. In this context, it is necessary that the E-Government Services are rethought and designed at European Union level to be suited not only to people' requirements but also to their digital abilities.

IT has now become a major pillar of Mauritian economic activity. It benefits every citizen in society of different ages or social situations. In Mauritius presently, the internet, mobile services and smartphone usage with applications in our daily lives have become faster and more trustworthy. In most, if not all of its ministries, government has focused on adopting e-services to facilitate processes. The advantages of early use of technology have been quickly realized by governments. As globalization has come, increased awareness and communication have prepared the way for methods to be developed to allow a civic-centered approach to the provision of all-round online services to the general public. This country has, to name a few, been more than useful in terms of empowering individuals by deploying online services in the fields of education, health, public service, transport, the judiciary, business, financial and security. This study explains the advantages that e-services can bring and highlights some obstacles to proper adoption. Some e-government services implementation is addressed and the merits, limitations and lessons that can be learned from each implementation can be highlighted (Sunassee et al., 2017).

The advances in information technology were significantly improved in today's globalization. Many people use IT to get information by having suitable information systems available. This leads to local governments developing electronic governments to inform the whole of Indonesian society. Several research studies have focused only on typology on developing e-government models. The goal of this study is to analyze the e-government aspects based on transparency and confidence in the provision of better information and information to the poor. This study also develops the concept of an e-government model of transparency and trust in Palembang. The quantitative research is utilized to gather data, with the highest proportion of pre-prosperous society, in 4 districts of Palembang. This research has resulted in a transparent and confident notion of e-government that the Palembang government might use to reach a public service especially for the poor (Antoni et al., 2017).

The Indonesian Ombudsman implements the electronic government, of which one is a public website. The website requires periodic assessments to improve the quality of public service. However, based on user views, the Ombudsman of the Republic of Indonesia has yet to assess the quality of services offered through the E-Government website. One of the primary criteria for achieving Good Governance is technological advancement. Through advancements in information technology, it is now possible to readily communicate information about state government to the general public. In addition, adult information is now easily accessible via a cell phone. As a result, delivering government information via e-government products benefits the community tremendously (Madyatmadja et al., 2010).

This study is intended to discover which factors influence the quality and improvement of the website services of the Ombudsman in the Republic of Indonesia. The results of this study show that the quality of e-government services is significantly affected by efficiency, dependability, public confidence, and support. There is a relationship between the quality and perceived efficiency of e-government services. The findings of this research can be utilized based on the needs of the entities concerned (Durachman et al., 2020).

Implementation in Indonesia and Overseas

Based on several studies that have been conducted by (Wahyu Sulistya et al., 2019), It can be claimed that e-government implementation is still not good in Indonesia. Indonesia remains well below other countries in EGDI's ranking. Presidential Regulation No. 95 on electronic-based governments had been enacted in Indonesia in 2018. The research conducted with the deployment of e-government has had a good impact on public services that highlight new values, agility and control, and accountability and cooperation.

A survey of 156 participants and qualitative methodologies through the Focus Group Discussion done by (Febriliantina et al., 2016), measures public impressions of Bandung's e-government deployment utilizing the Mix Method Research (MMR) system. Benefit and content sizes are viewed as good, however the other 6 characteristics are still to be improved in terms of cost, availability, reliability, technology, reporting and support. Therefore, efforts to improve the quality of public services are necessary to enable the successful deployment of e-government.

Several studies have been conducted to gain more knowledge about e-government. First, study from (Sari et al., 2018) examines the challenges and concerns of the implementation of e-complaints in Indonesia and analyzes them. During this investigation, the STOPE framework was used to analyze and keep the research objective in context. Ten STOPE framework analysis sub-domains as the obstacles and challenges of e-complaints are known in Indonesia. These include political bureaucracy and commitment, the advancement of strategy, security and privacy, a lack of organizational competence, team coordination, a lack of organizational training, poor citizen education, confidence, digital division, and social culture. E-complaint challenges and concerns in Indonesia can be analyzed to provide an overview of how a better e-complaint platform in Indonesia should be developed.

Based on a study by (Meiyanti et al., 2019) that examines the challenges of implementing e-government in developing countries in Asia and Africa, the challenges of implementing e-government can be divided into 5 which include IT infrastructure, managerial issues, digital culture, budgeting, laws and legislation, and human resources. IT Infrastructure challenge is the lack of integration, latest and updated hardware and software of IT infrastructure. Managerial Issues challenges consist of a lack of expertise, transparency, collaboration, and coordination in managing the implementation of e-government. Budgeting is a lack of funding and misuse of funds from the country. Human resources challenges consist of a lack of motivation, ability, education from developers or the state in implementing e-government. Indonesia itself faces 3 of the 5 challenges, namely IT infrastructure, management, and human factors. This also serves as a roadmap for the Indonesian government to develop computerized government services. Currently, most phases in developing e-government applications in Indonesia are focused on delivering websites and information application services (Madyatmadja et al., 2019).

Impact for the Policymaker

In the paper created by (Alkraiji, 2020), a model based on a mixture of successful information systems models was developed and empirically tested, together with a theory of trust. The findings indicate that the perceived utility of e-government and confidence mediated the indirect impact on citizens' satisfaction, both system quality and information quality. The results can be used by policymakers to adjust the resources needed to raise public satisfaction with compulsory education services.

Smart city challenges remain identified in Indonesia, with the goal not fully reached from 25 cities designated for the smart city program in 2017. In 15 cities that are regarded ready to become smart cities, the examination was undertaken. The outcome of the e-government system evaluated by these cities is more than 51 percent of the smart governance activities. Smart governance as a crucial aspect in the effective deployment of smart cities is demonstrated by this research. This contribution gives every decision-maker and policymaker in government vital benefits if they wish to manage smart cities in his city. And also to the reference cities, which are an example of how the smart city in Indonesia might be achieved (Anindra et al., 2018).

Another study did by (Elkheshin & Saleeb, 2017). The paper explores the determinations and factors necessary to enhance citizens' adoption of the e-government services of developing countries, in particular Egypt, using a set of political, social, and design constructions developed from different sources of research literature to extend the Technology Acceptance Model (TAM).

METHOD

Conceptual Framework

Figure 1. Conceptual framework

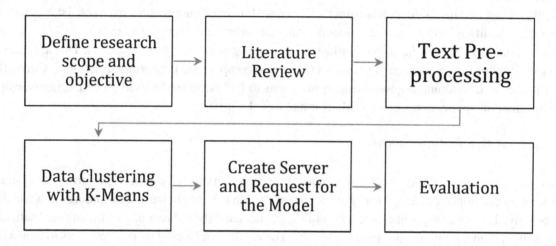

Conceptual Framework Explanation

Determine Purpose and Scope of the Research

Research objectives require a statement of the problem and summarize what is to be achieved in a study. The purpose of this study is to find out whether the K-Means Clustering method can be applied to determine the priority list of problems in Indonesia from the complaint data that is accommodated in the smart city Tangerang LIVE on the LAKSA feature. The purpose of using the smart city Tangerang LIVE is because we need data that can represent problems in regions in Indonesia. And in the smart city Tangerang LIVE itself, there is a LAKSA feature that has the concept of online complaints in text format so that the collection of complaints can be used as a data source.

Literature Review

A literature study is intended to search and evaluate the literature needed in the research or selected topic area. This indicates that the reader has a deep understanding of the subject and the direction of the research. At this stage, the author looks for various references related to the topic under study, namely categorization using the K-Means Clustering method, and looking for references about the method to be used, the type of data used, and integrating the information obtained in summary.

Text Pre-Processing

At the pre-processing stage, text cleansing and text filtering are carried out. Text cleansing is needed to remove unnecessary information such as numbers, formats, and formulas from the LAKSA complaint data. At this stage, case folding is also carried out to convert all words into lowercase letters and convert short words into full words using the python programming language. Furthermore, at the filtering stage, words are carried out to remove characters with no weight or provide information, such as numbers and punctuation marks. After that, it is also done to remove stopwords or non-descriptive words such as "and", "yang", "but", "at" to improve the speed and performance of grouping or classification. Before performing the clustering method, complaints that only contain keywords or keywords are given a label first. The label used is a label that has been created in the process of making class labels. The labels are divided according to their respective methods. The labels are divided into 5, namely "State Facilities", "PJU", "WNI Identity Documents", "PKL", and "PAM".

CLUSTERING USING THE K-MEANS METHOD

The K-means algorithm is an iterative algorithm that tries to partition the dataset into K predefined non-overlapping subgroups (clusters) where each data point belongs to only one group. This is to make the data points between clusters as similar as possible while also keeping the clusters as distinct (as far) as possible. It assigns data points to a cluster so that the sum of the squared distances between the data points and the cluster centroid (the arithmetic mean of all the data points included in that cluster) is minimum. The less variation we have within the cluster, the more homogeneous (similar) data points are within the same cluster.

An objective function, in this case a squared error function, is being tried to be minimized by this method. The objective function:

$$W\left(S,C\right)=\sum_{k=1}^{k}\sum_{i \in S_k} x^i - \mu_k^{\,2} \tag{1}$$

There are K clusters, each with a centroid c_k (k=1,2,...K), that are not empty and don't overlap with each other in the M-dimensional feature space. S is a K-cluster partition of the set of entities represented by the vectors y_i (i\inI) in the M-dimensional space.

There have been a variety of alternative recommendations in the literature for selecting the optimal K after several K-Means runs; we will focus on the following techniques MENDELEY CITATION PLACEHOLDER 20.

First technique (Kodinariya, T.M & Makwana, P.R, 2013) Elbow Method. The aim is to begin with K=2 and gradually increase it by 1, estimating your clusters and the cost associated with training. At a certain value for K, the cost reduces quickly, and then hits a plateau when the value is increased further. This is the desired K value.

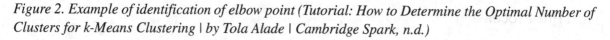

Figure 2. Example of identification of elbow point (Tutorial: How to Determine the Optimal Number of Clusters for k-Means Clustering | by Tola Alade | Cambridge Spark, n.d.)

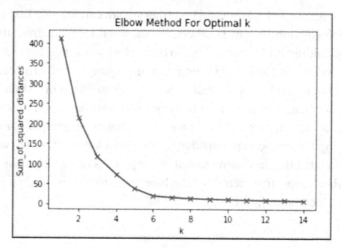

The argument is that we will expand the number of clusters after this, but the new cluster will be quite close to some of the existing clusters. In fig. 1, the distortion J () decreases fast as K increases from 1 to 2, and then from 2 to 3, until W reaches an elbow at K=3, at which point the distortion decreases extremely slowly. And then it appears as though three clusters is the optimal amount, as that is the elbow of this curve. Because distortion decreases fast until K=3 and thereafter very slowly, the number of clusters required for this data set is 3 (Kodinariya, T.M & Makwana, P.R, 2013).

Kaufman and Rousseeuw in (Kodinariya, T.M & Makwana, P.R, 2013) presented a well-balanced parameter, the silhouette width, that has demonstrated excellent performance in studies [13-14]. The term "silhouette width" refers to the difference between the tightness inside a cluster and its separation from the remainder. For entity iEI, the silhouette width s(i) is defined as:

$$s\left(i\right) = \frac{b\left(i\right) - a\left(i\right)}{max\left(a\left(i\right).b\left(i\right)\right)}$$

It says that $a(i)$ is the average distance between i and all other members of the cluster to which i belongs. Then, $b(i)$ is the average distance between i and all the members of all the other groups. It ranges from –1 to 1. If an entity has a silhouette width value that is close to zero, it means that the entity could also be part of a different group. If the silhouette width value is close to 1 and the object isn't what it should be, then it's not what it should be. If all of the silhouette width values in the set i are close to 1, it means that the set is well-grouped (Kodinariya, T.M & Makwana, P.R, 2013).

A clustering can be described by the average width of the silhouettes of each individual thing. Over different K, the number of clusters that have the widest silhouettes is the best.

In this phase, we build a model containing the k-means clustering algorithm to categorize various kinds of complaints into five predetermined categories.

The server functions to call the category results from the code model that has been built. The server here handles GET and POST requests, where GET is the method used to request data requests from the server and POST is a method for sending data for server processing. In making a server for the k-means clustering model, the author uses the flask web framework for making web services. Flask is a web framework written using the Python programming language. The author chooses to use the Flask web framework because Flask is designed to be easy to use and is a strong foundation for the creation of web applications with different complexities. After building the clustering and server model, the next step is to run the server by requesting requests on the server. This stage aims to see the results of the categorization of sentences that have been analyzed through the clustering model.

RESULT AND DISCUSSION

Research Result

The research is divided into several stages. The results of this study will explain each of these stages. Starting from data collection, text preprocessing to the final results of making clustering models and classification models using the Python programming language.

Data Collection

The data used in this study is data on complaints submitted by the public through a government application, namely smart city Tangerang LIVE on the LAKSA feature. This complaint data is a complaint submitted by the public through the LAKSA feature from April 2018 to April 2019. The data contains various kinds of information, ranging from complaints, accident information, suggestions to requests for assistance. There are 4,652 complaint data that the author obtained from the Tangerang LIVE smart city application on the LAKSA feature.

Table 1. Complaint data collection

isi_pengaduan
Jl. Hasyim Ashari berlubang
Menerima Kunjungan sekolah.
Depan perumahan mahkota II blok A5 jalan rusak bertahun tahun. Tidak ada warga baik aparat yang care
Sungai cantiga ini makin dangkal, selain material yang terbawa dari hulu, pedagang disisi sungai sering buang sampah sembarangan
Pemasangan Rambu Dilarang Parkir di depan Stasiun Kota Tangerang, smoga dpt memperlancar lalin di sekitar kawasan tsb.
Assalamualaikum bapak2 ibu2, ini drainase di depan warung ayah saya, h. Sadeli sepertinya mampet atau penuh kalau hujan deras air yang dari drainase masuk ke warung terima kasih

Text Pre-Processing

The results of the preprocessed data will be explained in more detail below using Data Cleansing and Filtering.

Data Cleansing

At this stage, the author records the data that is not needed and the needed data before the data is used for analysis using the Python language program. Here the author performs several steps, the first is to delete columns that are not needed, this is so that the data can be more easily read and reduce the data volume. The author only leaves a column containing a complaint sentence because only that column is needed for data analysis.

After deleting the unnecessary columns, the writer started cleaning the data using the Python Language program. Due to the inconsistent use of capital letters, the next step the author takes is case folding, which converts all text into lowercase or lowercase letters. In addition, the author also becomes an abbreviation so that it has the same meaning and word, for example changing all the words in the ID card.

Figure 3. Source code 1 conversion of abbreviations

```
#Replace Singkatan
ktp = lowerase.replace('ektp', "ktp")
kk = ktp.replace('kk', "kartu keluarga")
pju = kk.replace('pju', "penerangan jalan umum")
pkl = pju.replace('pkl', "pedagang kaki lima")
```

Table 2. After Data Cleansing

isi_pengaduan
jl. hasyim ashari berlubang
menerima kunjungan sekolah.
depan perumahan mahkota ii blok a5 jalan rusak bertahun tahun. tidak ada warga baik aparat yang care
sungai cantiga ini makin dangkal, selain material yang terbawa dari hulu, pedagang disisi sungai sering buang sampah sembarangan
pemasangan rambu dilarang parkir di depan stasiun kota tangerang, smoga dpt memperlancar lalin di sekitar kawasan tsb.
assalamualaikum bapak2 ibu2, ini drainase di depan warung ayah saya, h. sadeli sepertinya mampet atau penuh kalau hujan deras air yang dari drainase masuk ke warung terima kasih

Filtering

Removing unnecessary characters is essential to reduce data volume so that accuracy and speed in the trained model are also better, so instead of removing all numbers and punctuation in the data, this is because these numbers and punctuation marks will not be used when performing data clustering.

Figure 4. Source code 2. remove numbers and punctuation

```
#Import
import nltk
import string

#Remove Number
number = re.sub(r'\d+', '', text)
#print(number)

#Remove Punctuation
translator = str.maketrans('', '', string.punctuation)
stripped = number.translate(translator)
#print(stripped)
```

After removing numbers and punctuation, the next step is to delete Stopwords. Stopwords are removed to remove functional words that do not carry information. With the removal of Stopwords, the size of the dataset is reduced and the time it takes to train the model is also faster. In addition, eliminating stopwords can also improve performance because only a few meaningful words remain, increasing clustering accuracy. The removal of stopwords is done by using the Sastrawi library for data in Indonesian.

Figure 5. Library stopwords

```
['yang', 'untuk', 'pada', 'ke', 'para', 'namun', 'menurut', 'antara', 'dia', 'dua', 'ia', 'seperti', 'jika', 'jika', 'sehingga', 'kembali', 'dan', 'tidak', 'ini', 'karena', 'kepada', 'oleh', 'saat', 'harus', 'sementara', 'setelah', 'belum', 'kami', 'sekitar', 'bagi', 'serta', 'di', 'dari', 'telah', 'sebagai', 'masih', 'hal', 'ketika', 'adalah', 'itu', 'dalam', 'bisa', 'bahwa', 'atau', 'hanya', 'kita', 'dengan', 'akan', 'juga', 'ada', 'mereka', 'sudah', 'saya', 'terhadap', 'secara', 'agar', 'lain', 'anda', 'begitu', 'mengapa', 'kenapa', 'yaitu', 'yakni', 'daripada', 'itulah', 'lagi', 'maka', 'tentang', 'demi', 'dimana', 'kemana', 'pula', 'sambil', 'sebelum', 'sesudah', 'supaya', 'guna', 'kah', 'pun', 'sampai', 'sedangkan', 'selagi', 'sementara', 'tetapi', 'apakah', 'kecuali', 'sebab', 'selain', 'seolah', 'seraya', 'seterusnya', 'tanpa', 'agak', 'boleh', 'dapat', 'dsb', 'dst', 'dll', 'dahulu', 'dulunya', 'anu', 'demikian', 'tapi', 'ingin', 'juga', 'nggak', 'mari', 'nanti', 'melainkan', 'oh', 'ok', 'seharusnya', 'sebetulnya', 'setiap', 'setidaknya', 'sesuatu', 'pasti', 'saja', 'toh', 'ya', 'walau', 'tolong', 'tentu', 'amat', 'apalagi', 'bagaimanapun']
```

Figure 6. Source code 3. remove stopwords

```
#Stopword
from Sastrawi.StopWordRemover.StopWordRemoverFactory import StopWordRemoverFactory

factory = StopWordRemoverFactory()
stopwords = factory.get_stop_words()
#print(stopwords)

factory = StopWordRemoverFactory()
stopwords = factory.create_stop_word_remover()

#Remove Stopword
stop = stopword.remove(yang)
print(stop)
```

Building Machine Learning

After going through the Stopword process, the next step to take is to build Machine Learning into 2 (two) stages, namely by building the model that will be used, namely K-means Clustering, then building a server to handle requests from GET and POST and then returning the results. Which will then send the desired request using a web service or URL to get categorized results on the web immediately. Moreover, two files will be created, namely model.py and server.py. A document called model.py will be used to develop and train the model and on server.py, it will generate code that is used to handle GET and POST requests and return results.

Building Clustering Model

In the process of making the categorization model, the K-Means Clustering method will be used to categorize the complaint data obtained from Tangerang LIVE and the results of the complaint data that have been previously processed by Text Preprocessing. K-Means Clustering is a method that is often classified as an unsupervised learning method, because of that using python will produce data that maximize similarities between classes or documents on preprocessed complaint data and minimizes similarities between classes. This file will be named model.py. The first thing to do is to do coding using the python programming language to load the complaint data in CSV format which will be used in k-means clustering processing. The author uses Jupyter Notebook to run and execute the code that will be used as the model to be built.

After loading the complaint data, the CSV format or complaint data is replaced with a list format using pandas to manipulate the matrix and data so that the complaint data is easier to process and read the data into each line in one document that makes it easier and allows to produce data similarity and categorization maximum.

Figure 7. Change to list

```
dflist = df['aduan'].tolist()
print(dflist)
```

After the replacement is made into a list, it will produce results as shown in Figure 10 showing the complaint data that has become a list.

Figure 8. Complaint list

```
['terjadi kecelakaan anak perempuan usia  tahun sebuah kendaraan bermotor menyebabkan anak tersebut lukaluka ', 'dinas terkai
t menata merelokasi pedagang kaki lima parkir kendaraan bermotor dijln irigasi kampung gunung cipondoh kedalam biar terulang
kejadian ini', 'kapan sering sekali melaporkan banyaknya pedagang kaki lima didaerah hari terjadi kecelakaan anak perempuan u
sia  tahun sebuah kendaraan bermotor dinas terkait menata merelokasi pedagang kaki lima dijln irigasi kampung gunung cipondo
h', 'lampu jalan jalan mangga  kelurahan cibodasari kecamatan cibodas satu minggu menyala  ditangani ', 'jalan kalibawah konb
lok mulai bergelombang banyak hilang banyak warga membakar sampah rumah tangga mengakibatkan polusi udara', 'ktp perubahan da
ta minimal berapa bulan pakibu jadinya kec priuk desa gebang raya', ' pak kiki wibawa camat cipondoh ', 'mau kasih saran keba
pak saatnya pedagang dijalan irigasi kampung gunung sering menyebabkan kemacetan direlokasi masuk kedalam liat lahan menampun
g didalam', 'kenapa lama sekali penerbitan ktp pnya tetangga belakangan membuat jadii kok punya smpai terbit', ' segera pohon
beralamat blokno  perumahan cipondoh makmur segera ditebang mengganggu kebersihan halaman dikhawatirkan roboh kena hujan angi
n mengenai warga bangunan warga mengenai kendaraan bawahnya ', 'parkir mobil hari ijin mobilnya pernah dipakai', 'yth bpk wal
i kota mau tanya pemutihan sertifikat rumah kec batu ceper kpnkira dpt informasi sekarang sedang kec cibodas infonya wassala
m', 'minta bantuannya jalan sawo rt rw cipadu larangan coba bersikan kekurangan tenaga alat ', 'sekitar  meter tugu selamat d
atang jln daan mogot arah jakarta lubang cukup besar  buah diameter nya  sejajar membahayakan pengendara sepeda motor terkena
l lubang', 'tolong pak tiang mau rubuh membahayakan pengguna jalan  tiang hampir jatuh harap segera diperbaiki', 'ini hampir
jatuh tiang karatan harap diperhatikan diperbaiki pak', 'saya orang tangerang asli sulit masuk kerja daerah tanah kelahiran
bantuannya pak orang asli membangun kota kelahiran kota menolak saya', 'ini bagaimana katanya sdh sering sekali tertibkan ped
agang kaki lima jalan irigasi kampung gunung irigasi sipon kenyataan banyak bukan sdh bilang tegas cepatcepat ditata kuatir m
endekati ramadhan semakin penuh ', 'ini bagaimana katanya sdh sering sekali tertibkan pedagang kaki lima jalan irigasi kampun
g gunung irigasi sipon kenyataan banyak bukan sdh bilang tegas cepatcepat ditata kuatir mendekati ramadhan semakin penuh sai
```

Before entering the process of making predictions and categorization using k-means, Sum of Squares (SSE) analysis is carried out, to determine the best number of clusters for modeling to obtain optimal results. Presentation of SSE values using the Elbow method. The Elbow method is a useful graphical tool for estimating the optimal number of K for a given task. And, the author uses as many as 20 samples, to determine the optimal cluster.

Based on the results of the Elbow method, the elbow is found at k = 5, which indicates that k = 5, or the number of clusters of 5 is the appropriate number for the data of this document.

Then, the general step is often referred to as TF-IDF. TF-IDF is a combination of TF (Term Frequency) and IDF (Inverse Document Frequency). TF-IDF is a numerical statistic that counts the number of words that appear in a document. The results of the TF-IDF process are shown in Figure 12.

Figure 9. Elbow method result

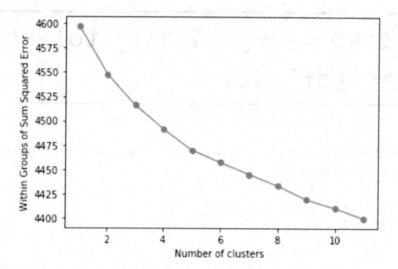

Figure 10. TF-IDF Process Result

A B	C
(0, 5218)	0.40083187440464707
(0, 9891)	0.17772598064824485
(0, 6105)	0.24904419642810274
(0, 1057)	0.2910097476513959
(0, 4358)	0.2313145234326555
(0, 8626)	0.30281816207368584
(0, 9429)	0.1944896258565943
(0, 10391)	0.3319460559165461
(0, 7547)	0.31510448744966923
(0, 266)	0.39580638746161934
(0, 4103)	0.264788721207724
(0, 9800)	0.20433147427432752
(1, 3446)	0.16035572679767307
(1, 4165)	0.24552282720801494
(1, 9950)	0.34960843862327606
(1, 1196)	0.2326089676380651
(1, 4134)	0.2794903677501063
(1, 1622)	0.16005219553161398
(1, 3121)	0.17327804926924248
(1, 3937)	0.16096946864110093
(1, 3512)	0.160508321252131
(1, 2121)	0.2680998444711118
(1, 6934)	0.2035750205899933
(1, 5117)	0.17145217094455897

After getting the numerical value from TF-IDF, the K-Means algorithm is analyzed or it can be called by determining the number of categories that will be used for labeling analysis later. This research will divide the number of categories and predictions into 5 parts. Then it provides a new document to the categorization or grouping algorithm and predicts the class for the received complaint data column.

Figure 11. Vectorizer result

```
n': 4358, 'bermotor': 1857, 'menyebabkan': 6185, 'tersebut': 9891, 'lukaluka': 5218, 'dinas': 2264, 'terkait': 9813, 'menat
a': 5731, 'merelokasi': 6165, 'pedagang': 7814, 'kaki': 3887, 'lima': 5117, 'parkir': 6934, 'dijln': 2121, 'irigasi': 3512,
'kampung': 3937, 'gunung': 3121, 'cipondoh': 1622, 'kedalam': 4134, 'biar': 1196, 'terulang': 9958, 'kejadian': 4165, 'ini':
3446, 'kapan': 3963, 'sering': 8936, 'sekali': 8705, 'melaporkan': 5582, 'banyaknya': 674, 'didaerah': 2036, 'hari': 3194, 'l
ampu': 4962, 'jalan': 3595, 'mangga': 5345, 'kelurahan': 4291, 'cibodasari': 1592, 'kecamatan': 4088, 'cibodas': 1591, 'sat
u': 8520, 'minggu': 6239, 'menyala': 6088, 'ditangani': 2507, 'kalibawah': 3904, 'konblok': 4665, 'mulai': 6365, 'bergelomban
g': 942, 'banyak': 673, 'hilang': 3265, 'warga': 10487, 'membakar': 5572, 'sampah': 8451, 'rumah': 8351, 'tangga': 9525, 'men
gakibatkan': 5827, 'polusi': 7877, 'udara': 18285, 'ktp': 4808, 'perubahan': 7787, 'data': 1782, 'minimal': 6246, 'berapa': 8
74, 'bulan': 1468, 'pakibu': 6847, 'jadinya': 3570, 'kec': 4085, 'priuk': 7969, 'desa': 1856, 'gebang': 2984, 'raya': 8171,
'pak': 6838, 'kiki': 4566, 'wibawa': 18535, 'camat': 1521, 'mau': 5444, 'kasih': 4010, 'saran': 8492, 'kebapak': 4058, 'saatn
ya': 8384, 'dijalan': 2111, 'kemacetan': 4299, 'direlokasi': 2388, 'masuk': 5406, 'list': 5101, 'lahan': 4905, 'menampung': 5
713, 'didalam': 2041, 'kenapa': 4550, 'lama': 4946, 'penerbitan': 7282, 'pnya': 7850, 'tetangga': 9963, 'belakangan': 808, 'm
embuat': 5621, 'jadii': 3565, 'kok': 4643, 'punya': 8065, 'smpai': 9166, 'terbit': 9724, 'segera': 8667, 'pohon': 7851, 'bere
lemat': 862, 'blokno': 1307, 'perumahan': 7711, 'makmur': 5291, 'ditebang': 2523, 'mengganggu': 5907, 'kebersihan': 4069, 'ha
laman': 3154, 'dikhawatirkan': 2161, 'roboh': 8298, 'kena': 4342, 'hujan': 3321, 'angin': 305, 'mengenai': 5890, 'bangunan':
638, 'bawahnya': 736, 'mobil': 6299, 'ijin': 3369, 'mobilnya': 6303, 'pernah': 7638, 'dipakai': 2287, 'yth': 10634, 'bpk': 13
84, 'wali': 18474, 'kota': 4734, 'tanya': 9559, 'pemutihan': 7204, 'sertifikat': 8946, 'batu': 721, 'ceper': 1568, 'kpnkira':
4765, 'dpt': 2657, 'informasi': 3435, 'sekarang': 8717, 'sedang': 8638, 'infonya': 3434, 'wassalam': 18511, 'minta': 6253, 'b
antuannya': 664, 'sawo': 8532, 'rt': 8323, 'rw': 8376, 'cipadu': 1617, 'larangan': 5010, 'coba': 1655, 'bersikan': 1108, 'kek
urangan': 4195, 'tenaga': 9660, 'alat': 182, 'sekitar': 8738, 'meter': 6195, 'tugu': 18226, 'selamat': 8778, 'datang': 1785,
```

The results of the vectorizer shown in Figure 13 explains that:

- Column A is the index of the indicated sentence, in this example the sentence index is 0, as shown in Figure 13.

Figure 12. Example of sentece index

```
In [9]:  dflist[0]

Out[9]:  'terjadi kecelakaan anak perempuan usia  tahun sebuah kendaraan bermotor menyebabkan anak tersebut lukaluka '
```

- Column B is a word index or ID for each word that has been automatically generated by the vectorizer. For example in Figure 13, the word "lukaluka" gets the number 5218 as the word index.
- Column C is the word probability that appears in one document. If the probability number is greater, then the word is more unique in the document and if the probability number is smaller, then the word often appears in one document. For example, for the word "lukaluka" which has a probability number of 0.4003187440464707, it shows that the word "lukaluka" is a unique word.

Then, the results of the k-means model that have been categorized and whose class has been predicted will be saved in SAV format using the pickle library which will later be used to call the model that has been built and created on the server which will display the results on the web. After creating the code that will provide Prediction results, a code that uses pickle is made to store the vectorizer and predictions on disk.

The pickle is used to serialize and deserialize the Python object structure, which python will then convert to a stream of bytes. The dump() method dumps the object to the file specified in the arguments. Figure 15 shows the results of grouping and prediction using K-Means Clustering using the python programming language. And in Figure 18, illustrates the results of the clustering model in the form of a scatter plot graph, which shows the results of the clusters of each complaint and shows that each cluster has similarities that are close to each other.

Figure 13. Source code 6. K-means clustering

```
#Clustering K-Means
from sklearn.feature_extraction.text import TfidfVectorizer
from sklearn.cluster import KMeans
from sklearn.metrics import adjusted_rand_score
import pickle


vectorizer = TfidfVectorizer()
X = vectorizer.fit_transform(dflist)


true_k = 5
model = KMeans(n_clusters = true_k, init = 'k-means++', max_iter = 100, n_init = 1)
model.fit(X)
```

Figure 14. Source code 7. saving the model and vectorizer and making predictions

	aduan	Prediction
0	terjadi kecelakaan anak perempuan usia tahun sebuah kendaraan bermotor menyebabkan anak tersebut lukaluka	[0]
1	dinas terkait menata merelokasi pedagang kaki lima parkir kendaraan bermotor dijln irigasi kampung gunung cipondoh kedalam	[3]
2	kapan sering sekali melaporkan banyaknya pedagang kaki lima didaerah hari terjadi kecelakaan anak perempuan usia tahun set	[3]
3	lampu jalan jalan mangga kelurahan cibodasari kecamatan cibodas satu minggu menyala ditangani	[1]
4	jalan kalibawah konblok mulai bergelombang banyak hilang banyak warga membakar sampah rumah tangga mengakibatkan pol	[0]
5	ktp perubahan data minimal berapa bulan pakibu jadinya kec priuk desa gebang raya	[2]
6	pak kiki wibawa camat cipondoh	[0]
7	mau kasih saran kebapak saatnya pedagang dijalan irigasi kampung gunung sering menyebabkan kemacetan direlokasi masuk ke	[3]
8	kenapa lama sekali penerbitan ktp pnya tetangga belakangan membuat jadii kok punya smpai terbit	[2]
9	segera pohon beralamat blokno perumahan cipondoh makmur segera ditebang mengganggu kebersihan halaman dikhawatirka	[0]
10	parkir mobil hari ijin mobilnya pernah dipakai	[0]
11	yth bpk wali kota mau tanya pemutihan sertifikat rumah kec batu ceper kpnkira dpt informasi sekarang sedang kec cibodas infor	[0]
12	minta bantuannya jalan sawo rt rw cipadu larangan coba bersikan kekurangan tenaga alat	[0]
13	sekitar meter tugu selamat datang jln daan mogot arah jakarta lubang cukup besar buah diameter nya sejajar membahayakan	[0]
14	tolong pak tiang mau rubuh membahayakan pengguna jalan tiang hampir jatuh harap segera diperbaiki	[0]
15	ini hampir jatuh tiang karatan harap diperhatikan diperbaiki pak	[0]
16	saya orang tangerang asli sulit masuk kerja daerah tanah kelahiran bantuannya pak orang asli membangun kota kelahiran kota	[0]
17	ini bagaimana katanya sdh sering sekali tertibkan pedagang kaki lima jalan irigasi kampung gunung irigasi sipon kenyataan banya	[3]

Building Server Model

After building a model that will be used as a reference for categorizing the complaint data, the next step that must be done is to create a server.py file, which is to build a server that will be used to handle GET and POST requests. There are two methods to request a response from the server, namely GET and POST. GET is used to request (request) data from the server and POST is used to send data to the server. The server to be built will use both methods to produce results on the web. To run this server, the flask library is also used as a web framework that will handle the existing methods.

Server development begins by importing the methods and libraries that will be used, in this case numpy, flask, request and jsonify. Then, create an instance of Flask() and load the previously created model into the model. To load the previously created SAV model, the pickle.load() method is used which loads the method and saves the deserialization byte into the model. Next, we will bind /api with the predict() method. Where the prediction method will get data from the flask request object that contains the URL request attribute and uses the args attribute. The args attribute is a dictionary containing the arguments from the URL. To get data that will be executed later, the get() method is used which will retrieve items from an existing dictionary or return a standard value.

Figure 15. K-means clustering and prediction results

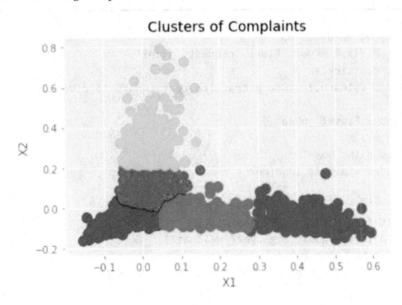

Figure 16. Scatter plot K-means clustering result. X1 describes cost function, X2 describes number of cluster

```
#Save the Model to Disk
filename = 'C:/Users/TINAPurbawati/Downloads/IBM/Binus/Susunan Skripsi/final_model_ok.sav'
pickle.dump(model, open(filename, 'wb'))

print("\n")

df['Prediction'] = df.apply(lambda x:model.predict(vectorizer.transform([x.aduan])), axis = 1)
pickle.dump(vectorizer, open('vectorizer.pickle', 'wb'))

df.to_csv(r'C:/Users/TINAPurbawati/Downloads/IBM/Binus/Susunan Skripsi/finalizedclustering_ok.sav')
```

Then, the predict_class class is created to label the predictions that have been obtained in the previous model creation. Before starting to create the predict_class class, load the vectorizer.pickle model that has been created so that the server reads the prediction results that have been made on model.py. After loading the vectorizer model, the predict_class class will contain an If-Else Statement that is used to label complaints that have been categorized into predictions and have been divided into 5 parts where for cluster 0 it is called "Fasilitas Negara" or State Facility, for cluster 1 it is called "PJU" or what can be referred to as Penerangan Jalan Umum or Public Street Lighting, for cluster 2 it is called "Dokumen Identitas WNI" or WNI Identity Documents, for cluster 3 it is called "PKL" or commonly referred to as Pedagang Kaki Lima or Street Vendors, and the last one for cluster 4 is called "PAM" or commonly called Perusahaan Air Minum or Drinking Water Company and returns the predicted variable to display the results later on the web.

Figure 17. Source code 8. create server

```
#Import Libaries
import numpy as np
from flask import Flask, request, jsonify
import pickle
from sklearn.feature_extraction.text import TfidfVectorizer

app = Flask(__name__)

#Load the Model
model = pickle.load(open('final_model_ok.sav', 'rb'))

@app.route('/api', methods = ['GET', 'POST'])
def predict():
    data = request.args.get('kalimat')
    #data = request.get_json(force = True)
    vectorizer = pickle.load(open('vectorizer.pickle', 'rb'))
```

Figure 18. Source code 9. prediction class

```
def predict_class(Prediction):
#get data from POST request
#data = request.get_json(force = True)
    if(Prediction == 0):
        predict = 'Fasilitas Negara'
    elif(Prediction == 1):
        predict = 'PJU'
    elif(Prediction == 2):
        predict = 'Dokumen Identitas WNI'
    elif(Prediction == 3):
        predict = 'PKL'
    else:
        predict = 'PAM'

    return(predict)
```

Next, a prediction is made which contains the model.predict() method which takes input from the vectorizer function which will call the data that takes the complaint item. The result of the model.predict() method will be stored in a variable named output and return this variable after converting into a json object using the flask jsonify() method.

After that, the server will be run using port 5000 and set debug=True because if there is an error can immediately debug and solve it. The server can accept requests.

Figure 19. Source code 10. create prediction dan set the port

```
ⓘ  127.0.0.1:5000/api?kalimat=dinas%20terkait%20menata%20merelokasi%20pedagang%20kaki%20lima
```

Running the Server and Receiving the Request

After the code for model.py and server.py has been built and the server is ready to accept requests, the next step is to try to request requests from the server for the prediction of sentences to be received.

This study uses a browser or web services to display the results of the complaint data received. To call server.py, run the server with Command Prompt or cmd. Then, to run server.py, you must enter the directory where the previously created SAV and pickle models are located.

Once python server.py is run it will start debugging, indicating that the Debugger is up and running on the browser shown on the cmd page.

On the sentence in cmd which indicates that server.py is already running on the pre-defined port. Next, the indicated URL and open the existing software browser.

Figure 20. Copying and entering complaints on the server

```
#Make prediction using model loaded from disk as per the data.
#prediction = model.predict([np.array(data['kalimant'])])
prediction = model.predict(vectorizer.transform([data]))

#print(prediction)
output = predict_class(prediction)
#output = prediction[0]
#return(predict_class)

return jsonify(output)

if __name__ == '__main__':
    app.run(port = 5000, debut = True)
```

After copying the URL in cmd, you must add the previously created /api on server.py, namely @app. route which is used to create a relationship between the URLs given as arguments and functions and in this study the /api decorator into the function that means that when the web browser requests the URL /

api, Flask will call this function and pass the return back to the browser in response.Running a URL that has been filled in by additional pre-existing complaint sentences, will produce results indicating if the previously received complaint data will enter the existing prediction group or cluster. In this case, because the data taken from the received complaint contains the sentence "Pedagang Kaki Lima", the prediction results that have been carried out indicate that the existing data belongs to the "PKL" group or cluster.

Figure 21. Prediction results of existing complaint data categories

Complaint Priority Analysis Results

From the results of clustering and predictions that have been made, the authors get the category with the most complaint data received in the LAKSA feature in the Tangerang LIVE application. Based on the results obtained, the category that has the most data on complaints is "Fasilitas Negara" or State Facility with a total of 3,415 complaints.

Then, the category that has the second most complaint data is the "PKL" complaint or commonly referred to as the Pedagang Kaki Lima or Street Vendors with 333 complaints.

The category that has the third most complaint data is "PAM" or commonly referred to as Perusahaan Air Minum or Drinking Water Company with 317 complaints.

The fourth most complaint data is "PJU" which is commonly called Penerangan Jalan Umum or Public Street Lighting with 301 complaints. And the category with the fewest complaints was "Dokumen Identitas WNI" with 290 complaints.

CONCLUSION

Tangerang City is one of the cities that applies the concept of e-Government in an application called Tangerang LIVE. The application has a feature called LAKSA which is used to receive complaints, complaints, suggestions, criticisms, and feedback from the people of Tangerang City. By using the data obtained from the LAKSA feature, this study uses the Clustering technique to determine the class prediction for each complaint data that has been received and will then be labeled so that the complaint belongs to a more specific group. The results of the predictions will be displayed in the browser using web services. From the evaluation results that have been obtained, there are several conclusions which are explained as follows:

1.   E-complaint makes it easier for the government to accommodate data on public complaints so that the government can be responsive in dealing with the problems that most often occur in the community

2. The number of kinds of complaints that are included in the LAKSA feature makes the government know which categories should be prioritized.
3. By using Data and Text Mining techniques, the government can find out which problems in which category must be addressed first.
4. From the results of the clustering model that has been built, there are five categories of complaint data classes, namely State Facilities, PJU, Indonesian Citizen Identity Documents, PKL, and PAM.
5. From the results of research based on the K-Means Clustering method, it can be concluded that the most complaints are in the "Fasilitas Negara" or State Facility category with a total of 3415 complaint data.
6. This indicates that the problems with the highest level of concern in the community are problems related to state facilities such as congestion, damaged roads, and others.
7. The second most problematic category is "PKL," or street vendors, which means that many people feel disturbed or have problems with the existence of street vendors.
8. For the third category, the most is the "PAM" category, which means that there are still many problems related to water problems, such as cloudy PAM water or irrigation problems. These three categories are the categories with the most complaints, so that their handling must be prioritized and resolved.

Further research can be done using supervised learning methods such as classification as a comparison of the results analyzed in this study so that it can be seen which method of use provides more accurate and efficient results. In addition, the algorithm relies heavily on good text-preprocessing. The text-preprocessing stage, which consists of case-folding, simple normalization, tokenization, stemming, filter stopwords, and manual data cleaning, can improve the accuracy of data classification.

REFERENCES

Alkraiji, A. I. (2020). Citizen Satisfaction with Mandatory E-Government Services: A Conceptual Framework and an Empirical Validation. *IEEE Access: Practical Innovations, Open Solutions, 8,* 117253–117265. doi:10.1109/ACCESS.2020.3004541

Anindra, F., Supangkat, S. H., & Kosala, R. R. (2018). Smart Governance as Smart City Critical Success Factor (Case in 15 Cities in Indonesia). *Proceeding - 2018 International Conference on ICT for Smart Society: Innovation Toward Smart Society and Society 5.0, ICISS 2018,* 1–6. 10.1109/ICTSS.2018.8549923

Antoni, D., Bidar, A., Herdiansyah, M. I., & Akbar, M. (2017). Critical factors of transparency and trust for evaluating e-government services for the poor. *2017 Second International Conference on Informatics and Computing (ICIC),* 1–6. 10.1109/IAC.2017.8280612

Darmawan, A. K., Siahaan, D. O., Susanto, T. D., Umam, B. A., & Bakir, B. (2020). Exploring Factors Influencing Smart Sustainable City Adoption using E-Government Services Effectiveness Evaluation Framework (E-GEEF). *2020 3rd International Conference on Information and Communications Technology (ICOIACT),* 234–239. 10.1109/ICOIACT50329.2020.9332140

Durachman, Y., Harahap, D., Rodoni, A., Faisal Bakti, A. M., & Mansoer, M. (2020). Analysis of Factors That Affect The Quality of E-Government Services: A Case Study in Ombudsman of the Republic of Indonesia. *2020 8th International Conference on Cyber and IT Service Management (CITSM)*, 1–7. 10.1109/CITSM50537.2020.9268796

Elkheshin, S., & Saleeb, N. (2017). A conceptual model for E-government adoption in Egypt. *Proceedings of 2016 11th International Conference on Computer Engineering and Systems, ICCES 2016*, 254–259. 10.1109/ICCES.2016.7822010

Febriliantina, R., & Ristekawati, S. F. (2016). The Study of e-Government Implementation in Improving the Quality of Public Services. *2016 International Conference on ICT For Smart Society, July*, 105–110.

Fitriani, W. R., Handoyo, I. T., Rahayu, P., & Sensuse, D. I. (2017). Intention to use smart city system based on social cognitive theory. *2016 International Conference on Advanced Computer Science and Information Systems, ICACSIS 2016*, 181–188. 10.1109/ICACSIS.2016.7872747

Ismail, A. (2016). Utilizing big data analytics as a solution for smart cities. *2016 3rd MEC International Conference on Big Data and Smart City (ICBDSC)*, 1–5. 10.1109/ICBDSC.2016.7460348

Kodinariya, T. M., & Makwana, P. R. (2013). Review on determining number of Cluster in K-Means Clustering. *International Journal of Advance Research in Computer Science and Management Studies*, *1*(6), 90–95.

Lytras, M. D., & Şerban, A. C. (2020). E-Government Insights to Smart Cities Research: European Union (EU) Study and the Role of Regulations. *IEEE Access: Practical Innovations, Open Solutions*, 8, 65313–65326. doi:10.1109/ACCESS.2020.2982737

Madyatmadja, E. D., Nindito, H., Verasius, A., Sano, D., & Sianipar, C. P. M. (2010). *Data Visualization of Priority Region Based On Community Complaints in Government*. Academic Press.

Madyatmadja, E. D., Olivia, J., & Sunaryo, R. F. (2019). *Priority Analysis Of Community Complaints Through E-Government Based On Social Media*. Academic Press.

Meiyanti, R., Misbah, M., Napitupulu, D., Kunthi, R., Nastiti, T. I., Sensuse, D. I., & Sucahyo, Y. G. (2018). Systematic review of critical success factors of E-government: Definition and realization. *Proceedings - 2017 International Conference on Sustainable Information Engineering and Technology, SIET 2017*, 190–195. 10.1109/SIET.2017.8304133

Meiyanti, R., Utomo, B., Sensuse, D. I., & Wahyuni, R. (2019). E-Government Challenges in Developing Countries: A Literature Review. *2018 6th International Conference on Cyber and IT Service Management, CITSM 2018*, 1–6. 10.1109/CITSM.2018.8674245

Razaghi, M., & Finger, M. (2018). Smart Governance for Smart Cities. *Proceedings of the IEEE*, *106*(4), 680–689. doi:10.1109/JPROC.2018.2807784

Sari, A. M., Hidayanto, A. N., Purwandari, B., Budi, N. F. A., & Kosandi, M. (2018). Challenges and issues of E-participation implementation: A case study of e-complaint Indonesia. *Proceedings of the 3rd International Conference on Informatics and Computing, ICIC 2018*, 1–6. 10.1109/IAC.2018.8780467

Sarker, M. N. I., Khatun, M. N., Alam, G. M. M., & Islam, M. S. (2020). Big Data Driven Smart City: Way to Smart City Governance. *2020 International Conference on Computing and Information Technology (ICCIT-1441)*, 1–8. 10.1109/ICCIT-144147971.2020.9213795

Sunassee, K., Vythilingum, T., & Sungkur, R. K. (2017). Providing improved services to citizens, a critical review of E-government facilities. *2017 1st International Conference on Next Generation Computing Applications (NextComp)*, 129–134. 10.1109/NEXTCOMP.2017.8016187

Tan, A.-H. (1999). Text mining: The state of the art and the challenges. *Proceedings of the Pakdd 1999 Workshop on Knowledge Disocovery from Advanced Databases*, 8, 65–70.

Tutorial: How to determine the optimal number of clusters for k-means clustering. (n.d.). Retrieved January 14, 2022, from https://blog.cambridgespark.com/how-to-determine-the-optimal-number-of-clusters-for-k-means-clustering-14f27070048f

Wahyu Sulistya, A. Q., Bastian Sulistiyo, B., Aditya, F., Aritonang, I. D., Amos Simangunsong, S., Shihab, M. R., & Ranti, B. (2019). A case study of Indonesian government digital transformation: Improving public service quality through E-government implementation. *Proceedings - 2019 5th International Conference on Science and Technology, ICST 2019*. 10.1109/ICST47872.2019.9166234

Chapter 9
Performance Measurement of Natural Dialog System by Analyzing the Conversation

Neelam Pramod Naik

SVKM's Usha Pravin Gandhi College of Arts, Science, and Commerce, India

ABSTRACT

The natural dialog system, Chatbot, plays an important role in business domains by properly answering customer queries. In the pattern matching approach of Chatbot development, the user input is matched with a predefined set of responses. The machine learning approach of Chatbot development uses the principles of natural language processing to learn from conversational content. This study focuses on the performance measurement of pattern-based and machine learning-based Chatbot systems. As per the user point of view, performance measurement parameters are the ability to answer quickly, accurately, and comprehensively; to understand questions clearly; user friendliness; personalization options; ethics followed; and ability to process user feedback. The comprehensiveness of the knowledge base, robustness to handle unexpected input, scalability, and interoperability are some of the parameters considered to evaluate the Chatbot system by expert point of view. In this study, the specially designed Chatbot Usability Questionnaire is used to measure the performance of the implemented Chatbot systems.

INTRODUCTION

One of the forms of natural dialog system between human and computer is a Chatbot. It is a software program that interacts with human being using natural language. Chatbots understands and responds intelligently to the user inputs. Even though natural dialog system, in terms of Chatbot is existed for a long time, its performance is improving day by day because of availability of data to be added to the knowledge base, better computing power and available open-source development platforms. Thus, it is seeking attention of business developers for its widespread implementation to improve the business. (Vijayaraghavan V. et al, 2020)

DOI: 10.4018/978-1-7998-9121-5.ch009

Chatbots are acquiring tremendous demand in the business domain as it reduces human efforts required to fulfill client services. Chatbots are available in various forms in social media forums and customer care platforms. The way customer communicates with the product manufacturer changed drastically after the evolution of artificial intelligence technology since 2016. Through social media platforms, many brands and services are publicized using Chatbot as messaging platform. Intelligent natural dialog system such as Chatbot is designed to imitate the act of the human expert while answering the queries raised by the user specific to that domain. The performance of the Chatbot is measured in terms of the quality of the answer more similar to the answer given by actual human expert. So, to achieve the smooth functioning of the system, it is necessary to test the Chatbot for its operations and interactions in a desirable manner. There is a need of comprehensive method that will focus on the assessment of the performance of the Chatbot system for its functionality based on user point of view and developer point of view. The success of Chatbot imitating human being, greatly depends on how much successfully and correctly Chatbot examines the query asked and generates appropriate response. Various quality attributes and assessment frameworks provide methods to measure Chatbot performance. The absolute list of quality attributes for evaluating Chatbots is not comprehensive. Again, the proper assessment of vast majority of quality attributes is difficult, time intensive and expensive also.

The present study concentrates on researching and implementing the comprehensive quality metrics which will quantify Chatbot performance. This will help in faster prototyping and testing of new Chatbot systems.

BACKGROUND

To decide the parameters to measure performance of the Chatbot system, it is equally necessary to understand categorization of Chatbot systems based on the range of knowledge access, primary goal of designing the Chatbot, method of response generation, dependency on human help and channels of communication. The Chatbot development approaches and its architecture, also decide the various parameters those can be considered for the performance measurement.

Categories of Chatbots

Various criteria are used for the categorization of the Chatbot. Single Chatbot may belong to more than one of these sub categories. Depending on the range of knowledge access, Chatbot is categorized as Open domain or closed domain. The open domain Chatbot responds to question in any domain, while closed domain Chatbot focuses on particular domain knowledge. The Chatbot which helps in railway reservation system is an example of closed domain. It particularly answers the questions about railway enquiry and the reservation of the tickets. (K. Nimavat et.al, 2017)

The primary goal of Chatbot categorizes it as informative, chat-based or task-based. In the informative Chatbot, the information is already stored or the information is made available from the fixed source. The information is retrieved by firing query on a database, or by performing string matching on already stored knowledge base. Mostly the static sources of the information are informative in nature. The example of such Chatbot is Frequently asked questions (FAQ) based Chatbot. The chat-based Chatbot converse with the user as another human being is conversing with the user. The techniques used by such Chatbot to continue the conversation are deference, evasion and cross questioning. Various algorithms for information retrieval, named entity extraction and relevance detection are used in chat-based Chatbots. Siri, Alexa are the examples of chat-based Chatbots. The task-based Chatbots are designed to perform conversation related to a particular task only. The actions needed to perform the task are hardcoded. The procedure to handle exceptional situation is also well defined. Such Chatbot is task specific. It is also intelligent enough to understand user's input related to that domain and also able to answer the user query smartly. Chatbot developed for the railway reservation system is considered as an example of task-based Chatbot. (K. Nimavat et.al, 2017)

According to the response generative method, Chatbot may be of Rule-based, Retrieval-based or Generative in nature. The rule based Chatbot development approach is based on the specified template. It maps the sentences with the patterns in collected input database. ELIZA, created by Weizenbaum in 1966 and PARRY, created by Colby in 1975 are the examples of rule-based Chatbots (Prissadang Suta et. al., 2020). The retrieval-based Chatbot is trained to give the best possible response from the database of predefined responses. On the basis of large amount of conversational training data, the generative Chatbot can generate new dialogue.

Depending on the intermediary human help requirement during the conversation, Chatbots are categorized as Human-aided or Autonomous. The fully autonomous Chatbot learns the new knowledge by itself. In case of human-aided Chatbot, the actual user of the system, such as full-time employee, or freelancer, can embody their actual live experience of the system, in the Chatbot system. Thus, the gaps in fully automated Chatbot systems are fulfilled by human intervention. (Adamopoulou E., 2020)

The communication channel creates Chatbot categories as Text-based or Voice-based Chatbots. The text-based messenger Chatbots exists on one or more messenger platforms. These messaging platforms are Short Message Service (SMS) based or web-based. The interaction of Chatbot with the user is through text or through button clicks. In voice-based Chatbots, it converses with the user using voice in natural language. The techniques used by voice-enabled Chatbot to response back is either text-to-speech conversion, using pre-recorded messages or using the mixture of both the techniques.

Chatbot Development Approaches

Depending on the techniques and algorithms adopted, there are two main approaches used for the development of a Chatbot. In pattern matching approach, rule-based Chatbot maps the user input with the rule patterns, selects an already defined answer from the set of already existing responses. The advantage of this approach is less response time and non-requirement of in-depth semantic and syntactic examination of the input text. The shortcoming of this approach is that the answers are repeated, automated and lack in spontaneity and originality. In the machine learning approach, Chatbot extracts user input using Natural Language Processing (NLP). It develops the ability to learn from conversations. The predefined responses are not used, instead it considers the whole dialog context to answer the query of the user.

Pattern Matching Approach

In case of pattern matching Chatbots, user input is matched with the pre-defined patterns. Using pattern matching algorithms, it chooses predefined answer from a collection of responses. ELIZA and Artificial Linguistic Internet Computer Entity (ALICE) are two famous Chatbots which are based on pattern matching approach. (Marietto et al., 2013). Some of the other Chatbots based on the pattern-matching approach are Chatterbot, Therapist III, PARRY, CONVERSE, HeX, and Jabberwacky. (Bradeško & Mladenić, 2012; Masche & Le, 2018)

As the knowledge is written in the form of already set conversational rules, in pattern-based Chatbots, the new answers are not created. The Chatbot answers user's questions satisfactorily if the rule database is exhaustive in nature. The limitation of such system is lack of rectification of grammatical and syntactical errors. Watson, Chatfuel and Cleverbot are the examples of rule-based Chatbots. (Ramesh, Ravishankaran, Joshi, & Chandrasekaran, 2017).

Pattern-based Chatbot is involved in a single-turn communication. The last response of the user is considered as a question for finding the related answer. In humanlike Chatbot, there is a multi-turn answer selection. Every response is considered as feedback to decide the answer which will be most appropriate for the entire context. (Wu, Wu, Xing, Zhou, & Li, 2016). The limitation of the pattern-based approach is that the answers are automated and repeated. Further, such answers do not have spontaneity of the actual human response. (Ramesh et al., 2017). The advantage of pattern-based Chatbot is that, it has very less response time as it does not perform, semantic and syntactical examination of the inputted text. (Jia, 2009).

Most Common Pattern-Based Chatbots Languages

The most commonly used pattern-based Chatbot languages are AIML, RiveScript and ChatScript.

Artificial Intelligence Markup Language (AIML)

The development in AIML, took place since year 1995 (Marietto et al., 2013). The pattern matching was possible through the building of the knowledge base. AIML is an Extensible Markup Language (XML) -based open-source language. For the world-famous Chabot ALICE, the knowledge base was built using AIML. AIML is the mostly used Chabot building language as it supports easy learning, easy execution of the code and versatile usability. There are pre-authored AIML collections available which provide the facility of reusability. (Arsovski, Muniru, & Cheok, 2017) Data objects in AIML consists of topics. Topics include relevant categories. Category is nothing but the rule of AIML. The rule has a pattern to represent user's input. Rule has template to describe the response of the Chatbot. The wildcard symbols, words and spaces can be included in the pattern. The object Graphmaster is used to store categories. This object has tree like structure. The internal nodes represent categories while the leaves represent template and it is actual response of the Chatbot. The depth first search algorithm is used to find the Chatbot's response in pattern matching technique. (Wallace, 2009). It is possible to improve the responses of the Chatbot by updating the value of variables during runtime. Many pattern matching languages like AIML, are combined together with Latent Semantic Analysis (LSA) technique. In such case, AIML answers the questions based on specific template while LSA produces responses for the questions which are not answered by LSA. (Nt, 2016).

RiveScript

RiveScript is a line-based scripting language, developed in year 2009. This language is used to build knowledge base in rule based Chatbots. It is open-source scripting language and it is compatible with Python and Java. In this language, symbol '+' is used to indicate user input and symbol '–' describes the Chatbot response. The interpreter is responsible for matching user input with stored responses. Interpreter also selects the most suitable response to the user input. This language supports wildcards and conversational redirects. (Gupta, Borkar, Mello, & Patil, 2015).

ChatScript

Released in 2011, ChatScript is an open-source scripting language. It is an expert system, which is used for the development of rule-based Chatbots. It is based on the principle of pattern matching. The tagger and parser in the system analyzes the user input and improves the semantics, syntax and grammar of the user input. (Wilcox & Wilcox, 2014). It uses the collections of similar words related to the other parts of the speech. The developer can use the existing database of concepts. It is case sensitive scripting language, and using lower case or upper case used by the user, it determines the emotions of the user. It has short term as well as long term memory. User information along with conjunctions and conditionals, responses are generated. (Ramesh et al., 2017). Suzette, Rosette, Chip Vivant, and Mistsuku are the Chatbots developed using ChatScript language. (Bradeško & Mladenić, 2012).

Comparative Analysis of Pattern Matching Languages

There are pros and cons of each and every scripting language used for the pattern matching based Chatbot development. The pros of AIML are that, while creating the content, AIML is straightforward and easy. But, while creating the large knowledge base using the AIML, the chatbot developer has to manually enter the knowledge in the Chatbot program. (Arsovski et al., 2017). The main limitation of AIML is that the chatbot developer has to write pattern for each and every possible query of the user. The quick and accurate response from the Chatbot depends only on the how accurately developer understands and implements the possible user queries in the knowledge base. The knowledge is stored in a file. So, as the knowledge base grows the file becomes bulky and difficult to maintain. AIML works on the principle of word matching rule-based system. So, the system will be either able to answer a fully contained pattern of words or answer according to the input word pattern. Thus, the system is highly inefficient. (Trivedi, Gor, & Thakkar, 2019). Again, if the knowledge is created using the webpage on the internet, then, it is mandatory to update the knowledge base manually. The automatic updating of the knowledge base content is not possible with AIML. RiveScript is efficient than AIML, as it has many built-in features and a greater number of tags than AIML. It uses the concept of inheritance in its topics. The additional configuration file is not required in case of RiveScript. To avoid the overhead in matching pattern, in AIML, user input is first converted into lower case. But this degrades the emotional flavors attached to the words when user uses upper case letters to express his or her emotions. The ChatScript overcomes these limitations. ChatScripts scripts are case sensitive. But at the same time, ChatScript is more complicated than AIML and RiveScript, as it involves parsed line-delimitations. ChatScript script is meaning based hence it is also used to manipulate human language.

Machine Learning Approach

Natural Language Processing (NLP) principles are used in case of Machine learning based Chatbot development. NLP principles are used to find patterns from the user input as it has ability to learn from the content generated through the conversation. Not only the current turn dialog is used for the interpretation of the user input but, the overall dialog context is also considered. The predefined question and answer patterns are not required here. The extensive training set is required for the learning process. The domain specific datasets are used for training purpose. In retrieval-based Chatbot development, neural network is used to assign scores to most likely responses from the pool of responses. In generative models based on machine learning uses the concept of deep learning to generate the response.

Natural Language Processing

As the part of Artificial Intelligence field, NLP looks into the interpreting and controlling the natural language text or speech. (Khurana, Koli, Khatter, & Singh, 2017). NLP algorithms are based on machine learning techniques. The process of natural language understanding includes understand the text and generate the natural language text. (Langner, Vogel, & Black, 2010; Perera & Nand, 2017)

Artificial Neural Network

Retrieval-based and generative-based Chatbots are based on Artificial Neural Network. The vector representation of input text is created. The word embedding process that is mapping the words into vector is done using deep learning techniques like Word2vec (Mikolov, Sutskever, Chen, Corrado, & Dean, 2013)

There are three steps of chatbot operations. These steps are understanding natural language input, producing relevant and automatic response, and constructing fluent and realistic natural language response. The improvements in the natural language processing capabilities of the chatbot can also improve its ability to understand context and content of user input and thus providing relevant response. (Prissadang Suta et. al., 2020)

Sample Case Study of Machine Learning Based Chatbot

International Business Machines (IBM) created a Watson chatbot in 2011. It is developed in IBM's DeepQA project. It is in the form of question-answering computer system and capable of giving answers to questions asked in natural language. This system was initially designed to answer questions in Jeopardy quiz show. Watson chatbot was able to win first place prize of one million dollar against quiz champions Brad Rutter and Ken Jennings. Watson's question answering computing system uses automated reasoning, knowledge representation, natural language processing, information retrieval and machine learning techniques. IBM's DeepQA software and Apache Unstructured Information Management Architecture (UIMA) are used for framework implementation. This system gathers data from dictionaries, newswire articles, literature and encyclopedias. it also uses databases, taxonomies and ontologies such as DBPedia, WordNet and Yago. Watson's question answering computing system parses questions into various sentence fragments and keywords. This system executes multiple languages analysis algorithms simultaneously. The possibility of the correct answer depends on the ability of finding same answer from most of the algorithms. The system generates a small number of potential solutions. This solution is verified against the existing entries in the supporting databases. (Ferrucci, David; et al., 2020)

The changes are made to Watson system to make it suitable for taking decisions in commercial applications related to lung cancer treatment. Around 90% of the Watson application users follow the guidance of it. To help doctors in healthcare diagnose diseases, Watson's advanced chatbot, Watson Health is designed. The only limitation of Watson chatbot is that it supports English language only for the communication purpose. Now a days Watson has extended its capabilities. Watson on IBM Cloud (Watson Assistant |IBM Cloud, 2020) provides deployment model to developers and researchers to create their own chatbots easily and quickly. This deployment model has machine learning capabilities and it also provides optimized cloud-based hardware. The extended capabilities of new generation Watson chatbot are seeing, hearing, reading, talking, tasting, interpreting, learning and recommending.

Chatbot Architecture

Various architectural Chatbot designs are proposed in the literature. Authors of this paper (Khanna et al., 2015) have proposed an architecture for rule-based Chatbot design. Authors of the paper (Wu et al., 2016) have suggested architecture for Retrieval-based Chatbots. In the paper of, (Zumstein and Hundertmark, 2017), authors have connected knowledge base with external databases and information systems. But sentiment analysis and ambiguity handling are not available in this design. The design by Khan (2017) is based on layered architecture. The paper lacks in explaining components of dialog management system. In the paper, (Nimavat & Champaneria, 2017), authors have provided a simplistic design of Chatbot. Authors of the paper, (Zhou et al., 2017), in their paper, described the architectural design consisting of Response Generation Module. This Chatbot generates emotionally logical and consistent responses. Authors of the paper (Hahm, Kim, an, Lee, & Choi, 2018) have provided the architecture of the Chatbot but without giving its in-depth details. Authors of the paper (S. and Balakrishnan 2018) provide an interesting design of integration of knowledge base of rule-based Chatbot with the big data source. Authors of the paper (Mislevics, Grundspen, k, is, and Rollande, 2018), have provided detailed design of Chatbot developed for the students. But this Chatbot has no sentiment analysis component. Authors of the paper (Zhou et al., 2019), have presented detailed architecture of XiaoIce ('little ice' in Chinese) Chatbot developed by Microsoft. The authors of the paper, (Villegas, Arias-Navarrete, and Palacios, 2020), explained the layered architecture of Chatbot but lacks in explaining detailed design of the Chatbot.

Figure 1. Generalized chatbot architecture

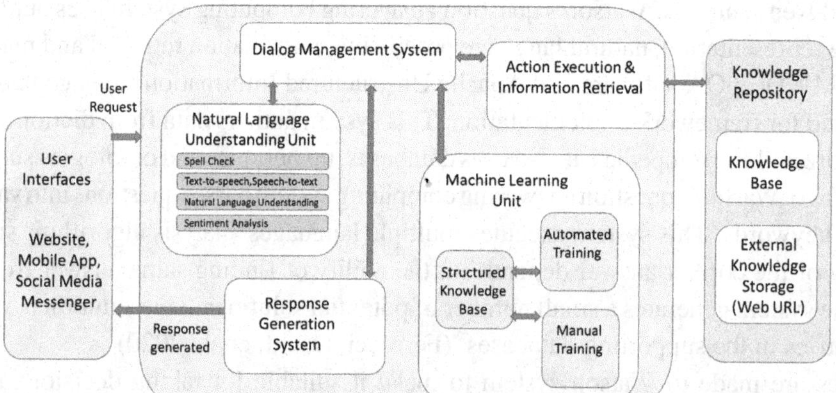

The figure 1 shows the generalized architecture of Chatbot. The process of communication starts with sending client request from any of the user interface such as website, mobile app or social media messengers such as Facebook or WhatsApp. The dialog management system of Chatbot receives this request. The Natural Language Understanding unit processes this input for spell check, or perform conversion from speech to text, or understands the sentiments and context of the text. Once the input is interpreted, action execution and information retrieval unit maps this input with knowledge stored in knowledge repository. At knowledge repository, the knowledge is stored in the form of knowledge base or external source such as web Uniform Resource Locator (URL). After retrieval of the information, response generation unit prepares the appropriate response with the help of machine learning unit and natural language understanding unit. The appropriate response is sent to the user through the user interface platform. (Adamopoulou E. & Moussiades L., 2020)

Even though the Chatbot is developed using any method, pattern-based or machine learning based, the performance evaluation of such Chatbot is needed to be done to make it operational. The following section discusses various parameters to measure the performance of the Chatbot.

Chatbot GDPR Compliant Issues

The Chatbot as a formal conversational agent has provided an opportunity for the human interaction and global engagement. An improvement the capability of this conversational agent, made this agent to collect and process a lot of personal information of the customer who is engaged in the conversation with it. This led to the crucial data protection issues. The rules imposed by General Data Protection Regulations (GDPR) are needed to be explored to achieve privacy of user information. European Union have made GDPR to establish robust regulations for the data protection in the digital world. The principles, rights and lawful bases are set by these regulations.

Principles

- Minimization of Data – The data controller must put control on the limited usage of the user data which is genuinely required for the processing purpose.
- Transparency – The data must follow the openness and honesty while processing the personal data of the user.
- Limitations on Storage – The data controller must specify that the data will be deleted after its usage and when it is no longer required for the processing purpose.
- Limitations of Purpose – The user's personal data should be collected by specifying its legitimate purpose.

Individual Rights

- Right to Access – According to this right, the user can ask for the replica of the data provided. User can also ask for the drive behind the processing of the data and third parties that are involved in the accessing the data provided.
- Right to Rectification – The inaccurate or the out-of-date information should be rectified or erased by the data controller.
- Right to be Informed – To maintain the transparency about the usage of the data, the user must be informed about what will be done with his or her data.
- Right to Erasure – If the user withdraws consent or there is no longer lawful basis available for the processing of the data then it is mandatory for the controller to delete the collected data.

Lawful Basis

- Legitimate Interest – In case of legitimate need of any specific data processing, controller can use the data available through the conversation without the consent of the user.
- Special Category Data – The special category data such as healthcare data, political opinion data, require highest level of protection.
- Consent – An explicit consent is required to be taken by the controller from the subject before actual processing of the data. Such agreement can be withdrawn any time.

GDPR is mainly applied on the applications developed in domains like cloud computing, blockchain technology and Internet of Things. But it is still in an elementary phase when it comes to protection of chatbot content. The open issues in chatbot design are related to the building of honest and open chatbot, incorporating consent practices, and handling user's unneeded personal information. All these open issues are needed to be considered by the data controller while designing any chatbot and the chatbot design must follow regulations imposed by GDPR. (Saglem R. B. & Nurse J. R.C., 2020)

Parameters to Measure Performance of the Chatbot

The use of Chatbot in the industry is growing with the tremendous rate. It is imperative to test, verify and validate the functionality of the Chatbot before launching it on commercial websites or the mobile apps so that, it won't fail during the actual operational phase. (Vijayaraghavan V. et al, 2020). The performance of the Chatbot is measured by providing it to the pilot users before launching it. The parameters for the performance measurement are needed to be shortlisted before testing the Chatbot.

Some of the parameters to measure the performance of Chatbot are scalability, passing the Turing test, interoperability and speed. A Chatbot is called to be scalable if it accepts large number of queries from the user and responds promptly and efficiently to the query. The Chatbot clears the Turing test if it exhibits intelligent behavior equivalent to human being. The ability of Chatbot to support and switch quickly between multiple channels is called an interoperability. The time taken by the Chatbot to generate efficient response to the user query decides the operating speed of the Chatbot.

As per the expert point of view, the quality attribute efficiency, is measured in terms of the performance of the Chatbot. The functionality and humanity decide the effectiveness of the Chatbot. The satisfaction gained by the use of Chatbot is measured in terms of effect of conversation, ethics followed and behavior of the Chatbot and accessibility of the Chatbot.

As per the user point of view, some of the characteristics of the Chatbot are considered as quality metrics. These are impression created, robustness, effectiveness, and navigability, ease of use, aid ability, clarity, comprehensiveness, naturalness, friendliness, visual look and process feedback.

The automatic measurable quality metrics are opinion mining (that measures sentiments, opinions, emotions, and attitudes from written language), response time, word count (number of words that occur in a message), turn Count (the number of dialogue acts that were sent during the conversation), readability, analytical thinking power, confidence to use the language, and authenticity.

The expectation of the particular performance parameter value determines the choice of Chatbot development approach such as pattern matching or machine learning.

Response Time

The Chatbot performance parameter, response time is measured in terms of the promptness in answering the user's query. A single Chatbot system may be handling multiple concurrent human queries at a time. The Chatbot response time is always much lesser than human response time. (IBM, 2017). But in case of Chatbot that provides 24/7 response service to concurrent human requests, the response time is also considered as one of the parameters to measure the performance. In general, it is presumed that the less response time improves the user satisfaction, but quick answers to the questions can also generate negative artificial feelings at user end. (Cas Jongerius, 2018)

Accuracy of Answers

The accuracy of the answer depends on the linguistically correct answer and its relevance to the asked question. Again, the readability of the text is also considered as one of the factors to measure the accuracy. Some of the well-known readability indices are: Flesch Reading Ease, Flesch-Kincaid, Grade Level, Gunning Fog Index, Coleman-Liau Index, Simple Measure of Gobbledygook (SMOG) Index and the Automated Readability Index. These indices provide insights of the complexity of a piece of text.

Number of Failures in Answering

The total number of failures in answering the question asked by users, is also considered as one of the performance metrics of the Chatbot. The trust on the automated virtual assistance system increases during the conversation if it is able to deliver correct answers to the user queries.

Completeness of the Answer

The answer provided by the Chatbot should be comprehensive. It should provide solutions to the all aspects of the question asked. Incomplete answer results in multiple further queries from the user, till user is satisfied with the answers.

Clarity in Understanding the Question

Misspelled words or typing errors in the questions are common. The challenge in front of the Chatbot is to overcome these mistakes. It is not always possible to rectify all errors in typed question, but virtual assistance system can remove mistakes from commonly used words and phrases. This avoids the user to ask for retyping the question.

Passing the Turing Test

Chatbot must be commercially expert in answering user queries. But at the same time, it should become believable in the eyes of users and user should feel like he or she is talking to the actual human being behind the screen. Therefore, the Chatbot must be equipped with the expertise as well as with the expression of personality. The personality touch is added to the communication by adding psychological deposits to the knowledge base of the virtual assistance. It includes adding personality individualities, expressed emotions and biological features. (Callejas et al., 2011)

User Friendliness and Ease of Use

The user interface design should be able to capture user attention before even the conversation begins. The charming and animated expressions in welcome screen fulfils this purpose. Uniform colour scheme and rounded border conversational bubbles create fresh look of chat window. Simple layouts enhance the beauty of the user interface and makes it easy for user to use it. The use of buttons, wherever necessary, makes the conversation easy. The clickable buttons help in continuing the conversation till the user get satisfied answer for his or her all queries.

Aid Ability

The virtual assistance can provide clickable links in its response. By clicking such links, user can navigate through the various parts of the website for additional information on the topic, he or she is interested in. The user gets immediate answer of the questions without typing the questions manually. Chatbot provides these embedded links dynamically, as tagged words or phrases. The static list of links to the various informative sections of the website is also provided below the Chatbot utterance. The Chatbot can also provide the facility of typing the term 'HELP' or pressing the button 'INFO' or 'i' for the further information on the term entered. After going through the additional information provided by the Chatbot, user can return to previous conversation window by clicking 'BACK' button or return to the main menu by clicking 'HOME' button (Kuligowska 2015).

Visual Look

The external appearance of the virtual assistance plays important and the major role in establishing overall influence about the conversation system. Human faces or animated human images representing Chatbot, proved to be beneficial while communicating with the Chatbot (Haake, 2009). The user involvement in the communication increases if Chatbot image resembles the living person. (Van Vugt et al., 2010). The social interaction, natural conversation plays very important role in securing fruitful communication between user and the Chatbot.

Easy Accessibility on Website or Mobile App

Embedding the Chatbot on the commercial website of the company increases the visibility of the Chatbot. The virtual assistants are included in the website as a floating window. The pull-out side tab is also provided in some cases. The flexible combination of built in Chatbot window and pull-out side tab are considered to be highly welcomed by the customers of websites of various commercial products (Kuligowska 2015).

Personalization Option

The personalization option provided to the user to modify the look and feel of the conversation window also creates positive impact on the user's qualitative conversation with the Chatbot. Even though this facility is illusion of customization, when user is allowed to select characteristics and appearance of the conversational agent, user finds it more pleasant, useful and trustworthy. (Xiao et al. 2007). The user will be provided with the personalization options such as changing the gender of the virtual agent, recalling the name of user and using it in further conversation, provision of adjustment of the conversational text and the window size, viewing the conversational history during the talk, or sending the conversation history through the email.

Effect of the Conversation

The effect of the conversation is measured in terms of the satisfaction gained by the user after the conversation. The appropriate greeting messages during the conversation and the pleasant personality of the Chatbot creates the effective conversation. Also, the ability to keep user engaged and entertaining increases the satisfaction level of user at the end of the conversation.

Ethics Followed

The Chatbot should be able to recognize offensive statements entered by the user. The ability of Chatbot not to get provoked by such statements provides the proof of following ethics by the Chatbot. The reaction of the Chatbot must be not to get provoked and to raise the level of anger and frustration of the user. Verbally abusive comments passed by the customer must be ignored by Chatbot tactfully and it should be able to divert the user attention towards main topic of the conversation. (Brahnam, 2005)

Ability to Process Feedback Given by the User

At the end of the conversation, user can be asked to provide feedback on the virtual assistance service or on the website or the customer's willingness to recommend product or service to other customers. The ability of Chatbot to process such feedback helps in evaluating customer satisfaction who were involved in virtual assistance-based conversation. (Kowalski et. al, 2013)

Comprehensiveness of the Knowledge Base

All the data, information and the knowledge about the virtual assistance is stored in the knowledge base. The knowledge base is the strong reason behind the existence of the Chatbot. (Kenny et al., 2007). The depth of the knowledge base decides the ability of the Chatbot to converse with the user on any related topic successfully. The comprehensive knowledge base includes the answer of on-domain as well as off-domain questions asked to the Chatbot (Sjödén et al., 2011). The knowledge base should include general information topics as well as specialized domain related knowledge. The exemplary questions based on general information are: what is today's date, what is the time, who are you, what is your name, how are you, how old are you, who is the prime minister of India, what is capital of India etc. The specialized knowledge included in the commercial Chatbot is comprehensive knowledge about the product of the company or the services of the organization. The use of such knowledge base, to answer satisfactorily to the user queries, depends on the successful implementation of the virtual assistance system.

Robustness to Handle Unexpected Input

Chatbot should be able to respond to unfamiliar situation. Such situation may occur when question asked by the user is not familiar to it, or question itself contains typo errors or grammatical errors. Even if the user's statement is difficult to understand for the Chatbot because of insufficient information in the knowledge base, it should be able to handle such situation intelligently. Providing an incorrect answer is not preferable. Some of the well-known Chatbots, handles such situations by asking user to, further search for the information, or by agreeing upon not availability of the answer and diverting user to some other topic.

Scalability

The ability of Chatbot to handle concurrent queries from the multiple users at a time is measured in terms of scalability. The scalable chatbot can deal with complicated scenarios in customer support. Such chatbot is available to the customer anytime and in any situation. On any e-commerce website, there are occasions such as festive seasons when purchase more and tend to have more and more queries. Unlike the regular days, chatbot may receive more than 500 chats a day. The automatic customer support system implemented through scalable chatbot can handle complex customer queries.

Interoperability

For a given organization, the Chatbot may be implemented on different platforms. These platforms could be website, Facebook Messenger, WhatsApp, Smart Speakers and many more. The interoperability refers to the ability of communicating these different Chatbots simultaneously for a specific user at a given point of time. It is an emerging concept and it will make Chatbot technology ease of use. For example, the user browsing a product on Facebook Messenger through chat can order the same product by instructing smart speaker later time. This will be possible if the all conversations are working synchronously. The interoperable Chatbot supports multiple channels simultaneously and easily and quickly shift between these available channels. The interoperable chatbot is always scalable as it handles complex queries from the multiple users simultaneously by using multiple platforms and channels.

Activation Rate

Activation Rate helps the organization to determine how quickly and effectively the new users are achieving perceived value. It counts the number of new users that have executed a predetermined "main action" within a predefined period of time, and the main action is assumed or known to deliver original customer value. In case of social media website such as Twitter, the key action might be in the form of following 7 other accounts or sending at least 3 more tweets. In case of the chatbot based website, key action will be in the form of user click on the appropriate link or menu to get actual information which user is searching for after getting the right information from the chatbot through conversation.

Interaction Rate

The interaction rate measures the communication rate between a customer and a company. The company gets a chance to connect with the customer through each interaction. This connection can be used for increasing customer retention and advocacy. The interaction rate is measured in terms of the number of interactions such as reactions, comments, shares divided by account size such as number of supporters or page likes, at the time of posting. In case of chatbot system if a single comment of chatbot gets 10 different customer reactions and the comment has 500 likes at the time of posting it already on the website then by considering even weight for each reaction, the interaction rate is calculated as (10 * 100/500 = 2%)

Retention Rate

Retention rate measures the percentage of customers who continue to reward the company their business compared to the percentage of customers who have churned out. To calculate the retention rate, the number of clients that remain at the end of the time period in assessment, compared to the number of clients that were present at the starting of the period are considered. In case of chatbot system the retention rate for one year is measured in terms of the number of users using the chatbot till the end of one year compared to the number of users that were started conversation with the chatbot at the beginning of the year.

Social Intelligence

Social Intelligence of the chatbot refers to its ability to produce adequate social behavior for the purpose of achieving desired goals. The social characteristics associated with social intelligence are moral agency, thoroughness, damage control, emotional intelligence, manners, and personalization. The ability of a chatbot to handle conflict or failure situation is called as damage control. In Graphical User Interface (GUI) based user interface, user communication takes place using visual controls such as links, menus, buttons. But in text-based conversational interface, language is the main tool of the communication. Thoroughness is an ability of chatbot to coherently use language and consistently present the expected style. The chatbot's behavior is considered to be full of manners if it adopts speech acts such as greetings, apologies, and closings. An ability of the chatbot technology to act according to the social notions of right and wrong, makes the chatbot socially moral. The ability to recognize user's feelings, and show respect, understanding and empathy makes the chatbot emotionally intelligent. Personalization ability of chatbot depends on the its capability to adapt interface, information and functionality to increase personal significance. (Chaves, A. P., & Gerosa, M. A., 2021)

Related Work

Authors of the paper (Mittal A. et. al., 2016), have evaluated the working of the well-known Chatbot systems such as ALICE, Jabberwacky and Rose. Various criteria used for the performance measurement are handling exceptional situations, knowledge base and conversational properties. The authors have concluded the work with the remark that even though Chatbot technique aid human in some situations but it cannot replace the human completely.

In the paper, (Hill J. et. al., 2015), authors have analyzed changes in the communication when person communicate with intelligent agent rather than another human being. The important observations from the are: person connected with the chatbot for stretched durations (but with shorter messages) than he communicated with another human being. It is also observed that the poverty of vocabulary in the human-chatbot communication.

In the paper, (Kuligowska, 2015), author has proposed measurement metrics to evaluate the usability, quality and performance of the conversational agents used in commercial applications. Some of the aspects of the performance measurement are the form of implementation on website, visual look, knowledge base, speech synthesis unit, conversational abilities, context sensitiveness, personalization options, and responses in emergency situations.

In the research paper, (Lin Li, 2020), authors have performed the study of Chatbots applied to many consumer-facing applications such as Online Travel Agencies and decided the quality dimensions and their effects on customer confirmation. It was observed that reliability, understandability, interactivity and assurance are the four qualities those contribute positively towards customer confirmation while technological anxiety moderately affects customer relationship.

In the paper, (Abdul-Kader, S. A., & Woods, J. C., 2015) authors have done a review on chatbot design techniques and compared these techniques. This study also elaborates that the development and improvement of Chatbot design is not growing at a predictable rate due to the variety of methods and approaches used to design a Chatbot.

In the paper (A. Przegalinska et. al, 2019), authors have proposed new method to track interaction between human and Chatbot. The Chatbot performance is measured in terms of ethical concern such as trust. The author of the paper (Thomas N T, 2016) has measured the performance of Chatbot that automatically generate responses to the user queries based on the data stored under FAQ category. This Chatbot is developed using the Latent Semantic Analysis (LSA) and Artificial Intelligence Markup Language (AIML).

The authors of the paper (Arsovski S., 2017) discuss similarities and difference in the implementing Chatbots using AIML and ChatScript.

Authors of this paper (Nagarhalli T. et.al, 2020) have performed a detailed study of recent Chatbot systems discussed in the literature and used in various application domains. The recent trends in developing technologies for the Chatbots is also debated in this paper. The authors of the paper (Santhana L., 2020) have studied various techniques of Chatbot development in detail. These techniques are based on natural language processing, deep learning and machine learning.

Authors of the paper (Mathew R. et. al., 2019) have proposed a medical system based on Chatbot which is an alternative to the conventional method of visiting a hospital, taking appointment of doctor, and get treated by the doctor. The techniques used to create the Chatbot is based on Natural Language Processing and machine learning. Chatbot is able to identify symptoms, predict the probable disease and provide the treatment. This system is really helpful to those patients who need to visit hospital for the treatment and consult the doctor on regular basis.

In all domains of the business, Chatbot technology is used to reduce the operational cost. The paper (Pablo R. et. al, 2018) presents the experiment results conducted to measure the trustworthiness of the Chatbot replacing the human work. The paper has studied the human behavior expressed while dealing with the Chatbot to get their queries solved. This behavior is also compared with the treatment given while dealing with human counterpart. The application of Chatbot system in the domain of mental health is incredible, as it helps patients to reach to the appropriate treatment method without facing many obstacles. Such method can collect detailed data of patients, and it can make accurate and timely diagnosis of the patient sufferings. Authors of the paper, (Ruyi W. et al, 2020) have proposed a Chatbot system to monitor and assess mental health of perinatal women in terms of depression, hypomania and anxiety.

EXPERIMENT CONDUCTED

In the literature it is found that, the educational virtual agents are developed to help improve learning outcomes (Kerly et al., 2007). In the present study, educational Chatbots are developed using both pattern-matching and machine-learning algorithms. These Chatbots are implemented on educational website. The students are asked to chat with the Chatbots and get their Java subject related queries, answered by these Chatbots. The figure 2 shows the design of the developed Chatbot using pattern-based approach. The main python file to implement pattern-based chatbot is PB_chatbot.py. Here letters PB stands for pattern-based. This file is responsible for providing appropriate response to the user's query by identifying whether the query is of general type or it is subject Java related query. PB_chatbot.py handles three files as shown in figure 2. Startup.xml is the starting point to communicate with the chatbot. As shown in figure 2, the next step is to accept input from human user. If the user input is general query, then such input is handled by general_chat.aiml file. And if the user input is subject Java related query, in that case, it is handled by subject_chat.aiml file. The output generated by any of these files by using the concept of pattern-matching, the chatbot provides the final response to the human user.

Figure 2. Design of the developed Chatbot using pattern-based approach

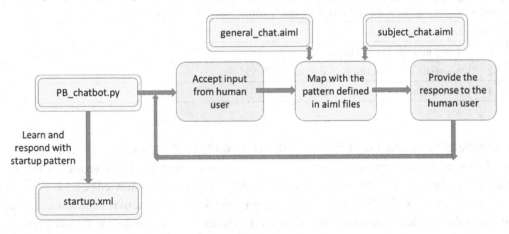

The various tasks performed by PB_chatbot.py python file are described in the figure 3. The first task performed by PB_chatbot.py file is to import AIML library. The chatbot based on the concept of artificial intelligence can easily be developed using python's AIML package. AIML is one of the forms of XML file. It defines rules to match patterns and accordingly the response is determined. As shown in figure 3, the next step is to load the kernel. AIML's Kernel () function is used to create kernel object. The kernel object is the publicly available interface to the AIML interpreter. The learn() method of kernel object is used to put the content of 'startup.xml' file into the kernel object.

```
kernel = aiml.Kernel()
kernel.learn("startup.xml")
kernel.respond("LOAD AIML B")
```

Here, "learn" method loads the contents of an AIML file into the kernel. While the "respond" method is used to get the response from the learned AIML file.

```
while True:
input_text = input(">Human: ")
response = kernel.respond(input_text)
print(">Bot: "+response)
```

As mentioned in Table 1, using while loop, input is accepted from the human user, response will be generated and printed on the screen by running general_chat.aiml file or subject_chat.aiml file in a continuous manner.

Table 1. Tasks performed by PB_chatbot.py

	PB_chatbot.py program flow	
1.	Import AIML library	
2.	Load the kernel by calling AIML's Kernel () function	
3.	Train the kernel by using startup.xml file	
4.	Provide the first response to the user using the kernel by referring the pattern defined in startup.xml	
5.	Within a continuous loop	
	5.1	Accept input text from the human user
	5.2	Provide the response to the input accepted in step 5.1
	5.3	Print the Chatbot's response on screen

The sample code of general_chat.aiml is shown in table 2. The program file general_chat.aiml is responsible for providing general queries asked by the human user to the pattern-based chatbot. The tag <category> defines the 'unit of knowledge' available in chatbot's knowledge base. <pattern> and <template> are sub-tags of <category> tag. <pattern> tag defines a pattern to match with human user's input given to the chatbot. <template> tag defines the chatbot's response to the human user's input. As shown in Table 2, if human input is 'HELLO' word followed by anything (indicated with wildcard *) then chatbot's response will be 'Well, Hello User!'. The general_chat.aiml file is responsible for producing chatbot's appropriate response by matching user's general questions with the already set patterns in the same file. Other similar questions are: 'WHO ARE YOU' and 'WHAT DO YOU DO' as shown in Table 2.

Table 2. Sample code - general_chat.aiml

general_chat.aiml program flow
`<aiml version="1.0.1" encoding="UTF-8">`

`<category>`
    `<pattern>HELLO *</pattern>`
    `<template>`
        Well, Hello User!
    `</template>`
`</category>`

`<category>`
    `<pattern>WHO ARE YOU</pattern>`
    `<template>`
        I'm a Chatbot!
    `</template>`
`</category>`

`<category>`
    `<pattern>WHAT DO YOU DO</pattern>`
    `<template>`
        I'm here to help you with you Java subject related queries!
    `</template>`
`</category>`

`</aiml>`

Table 3. Sample code - subject_chat.aiml

subject_chat.aiml program flow
`<aiml version="1.0.1" encoding="UTF-8">`

`<category>`
    `<pattern>platform independent</pattern>`
    `<template>`
        Java is called platform independent because of its byte codes which can run on any system irrespective of its underlying operating system.
    `</template>`
`</category>`

`<category>`
    `<pattern> wrapper classes in Java</pattern>`
    `<template>`
        Wrapper classes convert the Java primitives into the reference types (objects). Every primitive data type has a class dedicated to it. These are known as wrapper classes because they "wrap" the primitive data type into an object of that class.
    `</template>`
`</category>`

`</aiml>`

The sample code of subject_chat.aiml is shown in Table 3. This file contains many <category> tags to mention various <pattern> and corresponding <template>. These patterns are the probable Java subject related queries asked by human user to the chatbot. By considering various such queries, patterns and templates are created. Few such patterns and templates are shown in Table 3. For example, if the user asks the query about 'platform independence in Java' then the chatbot's response to this query will be 'Java is called platform independent because of its byte codes which can run on any system irrespective of its underlying operating system'.

The sample code of startup.xml is shown in Table 4. This is the starting XML file loaded by PB_chatbot.py python program in kernel object. The matched pattern is "LOAD AIML B". Hence after matching this beginning pattern, it will load two aiml files. The general_chat.aiml is for generating answers to the general queries of human user and subject_chat.aiml is for generating answers to Java subject related queries of the human user. Here <learn> tag is used to load these aiml files as shown in Table 4.

Table 4. Sample code - startup.xml

startup.xml program flow
<aiml version="1.0.1" encoding="UTF-8">
``` <category>   <!-- Pattern to match in user input -->   <!-- If user enters "LOAD AIML B" -->   <pattern>LOAD AIML B</pattern>   <!-- Template is the response to the pattern -->   <!-- This learns an aiml file -->   <template>   <!-- aiml file to answer general questions is added here -->   <learn>general_chat.aiml</learn>   <!-- aiml file to answer subject questions is added here -->   <learn>subject_chat.aiml</learn>   </template> </category> ```
</aiml>

The figure 3 shows the design of the developed Chatbot using Machine Learning based approach. In the preparatory step, various python libraries are installed and imported which are required for the functioning of machine-learning based chatbot. Natural language toolkit library, Natural Language Toolkit (nltk) library, is used to process human language data.

```
from newspaper import Article
import random
import string
import nltk
from sklearn.feature_extraction.text import CountVectorizer
from sklearn.metrics.pairwise import cosine_similarity
import numpy as np
import warnings
```

The functions used for web scraping articles are referred from newspaper3k python library. The punkt package from nltk library acts as a tokenizer. It divides the text into the list of sentences using unsupervised algorithm.

After loading all the required libraries, the conversation starts. The exit list is defined as shown below.

```
exit_list = ['exit','see you later','bye','quit','break']
```

If the user input exists in the exit list, it terminates the chat. Otherwise, the python program checks for the user input from greeting specific or subject specific lists. If the user input is from greeting_list, then it calls greetings_response function to generate the greeting message to the user. Else it searches the term in the already created web article (showing the Java related content) and corresponding text is presented as the response.

Figure 3. Design of the developed Chatbot using machine learning based approach

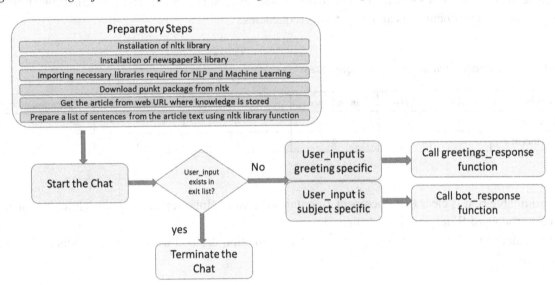

Table 5. Program flow of greeting_response function

Working of greeting response function	
1	Accept the user_input and convert it into lower case
2	Define the bot_greetings list of greeting words for Chatbot
3	Define the user_greetings list of greeting words for user
4	If the word entered by the user exists in user_greetings list then randomly displays the any word from bot_greetings list

Table 5 shows the working of greeting_response function which is used to greet user at the time of beginning of the conversation. The user input is converted into lower case text. The lists of chatbot's and user's greeting messages are created. If the user-entered greeting word exists in user_greetings list then the program will randomly display any greeting word from the bot_greetings list.

bot_greetings = ['howdy','hi','hey','hello','hola']
user_greetings = ['hi', 'hey', 'hello','hola','greetings','wassup']
for word in text.split():
if word in user_greetings:
return random.choice(bot_greetings)

Cosine Similarity Algorithm

The cosine similarity algorithm finds the similarity between two given vectors defined in an inner product space. Whether two vectors are pointing towards the same direction or not, that is decided by measuring angle of cosine between two vectors. This concept is also useful in defining the similarity between two text documents. The important words, key words and phrases in the document are considered as attributes of the document. The frequencies of such special words in the document are counted. The term-frequency vector is formed by such attribute frequencies. (Jiawei H. et.al, 2012). Table 1 shows the example of two documents and their term-frequencies.

Table 6. Documents and their term-frequencies

Document	Object	Class	Inheritance	Polymorphism	Abstraction	Encapsulation
Document 1	9	2	8	0	2	3
Document 2	7	1	7	1	8	4

From table 6, it is clear that document 1 contains the word 'Inheritance' 8 times while document 2 contains the word 'Encapsulation' 4 times.

Consider the two vectors x and y. The similarity function defined using cosine similarity is given by equation 1.

$$\text{sim}(x, y) = \frac{x.y}{\|x\| \|y\|} \quad \ldots\ldots\ldots \tag{1}$$

‖x‖ is a Euclidean norm of vector x = (x1, x2,...xp) and it is defined by equation 2.

$$\|x\| = \sqrt{x_1^2 + x_2^2 + \ldots + x_p^2} \quad \ldots\ldots\ldots \tag{2}$$

Similarly, ‖y‖ is a Euclidean norm of vector y.

Similarity function sim(x, y) is the cosine ratio of the angle between two vectors x and y. If the cosine value is almost zero then two vectors are orthogonal to each other and there is no similarity between them. If the cosine of the angle is towards one then there is maximum similarity between two vectors.

The machine learning based Chatbot algorithm uses the concept of cosine similarity to calculate the closeness of two sentences. These sentences are, the sentence of user query and each statement in the available knowledge base. If the user query contains the maximum number of words (with high frequencies) similar to the sentence in the knowledge base then the later sentence is considered as the answer to the user query.

Table 7 shows the working of bot_response function which is based on Cosine Similarity algorithm.

Table 7. Program flow of bot_response function

	Working of bot_response function	
1.	Accept the user_input sentence and convert it into lower case	
2.	For each sentence in knowledge source:	
	2.1	Find out the similarity vector for the frequencies of the special words in user_input
	2.2	Calculate similarity score of each sentence using cosine similarity with user_input sentence
	2.3	Make a list of sentences found in step 2.2
3.	Print all the paragraphs associated with the list of sentences found in step 2.3	

Chatbot Performance Measurement

There are two types of Chatbot performance measurement methods, questionnaire-based and automatic metrics based. Many researchers have used questionnaire-based method to evaluate Chatbot system. Again, experts as well as the users of Chatbot system are asked to fill the questionnaires. Radziwill and Benton (2017) have considered effectiveness, efficiency and satisfaction as three main categories of performance attributes. Semeraro et.al (2002) have designed a questionnaire to measure performance as per user point of view. They have considered performance measuring attributes as comprehension, ability to aid, navigability, an impression, and an ability to learn and command.

But it is also proved by some researchers that the questionnaire having the combination of expert-based and user-based questions, is effective and helps in getting overall understanding of the system (Desurvire, 1994). Therefore, in this experiment, the designed questionnaire contains the questions which will be answered by the user of the system as well as by the expert. These Chatbots are able to answer the queries of graduate students of information technology discipline. Around 214 students, learning Core and Advanced Java as a subject, are chosen to converse with Chatbot on educational website. The performances of these Chatbots are measured and compared on the basis of above-mentioned performance metrics. The questionnaire is circulated to students and their responses are collected. For each question, the Likert scale of 1-5 is assigned. The number 1 corresponds to 'Strongly disagree' while number 5 corresponds to 'Strongly agree'. The questionnaire prepared for the assessment of the performance of the Chatbots is shown in Table 8.

The questions related to parameters number 1 to 14 are asked to the actual user of the Chatbots. The question under the parameters 15 to 22 are asked to the experts of the domain. For each parameter, there are two questions. One is positive and another is negative. So, there are total 28 questions asked to each user. To give an example, the question such as: 'The answers given by Chatbot were complete.' was asked to actual user of the chatbot to judge the completeness of the answer. Similarly, to measure the Chatbot scalability and interoperability as mentioned in question number 17 and 18, all experts are asked to simultaneously converse with the chatbot, also each expert is asked to with the chatbot using multiple channels such as website and mobile application.

A new custom-built tool for measuring Chatbot usability is used here to calculate the Chatbot Usability Questionnaire (CUQ) score of each response. (Samual Holmes et.al, 2019) The steps of the CUQ score calculation is described in Table 9.

Table 8. Questionnaire for the evaluation of the performance of the Chatbots

S. No.	Parameter	Questions
1	Response time	Chatbot answered my questions quickly
		Chatbot took time to answer my questions
2	Accuracy of answers	The answers given by Chatbot were accurate
		Chatbot gave wrong answers of few questions asked by me
3	Failures in answering	Most of the times Chatbot answered my questions
		Only few times Chatbot answered my questions
4	Completeness of the answer	The answers given by Chatbot were complete
		The answers given by Chatbot were having missing parts
5	Clarity in understanding the question	Chatbot understood my questions very well
		Chatbot got confused in understanding my questions
6	Passing the Turing Test	The personality of the Chatbot was realistic and engaging
		The Chatbot looked more like robotic machine
7	User friendliness and ease of use	It was easy to navigate through various options provided by the Chatbot
		It was difficult to navigate through various options provided by the Chatbot
8	Aid ability	Chatbot provided the links and buttons for easy access of the information on website
		I could not find links and buttons for easily getting further information
9	Visual look	Look and feel of the Chatbot was interesting
		Chatbot had very simple and unattractive user interface
10	Easy accessibility on website or Mobile App	Chatbot was part of website from where I wanted to get information
		Chatbot was totally separate entity and not a part of the website from where I want to seek information
11	Personalization options	It was possible to change Chatbot image and background as per my choice
		There was no option available to change background and Chatbot image
12	Effect of the conversation	The Chatbot explained its scope and purpose well
		The Chatbot gave no indication as to its purpose
13	Ethics followed	The Chatbot welcomed me before the beginning of the actual conversation
		Chatbot seemed very impolite
14	Ability to process feedback given by user	Chatbot implemented or agreed to implement suggestions given by me for the improvement of the virtual assistance service
		Chatbot ignored the suggestions given by me for the improvement of the virtual assistance service
15	Comprehensiveness of the knowledge base	The knowledge base of Chatbot was comprehensive to cover all aspects of the domain
		There were few missing topics in the knowledge base of the Chatbot
16	Robustness to handle unexpected input	Chatbot was able to handle unexpected user input
		Chatbot got confused by unexpected user input
17	Scalability	This Chatbot could work for concurrent multiple user requests
		Chatbot was able to handle one user at a time
18	Interoperability	I could view the Chatbot on multiple channels such as website, messenger at the same time
		Chatbot was available only on the website

continues on following page

Table 8. Continued

S. No.	Parameter	Questions
19	Activation Rate	Through the chatbot conversation, it was possible to get required information available on the website.
		Through the chatbot conversation, it was not possible to get required information available on the website.
20	Interaction Rate	Chatbot was able to provide comments that led to perform multiple appropriate actions on the website.
		Chatbot was able to provide comments but it did not lead to perform multiple appropriate actions on the website.
21	Retention Rate	Chatbot made me to visit the website once again.
		I do not have any plan to visit the website once again.
22	Social Intelligence	Chatbot was able to show social intelligence by following manners, morals and emotional intelligence.
		Chatbot was not socially intelligent.

Table 9. Calculation of CUQ (Chatbot usability questionnaire) score

			Step of the Calculation
1.			Initialize Sum = 0;
	1.1		For a single user response from R1 to R214, consider Ri (i varies from 1 to 214)
		1.1.1	For each Q1 to Q28 questions, score from 1 to 5, is assigned by the user. Score 5 refers to 'strongly agree' while score 1 refers to 'strongly disagree'. 'Neutral' is worth score 3.
		1.1.2	S1= The sum of scores for all odd numbered that is positive questions
		1.1.3	S2= The sum of scores for all even numbered that is negative questions
		1.1.4	S3 = S1 - 14
		1.1.5	S4 = 70 – S2
		1.1.6	S5 = S3 + S4
		1.1.7	S5 score is out of (14*14 = 196) Calculate the percentage score of S5 S6 = S5*100/196
	1.2		(CUQ)i = S6
	1.3		Sum = Sum + (CUQ)i
2.			Average CUQ score for all responses = Sum/214
3.			Display the Average CUQ score for the Chatbot implementation method

Table 10 shows the result of the calculation of CUQ score for user and expert responses. For the user review related questions, which are parameter number 1-14 questions, responses from users are received. The CUQ score is calculated for each response. The average calculated CUQ score for the pattern based Chatbot is **64.29** while for Machine Learning based Chatbot is **71.43**.

For the expert review related questions, which are parameter number 15-21 questions, responses from the experts are received. The CUQ score is calculated for each expert's response. The average calculated CUQ score by the experts for pattern based Chatbot is **61.46** while for Machine learning based Chatbot is

67.17. The threshold value for acceptance of the CUQ score is **50%**, as for each performance parameter there are positive and negative question.

Table 10. CUQ of the Chatbots

Category of Chatbot	Average CUQ (User based questions)	Average CUQ (Expert based questions)
Pattern based	64.29	61.46
Machine learning based	71.43	67.17

FUTURE RESEARCH DIRECTIONS

The present study considers the performance measurement of the Chatbots developed using the techniques such as pattern-matching and machine-learning. The advanced technique, deep learning for Chatbot implementation, can also be used. This study can be extended in future by comparing Chatbot performance developed using pattern-matching, machine learning and deep learning techniques.

For the modelling of complex relationships between semantics of the language, Natural Language Processing technique is used. By using traditional machine learning techniques and NLP, if such models are developed then these models are not generic in nature. If the semantics of the language are modelled using NLP and Deep Learning then, it is easier to create generic model by handling NLP complexities.

On the basis of concepts such as NLP and Deep Learning, chatbot can be developed using Multi-layer Perceptron, Convolutional Neural Network, Sequence to Sequence model and Long Short-Term Memory. These techniques overcome the limitations of the context recognition which is the essential part of any NLP-based model. The performance of these deep learning based chatbots can be compared with pattern-matching based chatbot and the machine-learning based chatbot.

The various chatbots developed using these techniques, can be implemented on actual real time websites and portals of products and service providers. The responses can be gathered from the users and domain experts of these websites. On the basis of these responses, the performance-wise superior chatbot can be decided by considering various chatbot performance measurement metrics mentioned in the current study.

CONCLUSION

The study shows that the machine learning technique of Chatbot implementation is more superior than pattern-based technique, as machine learning based technique, adds more and more information to the knowledge base through self-learning. The machine learning based Chatbot development algorithms tries to understand and interpret sentiments of user's query by reading topics, themes and entities. These algorithms also divide the user input string into linguistically symbolic tokens. The preprocessing techniques used by machine learning based Chatbot development algorithms such as an identification of named entities, removing spelling as well as typographical errors, applying method of dependency parsing to find dependent and related terms, make this more superior than the traditional pattern-based Chatbot development method.

As per user point of view, the Chatbot performance evaluation parameters such as Chatbot's visual look, ability of Chatbot to understand the user query clearly and accuracy of the Chatbot answers. As per the expert point of view, the Chatbot performance is greatly affected by robustness of Chatbot to handle unexpected user input and the comprehensiveness of the knowledge base.

This study definitely provides platform to the Chatbot developers to identify the design and performance parameters those are really needed to be emphasized on.

ACKNOWLEDGMENT

I sincerely thank Dr. Seema Purohit, Principal, Brihan Maharashtra College of Commerce, Pune, Maharashtra, India for useful discussions and advice.

REFERENCES

Abdul-Kader, S. A., & Woods, J. C. (2015). Survey on chatbot design techniques in speech conversation systems. *International Journal of Advanced Computer Science and Applications*, 6(7).

Adamopoulou, E., & Moussiades, L. (2020). An Overview of Chatbot Technology. In I. Maglogiannis, L. Iliadis, & E. Pimenidis (Eds.), *Artificial Intelligence Applications and Innovations. AIAI 2020. IFIP Advances in Information and Communication Technology* (Vol. 584). Springer. doi:10.1007/978-3-030-49186-4_31

Przegalinska, Ciechanowski, Stroz, Gloor, & Mazurek. (2019). *In bot we trust: A new methodology of Chatbot performance measures*. Kelley School of Business, Indiana University. / doi:10.1016/j.bushor.2019.08.0050007-6813

Arsovski, S., Muniru, I., & Cheok, A. (2017). Analysis of the Chatbot open-source languages aiml and chatscript. *RE:view*. Advance online publication. doi:10.13140/RG.2.2.34160.15367

Bradeško, L., & Mladenić, D. (2012). *A survey of Chatbot systems through a loebner prize competition*. Academic Press.

Brahnam, S. (2005). Strategies for handling customer abuse of ECAs. *Proceedings of the INTERACT 2005 Workshop on Abuse: The darker side of Human-Computer Interaction*.

Callejas, Z., Griol, D., & López-Cózar, R. (2011). Predicting user mental states in spoken dialogue systems. *EURASIP Journal on Advances in Signal Processing*, 6(1), 2011a. doi:10.1186/1687-6180-2011-6

Jongerius, C. (2018). Quantifying Chatbot Performance by using Data Analytics. Center for Organization and Information Department of Information and Computing Sciences, Utrecht University.

Chaves, A. P., & Gerosa, M. A. (2021). How should my chatbot interact? A survey on social characteristics in human–chatbot interaction design. *International Journal of Human-Computer Interaction*, 37(8), 729–758. doi:10.1080/10447318.2020.1841438

Desurvire, H. W. (1994). Faster, cheaper!! Are usability inspection methods as effective as empirical testing? In J. Nielsen & R. L. Mack (Eds.), *Usability inspection methods* (pp. 173–202). John Wiley & Sons, Inc.

Ferrucci, Brown, Chu-Carroll, Fan, Gondek, Kalyanpur, Lally, Murdock, Nyberg, Prager, Schlaefer, & Welty. (2010). The AI Behind Watson – The Technical Article. *AI Magazine*.

Haake, M. (2009). *Embodied Pedagogical Agents: From Visual Impact to Pedagogical Implications* (Doctoral thesis). Lund University.

Hahm, Y., Kim, J., An, S., Lee, M., & Choi, K.-S. (2018). Chatbot who wants to learn the knowledge: kb-agent. *Semdeep/NLIWoD@ISWC*, 4.

Hill, J., Ford, W. R., & Farreras, I. G. (2015). Real conversations with artificial intelligence: A comparison between human–human online conversations and human–chatbot conversations. *Computers in Human Behavior, Elsevier, 49*, 245–250. doi:10.1016/j.chb.2015.02.026

IBM. (2017). *How Chatbots can help reduce customer service costs by 30%*. Retrieved from https://www.ibm.com/blogs/watson/2017/10/how-Chatbots-reducecustomer-service-costs-by-30-percent/

Jia, J. (2009). CSIEC: A computer assisted English learning Chatbot based on textual knowledge and reasoning. *Knowledge-Based Systems, 22*(4), 249–255. doi:10.1016/j.knosys.2008.09.001

Han, Kamber, & Pei. (2012). *Data Mining: Concepts and Techniques*. Morgan Kaufmann. doi:10.1016/C2009-0-61819-5

Kenny, P., & Parsons, T. D. (2011). Embodied Conversational Virtual Patients. In Conversational Agents and Natural Language Interaction: Techniques and Effective Practices. IGI Global. doi:10.4018/978-1-60960-617-6.ch011

Kerly, A., Hall, P., & Bull, S. (2007). Bringing Chatbots into education: Towards natural language negotiation of open learner models. *Knowledge-Based Systems, 20*(2), 177–185. doi:10.1016/j.knosys.2006.11.014

Khan, R. (2017). Standardized architecture for conversational agents a.k.a. Chatbots. *International Journal of Computer Trends and Technology, 50*(2), 114–121. doi:10.14445/22312803/IJCTT-V50P120

Khanna, A., Pandey, B., Vashishta, K., Kalia, K., Bhale, P., & Das, T. (2015). A study of today's A.I. through Chatbots and rediscovery of machine intelligence. *International Journal of U- and e-Service Science and Technology, 8*(7), 277–284. doi:10.14257/ijunesst.2015.8.7.28

Khurana, D., Koli, A., Khatter, K., & Singh, S. (2017). *Natural language processing: State of the art, current trends and challenges*. Retrieved from https://arxiv.org/abs/1708.05148

Nimavat, K., & Tushar, C. (2017). Chatbots: An Overview Types, Architecture, Tools and Future Possibilities. International Journal for Scientific Research & Development, 5(7).

Kowalski, S., Pavlovska, K., & Goldstein, M. (2013). *Two Case Studies in Using Chatbots for Security Training*. Information Assurance and Security Education and Training, IFIP Advances in Information and Communication Technology. doi:10.1007/978-3-642-39377-8_31

Kuligowska, K. (2015). Commercial Chatbot: Performance evaluation, usability metrics and quality standards of embodied conversational agents. *Professionals Center for Business Research*, 2(02), 1–16. doi:10.18483/PCBR.22

Langner, B., Vogel, S., & Black, A. (2010). *Evaluating a dialog language generation system: Comparing the MOUNTAIN system to other NLG approaches. Academic Press.*

Li, L., Lee, K. Y., Emokpae, E., & Yang, S.-B. (2019). What makes you continuously use Chatbot services? Evidence from Chinese online travel agencies. *Electronic Markets*. Advance online publication. doi:10.100712525-020-00454-z

Marietto, M., Varago de Aguiar, R., Barbosa, G., Botelho, W., Pimentel, E., Franca, R., & Silva, V. (2013). Artificial intelligence markup language: A brief tutorial. *International Journal of Computer Science and Engineering Survey, 04*(3), 1–20. Advance online publication. doi:10.5121/ijcses.2013.4301

Masche, J., & Le, N.-T. (2018). *A review of technologies for conversational systems.* doi:10.1007/978-3-319-61911-8_19

Binu, M. R., Varghese, S., Joy, S. E., & Alex, S. S. (2019). Chatbot for Disease Prediction and Treatment Recommendation using Machine Learning. *Proceedings of the Third International Conference on Trends in Electronics and Informatics (ICOEI 2019).*

Mikolov, T., Sutskever, I., Chen, K., Corrado, G. s., & Dean, J. (2013). Distributed representations of words and phrases and their compositionality. *Advances in Neural Information Processing Systems*, 26.

Mislevics, A., Grundspen, K., Is, J., & Rollande, R. (2018). *A systematic approach to implementing Chatbots in organizations—RTU leo showcase.* BIR Workshops.

Amit, M., Agrawal, A., Chouksey, A., Shriwas, R., & Agrawal, S. (2016, March). A Comparative Study of Chatbots and Humans. *International Journal of Advanced Research in Computer and Communication Engineering, 5*(3).

Nagarhalli, T., & Vinod Vaze, N. K. (2020). A Review of Current Trends in the Development of Chatbot Systems. *6th International Conference on Advanced Computing & Communication Systems (ICACCS).* 10.1109/ICACCS48705.2020.9074420

Nimavat, K., & Champaneria, T. (2017). Chatbots: An overview types, architecture, tools and future possibilities. *International Journal for Scientific Research and Development, 5*(7), 1019–1024. http://www.ijsrd.com/

Nt, T. (2016). *An e-business Chatbot using AIML and LSA.* doi:10.1109/ICACCI.2016.7732476

Rivas, P., Holzmayer, K., Hernandez, C., & Grippaldi, C. (2018). Excitement and Concerns about Machine Learning-Based Chatbots and Talkbots: A Survey. *IEEE International Symposium on Technology in Society (ISTAS) Proceedings.* 10.1109/ISTAS.2018.8638280

Perera, R., & Nand, P. (2017). Recent advances in natural language generation: A survey and classification of the empirical literature. *Computer Information, 36*(1), 1–31. doi:10.4149/cai_2017_1_1

Suta, Lan, Wu, Mongkolnam, & Chan. (2020). An Overview of Machine Learning in Chatbots. *International Journal of Mechanical Engineering and Robotics Research, 9*(4).

Ramesh, K., Ravishankaran, S., Joshi, A., & Chandrasekaran, K. (2017). A survey of design techniques for conversational agents. In *Information, communication and computing technology* (Vol. 750, pp. 336–350). Springer. doi:10.1007/978-981-10-6544-6_31

Radziwill, N. M. & Benton, M. C. (2017). *Evaluating Quality of Chatbots and Intelligent Conversational Agents*. Academic Press.

Wang, Wang, Liao, & Wang. (2020). Supervised Machine Learning Chatbots for Perinatal Mental Healthcare. *International Conference on Intelligent Computing and Human-Computer Interaction (ICHCI)*.

Holmes, S., Moorhead, A., Bond, R., Zheng, H., Coates, V., & Mctear, M. (2019). Usability testing of a healthcare chatbot: Can we use conventional methods to assess conversational user interfaces? In *Proceedings of the 31st European Conference on Cognitive Ergonomics (ECCE 2019)*. ACM. 10.1145/3335082.3335094

Santhana Lakshmi, V. (2020). A Study on Machine Learning based Conversational Agents and Designing Techniques. *Proceedings of the Fourth International Conference on I-SMAC (IoT in Social, Mobile, Analytics and Cloud) (I-SMAC)*.

Semeraro, G., Andersen, H. H., Andersen, V., Lops, P., & Abbattista, F. (2002). Evaluation and Validation of a Conversational Agent Embodied in a Bookstore. In N. Carbonell & C. Stephanidis (Eds.), *Universal access*. doi:10.1007/978-3-642-23196-4

Sjödén, B., Silvervarg, A., Haake, M., & Gulz, A. (2011). Extending an Educational Math Game with a Pedagogical Conversational Agent: Facing Design Challenges. *Communications in Computer and Information Science, 126*. doi:10.1007/978-3-642-20074-8_10

S., R., & Balakrishnan, K. (2018). Empowering Chatbots with business intelligence by big data integration. *International Journal of Advanced Research in Computer Science, 9*(1), 627–631. doi:10.26483/ijarcs.v9i1.5398

Thomas, N. T. (2016). An E-business Chatbot using AIML and LSA. *Intl. Conference on Advances in Computing, Communications and Informatics (ICACCI)*. 10.1109/ICACCI.2016.7732476

Van Vugt, H., Bailenson, J., Hoorn, J., & Konijn, E. (2010). Effects of facial similarity on user responses to embodied agents. ACM Transactions on Computer-Human Interaction, 17(2). doi:10.1145/1746259.1746261

Vijayaraghavan, Cooper, & Leevinson. (2020). Algorithm Inspection for Chatbot Performance Evaluation. *Procedia Computer Science, 171*, 2267–2274.

Villegas, W., Arias-Navarrete, A., & Palacios, X. (2020). Proposal of an architecture for the integration of a Chatbot with artificial intelligence in a smart campus for the improvement of learning. *Sustainability, 12*(1500), 1500. Advance online publication. doi:10.3390u12041500

Wallace, R. S. (2009). The anatomy of a.l.I.C.e. In R. Epstein, G. Roberts, & G. Beber (Eds.), *Parsing the turing test: philosophical and methodological issues in the quest for the thinking computer* (pp. 181–210). Springer Netherlands. doi:10.1007/978-1-4020-6710-5_13

Watson Assistant IIBM Cloud. (2020). https://www.ibm.com/cloud/watson-assistant/

Wilcox, B., & Wilcox, S. (2014). Making it real: Loebner-winning Chatbot design. *Arbor, 189*(764), a086. Advance online publication. doi:10.3989/arbor.2013.764n6009

Wu, Y., Wu, W., Xing, C., Zhou, M., & Li, Z. (2016). *Sequential matching network: A new architecture for multi-turn response selection in retrieval-based Chatbots.* Retrieved from https://arxiv.org/abs/1612.01627

Xiao, J., Stasko, J., & Catrambone, R. (2007). The Role of Choice and Customization on Users' Interaction with Embodied Conversational Agents: Effects on Perception and Performance. *Proceedings of CHI 2007.* 10.1145/1240624.1240820

Zhou, H., Huang, M., Zhang, T., Zhu, X., & Liu, B. (2017). *Emotional chatting machine: emotional conversation generation with internal and external memory.* Academic Press.

Zhou, L., Gao, J., Li, D., & Shum, H.-Y. (2019). *The design and implementation of xiaoice, an empathetic social Chatbot.* Retrieved from https://arxiv.org/abs/1812.08989

Zumstein, D., & Hundertmark, S. (2017). Chatbots – an interactive technology for personalized communication. *Transactions and Services. IADIS International Journal on WWW/Internet, 15*, 96–109.

Chapter 10
Social Network Mining, Analysis, and Research Trends:
A Case Study

Abhijit Banubakode
🆔 https://orcid.org/0000-0003-4389-0026
MET Institute of Computer Science, India

Chhaya Gosavi
🆔 https://orcid.org/0000-0002-2348-0698
MKSSS's Cummins College of Engineering, India

Meghana Satpute
University of Texas at Dallas, USA

ABSTRACT

Social media has altered the way we interact with the world around us. Social media usage has taken the world by storm the previous couple of years, and the wide variety of users has grown manifold. The analysis of social networks has been given special attention in recent years, mainly because of the success of online social networks and media sharing sites. In intelligence management, social structures need to be revealed to see social behaviour and social change based on the interactions that have taken place between the social members. Social network mining is very important because of various reasons. For example, studying and analysing social networks allows us to understand social behaviours in different contexts. In addition, by analysing the roles of the people involved in the social network, we can understand how information and opinions spread within the network, and who are the most influential people. This chapter presents a methodical review of social media and mining by applying data mining algorithms to study social networks.

DOI: 10.4018/978-1-7998-9121-5.ch010

INTRODUCTION

People are basically social creatures. Every single day in our life is replete with social interactions; be it family and friends, colleagues, and even routine exchanges made while shopping or travelling (Lee & Chen, 2013). The advent of social computing in the 21st century has now re-created these interactions in the virtual world enabling varieties of endeavours previously unheard of. It has modified the very nature of computation. In recent years, social community studies have been completed using facts collected from on-line interactions and from explicit relationship links in online social network platforms (e.g. facebook, LinkedIn, flickr, on the spot messenger, and so forth.) (Messinger, Stroulia, Lyons, Bone, Niu, Smirnov and Perelgute 2009), (Wang, 2008). The capability to gather this kind of information by using technological manners has implied a full-size shift in social community research, central to the emergence of a "new," "computational social technological know-how" (Zhang, Y. Jin, W. Jin, Liu, 2015) (Agrahari & Rao, 2017). On one hand, it has had a massive increase in the availability and in how big is social network data, and on one other hand it's completely redefined the forms of data that may be collected and analysed. This shift in the capability to collect data has additionally broadened all of the disciplines causing the advance of social network research. As per the authors, social network extraction can be used for social engineering (Nasution, 2019). Social network mining and research result are discussed by (Yeung, 2011). (Kim,2006) discussed various do's and don'ts of using social media for brand monitoring. Massiveness of data and importance of data mining is presented by (Tepper, 2012). (Goldberg & Zhu, 2006) presented graph-based semi-supervised learning algorithm to address the sentiment analysis task of social media data. (Jackson, 2010) has given detailed introduction to social and economic networks. (Liu & Lee, 2009) developed a way to increase recommendation effectiveness by incorporating social network information into collaborative filtering. (Kaschesky, Pawel Sobkowicz & Guillaume Bouchard, 2011) proposed an opinion formation framework based on content analysis of social media and socio-physical system modelling. (Pang and Lee, 2008) proposed technique of using simple statistics in an unsupervised fashion to re-rank search engine results when review-oriented queries are issued. Nanayakkara (2021) mainly focused on datamining techniques to findout trends in social media.

Figure 1. Various spheres of social computing and technologies

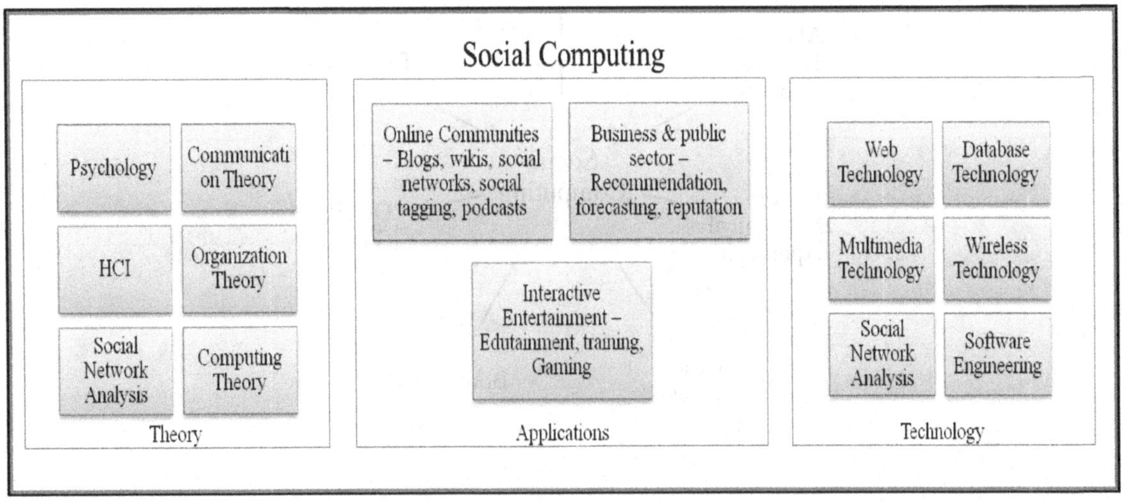

Social Computing relies on a strong theoretical background encompassing psychology, communication, Human Computer Interface (HCI), Organization and Computing Theory as these areas support social interaction. To enable this, an expanse of technologies are required ranging from Web, Database, Multimedia, Wireless Technologies to Software engineering (Wang, Carley, Zeng & Mao, 2007).

Essentially the convergence of Theory, Application and Technology; these three spheres has led to the extraordinary expansion in social computing. This collaboration has led to a host of applications in every known field – from blogs, social networks, medicine, forecasting, education, and training to gaming. When social computing is compared to any traditional form of computing these are following distinguishing characteristics:

1. **Decentralization:** Most forms of social computing are not centralized in terms of control.
2. **Real Time:** There is a constant update of the content reflecting the dynamic world as it is. This also allows for immediate propagation of information.
3. **Quality Control:** In contrast to standard protocols kept in place to monitor quality of content; social channels use feedback from their peers to manage their content. Certain forms do however have moderation of content.
4. **Bottom-Up Structure:** Traditional forms of computing exist in a top-down structure; while social computing typically works in a bottom-up fashion.
5. **Varied Interests:** Previously, structures maintained singularity in their methodology, but social computing offers avenues for people of different interests.
6. **Non-Hierarchical Approach:** The hierarchical structures present are a thing of the past, as we move towards flexible and evolving approaches.
7. **Alternate Revenue Methods:** Revenue is no longer generated in the typical consumer producer fashion but generated from advertisements (Parameswaran & Whinston, 2007).

Figure 2. Characteristics of social computing

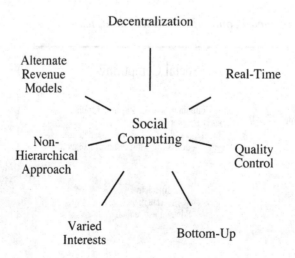

In this chapter the authors discuss data acquisition and preparation, usage of social computing, through a survey. In addition, the authors provide insights on future research directions with a particular focus on business impact. More specifically, the main contributions of this chapter can be summarized as follows

- The authors present a data acquisition and preparation.
- The authors provide insights usage of social computing, through a social network survey and mining methods.
- The authors provide detailed future research directions in social network analysis and mining from the viewpoint of trade applications.

The research work is planned as follows. In Social communication inputs section the authors introduce social communication inputs with direct and indirect connections

In Data Procurement and Composition section the authors discuss method of data preparation those includes data acquisition and anonymization. In Methodology section the authors focus on reputation, trust, and methods of finding experts and assembling teams. In implementation of Apriori Data Mining Algorithms section, the authors discuss the detection of communities in social networks, models of graph evolution, and link formation. Shifting Paradigm Section focuses on information propagation in social networks, considering influence, information propagation, and churn. Finally, in Future direction section the authors summarize potential business applications and future research directions. Finally Conclusions and future work are presented.

SOCIAL COMMUNICATION INPUTS

Social communication data can often be derived from multiple data sources, thus the preparation and collection of social network data required special attention as it continues to be a major hurdle in industrial applications. In this study we have collected data by implementing survey form. This study was carried out on a sample of 173 participants in the age group 18 years and above. A questionnaire regarding their use, frequency was shared and data collected. In the following section the results of this study have been detailed and briefly mention some of the most important issues.

Direct and Indirect Connections

Social communication can be represented as a graph $G = (V, E)$. Every node in the set V represents a user or customer in the network, and an edge (u, v) in the set E models a certain type of interaction between the users or customers represented by nodes u and v. Depending on the type of relationship modelled the edges may be *directed* or *undirected*.

In many domains, the social network structure includes links that are directly declared by users and links that are indirect and have to be inferred. For instance, in online social networking platforms, individuals can declare directly their "friends" or connections "join" a group, "follow" a user, accept a "friendship" request, etc. However, these directly declared links may be incomplete and not describe entirely all of the relationships in the network.

Indirect connections can be revealed from user's activities by analyzing wide-ranging and repeated interactions between users. In social media sites, this may include voting, sharing, bookmarking, tagging, and/or commenting items from a specific user or set of users, or other type of repeated interactions between individuals. In telecommunications networks, Short Message Service (SMS) and repeated calls between individuals can be mined from call-detail records and interpreted as relationships. Indirect connections can also be discovered from user's similarity. For instance, in social media sites, users that use the same tags often can be described as similar and connected through links, and such implicit connections can be used for business applications.

DATA PROCUREMENT AND COMPOSITION

In the early days of social network analysis research the biggest hurdle was collection of relevant data. There were no "automatic" methods to collect data and, as in most of social science research, data collection was done by performing interviews and often small-scale group studies with volunteers. Nowadays, the collection of raw data is done from online sources (e.g., Web) and offline sources (e.g., call data) is much easier, and while data quality has always been an important issue and approaches to address it have been studied since the early 1950's [Winkler 2003], there are new challenges specific to social networks that include the computational complexity in analyzing networks of millions or billions of nodes and the integration of various data sources in treating implicit connections. In addition, due to the sensitivity of information on social relationships, additional privacy issues arise.

Social network data from online networks may suffer additional problems including the following:

- Duplicate nodes, for example, a single person having two email addresses;
- Inactive nodes: individuals who do not explicitly remove their profile, but no longer access it (one case occurs when people pass away and their profiles remain active though);
- Artificial nodes for example, automated agents, possibly malicious ones.

Now, once we have the data, we need to pre process it which includes cleaning of data and preparation of the data for data analysis. This data has a lot of discrepancies like incorrect data, missing values, abrupt values and blank columns which need to be cleaned. In this chapter, the authors have organized the data into a single table, with different attributes which makes it look more structured.

Rahm and Do [2000] classify the problem into two basic categories namely *Single-source* and *multiple-source* problems. Those are further divided into *schema* and *instance* levels. The process of data cleaning is characterized into several phases like: data analysis, definition of transformation workflow and mapping rules, verification, transformation, and backflow of cleaned data. Although their framework is not specific to social networks, the issues in data cleaning for social network analysis can be clearly identified from their perspective (Bonchi, Castillo, Gionis & Jaimes, 2011). Social media the big umbrella, encompassing various players has contributed towards the growth of social computing. Here we discuss a few of the giant players of social media based on the data collected through our survey form. Facebook one of the oldest social networking site which was originally developed by University students. It is responsible to creating the virtual social village. It gives an opportunity to small social groups to share information for social cause; moreover, it provides a platform for product brands to connect to their users at personal level. Facebook allows producers to reach out to their audience online. In spite of being one of the oldest social networking sites, it has still maintained its popularity. On the basis of survey, data collected shows that Facebook is still choice of 39.7% of people which they use for socializing and as per survey it is identified that 76.4% are using it for the same.

The sea of blue colour in the graph below shows the popularity of Facebook worldwide, which strongly supports the results of the survey done by us. In spite of being one of the oldest social networking sites, it still has the major stake in the world of social networking.

Figure 3. Graph showing percentage of various social media platform used by sample size of 73 responses, the graph shows that of Facebook is the most popular social media which is 39.7%

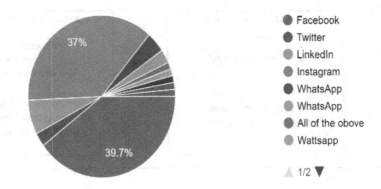

METHODOLOGY

To generate perception finding, we are using raw data collected from different social media sites. The proposed methodology is divided into three phases such as Text pre-processing, Association rule mining and Perception Findings are shown in Figure 4.

In text pre-processing phase we first tokenize the input document in to tokens after that tokens are filtered by removing end word as they do not carry any meaningful information. Normally token contains many affixes and it is required to remove all the affixes to achieve better result in perception finding.

Then the tokens are indexed using TFIDF (Term Frequency Inverse Document Frequency) values. The Association rule mining phase creates association rules based on weighting scheme TF-IDF, which depends on the user's requirement, the high frequency keywords are selected to generate association rules. The last phase is to generate perception finding using those generated association rules.

Text Pre-Processing Phase

Pre-processing is an essential part of the analysis process. In which, unstructured data is reformatted into a uniform and standardized form. Identification of the sentences, words and characters are done at this stage, which are the elementary units communicated to all further processing stages. The high-quality of the pre-processing has a big impact on the end result of the complete system.

Figure 4. Proposed system block diagram

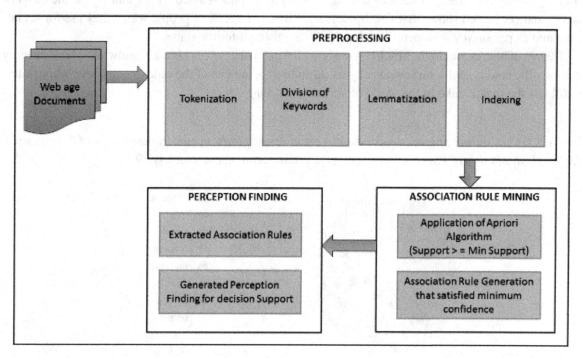

Web data is in unstructured format and the data usage generated everyday on social media, hence to mine such large documents it is mandatory to pre-process the input document is stored into structured format which can be further used for pre-processing and generating association in it.

The text pre-processing phase involves the following phase shown below:

- **Tokenization:** Normally web pages contain information in unstructured format. This creates a concern for the process of text mining and it also consumes lot of memory as well as time to process the same. Tokenization process converts an important portion of data into token, e.g. an account number when tokenized it is converted into a random string of characters which do not have significant value, if breached. The main role of this process is to convert unstructured document into structured document.

- **Division of keywords:** To generate accurate knowledge from the raw data collected, the user needs to find out relationship between all the keywords. This task becomes very tedious if we do not remove redundant and inefficient data. Finding relationship becomes very difficult if that document is not filter well, thus filtration of raw data can be done by removing stop words (does not have meaningful information) and suffixes (attached with the same word but with different form).

- **Lemmatization:** Lemmatization is the process which trims down the words to a word existing in the language. Either Stemming or Lemmatization can be used. Stemmers and lemmatizers are implemented in the libraries like nltk, and spaCy. Lemmatization replaces the entire match suffix from the keywords with replacement character and words. The reasons for using stemming are it changes the meaning of term even main route word is same, ambiguous association rule are generated, it make data complex and occupy extra memory

- **Indexing:** After applying the above process the weight scheme Term Frequency, Inverse Document Frequency (TF-IDF) is used to allocate weight to distinguish expressions in the document. Frequency is the count that represents how many times of keywords has occurred in that document whereas inverse document frequency is the count that represents the total number of documents that contains the keywords at least once. The authors have used this weighting scheme to select higher frequency keywords for generating association rules. In the next section apriori algorithm is used for association rules generation.

IMPLEMENTATION OF APRIORI DATA MINING ALGORITHM

Apriori algorithm which was intended to work on databases was developed by Agarwal and Srikant

In Association rule mining the association rules are referred as simple if then statement that helps to discover relationships between apparently independent relational databases or other data repositories.

Association rule mining is a process which intends to examine frequently occurring patterns, correlations, or associations from datasets found in various kinds of databases. The databases are like relational, transactional, and other type of repositories. Association rule mining is a technique that shows how items are associated to each other. Association Rule Mining analyses important relationships associated between the various social sites. We cannot say by our own any relationship exists. We have to analyse millions of transactions and search patterns between them. If you look at the user who opens an account on Facebook then there is a possibility to open an account on Histagram.

This section explains how algorithm works. In association rule mining if you open account on social media A, then you open account on social media B. This type of one social media account to another social media account relationship is called a Single Cardinality Rule.

There are customers who open social media account A, social media account B, they can also open social media account on C or customer who open social media account on A, B and C can also open social media account on D in this Rule Cardinality is increased and there are many such combinations. Hence customers having multiple social media accounts on various social media are identified as increased cardinality.

Suppose if you are having many social media then just imagine how many rules you are supposed to design. Before understanding the algorithm we understand math behind this algorithm there are three important parameters are support, confidence and lift. Support, indicates how frequently the if/then relationship appears in the database. Confidence, tells about the how many times these relationships have been found to be true and lift is a measure of the performance of an association rule at forecasting or classifying cases as having an enhanced response, calculated against a random choice targetingmodel. Apriori Algorithm uses the frequent web page sets to generate the association rule. And it is based on the concept that a subset of a frequent web page set must also be a frequent web page set.

Now this raises the question what exactly is a frequent web page set? So frequent web page set is an web page set whose support value is greater than the threshold value just now the authors discussed that the marketing team according to the sales have a minimum threshold value for the confidence as well as the support. So frequent web page set is that web page set whose support value is greater than the threshold value already specified example, if A and B is a frequent web page sets than A and B should also be frequent web page sets individually.

Now, let's consider the following social file transaction to make things a little easier. Suppose, we had transactions 1, 2, 3, 4, 5 and these web pages are there. So T1 has P1, P3 & P4, T2 has P2, P3 and P5, T3 has P1, P2, P3, P5, T4 has P2 P5 and T5 has P1, P3, P5.

Figure 5. Apriori algorithm: 1st iteration and 2nd iteration

Now the first step is to build a list of web page sets of size 1 by using this transactional data. Here the minimum support count given is 2. Let's suppose its 2 so the first step is to create web page sets of size 1 and calculate their support values. So as you can see here, we have Table A1 in which we have the web page sets 1, 2, 3, 4, 5 and the support values. The support is calculated using frequency division by the total number of occurrences. Hence accordingly here for the web page set 1 the support is 3 as you can see here that web page set 1 appears in T1, T3 and T5. So as you can see, it's frequency is 1, 2 & 3 now as you can see here the web page set 4 has a support of 1 as it occurs only once in transaction 1 but the minimum support value is 2 that's why it's going to be eliminated. So we have the final table, which is Table B1 as indicated in figure 5. Here the web page sets 1, 2, 3 and 5 and we have the support values 3, 3, 4 and 4.

Now the next step is to create web page sets of size 2 and calculate their support values. Now all the combinations of the web page sets in the B1, which is the final table in which we discarded the 4, are going to be used for this iteration. So we get the table A2 so as you can see here we have {P1, P2}, {P1, P3}, {P1, P5}, {P2, P3}, {P2, P5} and {P3, P5}. Now, if you calculate the support here again, we can see that the web pages set {P1, P2} have a support of 1 which is again less than the specified threshold. So we're going to discard that so if we have a look at the table B2 we have {P1, P3}, {P1, P5}, {P2, P3}, {P2, P5} and {P3, P5}.

Figure 6. Apriori algorithm: 3st iteration (pruning) and 4nd iteration

TRANSACTION	WEB PAGE
T1	P1 P3 P4
T2	P2 P3 P5
T3	P1 P2 P3 P5
T4	P2 P5
T5	P1 P3 P5

WEB PAGE	SUPPORT
{P1,P2,P3} {P1,P2},{P1,P3}, {P2,P3}	NO
{P1,P2,P5} {P1,P2},{P1,P5},{P2,P5}	NO
{P1,P3,P5} {P1,P5},{P1,P3},{P3,P5}	YES
{P2,P3,P5} {P2,P3},{P2,P5},{P3,P5}	YES

TABLE A3

TABLE B3

WEB PAGE	SUPPORT
{P1,P3,P5}	2
{P2,P3,P5}	2

WEB PAGE	SUPPORT
{P1,P3}	3
{P1,P5}	2
{P2,P3}	2
{P2,P5}	3
{P3,P5}	3

TABLE B2

WEB PAGE	SUPPORT
{P1,P2}	1

TABLE A4

TRANSACTION	WEB PAGE
T1	P1 P3 P4
T2	P2 P3 P5
T3	P1 P2 P3 P5
T4	P2 P5
T5	P1 P3 P5

Again the authors are going to move forward and create the web page set of size 3 and calculate their support values. Now, all the combinations are going to be used from the web page set B2 for this particular iterations. Now before calculating support values, let's perform pruning on the data set. Now what is pruning? Now after the combinations are being made. The authors' device A3 web page sets to check if there is another subset whose support is less than the minimum support value.

That is what frequent web page setsmean. So if you have a look here the web pages that authors have is {P1, P2, P3}, {P1, P2}, {P1, P3}, {P2, P3} for the first one Because as you can see here, if one look at the subset of {P1, P2, P3}, then we have {P1, P2} as well [we discard in earlier step], so authors are going to discard this whole web page set same goes for the second one. The data includes {P1, P2, P5}, we have {P1, P2} in that, which was discarded in the previous set or the previous step. That's why authors are going to discard that also which leaves us with only two factors, which is {P1, P3, P5} web page set and the {P2, P3, P5} and the support for this is 2 and 2 as well now. Table A4 is created using four elements, we're going to have only one web page set which is P1, P2, P3 and P5 and then we have a look at the table where the transaction table 1, 2, 3 and 5 appears. So the support is 1 and since A4 the support of the whole table A4 is less than 2 so the process is stopped here and return to the previous web page set i.e. T3.

So the frequent web page sets have {P1, P3, P5} and {P2, P3, P5}. Now, let's assume our minimum confidence value is 60 percent. Hence the authors are going to generate all the non-empty subsets for each frequent web page sets. Now for I equal {P1, P3, P5} which is the web page set. We get the subset {P1, P3}, {P1, P5}, {P3, P5}, {P1}, {P3} and {P5} similarly for {P2, P3, P5} we get {P2,P3}, {P2, P5}, {P3,P 5}, {P2}, {P3} and {P5} now this rule states that for every subset S of I the output of the rule gives something like S gives I to S that implies S recommends I of S and this is only possible if the support of I divide by the support of S is greater than equal to the minimum confidence value.

Figure 7. Association rule generation for decision support

RULE1: {P1, P3} gives {P1, P3, P5} and {P1, P3}. It means P1 and P3 is P5 so the **confidence** is equal to the **support of** {P1, P3, P5} divided by the **support of** {P1, P3} that equals 2/3 which is 66% and which is greater than the 60 percent. So the **Rule 1** is selected.

RULE2: {P1, P5} gives {P1, P3, P5} and {P1, P3}. It means P1 and P3 is P5 so the **confidence** is equal to the **support of** {P1, P3, P5} divided by the **support of** {P1, P5} that equals 2/2 which is 100% and which is greater than the 60 percent. So the **Rule 2** is selected.

RULE3: {P3, P5} gives {P1, P3, P5} and {P3, P5}. It means P3 and P5 is P1 so the **confidence** is equal to the **support of** {P1, P3, P5} divided by the **support of** {P3,P5} that equals 2/3 which is 66% and which is greater than the 60 percent. So the **Rule 3** is selected.

RULE4: {P1} gives {P1, P3, P5} and {P1}. It means P1 is P3 and P5 so the **confidence** is equal to the **support of** {P1, P3, P5} divided by the **support of** {P1} that equals 2/3 which is 66% and which is greater than the 60 percent. So the **Rule 4** is selected.

RULE5: {P3} gives {P1, P3, P5} and {P3}. It means P3 is P1 and P5 so the **confidence** is equal to the **support of** {P1, P3, P5} divided by the **support of** {P3} that equals 2/4 which is 50% and which is less than the 60 percent. So the **Rule 5** is Rejected

RULE6: {P5} gives {P1, P3, P5} and {P5}. It means P5 is P1 and P3 so the **confidence** is equal to the **support of** {P1, P3, P5} divided by the **support of** {P3} that equals 2/4 which is 50% and which is less than the 60 percent. So the **Rule 6** is Rejected

---

Now applying these rules to the web page set of B3 we get

RULE1: {P1, P3} gives {P1, P3, P5} and {P1, P3}. It means P1 and P3 is P5 so the confidence is equal to the support of {P1, P3, P5} divided by the support of {P1, P3} that equals 2/3 which is 66% and which is greater than the 60 percent. So the Rule 1 is selected.

Now if we come

RULE2: {P1, P5} gives {P1, P3, P5} and {P1, P3}. It means P1 and P3 is P5 so the confidence is equal to the support of {P1, P3, P5} divided by the support of {P1, P5} that equals 2/2 which is 100% and which is greater than the 60 percent. So the Rule 2 is selected.

But again, if you check Rule 5 and Rule 6 have similarity, if we select P3 gives {P1, P3, P5} and {P3} it means if you have P3, we also get P1 and P5. So the confidence for this comes at 50% which is less than the given 60 percent target. So we're going to reject this Rule and the same is applied for rule number 6.

Now the thing to remember is that although the Rule 1 and Rule 5 look a lot similar they are not. So it really depends what's on the left hand side of the arrow and what's on the right hand side of the arrow is the if-then possibility.

SHIFTING PARADIGM

This chapter contributes insights to knowledge on how social media platforms can be used to increase the quality of life of the elderly and which is the popular social media platform used by the elderly respondents of this study. Defining age can be difficult and complex due to its multi-dimensionality. Ageing can be conceptualized with the perspective of a four-dimensional model based on biological, cognitive, social (actions) and psychological functional areas of self (Barak, Mathur, Lee, & Zhang, 2001). The increase in life span of human beings due to advances in health and medicine has sparked a global ageing phenomenon that has resulted in an energetic older population (compared to a few decades ago), thereby questioning traditional definitions and boundaries. But, typically, chronological age has been used to define the elderly, predominantly for research on ageing and communication, as it is easy to measure. Elderly are therefore defined as those aged sixty and above for the purpose of this study.

Loneliness and Social Isolation: Effects

Loneliness and social isolation depressingly impact overall health, especially in an older age group, which virtues the attention placed on how social benefits can be derived from technology and social media engagement. Social media engagement can help to reduce loneliness by providing various platforms to connect with loved ones. Platforms like WhatsApp, Facebook and Twitter are easily accessible at a relatively low-cost to keep the elderly socially engaged.

The purpose of use of social media may differ from person to person. Reducing social isolation and loneliness and a strong willingness to be involved of their family lifestyles are the important motivators for seniors to go on social media. Participation in communities, creating new social circles and establishing new relationships on-line also cause them to use social media. Putting round on facebook, twitter or instagram offers more price than just conversation (chatting/talking) with buddies or posting pictures.

The utilization of social media is pervasive amongst younger people; but still elderly people are still lagging behind the younger demographic (Norval, 2012). Research has revealed that lack of social contact as a result of living alone or of having limited social networks, could lead to social isolation and ultimately impact negatively on the health of senior citizens. Nevertheless, by using social media people are able to remain socially connected irrespective of physical distances or most significant impairments brought about by old age (Bell, Fausset, Farmer, Nguyen, Harley & Fain, 2013). It stands to reason that, with a growing ageing population increasingly making use of social media and understanding its use, there is a positive impact on the quality of life. This is also changing the contours of social interactions and is of great value to society at large.

Table 1. Responses on the use and preference of social media

Social Media Type	Responses	Percentage
Facebook	98	78.40%
Whatsapp	125	100%
Instagram	90	72%
Twitter	92	73.60%
Linkedin	57	45.60%

Figure 8. Graphical representation of use & preference of social media

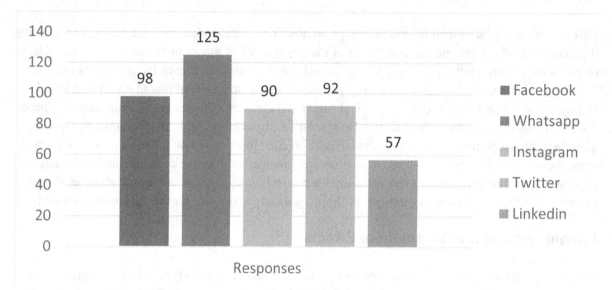

In this study, the responses of the target group on use of social media and preferred media platforms were recorded and the same are presented below in Table1.

Figure 8 shows the results that WhatsApp is the most popular medium used followed by Facebook, Twitter, Instagram and LinkedIn. All respondents found WhatsApp quite easy to use and very quick in getting a personalized response. The respondents expressed that WhatsApp is one of the most popular messaging and video calling apps and is available for free. Group and individual chatting and video calling, posting pictures and updating latest happenings have made it most popular among the respondents. It was found that LinkedIn is mostly used by those who are still working or are self-employed; hence its users were less as compared to other social media platforms.

It is prominent however, that social and cognitive ability are linked. For example, solitude and social isolation are predictors of cognitive decreases among individuals over the age of 65 years (James, Wilson, Barnes, & Bennett, 2011; Tilvis et al., 2004; Wilson et al., 2007). Social media is a powerful tool that can also forge new friendships and inspire civic engagement. At present, 34% use social networks against 12 percent five years ago.

Results of another anonymous survey have confirmed that respondents were light users of Facebook, using only a limited number of features. It also revealed that the respondents used Facebook primarily to stay socially engaged with their friends, family and community which adds happiness to their lives.

Indian Social Media Landscape

With the ease of internet access, the wide variety of lively social media users in India stood at 330 million in 2019 and it's far anticipated to reach 448 million via 2023. Facebook and YouTube are the most famous social media networks in India, the access of whatsapp into India's digital marketplace boosted app utilization, with a doubling in rural regions in recent years. Data suggests that the reach of the messaging provider extends wider than simply city regions. Indians now download more apps than citizens of any other country – over 19 billion apps have been downloaded by Indian users in 2019, which results in a 195% boom over 2016 facts. The common Indian social media consumer spends 17 hours on the system/device every week, which is more than China and United States social media users. Indian net users' experience of social media consistently increasedin the last few years. In 2021, it's widely predicted that there can be around 448 million social network customers in India, a vast increase from 2019 wherein it figured at 351 million. There are about 270 million facebook users in India as of 2019, setting India as the United States of America with the biggest facebook consumer base in the international.

Survey of the Use of Social Media

The use of technology has transformed peoples living style nowadays. For this study we selected 125 senior respondents who were older than 60 years and using social media platforms in their personal life. Respondents were given a questionnaire in Google Form to study the use of social media platforms such as WhatsApp, Facebook, Twitter, LinkedIn and Instagram to find out how these platforms are helping the elders keep socially, mentally, emotionally and cognitively active and healthy. Figure 9 reveals that all the respondents of this study are using social media at different levels.

Figure 9. Usage of social networking sites

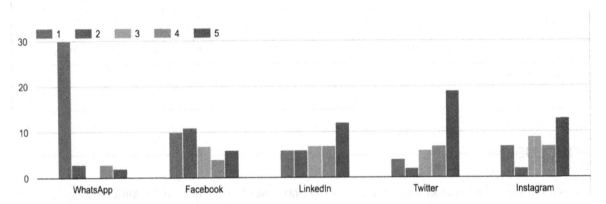

FUTURE DIRECTIONS

The survey conducted questioned users on where they think the future lies. A sample is shown in figure 10 below.

The general contention is that the growth of social media will continue to escalate and takes its place as the primary player in various fields. Some points to note are:

- The field will depend more on multimedia than text.
- Influencer marketing will continue to create its own niche.
- Social media may play a more defined role in the economy.
- Platform for education
- Social media uses less personal content than memes.

- Messaging via audio clips which in turn leads to speech recognition and personalized communication environment using AR and VR for them.
- Brands connect with the audience rather than bombarding with advertisements.
- It has changed the way we work and will continue to evolve.

Figure 10. Forecast about future of social media by sample population (73 users)

Future of social media

73 responses

Very promising

Till 2050, social media platforms will be the main source of communication around the globe due to accessibility and various people belonging to various sects will adapt platform according to their need. This will divide the social media into 2 or 3 groups according to usability.

For social connectivity

It will continue to grow..and probably there would some new kind of social media app that would be famous.

It will get more popular

Unbeatable

The future of social media seems like it will grow more and help make connecting to people easier

More broader

CONCLUSION

Age should never be a barrier when it comes to technology. User friendly and simple apps make social media very popular among different age groups. Sometimes it may be difficult for the elderly people to keep pace with the ever-changing world of technology and social media. There may be some negatives of using social media and the online world, but the benefits of being active on social media are far more important than the negative aspects of it. This study finding indicates that the potential for positive consequences is high: social media participation can advance health-related knowledge on prevention, avoidance, diagnosis, and treatment of conditions and disorders. In terms of meaningful social exchange, social media can be used as a means to provide and receive social support, overcome loneliness and to enhance feelings of control and self-efficacy.

The study found that 100% participants of the target group feel that social media platforms are user friendly, 94.7% felt that the use of social media helps in updating of knowledge and 65.8% felt that it is useful for getting medical and health care benefits. Only 34.2% felt that these platforms were not useful. Apriori Algorithm uses the frequent web page sets to generate the association rule. It is based on the concept that a subset of a frequent web page set must also be a frequent web page set itself. The outcomes help to identify the interest of the user, so that unwanted, unnecessary information will not be communicated to the users in future. The brands can use the association to identify the similar interest customers and can form a better connection with them. Sharing improves the overall use of social media.

FUTURE WORK

This chapter explains the social media network data analysis and trends whereas the future work is totally based on user oriented enhancement. Currently social media is used for messaging, posting pictures, videos, sharing views etc. The future of social media is mostly based on one on one communication with followers, fans. The mining algorithms are used to identify the association between the brands and users, it unites people with common interests. Users can interact or share information with members of any other group, parents, entrepreneurs etc. Basically social media has become more user centric and user oriented.

REFERENCES

Agrahari & Rao. (2007). Association Rule Mining using RHadoop. *Proceedings of the International Research Journal of Engineering and Technology, 4*(10).

Barak, B., Mathur, A., Lee, K., & Zhang, Y. (2001). Perceptions of age–identity: A cross- cultural inner-age exploration. *Psychology and Marketing, 18*(10), 1003–1029. doi:10.1002/mar.1041

Bell, C., Fausset, C., Farmer, S., Nguyen, J., Harley, L., & Fain, W. B. (2013). Examining social media use among older adults. *Proceedings of the 24th ACM Conference on Hypertext and Social Media*, 158-163. 10.1145/2481492.2481509

Bonchi, Castillo, Gionis, & Jaimes. (2011). Social Network Analysis and Mining for Business Applications. *ACM Transactions on Intelligent Systems and Technology, 2*(3).

Ching-man. Yeung, & Iwata. (2011). Research on Social Network Mining and Its Future Development. *NTT Technical Review, 9*(11). doi:10.1088/1742-6596/1235/1/012111

Goldberg, A., & Zhu, X. (2004). Seeing stars when there aren't many stars: Graph-based semi supervised learning for sentiment categorization. *HLT-NAACL 2006 Workshop on Textgraphs: Graph-based Algorithms for Natural Language Processing.*

Jackson, M. O. (2010). *Social and economic networks.* Princeton University Press.

Kaschesky, M., Sobkowicz, P., & Bouchard, G. (2011). Opinion Mining in Social network: Modelling, Simulating, and Visualizing Political Opinion Formation in the Web. *Proceedings of 12th Annual International Conference on Digital Government Research.*

Kim, P. (2006). *The Forrester Wave: Brand Monitoring, Q3 2006.* Forrester Wave.

Lee & Chen. (2013). Understanding social computing research. *IT Professional, 15*(6), 56-62.

Liu, F., & Lee, H. J. (2010). Use of social network information to enhance collaborative filtering performance. *Expert Systems with Applications, 37*(7), 4772–4778. doi:10.1016/j.eswa.2009.12.061

Messinger, P. R., Stroulia, E., Lyons, K., Bone, M., Niu, R. H., Smirnov, K., & Perelgut, S. (2009). Virtual worlds—past, present, and future: New directions in social computing. *Decision Support Systems*, *47*(3), 204–228. doi:10.1016/j.dss.2009.02.014

Messinger, Stroulia, Lyons, Bone, Niu, Smirnov, & Perelgute. (2009). Social computing: An overview. *Communications of the Association for Information Systems, 19*(1), 37.

Nanayakkara, Kumara, & Rathnayaka. (2021). A Survey of Finding Trends in Data Mining Techniques for Social Media Analysis. *Sri Lanka Journal of Social Sciences and Humanities*, *1*(2), 37–50.

Nasution, M. K. M. (2019). Social Network Mining: A discussion. *Journal of Physics: Conference Series*, 1235.

Norval, C. (2012). Understanding the incentives of older adults' participation on social networking sites. *ACM Sigaccess Accessibility and Computing*, *102*(102), 25–29. doi:10.1145/2140446.2140452

Pang, B., & Lee, L. (2008). Using very simple statistics for review search: An exploration. *Proceedings of the International Conference on Computational Linguistics (COLING)*.

Tepper, A. (2012). *How much data is created every minute?* https://mashable.com/2012/06/22/datacreated-every-minute/

Wang, F.-Y. (2008). Social computing: fundamentals and applications. In *2008 IEEE International Conference on Intelligence and Security Informatics*. IEEE. 10.1109/ISI.2008.4565016

Wang, F.-Y., Carley, K. M., Zeng, D., & Mao, W. (2007). Wang, Fei-Yue (2008). "Social computing: From social informatics to social intelligence. *IEEE Intelligent Systems*, *22*(2), 79–83. doi:10.1109/MIS.2007.41

Zhang, J., Jin, & Liu. (2015). Study of Data Mining Algorithm in Social Network Analysis. *3rd International Conference on Mechatronics, Robotics and Automation (ICMRA 2015)*.

Chapter 11
User Interface Design With Data Visualization Technique:
Case Study of the COVID-19 Pandemic in India

Reshma Nitin Pise
Vishwakarma University, India

Bharati Sanjay Ainapure
Vishwakarma University, India

ABSTRACT

User experience designers have to put in tremendous effort to convey complex information such that it can be easily understood and be visually appealing to the users. In today's world of big data, visualization techniques are essential to analyse massive amounts of complex data and make data-driven decisions. To support better decision making, visualization technologies enable users to uncover hidden patterns. During the COVID-19 pandemic, these techniques have been used as user interface in order to communicate the impact of the pandemic on the public. Considerable effort has been devoted to monitor the spread of the disease across the world and understand the various aspects of the pandemic. This chapter emphasizes the role of the data visualization technique as an effective user interface. Visualization of COVID-19 data is performed in the form of interactive dashboards, which can be beneficial to healthcare users and policy makers to plan the resource allocation and implement strategies to mitigate the effects of the pandemic.

INTRODUCTION

In today's digitized world, everyday huge amount of data is generated over the internet. As per survey ("How Much Data Is Created Every Day? [27 Powerful Stats]," n.d.) per day 1.145 trillion MB data is created all over the world. With the growth of internet users there is a huge increase in the data being generated. History of internet started from 1960 with email facility and then expanded its use for file

DOI: 10.4018/978-1-7998-9121-5.ch011

sharing in the year 1970. In the year 1989, revolution was created with the invention of world wide web (WWW). Tim Berners Lee was the scientistist who invented the WWW, which made us to share the information using network of computers. Since then, a plethora of sources have been available on the internet for people to share data. This massive amount data is called as big data. There are three major sources from which the data is generated day-by-day over the internet: 1. Transactional data, 2. Social media data and 3. Machine generated data. Apart from this public data, the private data is also generated from oganizations. This type of data resides behind the firewall.

Figure 1. Yearwise voume of data ("How Much Data Is Created Every Day? [27 Powerful Stats]," n.d.)

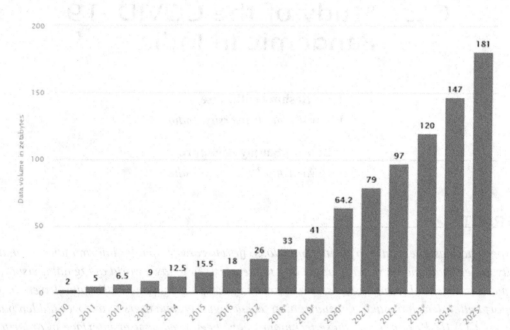

Figure 1 shows the volume of data being created every year. Due to easy access of internet, users digital footprint has resulted in rapid growth in the data and the data size is measured in megabytes, gigabytes, and terabytes, petabytes to zetabytes. As per source ("Total data volume worldwide 2010-2025 | Statista," n.d.) it is expected that till 2025, 181 zetabytes of data will be genearted. Since 2019, data usage has increased due to COVID-19 pandemic. During the countrywide lockdown, people work from home and internet usage has increased. Huge number of users are joining various social network sites to share their views. From the graph, it is clear that there is a large amount of data generated from the year 2019. There is a sudden increase from 42 zetabytes to 64.2 zetabytes. It is very important to know whether, the data generated over the internet or within organization is structured or unstrcuted. Unstrstured data needs a lot of efforts to make sense of it.

The graph ("Volume of data generated in a single year for various sources. | Download Scientific Diagram," n.d.) in Figure 2 shows the data generated from different types of sources that is used in data science for analysis. Out of all the data souces, 64% of the transactional data is used by many professional oganizations for analysis.

Figure 2. Sources of data ("Volume of data generated in a single year for various sources. | Download Scientific Diagram," n.d.)

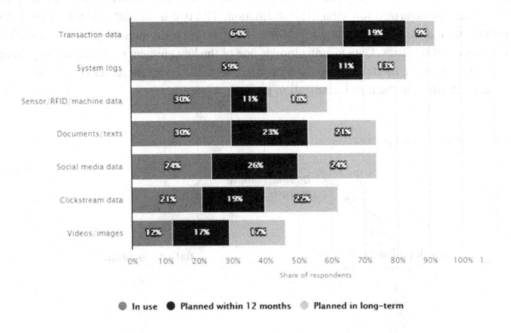

Eventhough huge amount of data is created everyday, if we don't know how to use and represent huge amount data strategically, then it is of no use. We should represent the data in an understandable form to gain actionable insights of huge and complex data.This type of representation can be done with the help of data visualization. When huge data is in the form text or any other structured or unstructured form, it is very difficult to understand it. We can call this data as information. To convert this information into understandable and interpretable form, data visuazilation is required.

This book chapter provides an insight of data visualization elements, techniques, its application areas and some of the popular data visualization tools. The chapter explores the online COVID -19 datasets of confirmed covid cases, recovered and deceased cases, data of hospitals, beds available and COVID -19 test data i.e., the number of tests conducted, number of positive cases across different states in India.

The key contributions of this book chapter are:

1. Emphasize the role of data visualization techniques as an effective user interface.
2. Apply visualization techniques for COVID-19 data (both Quantitativeand Qualitative) using Python libraries, PowerBI and Tableu to gain a better understanding of the pandemic situation.
3. c. Design appropriate visuals such as charts, word clouds and dashboards so that the users, policy makers and healthcare workers can easily compare data, detect relationships, predict future trend and use it for better decision making.

What is Data Visualization?

Data visualization is the use of graphical representations to explore, interpret, communicate massive amount of data. Visual elements like charts, tables, graphs, and maps are used to present the data. Visualization is essential to detect and analyse meaningful patterns in the raw data and make data-driven decisions (Few, 2007). It is also referred to as information visualization since visualizations generally depict aggregated, summarized raw data i.e., information. The two terms data visualization and information visualization are used interchangeably. Data visualization is an intersection of various fields of graphics, science and statistics. Data visualization is one of the key element of data science. Along with data collection, extraction, modeling visualization helps to make conclusions about the data. Figure 3 shows the steps involved in the data visualization process.

Figure 3. Data visualization process

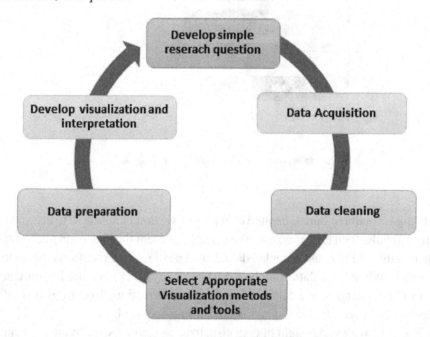

Before creating the visualization, one need to understand how data visualization will help the user or what type of research questions are to be answered. Clear research questions will avoid data visualization problems. For example Figure 4 shows an example of bad visualization. This figure depicts COVID-19 related data visualization, in which all the parameters are included in one chart. This type of visualization makes it hard to read and understand, especially when multiple y-axes are present. It is not clear from the graph which parameter corresponds to which axis. The graph does not even present clear-cut stastistics about COVID-19 records from different countries.

The second step of data visualization is the data acquisition. This is the process of data collection or generation. In this phase one can use the available data or can collect the data based on specific requirement. Some of the self data collection methods include: surveys, questionnaire, interviewing the users, group discussion, observations etc.

There are three basic data types (COWAN & Siegen, 2019):

1.   Quantitative: Data is a numerical measurement or a count. It has an implicit ordering among the values:

For example, i) price in Rupees: 100, 500, 2000 ii) age in years: 2, 18, 46

2.   Ordinal / Qualitative Data: It is not a numeric quantity but has some kind of order /rank i.e., it can be ordered and compared :

For example i) months in a year ii) user's rating of a movie: poor, average, good, very good

3.   Nominal / Categorical: Data are qualitative. It is a non-numerical data without any intrinsic order-ing. for example i) names of the countries: India, China, Japan ii) names of the fruits: bananas, apples, oranges, mangoes iii) Colors: red, blue, green, black.

Figure 4. Example of a bad visualization

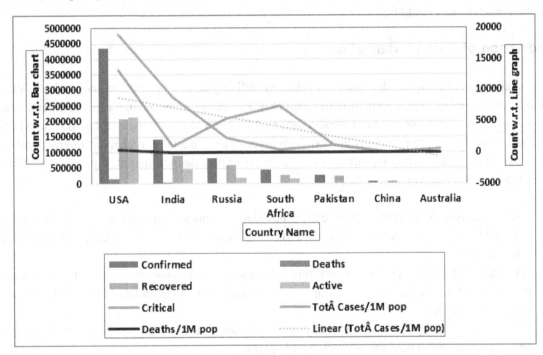

Data extraction is the data collection from different web pages or using the available sources to download the data. Whether data is acquired from other sources or collected on own, data need to be cleaned in order to make it useful. Next step in the visualization process is data cleaning. Preprocessing is another name used for data cleaning. In this phase, fixing of incomplete, inccorrect, missing values, outliers and duplicate values in the dataset is carried out. When data is gathered from several sources, there's a good risk it won't be exactly what we want. If we use incorrect data, outcome of data analysis and visualization becomes unreliable. In general there is no any specific way to do the data cleaning, but one can use data cleaning tools like Python, R etc.

Next step in data visualization process is to choose the correct data visulalization techniques and tools. Depending on the type of data or what you need to visualize, different techniques such as charts, plots, maps, dash boards, reports, tables, word clouds, network diagrams etc. are designed to present the data. These techniques can be implemented using the visualization tools e.g., PowerBI, Tableau, Qlik view, Sisense, DataBox, MS- Excel, DataWrapper or libraries of programming languages like Python, R etc.

Data preparation is one of the important step in data visualization. This includes: data reformatting, use of appropriate units to convert the values, data filtering, grouping of data, applying aggregate fucntions like, mean, mode, average. Data preparation ensures that the appropriate information is delivered to the intended users. This also makes the data enriched and optimized.

Final step is visualization and interpretation. The outcome of data analytics is displayed via data visualization. We can use one or more of the above mentioned methods and tools to design the visualization. The type of visualisation is determined by the data you're working with and the story you want to convey. Finally, data interpretation allows you to interpret the analysis and visualization. This is when you go beyond simply providing the data and explore it through the lens of your knowledge and experience. Interpretation could include not just a description or explanation of what the data shows, but also what the consequences could be.

Importance of Data Visualization

Data visualization improves understanding of data by utilising human perception and intellect. Visualization helps people analyse information more quickly. For example, in Business Environment, visualization aids in the communication of business data to decision makers, allowing them to respond faster than if the same facts were presented in reports. Widgets enable decision-makers to interact with data and uncover the questions they should be asking in order to gain deeper insight. Following are the few points that focus on importance of visualization:

- It assists decision-makers in comprehending how data is evaluated in order to make right decisions.
- Getting the target spectators to concentrate on insights of data in order to identify areas that need to be addressed.
- Using a visual representation of enormous volumes of data to provide a summary of previously unknown patterns in the data, exposing insights and the history behind the data in order to establish a decision goal.
- By making sense of your data, you may visualise company or organization data to monitor performance and transform patterns into achievable plans.
- It reveals previously ignored crucial information about the data sources in order to assist decision makers in the creation of data analysis reports.

Data visualisation is not just crucial for data scientists and analysts; it is also necessary for everybody in any profession. You need to visualise data whether you work in finance, marketing, technology, design, or anything else. This fact proves the importance of data visualization.

DATA VISUALIZATION TECHNIQUES AND ELEMENTS

We can create visualizations to represent amount (quantitative data: numerical values associated categories), deviation, distribution, proportions, ranking, correlation, geospatial information, x–y relationships, timelines etc. The designer has to determine what type of chart is most appropriate to represent his data or which graph gives the analysis desired for their specific query. Visualization can be static or interactive. Static type provides single dimensional data analysis whereas in interactive type, data can be visualized in multiple dimensions (Wilke, 2019)("Ebook I Visualize It!: A Comprehensive Guide to Data Visualization," n.d.). The following section presents the description of different types of charts and graphs that are commonly available in visualization tools.

Line Chart: Line charts are the most basic and frequently used graphs to show the relationship between two variables. In this chart, x-y axes (horizontal and vertical) are used to map quantitative variables. They are ideal choice to display changes or trends in data over a period of time (with x-axis representing time) ("Ebook I Visualize It!: A Comprehensive Guide to Data Visualization," n.d.).

Figure 5. Line chart for COVID cases

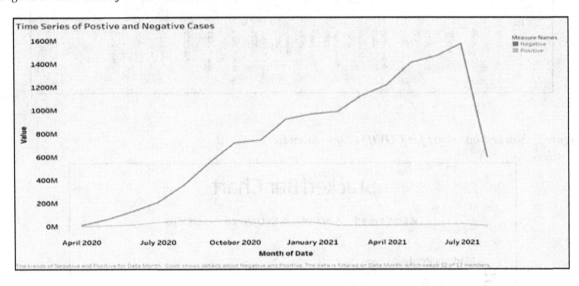

The line graph in Figure 5 shows the change in the number of COVID cases (positive and negative) over a period of 6 months from April 2020 to July 2021. The Y-axis represents number of people in millions and X-axis represents the time period in months.

Bar Chart: Bar charts are the most popular visuals to represent nominal or numerical data distributed into multiple discrete categories. We can quickly compare trends across different categories. Bar charts can be of 3 forms (COWAN & Siegen, 2019):

- Vertically aligned: Used for chronological data in left to right direction. Figure 6 shows a bar chart for the number of COVID negative cases month-wise for a period April 2020 to August 2021
- Horizontally aligned: Used to represent and compare different categories.
- Stacked bars: To show multiple categorical variables at the same time in a single chart. The horizontal stacked bar chart in Figure 7 displays the number of four categories of COVID cases (Confirmed, Active, Recovered and Deaths) across different states.

Figure 6. Bar chart for COVID cases monthwise

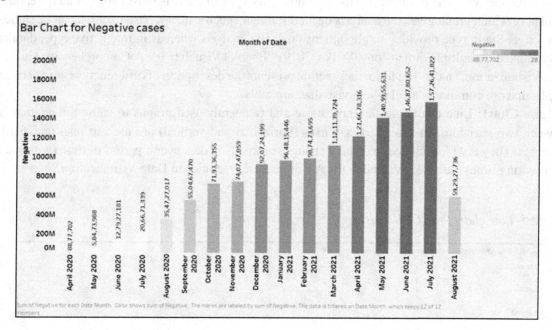

Figure 7. Stacked bar chart for COVID cases statewise

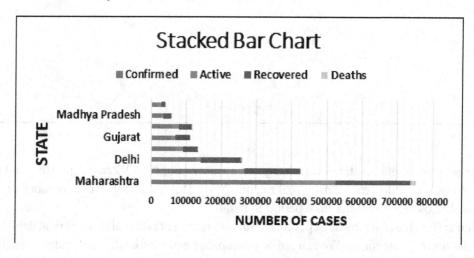

Pie Chart: Pie charts are visually attractive charts that are useful to showcase the relative proportions of a specific measure across multiple categories. They can be used with discrete or continuous data. A piechart consists of a circle divided into parts such that the area of each part is proportional to the fraction of the total being represented (Wilke, 2019). In general pie charts are ideal to illustrate small number of categories (upto 4) and to represent simple fractions, such as one-half, one-third, or one-quarter. Figure 8 is a piechart to present statewise number of COVID 19 confirmed cases where each slice of the circle corresponds to a different state. We can see from the chart, that maximum number of cases are from Mahrashtra followed by Tamilnadu and so on.

Figure 8. Pie chart for statewise COVID confirmed cases

Donut Chart / Ring Chart: It is a minor variation of piechart with space in the center of the circle. It is quick and easier to understand the proportion of the slice in a donut chart. Figure 9 shows a donut chart corresponding to the above pie chart.

Figure 9. Donut chart for statewise COVID confirmed cases

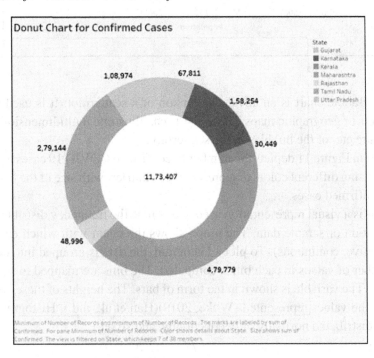

Scatter Plot: A scatter plot is an effective to analyze correlation between two or three variables, identify trends, clusters and outliers in the given large dataset (Han, Kamber, & Pei, n.d.). The chart includes independent points plotted on a cartesian plane. For example with two factors, a scatter plot can be used to explore the relationship between height and weight of a group of students. Generally a trend line referred to as line of regression (best fit line through the data points) is added to the scatterplot to visualize the nature of relationship between the variables. Figure 10 presents a scatterplot to explore the relationship between the number of COVID deaths and total population across different countries.

Figure 10. Scatterplot for countrywise COVID deaths

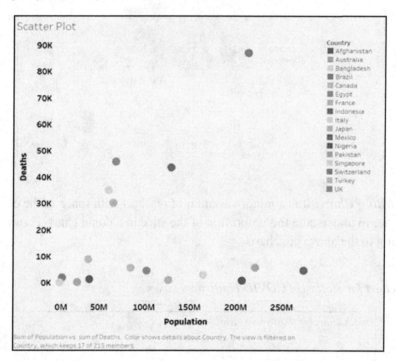

Bubble Chart: Bubble chart is an advanced version of a scatterplot. It is used to enrich the data shown in scatter plots or geographic maps.These charts can illustrate multidimensional data by varying the size, color, texture etc. of the bubbles in the scatterplot.

The Bubble chart in Figure 11 depicts the number of confirmed COVID 19 cases against total population of countries by using different colors to represent the countries, with size of the bubbles proportional to the number of confirmed cases.

Histogram: This is a visual representation used to examine the frequency distribution of a particular variable in a population or sample data. The graph shows the count with which each value occurs in the dataset (quantitative, continuous). To plot a histogram, the data is grouped into equal interval bins/ ranges and the number of values in each bin is computed. The bins are mapped to x-axis and the count is mapped on y-axis. The variable is shown in the form of bars. The heights of these bar are proportional to the frequency of the values represented (Wilke, 2019)(Han et al., n.d.). Histogram helps to quickly check if the data is distributed normally or exponentially, and so on.

Figure 11. Bubblechart for population and countrywise COVID cases

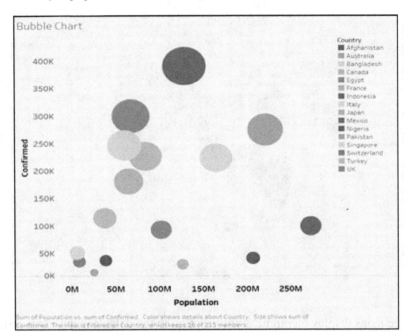

Figure 12. Histogram for COVID cases statewise

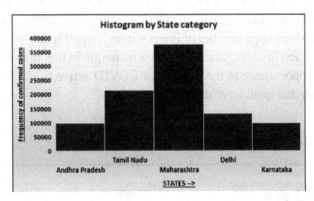

Figure 12 is a histogram to show the statewise distribution of COVID 19 confirmed cases where each bin reprents a state. We can quickly analyze which state is the most or the least affected.

Geographic Maps: These are useful to plot the geospatial i.e., location information present in the dataset like state or city names, latitude/ longitude values, zipcodes. The data is plotted locationwise on a map. Information such as population, literacy, income distribution, percentage of voting etc.) can be visualized better with a geographic map (Chen, n.d.). Geographic maps are useful to visualize qualitative geospatial data such as demographic information.

For example, we can plot a geographic map to show the total number of COVID 19 cases in India statewise as shown in Figure 13.

Figure 13. Geographic map for COVID cases statewise

Tree Map: Tree maps display hierarchical information in the dataset using a tree structure as nested rectangles in a plane. They are created by iteratively partitioning an area alternatively in a vertical and horizontal direction (Chen, n.d.)(SHARDA, DELEN, & TURBAN, 2018). Surface areas of the rectangles obtained are proportional to the data that they represent. Rectangles at the leaf level, are colored to show a different dimension of the data and uncover the patterns present in the data set. Advantage of tree maps is that they can show large number of items within a small space. Figure 14 shows a tree map for number of COVID 19 active cases, statewise. Each rectangle in this map represents a state and the size of the rectangle is proportionate to the number of COVID active cases. Tree maps can be used to visualize both quantitative and qualitative data.

Figure 14. Tree map for COVID cases statewise

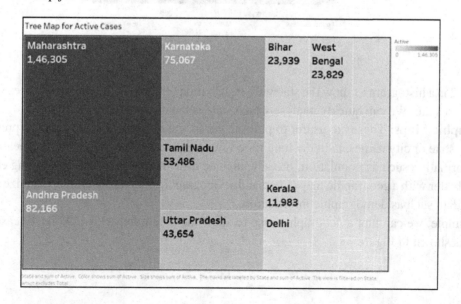

Heat Map: Heat maps are used to represent the quantitative value of a variable in the form of a matrix / map/ a customized image, across two categories using different colors or color intensities. Intense colors are used to show higher values and additional dimensions are visualized with size and color. The viewer can easily compare the data across two different categories at a glance(SHARDA et al., 2018).

Highlight Table: A highlight table is a 2D matrix. Like a heat map, gradient of colors are used to compare categorical data. In addition the table is populated with numerical values of the variable being represented.

Figure 15. Highlight table for COVID cases statewise

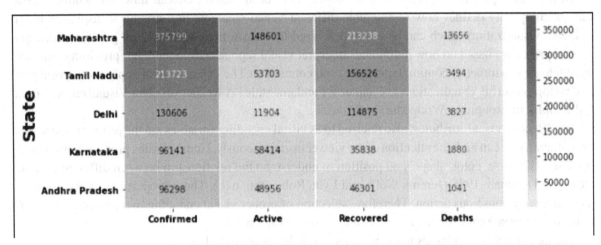

For instance, we can plot a highlight table as in Figure 15 to represent the number of COVID 19 patients across different states and patient category (confirmed, active, recovered cases and death).

There are many other specialized graphs and charts used for specific visualization purpose. They are derived from basic graphs and also there is a trend to combine the charts listed above to create more attractive, informative visualizations by adding animation to present complex data. Charts like Gantt charts and PERT (Network) charts find application in planning and scheduling of big projects. They are appropriate for portraying project schedule, actitity duration/ completion, resource allocation and task dependencies (SHARDA et al., 2018). Bullet graphs, a variation of a bar charts are used to showcase progress / achievement towards a goal. Dashboards is a form of visualization technique extensively used for business performance management and business intelligence. Dashboard provides visual information about important performance metrics in a consolidated view so that information can be understood easily and quickly in a single view and explored futher in depth (Few, 2005).

BASIC PRINCIPLES OF DATA VISUALIZATION

The primary objective of data visualization is to aid the users understand and analyze the data we are trying to portray. Data visualization is a platform for communicating stories and exploring the objects being represented. It emphasizes on effective communication through perception. Therefore, it is essential to have a comprehensive understanding of how to create data visualizations in order deliver simple, meaningful and effective charts, reports, infographics, and dashboards. It is also important to adhere to a set of best practices to format and design attractive visualization. Communicating the data effectively requires both artistic and scientific skills.

The most commonly used perceptual properties in information visualization are based on

- Gestalt Laws
- Pre-attentive attributes

Gestalt Laws play an important role in information visualization . Gestalt Law, also known as the Law of Simplicity defines how to assemble different visual elements in a graphical display in order to create visualization which can be easily perceived by human brain. The Gestalt guidelines specify several principles based on how individuals interpret visual representation namely - proximity, similarity, enclosure, symmetry, continuity, closure, and connection.The designers can apply these principles to develop powerful visualizations ("Chapter 2 Fundamentals | A Reader on Data Visualization," n.d.) ("Principles of grouping - Wikipedia," n.d.).

Pre-attentive visual attributes, also referred to as visual encoding variables are the properties of visual presentation that can grab the attention of the viewer instantaneously. Human brains process certain characteristics like size, color, shape, and position to understand the relationship between different graphic elements(Treisman, 1985)(Jeremy Wolfe and Lynn Robertson, n.d.). These properties are perceived by us without any conscious action. Therefore, selection of proper visual encoding to represent our data is important to create easy to understand visualizations (Ware, n.d.).

The key visual design issues to be considered are discussed as below.

Spatial Elements (Structure, Layout)

This refers to the space in which the information is represented and the structure, layout / organization of the visualization. "Layout" is a plan for placing graphical elements in order to organize the space effectively and according to users' needs for navigationg, scrolling filtering information. The structure of a visualization should highlight some aspect of the underlying data. The most important view is placed at the top or in the upper left corner. The human eyes tend to see that part initially, while looking at the presentation (Card, 2009) ("Visual Mapping – The Elements of Information Visualization | Interaction Design Foundation (IxDF)," n.d.).

Most commonly two dimensional space (2D with x and y axes) is chosen to visualize the information. The best way to present quantitative data is in a 2D space which can be processed visually and understood. To explore multivariate dataset, three or hyper dimensional representations are needed. Data is mapped to axes based on the type.

Visual Elements: visual elements are the basic geometric elements that will appear in our visualization. These are the building blocks of visualization which portray a quantitative message. There are four types of visual elements as shown in Table 1. Appropriate visual elements should be chosen for effective communication of data ("Visual Mapping – The Elements of Information Visualization | Interaction Design Foundation (IxDF)," n.d.).

Table 1. Visual elements

Points	· ● ▲
Lines	- - - ╱
Surfaces	▭ ▱
Volumes	⬭ ▱

Visual Encoding Variables

These are the graphical properties (also known as retinal variables) which can be applied to the visual elements. They are used to make the visual elements more or less perceptible to the human eye. They provide a "call to attention" to the eye. Visual encoding means mapping data (quantitative or categorical) into visual attributes such as size, position, shape or color (Bertin & Berg, 2011)(White, 2017) (joel laumans, n.d.) .

Figure 16. Visual variables

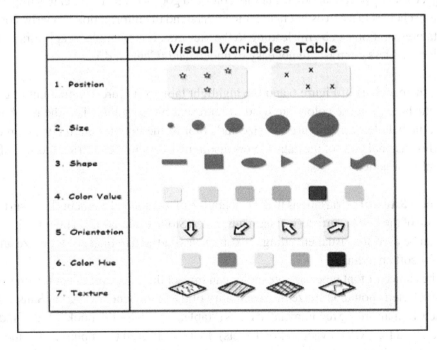

Figure 16 displays the most commonly used graphical properties in visualization (White, 2017)

1. **Size –** Size is a good visual attribute to present quantitative type of data. The variation in the size of a point, line, plane or volume can convey information about measure/quantity of data being represented. For example line with longer length indicates greater quantity(Stolte, Tang, & Hanrahan, 2002) (joel laumans, n.d.). For e.g., in the tree map in Figure 14, size of rectangles is propotional to the quantity i.e. number of COVID 19 active cases, statewise.

2. **Position –** Refers to the spatial location of an element e.g., position on x-y axis or in 3D space. For instance, important elements can be placed at top left corner in a visualization.

3. **Proximity -** Distance between objects can be a visual encoding e.g., similar objects are placed at adjacent positions.

4. **Shape -** Shapes such as circles ¡, triangles △, stars ☆, solid rectangles ■ etc. can be used to encode different categories / classes (Stolte et al., 2002).

5. **Color -** Color is one of the extensively used visual property to present and discriminate data. It is a good option for encoding qualitative data into separate categories. There are three standard scales in which color can be represented : HSL (Hue, Saturation and Lightness), RGB (Red, Green, Blue) and CMYK (Cyan, Magenta, Yellow and Key). HSL is most widely used in visual encoding. The Hue and intensities are effective preattentive visual variable(joel laumans, n.d.).

    a. Hue: Hue of an object is what we normally imagine when we think of color. It is a measure of the color that we give a name to such as e.g., red, green, black and so on.

    b. Saturation: this is a measure of the intensity of a given color's hue. It varies based on the brightness. Darker colors are less saturated and less saturated color gets closer to a neutral (hueless) color.

    c. Brightness - It is measure of the color's luminosity i.e. the amount of light reñected by one object with respect to another. Though color is a good visual attribute, it is important to apply color schemes in a consistent manner to understand the information properly. Poorly-encoded data presentation can be misleading to the viewers . For example. graphs drawn with similar colors and less contrast are not easy to understand (Chen, n.d.).

For e.g., in the bar chart of Figure 6 and the highlight table of Figure 15, gradient of colors is used as the visual attribute . Intense colors are used to represent higher values i.e., the number of COVID 19 patients. In the bubble chart (Figure 11) size and color of the bubbles are the visual properties that provide multidimensional view of the data. Colors distinguish different countries and size of the bubbles represents number of patients.

6. **Orientation & texture-** Variations in the orientation of a graphical element (line / surface) indicate the purpose of the line or surface(joel laumans, n.d.) (Stolte et al., 2002). Though it is less common, texture can be used for visual encoding. Texture is less attractive than color or size and hence can be used for soft encoding.

7. **Font -** The choice of font type, size and color can impact the effectiveness of the presentation. The font type selected should optimize the readability of the text. Generally Arial, Sans serif, Georgia, Times New Roman are the recommended types ("tableau-visual-guidebookTableu," n.d.). In Figure 19 (Word cloud for COVID vaccination tweets), font size is used to emphasize the most frequently occurring words in the vaccination tweets.

APPLICATIONS OF DATA VISUALIZATION

In the recent years data visualization is being used across numerous domains from business to social science to understand and analyze the huge amount of data generated. The insights gained can help in planning, better decision making and policy development.

1. **Business:** This is the predominat application area of information visualization. Companies use data visualization to evaluate business performance and make data driven decisions. The management people, CEOs, business analysts monitor the KPIs: (Key Performance Indicators) using dashboards and scorecards. A KPI is a measure which indicates the performance of an organization towards achieving a business objective. KPIs are used to assess the progress and make better decisions to accomplish business goals. They are used in almost all the business areas including production, sales, marketing, finance, Human Resources (HR), logistics and project management. KPIs are customized based on the type of business and the specific objectives that we want to monitor. Most commonly tracked KPIs are: revenue generated, sales amount, customer satisfaction, outcome of marketing policies, qualityof service, employee performance etc. in sales, marketing department (SHARDA et al., 2018).

   The following points are considered while developing KPIs (Parmenter, n.d.)

   a. KPIs chosen should assist the organization to achieve key business objectives.
   b. KPIs need to be properly communicated to all the stakeholders of the organization.
   c. It is important to evaluate and fine tune the KPIs on a regular basis to incorporate the varying business requirements.
   d. The KPI chosen should be is actionable and attainable.

2. **Politics:** Data visualizations can help government develop policies and can also influence the political situation. With effective visualization, common people can easily understand election results, political donations e.g., a graph showing country GDP over a time period, geographic map that shows the statewise results of election or percentage of voting done in each state.

3. **Healthcare:** Health care professionals and management need to monitor the patient profile, operational data and resource utilization within the hospitals. With visualization they can track the performance metrics using an effective dashboard. Commonly used metrics are number of patients being admitted, average time these patients have to wait, patient satisfaction level, room availability etc. Visulaization can help to take necessary action to improve these metrics. For e.g., a dashboard to monitor the healthcare infrastructure utilization during COVID 19 pandemic ("Chapter 2 Fundamentals I A Reader on Data Visualization," n.d.).

4. **Research:** Scientific visualization help academicians and researchers to gain a better insight from their research / experimental data. Data scientists create visualizations using tools or programming language libraries. This helps them understand the large data sets, detect outliers and identify correlation and patterns.

5. **Finance:** Finance professionals have to collect data from multiple sources such as balance sheet, profit and loss and cashflow statements, then analyze this data to detect the trends, exceptions and investment opportunities. These findings will aid in strategic decision making. Financial dashboards

in the form of charts, graphs, maps etc. can help easily understand, compare performance and make optimal investment decisions. For instance a dashboard to communicate and analyze stock market upadates.

DATA VISUALIZATION TOOLS

Good information visualization tool or software is essential to create easy to interpret, interesting and engaging presentation. There are many software available in the market. They can be used for different purposes depending on our requirement and preference . Most commonly visualization software is used as business intelligence (BI) reporting tool to create dashboards scorecards to monitor the business KPIs (SHARDA et al., 2018).

This following section provides a details of some of the top data visualization tools.

Microsoft Excel: Excel is the most simple, common and flexible tool for data preparation and visualization. Chart wizard in Excel supports numerous charts and graph options from simple line and bar charts to histograms, funnel charts,waterfall charts and sun burst diagrams.

Tableau: Tableu the most popular and the market leader in visualization, widely used for business intelligence (BI) and data analytics. It provides a wide range of charts, maps, graphs to create interactive dashboards and worksheets to know business insights. The drag-and-drop interface of tableau makes it very easy to clean, analyze, and visualize data, Tableau is compatible with various data sources, including Excel, MS SQL Server, MySQL, Hadoop and cloud-based data repositories and it can connect with R . We can choose from Tableau Desktop, Tableau Public, or Tableau Online for visualization as per requirement. The visualization capabilities of Tableau are quite diverse and poweful, giving it an edge over others("Chapter 2 Fundamentals | A Reader on Data Visualization," n.d.).

Qlik View: It is another quite popular and powerful tool for visualization in business intelligence applications. It offers a various visualization features that are easy to learn and create dashboards to gain deeper business insights. It supports multiple data sources e.g., MS SQL Server, My SQL, Amazon Vectorwise,Redshift, Cloudera Hadoop and Hadoop, IBM Netezza, MicroStrategy and many more. With Qlik, we can perform data analysis at a high speed which enables faster decision making.

Microsoft Power BI: Power BI is an easy to use platform to create business intelligence reports and personalized dashboards. Power BI Desktop is a freely downloadable application It can integrate with a broad range of data sources to build a data model. With PowerBI, we can create attractive dashboards using numerous charts such Ribbon, Waterfall, Map, Funnel and Gauge chart etc ("Data Visualization | Microsoft Power BI," n.d.).

Google Charts: It's an open-source, that allows to create dynamic visualization embedded onto a web page. The charts created are rendered to HTML5/SVG format and are compatible across various browsers. It provides a rich set of charts such as bar, pie, line, map, and gauge charts. It is flexible and user friendly like Excel. Google charts are used to generate business, financial, educational website reports.

There are several other visualization software and tools that are listed as follows: D3.js, Infogram, MicroStrategy, IBM Cognos Analytics, Jupyter, Plotly, Datawrapper, R Shiny and IBM Watson Analytics. The Python language has a rich set of libraries for creating stunning interactive web visualizations. The list of libraries includes: Bqplot, Bokeh, Seaborn and Plotly and many more.

DATA VISUALIZATION: CASE STUDY OF COVID 19 PANDEMIC IN INDIA

Due to the propagation of Novel Coronavirus, the pandemic has lasted for more than a year and a half. Every country in the world has gone through surges at different times. We are in desperate need of narratives and information to assist us grasp what is going on as a result of a worldwide health catastrophe. This has lead to research studies aimed at better understanding the pandemic's effect.Many researchers are putting a lot of efforts to figuring out how the disease spreads in different parts of the world. The rapid spread of the disease around the world needs quick solutions to understand and predict disease transmission. Therefore, data visualization is crucial to understand and analyze pandemic situation for better decision making.

For the first time on 11th March 2021, John Burn-Murdoch("How John Burn-Murdoch's Influential Dataviz Helped The World Understand Coronavirus | by Jason Forrest | Nightingale | Medium," n.d.) developed initial log scale chart. Through this chart he displayed the trajectory of infection rates between countries. This chart enabled millions of people throughout the world comprehend that the pandemic was getting started in England and the United States. John continued to develop dashbords and reports which could show information about COVID cases and deaths in United States.

During pandemic situation, data visualisation is useful for more than just communicating, it may also be used to influence people to change their habits("CSSEGISandData · GitHub," n.d.). In this chapter, different data visualization ap proaches are applied to analyse the COVID-19 data of India.

Figure 17 shows a dynamic dashboard created to understand COVID-19 cases in India. This dashboard consists of 7 elements. It presents information about COVID cases across the world, day to day confirmed cases, total number of active cases and confirmed cases (within last 30 days) in India. The dashboard is created using Python libraries: Dash, Plotly and pandas.

Three different live data sources: 'time_series_covid19_confirmed_global.csv', 'time_series_covid19_deaths_global.csv', 'time_series_covid19_recovered_global.csv' were collected from github to create dashboard("GitHub - CSSEGISandData/COVID-19_Unified-Dataset: Unified COVID-19 Dataset," n.d.). Features like 'Province/State','Country/Region','Lat','Long' were extracted and preprocessed.

Figure 17. Dashboard created using Python libraries

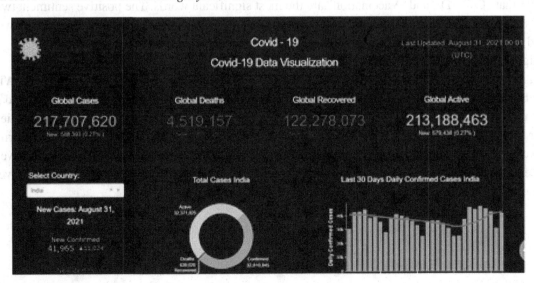

Another visualization technique is used to show the COVID-19 vacciantion related tweet analysis in the form of funnel chart. Figure 16 displays the funnel chart generated. In the chart you can see three different sentiment types of tweets: postive, negative and nuetral. To create this funnel chart, dataset (Tweeter_Data_IN.csv) ("Covid Vaccine Tweets | Kaggle," n.d.) containing tweets about COVID-19, posted from India, for the time period from March 2020 to May 2020 is used.

Figure 18. Funnel chart for sentiments of COVID vaccination tweets

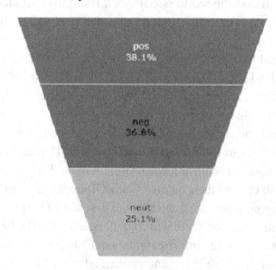

Wordclouds are a great choice to visualize qualitative information such as important textual data points. They emphasize the most frequently occurring words in the text by using fontsize. The magnitude of each word represents its frequency or relevance in a wordcloud ("What are Word Clouds? The Value of Simple Visualizations | Boost Labs," n.d.). The above metioned dataset is processed to visualize the words present in the tweets. Python modules like matplotlib, pandas and wordcloud are used to create wordcloud. Figure 19 shows the WordCloud for vaccination related words from tweets. From the chart it is clear that "COVID " and "Vaccination" are the most significant words. The positive sentiment tweets have significant references to words such as need, take, good, thank and hope whereas significant words found in negative sentiment tweets are: death, died, side effets, government.

Figure 20 shows the code snippet written to create WordCloud.

Figure 21 is a dashboard created using PowerBI for Indian dataset ("COVID-19 INDIA DATA | Kaggle," n.d.). The dashboard depicts the number of patients both state and date wise. Clustered Bar chart indicates the number of patients in Delhi, Kerala, and Andhra Pradesh. Based on the Total patient's slicer inputs, the charts get updated dynamically. The donut chart presents the number of confirmed, recovered and deceased cases in Maharashtra. The line chart indicates number of cases that have increased for March and April day by day. The funnel chart shows the number of confirmed, recovered and deceased cases in Kerala.

Figure 19. Word cloud for COVID vaccination tweets

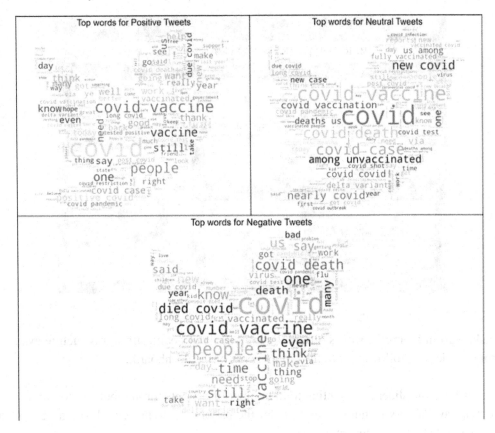

Figure 20. Python code to create to Word cloud

```
d = path.dirname(__file__) if "__file__" in locals() else os.getcwd()

twitter_mask = np.array(Image.open(path.join(d, "twitter_mask.png")))

wc = WordCloud(
    background_color='white',
    max_words=200,
    mask = twitter_mask
)
wc.generate(' '.join(text for text in data.loc[data['sentiment'] == 'neg', 'text']))
plt.figure(figsize=(18,10))
plt.title('Top words for negative Tweets',
          fontdict={'size': 22, 'verticalalignment': 'bottom'})
plt.imshow(wc)
plt.axis("off")
plt.show()
```

User Interface Design With Data Visualization Technique

Figure 21. Dashboard for patients record

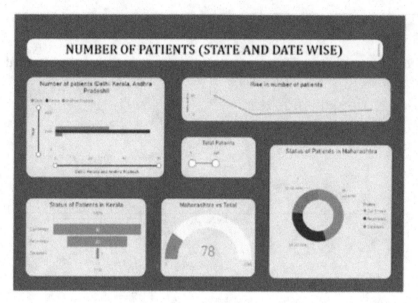

The dashboard in Figure 22 shows different components of healthcare infrastructure availability in India during pandemic. Followings are the components of the dashboard.:

- Slicer: Adjustable slicer representing total number of patients throughout the country.
- Tree map: availability of number of beds for the patients are represented. Bigger block showing more available beds than its counterpart.
- Funnel: Funnel chart represents how many new people are trained and how many are placed on active duty to support the health care.
- Key Performance indicator (KPI) - 1: Represents maximum and live count of patients recovering daily.
- Key Performance indicator - 2: Represents number of beds added to the infrastructure to meet requirement.
- Ring chart: Chart represents percentage of population across each state who are confirmed positive and still active.

The dashboard illustrates how healthcare infrastructure is scaled up to meet the requirement of increasing number of COVID positive patients. The gauge chart provides an idea of how many more young people are kept on stand by whenever healthcare needs some support. KPIs are used to keep track of number of patients recovering and the number of beds added. It also indicates the goal set for helping active and positive patients for maximum recovery.

Figure 22. Dashboard for healthcare infrastructure in India during pandemic

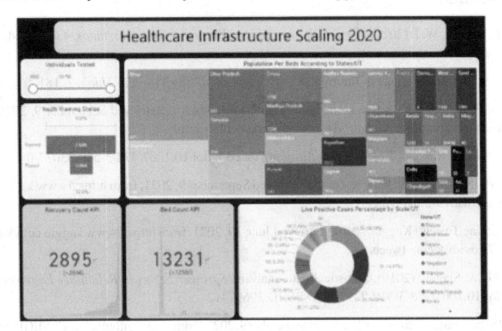

CONCLUSION

The field of data visualization is playing a key role in almost all the domains. Colors and patterns draw human attention. Everything in our culture is visual, from art and marketing to television and movies. One can easily identify trends, patterns and outliers while looking at a presentation. Therefore this book chapter explores the data visualization principles, popular tools and techniques. This chapter has illustrated the design of different user interfaces with the help of data visualization techniques such as charts, plots, maps, reports, tables, word clouds, dashboards etc. to understand and analyse COVID-19 pandemic situation. This visualization can help healthcare workers, policy makers to make better decisions and communicate the current situations to common public in an effective manner. Different tools like PowerBI and libraries from programming languages such as Python and R are used to visualize the effect of COVID-19 pandemic. The visualizations are created using datasets that are available on Kaggle and GitHub.The dashboard designed in PowerBI presents the healthcare infrastructure status during the pandemic situation in India. Analysis of COVID-19 vaccination related tweets is visualized in the form of a funnel chart and word cloud. The chapter discussed the application of data visualization techniques in order to explore the different aspects of the pandemic.In future authors may integrate the current work with machine learning algorithms for better understanding and analysis of data. The dashboards can web based and interactive to give real-time perception of key performance indicators and help users to understand, select, and provide deep insights into the data.

REFERENCES

Bertin, J., & Berg, W. J. (2011). *Semiology of graphics : Diagrams, networks, maps, 438* (1st ed.). ESRI Press.

Card, M. S. (2009). Readings in Information Visualization. *Using Vision to Think, 2*, 181.

Chapter 2 Fundamentals | A Reader on Data Visualization. (n.d.). Retrieved September 9, 2021, from https://mschermann.github.io/data_viz_reader/fundamentals.html

Chen, C. (2008). *Handbook of data visualization* (1st ed.). doi:10.1007/978-3-540-33037-0

COVID-19 INDIA DATA | Kaggle. (n.d.). Retrieved September 9, 2021, from https://www.kaggle.com/ashkhagan/covid19-india-data

Covid Vaccine Tweets | Kaggle. (n.d.). Retrieved June 29, 2021, from https://www.kaggle.com/kaushik-suresh147/covidvaccine-tweets

Cowan, G., & Siegen. (2019). Statistical data analysis. *Springer Series in Reliability Engineering, 0*, 53–81. doi:10.1007/978-3-319-92574-5_3 PMID:30691412

CSSEGISandData GitHub. (n.d.). Retrieved September 9, 2021, from https://github.com/CSSEGISandData

Data Visualization | Microsoft Power BI. (n.d.). Retrieved September 9, 2021, from https://powerbi.microsoft.com/en-us/

Ebook | Visualize It!: A Comprehensive Guide to Data Visualization. (n.d.). Retrieved September 9, 2021, from https://www.netquest.com/en/download-ebook-data-visualization

Few, S. (2005). Dashboard Design: Beyond Meters, Gauges, and Traffic Lights. *Business Intelligence Journal, 10*(1), 18–24.

Few, S. (2007). *Data Visualization - Past.* Present, and Future.

GitHub - CSSEGISandData/COVID-19_Unified-Dataset: Unified COVID-19 Dataset. (n.d.). Retrieved September 9, 2021, from https://github.com/CSSEGISandData/COVID-19_Unified-Dataset

Han, J., & Kamber, M. (2006). Data Mining: Concepts and Techniques (2nd ed.). Academic Press.

How John Burn-Murdoch's Influential Dataviz Helped The World Understand Coronavirus | by Jason Forrest | Nightingale | Medium. (n.d.). Retrieved September 9, 2021, from https://medium.com/nightingale/how-john-burn-murdochs-influential-dataviz-helped-the-world-understand-coronavirus-6cb4a09795ae

How Much Data Is Created Every Day? [27 Powerful Stats]. (n.d.). Retrieved September 9, 2021, from https://seedscientific.com/how-much-data-is-created-every-day/

Jeremy Wolfe and Lynn Robertson. (n.d.). *From Perception to Consciousness: Searching with Anne Treisman - Oxford Scholarship.* Retrieved September 9, 2021, from https://oxford.universitypressscholarship.com/view/10.1093/acprof:osobl/9780199734337.001.0001/acprof-9780199734337

Laumans. (2016). *Visualizing Data.* Academic Press.

Parmenter, D. (2010). *Key performance indicators* (2nd ed.). Wiley.

Principles of grouping - Wikipedia. (n.d.). Retrieved September 9, 2021, from https://en.wikipedia.org/wiki/Principles_of_grouping

Sharda, R., Delen, D., & Turban, E. (2018). Business intelligence and analytics. *Higher Education Strategy and Planning.* doi:10.4324/9781315206455-12

Stolte, C., Tang, D., & Hanrahan, P. (2002). Polaris: A system for query, analysis, and visualization of multidimensional relational databases. *IEEE Transactions on Visualization and Computer Graphics*, *8*(1), 52–65. doi:10.1109/2945.981851

tableau-visual-guidebookTableu. (n.d.). Retrieved September 9, 2021, from https://www.tableau.com/learn/whitepapers/tableau-visual-guidebookTableu

Total data volume worldwide 2010-2025 | Statista. (n.d.). Retrieved September 9, 2021, from https://www.statista.com/statistics/871513/worldwide-data-created/

Treisman, A. (1985). Preattentive processing in vision. *Computer Vision Graphics and Image Processing*, *31*(2), 156–177. doi:10.1016/S0734-189X(85)80004-9

Visual Mapping – The Elements of Information Visualization | Interaction Design Foundation (IxDF). (n.d.). Retrieved September 9, 2021, from https://www.interaction-design.org/literature/article/visual-mapping-the-elements-of-information-visualization

Volume of data generated in a single year for various sources. The size... | Download Scientific Diagram. (n.d.). Retrieved September 9, 2021, from https://www.researchgate.net/figure/olume-of-data-generated-in-a-single-year-for-various-sources-The-size-of-Single_fig1_271839316

Ware, C. (2020). Information visualization : Perception for design (4th ed.). Academic Press.

What are Word Clouds? The Value of Simple Visualizations | Boost Labs. (n.d.). Retrieved September 9, 2021, from https://boostlabs.com/blog/what-are-word-clouds-value-simple-visualizations/

White, T. (2017). Symbolization and the Visual Variables. *Geographic Information Science & Technology Body of Knowledge, 2017*(Q2). doi:10.22224/GISTBOK/2017.2.3

Wilke, C. O. (2019). Fundamentals of data visualization Aitor Ameztegui Data visualization (1st ed.). Academic Press.

Chapter 12
Integrating Multiple Techniques to Enhance Medical Data Classification

Balasaheb Tarle

https://orcid.org/0000-0001-9656-7834

MVPS's KBT College of Engineering, India

M. Akkalakshmi

School of Technology, GITAM University, India

ABSTRACT

Improving classification performance is an essential task in medical data classification. In the current medical data classification technique, if data pre-processing is not performed, the approach is more time consuming and has less classification accuracy. Here, the authors proposed two pre-processing techniques for enhancing the classification performance on medical data. The first pre-processing technique is noise filtering to improve the data quality. The second pre-processing bag of words technique is used for better feature selection. Subsequently, the hybrid fuzzy neural network approach is used for classification to handle data imprecision during classification. This arrangement of data pre-processing and the fuzzy neural classifier method improve classification accuracy.

INTRODUCTION

This chapter proposes two algorithms; the first algorithm (BNFC) applies the bag of words approach for feature subset selection as a pre-processor to the Neuro Fuzzy Classifier (NFC). We have abbreviated it as BNFC. In the second algorithm (FBNFC), we have applied a data filter to remove noise from data as a pre-processor to the BNFC algorithm, and we have abbreviated it as FBNFC. Improving classification performance is an essential task in medical data classification. The current medical data classification technique is time-consuming and performs poorly if data pre-processing is not performed. Here, in this chapter, two-staged pre-processing methods are proposed to increase the quality of the classification of

DOI: 10.4018/978-1-7998-9121-5.ch012

medical data. The first pre-processing method filters the noise to enhance data accuracy. The second technique for the pre-processing bag of words improves the range of features. The neuro-fuzzy classifier technique is then used to identify unreliable data during classification. This pre-processing and classification system for the neuro-fuzzy classifier offers higher classification accuracy.

Further, a data-cleaning technique is implemented in the suggested algorithm to enhance data consistency as a primary tool, along with the bag of words as a feature selection technique and the neuro-fuzzy classifier. This methodology classifies clean filtered data, leading to an accurate classification compared to the current methods, with the correctly reduced feature set. In this way, the proposed approach deals with three challenges: eliminating data noise, selecting features, and controlling data imprecisions. The comparative analysis on many medical databases using accuracy as a performance measure shows that the suggested approaches work more appropriately than the present techniques and improve.

BACKGROUND

The real-world data contains irrelevant or meaningless data termed noise which can significantly affect various data analysis tasks of data mining. The erroneous training data results in low classification performance of a classifier; it increases the algorithm's time complexity. Several researchers have proposed various techniques for data cleaning. Those techniques include neural networks, filters, Occam's razor and other methods. There is a somewhat growing field of real-life science, mostly interpreting patient data and evidence for a precise clinical illness diagnosis. Over recent decades, the medical decision-making support processes have evolved as a central area throughout medical sciences, which aid physicians in their treatment and medical diagnosis (Sumalatha, 2013) (Garcia et al., 2017). Machine learning, image processing, and data mining-based approaches are effectively employed in numerous medical data classification (Sharma, 2013) (Tarle et al., 2016). The general workflow of analytical medical data processing involves: (a) input (typically includes medical data), (b) modules for pre-processing of datasets, and (c) relevant data mining approaches which are capable of learning from training data and carrying out the classification of test data which is unseen for the trained model (Zhao, 2018). Cleaning noise in data and choosing a subset from the available set of features are critical pre-processing measures to enhance the classification model's efficiency (Mohammed, 2013) (Garcia, 2021).

A short overview of several latest advancements in medical data classification is mentioned in this sub-section.

Removing Noise from Data

The authors demonstrated a classifier filter that removes all noisy tuples from the training dataset and an unclassified training sample. They have (Guyon et al., 2003) presented the training of neural networks in which an approach about the sharing of the weights between neurons is discussed. The neural network has a minimum mean-square-error expense feature for the BP algorithm. Impure data is used as input, and various layers of data cleaning are forced. The goal function used is a minimal mistake. This chapter also presented the application of Occam's razor to reduce noise. The Occam razor is likely to improve inferred knowledge in the data and improve efficiency in classifying test data (Gamberger et al., 1997).

The suggested saturation filter focuses on the premise that noisy training data instances are observed and removed to produce less complicated and more accurate theories (Tarle et al., 2019). Elimination of noisy samples from training data eliminates the complexity and importance of CLCH. With the CLCH value, the saturation filter monitors the saturation of the training data. In a given problem domain, the accuracy of the description is the root of all possible correct cases. The objective theory should be a valid interpretation of the hypothesis empiric idea. The principle of stable targets is concluded using saturated training data collection.

Tuba et al. also introduced an explicit form of noise learning. The device detects compromised fields for subsequent modeling and analysis and uses non-corrupted fields (Tuba et al., 2019). In classification problems, Verbaeten and Assche proposed three set-based noise elimination approaches (Verbaeten & Assche, 2003). The first is an ILP expansion of the C4.5 based classification algorithm. Instead of using attribute values for test nodes, this extension utilizes logical queries. The second technique for filtering is that the voting filter is removed if most classifiers misclassify the instance. The latest approach increases Adaboost filters by removing the maximum mass samples after n rounds (Husam et al., 2017).

Sequential Floating Forward Selection

Sequential Floating Forward Selection (SFFS): Sequential feature selection algorithms are a family of greedy search algorithms that are used to reduce an initial d-dimensional feature space to a k-dimensional feature subspace where $k < d$. The motivation behind feature selection algorithms is to automatically select a subset of the most relevant features to the problem. Sequential Floating Forward Selection (SFFS) can be extended to the simpler SFS algorithm. The floating algorithms have an additional exclusion or inclusion step to remove features once they were included (or excluded) so that a larger number of feature subset combinations can be sampled. It is important to emphasize that this step is conditional and only occurs if the resulting feature subset is assessed as better by the criterion function after the removal (or addition) of a particular feature (Xu et al., 2017).

Semi-Supervised Feature Selection

Semi-Supervised Feature Selection (LSFS): It is focused on maximizing data effectiveness by using labeled and unlabeled data together. In this case, the amount of unlabeled data is much more significant than that of labeled data. Semi-supervised algorithms have attracted attention for their ability to model the intrinsic structure of data. Most supervised feature selection methods are dependent on labeled data. Unfortunately, it is difficult to obtain sufficient labeled data for audio classification, while unlabeled data is readily available. Semi-supervised feature selection methods can make good use of labeled and unlabeled data; thus, this approach is more practical (Setiawan et al., 2018).

Handling Missing Data

The following subsections present information on the randomness of missing data and handling missing data.

The Randomness of Missing Data

The randomness of missing data is classified (Little & Rubin, 1989) into three following classes:

- *Missing entirely at Random* (MCAR): Missing values are scattered randomly across all instances. In this type of randomness, any missing data handling method can be applied without the risk of introducing bias on the data. It occurs when the probability of an instance having a missing value for an attribute does not depend on either the known values or the missing data. MCAR can be verified by separating cases into those with and without missing data. Then, t-tests of mean differences on attributes establish that the two groups do not differ significantly.
- *Missing at Random* (MAR): It is a condition that happens when missing values are not uniformly altered at all stages of observation but are randomly distributed through one or more groups (e.g., missing more white than white, but random in all groups). The possibility that an instance would get a missing value depends on the established values rather than the amount of the missing data.
- *Not missing at Random* (NMAR): the challenge will not be missing; it happens while random observations do not modify the forgotten values. It is often referred to as failure as not being apparent. The possibility of an example with a missed value could depend on the attribute's value.

Techniques for Handling Missing Data

Methods for handling missing data are as follows.

- *Ignoring data*: There are two essential methods available to remove missing data. The solution is the complete case study and discarding. These procedures are only carried out where the missing data is random. The elimination of instances is dangerous (Little and Rubin, 1989). Elimination of the deleted records assumes that the complete dataset is relatively small and that the cases are random. The exclusion will lead to significant distortions in the experiment. The small sample size may also seriously obstruct the analysis. If datasets have more than 5% of instances with missing attribute values, the thumb rule for deleting must not delete these instances (Tarle & Akkalakshmi, 2019).
- *Imputation*: An imputation-based process imputes lost values equally to possible values instead of being excluded. The goal is to use proven associations to estimate missing costs more accurately (Schafer & Graham, 2002).
- *Multiple Imputations*: This approach gives several simulation values for each missing piece of information and then transmits the data instance for each simulated value substituted at each round (Little & Rubin, 1989). Five imputation duplications are often appropriate for a limited amount of missed information. Other methods involve, for example, the substitution of missing values with the mean mode of neighboring points, or the linear interpolation of previous and subsequent known issues, or the replacement of the sum of the linear regression pattern by one end between adjacent valid values above and below one missing.

Feature Subset Selection

Various studies have used multiple data reduction techniques; a variety of methods are discussed here.

Anwar et al. have given a set of attributes using an updated genetic algorithm. High-dimensional outcomes are a system that focuses on a specific representation scheme for the scale of features, and the modified form of genetic operators is being introduced here (Anwar et al., 2011) (S. Murugesan et al., 2021).

Kumar et al. discussed widespread structures, their importance, the measurement criteria, and the set of attributes (Kumar et al., 2014). A dimensional data reduction approach has been present to check the class standard based on the correction technologies for the results given. Recommended structure picks up Eigenvector and Eigenvalues matrix have been revised for high dimensional reduction with PCA (Ludmila et al., 2014). Jayanthi and Saisikal are proposed analytical methods for the productive extraction of the classification method by the PCA. This technique eliminates dimensionality by deleting features and performs a high-precision data classification (Jayanthi et al., 2014). They have proposed classifying medical information that depends on OLPP and its conjunction with a classifier to increase medical data mining efficiency. ANN recycles the ABC algorithm for classification purposes. The reduction of measurements without accuracy is applied here (Tarle & Jena, 2019). They have suggested a mixture of theorem bays and a balanced difference based on the cross-selection process. The recommended approach was applied to the problem of hyperactive pressure (Park et al., 2017).

Peng et al. have applied a new approach to selecting biomedical data classification functions concerning high-dimensional issues. Selection approaches for feature subsets are divided into three main types: (i) filter, (ii) wrapper, and (iii) hybrid. The filtering method chooses attributes independent of the model, whereas the wrapper technology requires a predetermined labeling tool to separate attributes (Peng et al., 2010) (Dasgupta et al., 2019). Sánchez et al. filtering methods have been used for imitation recording sets with several appropriate characteristics and output noise ranges, attribute communication, and growing sample volumes (Sánchez et al., 2006) (Singha et al., 2019) in combination with various filters selection attribute techniques. The filters are compared and addressed based on the results of these filters. A hybrid approach for the collection of attributes is proposed to create high-quality filters. Hany et al. proposed key strategies for supplying features, such as filters and wrappers for Particle Swarm Health Optimization. The output is used to compare the attribute collection techniques. The precision of classification is improved relative to the GA-based method (Hany et al., 2014) (Xiao Liu et al., 2015). A systematic cross-selection approach has been proposed by Alzubi et al. The suggested algorithm is concentrated on the embedded method. Maximization and removal of the SVM attribute using Conditional Mutual Information (Alzubi et al., 2018) (Anand & Neelanarayanan, 2019).

MAIN FOCUS OF THE CHAPTER

This chapter study finds various issues in prior research and approaches to overcome these drawbacks. The common problem in the existing definition of medical details is seen below. Feature selection is a pre-processing technique used in machine learning to remove irrelevant and redundant attributes to increase learning accuracy. Feature selection is necessary because the high dimensionality and vast data pose a learning task challenge. In the presence of many irrelevant features, some features do not add much value during the learning process. Learning models tend to become computationally complex, overfitting becomes less comprehensible and decrease learning accuracy. Feature selection is one effective way to identify relevant features for dimensionality reduction. However, the advantages of feature selection come with extra effort to get an optimal subset that will be an accurate representation of the original dataset.

We need to formalize some new techniques for feature subset selection.

The authors also introduced a data-cleaning technique in the suggested algorithm to improve data accuracy as a primary method, along with the term bag of words as a feature selection method and the NFC. This methodology classifies clean filtered data, contributing to a reliable classification instead of the existing methods, with the correctly reduced feature set. In this way, the authors have attempted with the suggested solution to handle three problems, remove noise present inside the data, unique features, and observer data imprecisions. The comparative study of the accuracy of multiple medical data sets reveals that the proposed techniques perform well than the current strategies and that progress is accomplished. We also need to handle imprecision in data. In data classification, we need to improve the classification performance of the classifier by applying some optimization techniques during the learning phase.

PROBLEM STATEMENT

1. Data processing and the development of classification efficiencies are critical concerns in medical data classification. To address these problems, they need to address other issues such as noisy data, overall data selection, and imprecision. This chapter introduced two algorithms that combine various methods to improve overall classification performance. In the first BNFC method, they used the terms Neuro-Fuzzy Classifier with the Bag of Words (BOW) method.

2. These methods to enhance the efficiency of each classification have been integrated into the second proposed FBNFC technology. FBNFC operates in three stages, including data filtering, removing noise data from training data, using BOW methods to select subsets, and finally identifying Neuro-Fuzzy at the classification level.

3. Initially, this technique excludes noise and imperfections from the necessary medical information collection of the data filter. After this function, this range is made. The method for properly sorting the feature subset is included in the suggested Bag of Words framework. The classification can be done with the help of a combined Fuzzy-Neural system. As stated above, it handles data imprecision due to fuzzy techniques and thus increases the data quality. Therefore, the proposed FBNFC methodology offers more reliable results than the methods currently in use. The suggested structure is contrasted with two LSFS, and SFFS selection approaches.

PROPOSED METHODS

The authors suggested two methods to increase the performance of the classification of medical data. The BNCF first and the FBNFC second in this proposed BNFC algorithm have implemented the Neuro-Fuzzy Classifier to select subset attributes utilizing the term bag of words methodology.

In the second proposed algorithm FBNFC, our main contribution FBNFC Algorithm, classification filter for noise removal, is subsequently used as a bag of words technique for feature subset selection and NFC. A further pre-processing step, the noise removal data filtering, boosts the proposed BNFC algorithm's classification efficiency. The summaries of both methods are explained in the following subsections.

BNFC ALGORITHM

We have proposed two algorithms to increase the performance of medical data classification. The BNCF first and the FBNFC second in this proposed BNFC algorithm have implemented the NFC to select subset attributes utilizing the term bag of words methodology.

The classification of medical data in our proposed algorithm takes place in two steps: the collection of pre-processing features and the next phase of classification. As far as our understanding was concerned, no one proposed this model, and we combined all the strategies to ensure optimal functionality and data imprecision, as mentioned above. Figure 1 illustrates the possible classification of medical data details for subsets collection using the NFC with the bag of words method. The collection of subsets is conducted as a pre-processing step. The selection of features is also referred to as selecting vector subsets, and a subset of suitable features can be chosen. For this purpose, the bag of words method is used. When feature selection is over, classification is carried out. The NFC's goal has been accomplished. The reliability of the classifiers is calculated using the statistical accuracy of the classifier. The following subsection of the BNFC algorithm contains information on how the subset selection algorithm works. The Neuro-Fuzzy Classifier is discussed in the following segment. The bag of words model is used in the document classification method, where each word is used to train the classifier at its frequency of occurrence. Similarly, we have used the bag of words algorithm to establish the relationship between specific class labels and corresponding feature values to calculate the weight for individual feature values. The frequency of occurrence of attribute values is also computed. Features with similar frequency and weights are selected. Thus we have used the bag of words approach for feature selection.

Neuro-Fuzzy Classifier

The neuro-fuzzy is getting used for classification purposes. The NFC input is the extracted features defined for categorising all provided data. The NFC's basic form is three-fold, whereas the detailed design of the NFC system is present in Figure 1. A neural network learning algorithm gets trained as a fuzzy system (Quang & Jeng, 2013). The Neuro-Fuzzy Classifier algorithm uses training data for learning and allows for local improvements using the fuzzy system. Overall, the NFC paradigm offers compelling solutions rather than essential machine elements (Juhola et al., 2014). The following section explains the neuro-fuzzy hybridization.

Fuzzification

The input values are extract properties or features, and then these attributes vary based on the membership function (MF). The system finds them to be feedback. The MF sets up different groups for each purpose. It is getting used to capture invisible and interrelated information characteristics, which means that the neuro-fuzzy system needs to be sorted with extra care.

The authors have used the π type membership function to classify the data. The MF (π type) has an optimized factor relative to the need for a problem. This allows simplification by choosing the correct value from the fuzzifier and adding it to the data sorting process. A difference in the varying fuzzifier value will calculate the gradient of the Gaussian function. The MF is predictable in the membership matrix after the Fuzzification phase. All rows and columns are cascaded and converted into a vector in the membership matrix. This vector created is the input of the neural network.

Figure 1. The architecture of neuro-fuzzy classifier

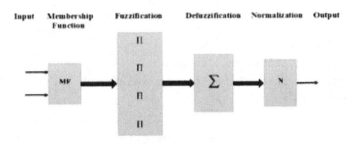

Neural Network

This neural network stage uses a multi-layer feed-forward perceptron classifier with a 3-layer; input to hidden then output layers. The cumulative sum is the same as the number of attributes and the input nodes of modular groups in the neural network. The cumulative sum of neural network output nodes refers to the number of phases (Gorzałczany et al., 2016). The whole amount of hidden nodes is similar to the input and output nodes' product square root (Liu et al., 2016).

The Defuzzification

This method translates the number of attribute memberships into strong statistical values in unwritten locations based on the neural network's output nodes. The Neuro-Fuzzy Classification algorithm is incorporated in Figure 1, and Figure 2 shows the Architecture of the BNFC System.

Figure 2. The Architecture of the BNFC System

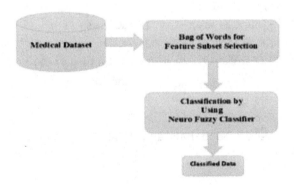

The suggested architecture of the BNFC system is explained in the form of an algorithm.

Algorithm BNFC

```
Begin
Load the dataset contents
Count no of Instances, Attributes, Classes
Create a Bag Matrix, and initialize it with weights
For i=1: numAttributes
End for
```

This Mat matrix is used to calculate the weights of features associated with the individual bag

1. *Total =$\sum$ x/NumOfInstances*

Calculate the feature values. These feature val

```
For j=1: NumClasses
R=find (data==i);
Y (i,j)=mean X(r,j);
```

$$Mat= \sum \left[X\left(r,i\right) - Y\left(i,j\right) \right]^2 /SamplePerClass\text{-}1$$

```
End for
```

These feature values are used to build a relation between the bag and attributes.

```
For i=1: NumFeatures
        J=1;
        While (j<=NumClasses)
                W (I,j)=SamplePerClass(j)/Mat(I,:);
                H (I,:) =W (I,:) / ∑ W (I,:);
                F=∑h (I,:)-Y (I,:);
                Fact=2-(numClasses-inv (NumClass+ 1);
                Num = (W (i)*Y (i)-F) ^2
    Demo= (numClass-1)*fact+∑1/ (SamplePerClass (j)-1)*(h (I,:) ^2;
                        F (i) = ∑Num/Demo;
End while
                End for
Now Count frequency value of each bag and filter it
                Count=0;
For i=1: size Of (F)
        If (F (i)>total)
                New (i) = F (i);
                Count++;
                New (i) =0;
End if else


Else
```

```
End for
  Sort data in descending order to generate ranks for each feature set.
  Input pre-processed data to Neuro-Fuzzy Classifier
  Apply NN on Fuzzy data Classification
  Process the result
  End
```

FBNFC ALGORITHM

In the second proposed algorithm FBNFC, a classification filter is applied for noise removal; subsequently, a bag of words technique is used for feature subset selection. The resulting processed dataset is used to train the Neuro-Fuzzy Classifier. In the abbreviation FBNFC "F" stands for Data Filter. To boost the proposed BNFC algorithm's classification performance, we have added the "data filter" before the pre-processing step. The data filtering strategy removes noise from data and improves data quality. Thus, the proposed algorithm incorporates three methods: data filter, BOW, and NFC.

The "data filter" removes noisy data from the training data (George et al., 1995). This process improves data quality, which helps increase the classification performance of the classifier. Classifier learning is done on the training dataset; subsequently, a single record from training data is tested on the filter. If it is classified, then it is not noisy and will continue as a training data member; otherwise, it removes a noisy record from training data. The learning process is done again on new training data. The training and testing process is repetitive until all noisy tuples are removed from training data. It is an iterative process and time complexity is more. Figure 3 shows the overall diagram for the data filter.

The classifier filter used to eliminate noise varies slightly from the John filter in the proposed method. The training data is obtained for the classifying, and the same information is used to test the classifiers filter directive. We have to use the training dataset as test data to find out the noise from the training data. John George (George et al., 1995) used a single tuple for testing, whereas we tested all tuples in training data at a time. The classifier cannot classify the data tuples as noisy data tuples and remove them from the training data.

Figure 3. The noise removal data filter

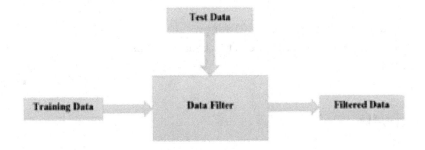

The training record classified on the classifier filter is not noisy data. The result is compressed data, and the noise from the training data is omitted. The precision of the data is improved by filtering, which improves the classification's reliability. The FBNFC algorithm has been established and modified compared to the BNFC algorithm to cope with noise in training results, resulting in enhanced rating accuracy.

Figure 4. The architecture of FBNFC with data filter

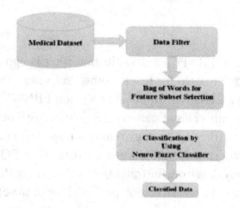

The suggested architecture of the FBNFC system is in Figure 4 and is explained in the form of an algorithm.

Algorithm FBNFC

```
Begin
Input medical data for cleaning to the data filter
Apply input data for learning.
Apply the same data for testing on the learned classifier.
The classified data is clean.
Unclassified is noisy data.
Load the dataset contents;//Apply for feature Subset selection on filtered
clean data
Count no of Instances, Attributes, Classes
Create a Bag Matrix, and initialize it with weights
For i=1: numAttributes
For j=1: NumClasses
R=find (data==i);
Y (i,j)=mean X(r,j);
```

$$Mat = \sum \left[X(r,i) - Y(i,j) \right]^2 / SamplePerClass-1$$

```
End for
End for
```

This Mat matrix is used to calculate the weights of features associated with the individual bag

1. *Total =$\sum$ x/NumOfInstances*

Calculate the feature values. These feature values are used to build a relation between the bag and attributes.

```
For i=1: NumFeatures;          J=1;
        While (j<=NumClasses)
                W (I,j)=SamplePerClass(j)/Mat(I,:);
                H (I,:) =W (I,:) / ∑ W (I,:);
                F=∑h (I,:)-Y (I,:);
                Fact=2-(numClasses-inv (NumClass+ 1);
                Num = (W (i)*Y (i)-F) ^2
        Demo= (numClass-1)*fact+∑1/ (SamplePerClass (j)-1)*(h (I,:) ^2;
                                F (i) = ∑Num/Demo;
End while
                End for
Now Count the frequency value of each bag and filter it         Count=0;
For i=1: size Of (F)
        If (F (i)>total)
                New (i) = F (i);
                Count++;
Else
                New (i) =0;
End if else
End for
```

Sort data in descending order to generate ranks for each feature set.
Input pre-processed data to Neuro-Fuzzy Classifier
Apply NN on Fuzzy data Classification
Process the result
End

METHOD OF EXPERIMENTATION

Experimental Setup

This chapter proposed two algorithms: BNFC and FBNFC algorithms. In the BNFC algorithm, eight benchmark medical datasets from the UCI repository (Dua & Graff, 2019) are used for conducting the experiments. These are well-known medical data sets. The feature subset selection method bag of words is applied as a pre-processing step. A bag of word algorithm is applied, implemented in Matlab2015b. After pre-processing the mentioned eight datasets, the resulting processed data set is used for further experimentation. In the next step, the NFC classifier is used for the experiment, and the fuzzy-neural network method is used for classification that can handle imprecision in data during classification.

The authors evaluated the proposed algorithm's performance using 5-fold cross-validation for eight of the UCI datasets. The results presented are accuracy, sensitivity, specificity, F-score, and precision, where averaged values are calculated across all 5-fold cross-validation experiments. In the next stage, two existing feature selection methods are compared with the bag of word feature selection method.

Table 1 presents a Neuro-Fuzzy classifier with a filter using a bag of words representing A_{FBNFC} (Accuracy). The comparative study is shown in Table 1. It shows accuracy as a performance measure on an NFC with a data filter using a bag of words, SFFS, and LSFS feature selection techniques, correspondingly, i.e., A_{FBNFC}, A_{FLNFC}, A_{FSNFC}. It shows that the proposed bag of words feature selection method works better than the other two techniques. When compared with the other two methods, it is proved that BOW is more efficient.

Table 1. The comparative analysis presents a neuro-fuzzy classifier with data filter using a bag of words representing A_{FBNFC} (accuracy)

Datasets	AFBNFC (BOW)	AFLNFC (LSFS)	AFSNFC (SFFS)
Cleveland	98.33	94.71	91.20
Hungarian	97.64	94.61	92.54
Switzerland	98.74	93.66	90.77
Chronic-kidney	98.40	94.74	91.33
Hepatitis	98.17	94.47	91.35
Liver	98.94	94.50	91.04
Migraine	98.49	91.97	93.00
Dengue	97.62	92.78	90.37

RESULTS AND DISCUSSION

Different methods are getting used for calculating the accuracy of the classifier. The k-fold cross-validation method is used to calculate the accuracy of the classifier. To calculate the accuracy of the classifier, they have used a 5-fold cross-validation technique. Here the data set is split into two groups: training and testing set.

Table 1 depicts a comparison of predicted and current approaches. The existing medical data classification technique is an Artificial Neural Network (A_{NN}), Neuro-Fuzzy Classifier (N_{FC}), compared to the two predicted algorithms BNFC and FBNFC. They have used eight benchmark medical datasets from the UCI repository. The accuracy of classification is calculated according to the amount of performance. The predicted system's classification accuracy (A) is represented as A. Table 2 shows accuracy (A) as A_{NN}. The performance indicates NFC, BNFC, and FBNFC methods are defined as A_{NFC}, A_{BNFC}, and A_{FBNFC}. It is experimental that NFC classification performance is enhanced compared to ANN. The classification performance of the BNFC approach is also improved compared to the classification performance of Neuro-Fuzzy Classifier, as a BOW is used to select the proper subset.

Enhancement in classification performance in FBNFC with reference to NFC is calculated as Δ_1, and is indicated in equation (1).

$$\Delta_1 = \left(\left(A_{FBNFC} - A_{NFC} \right) / A_{NFC} \right) * 100 \tag{1}$$

Classification performance (on FBNFC vs. NFC) improved by 1% to 10% across all data sets, with an average improvement of 5.81%.

Also, delta (Δ_2) is considered; it is denoted in equation (2). On all datasets, it compares the proposed FBNFC technique's classification performance to that of the existing ANN method.

$$\Delta_2 = \left(\left(A_{FBNFC} - A_{NN} \right) / A_{NN} \right) * 100 \tag{2}$$

The performance with the proposed FBNFC is enhanced by around 14% to 20%, and the enhancement is about 17.43%. Due to noise removal by Data/classification filter, the enhancement achieved is that BOW selects appropriate features from the dataset, and Fuzzification handles imprecision. Thus integrating multiple techniques help us to improve classification performance. The results are also shown graphically to visualize the enhancements achieved.

The graph in Figure 6 shows the medical data classification values among the proposed FBNFC, BNFC, NFC, and ANN methods.

The performance of the suggested method based on the time required for execution is presented in Table 3. As a filter is applied to remove the noise, the time needed for learning (Time for FBNFC) is reduced for BOW with a filter compared to BOW without a filter (Time for BNFC). Also, a comparison of the time required with Bag of Words (BOW) and the other two feature selection methods is also presented in the table. The methods are Linear Semi-supervised Feature Selection (LSFS) (Xu et al., 2017), and Sequential floating forward selection (SFFS) (Setiawan et al., 2018). It is found that LSFS and SFFS need more time as compared to the BOW for feature selection.

Figure 5. The comparative analysis of accuracy with various feature selection techniques

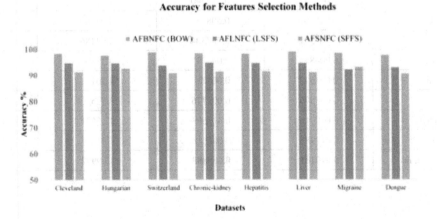

Table 2. The comparison shows the predicted and present methods in the form of accuracy measured

Datasets	A_{NN}	A_{NFC}	A_{BNFC}	A_{FBNFC}	Δ_1	Δ_2
Cleveland	81.89	96.36	97.93	98.33	2.04	20.07
Switzerland	82.40	91.06	94.83	97.64	7.22	18.49
Hungarian	86.05	96.19	97.35	98.74	2.64	14.74
Chronic kidney	82.74	97.26	97.18	98.40	1.17	18.93
Hepatitis	85.17	92.00	94.77	98.17	6.70	15.26
Liver	86.19	96.81	97.44	98.94	2.20	14.79
Migraine	80.30	85.97	97.47	98.49	14.57	22.66
Dengue	85.27	88.78	98.52	97.62	9.96	14.49
The average accuracy					5.81	17.43

Figure 6. The comparison shows the predicted and present methods in the form of accuracy measured

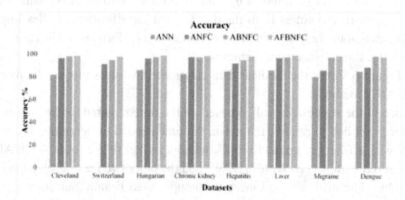

Table 3. Comparing execution time of BOW, LSFS, and SFFS with filter and without a filter in milliseconds (ms)

Datasets	FBNFC (time in ms)	BNFC (time in ms)	LSFS (time in ms)	SFFS (time in ms)
Cleveland	0.022543	0.212540	11.7711	3.2027
Switzerland	0.006169	0.008358	4.76160	0.8426
Hungarian	0.007357	0.007304	25.4186	1.7711
Chronic kidney	0.008854	0.008291	41.1802	6.5399
Hepatitis	0.004643	0.008717	4.76161	1.9973
Liver	0.003576	0.002776	8.72520	0.7949
Migraine	0.010316	0.417503	13.5631	1.8125
Dengue	0.017983	0.005618	1.81251	1.1769
Average Time in ms	**0.010181**	**0.083888**	**13.9992**	**2.2672**

Performance Measure

Any classifier model's performance is calculated using many measures like training accuracy, testing accuracy, sensitivity, specificity, precision, misclassification rate, F-score, etc. Here they have used testing accuracy, sensitivity, specificity, and precision. These parameters are explained in detail. The objective to evaluate the success of the proposed approach, the utilization of approximation metrics is done. It consists of a collection of parameters that indicates a standard estimation design. The authors have chosen a few parameters for performance evaluation. Four possible results are expected when any test is done using a classifier. If the instance is positive and classified as positive, it is considered True Positive (TP). If the example is positive and classified as negative, it is considered False Negative (FN).

- *Overall Accuracy*: It is the overall accuracy of the model, meaning the fraction of the total samples that were correctly classified by the classifier.

$$Overall\ Accuracy = \frac{TP + TN}{TP + FN + FP + TN} \tag{3}$$

- *Specificity*: It is measured as the True Negative Rate (*TNR*). Specificity measures the ability of the proposed method to identify typical cases.

$$Specificity = \frac{TN}{FP + TN} \tag{4}$$

- *Sensitivity*: It is also observed as True Positive Rate (*TPR*). It methods the ability of the proposed approach to identify abnormal cases.

$$Sensitivity = \frac{TP}{TP + FN} \tag{5}$$

- *Precision*: Precision is defined as the ratio of the total number of correctly classified positive classes divided by the total number of predicted positive classes.

$$Precision = \frac{TP}{TP + FP} \tag{6}$$

- *The F-score*: It is also called the F1-score, which measures a model's accuracy on a dataset. The F-score combines the precision and recall of the model, and it is defined as the harmonic mean of the model's precision and recall. The F-score is the geometric mean of precision and recall.

$$F - Score = \frac{2TP}{2TP + FP + FN} \tag{7}$$

Tables 4 and 5 show the experimental results on eight datasets, and Figure 7 shows the medical data classification values of performance measures.

Table 4. Performance measures of FBNFC method using the medical datasets

Sr. No.	Datasets	TP	TN	FP	FN	FPR	FNR
1	Cleveland	190	1	2	1	66.67	0.52
2	Kidney	362	4	4	2	50	0.55
3	Hepatitis	305	1	4	2	80	0.65
4	Liver	342	2	2	2	50	0.58
5	Switzerland	63	19	1	1	5	1.56
6	Hungarian	242	2	2	1	50	0.41
7	Migraine	3623	12	30	26	71.43	0.11
8	Dengue	81	1	1	1	50	1.22

Table 5. Performance measures of FBNFC method using the medical datasets

Sr. No.	Datasets	Sensitivity	Specificity	Precision	Accuracy	F-Score
1	Cleveland	99.48	33.33	98.96	98.45	99.22
2	Kidney	99.45	50.00	98.91	98.39	98.18
3	Hepatitis	99.35	20.00	98.71	98.08	99.03
4	Liver	99.42	50.00	99.42	98.85	99.42
5	Switzerland	98.44	95.00	98.44	97.62	98.44
6	Hungarian	99.59	50.00	99.98	98.79	99.38
7	Migraine	99.29	28.57	99.18	98.48	99.23
8	Dengue	98.78	50.00	98.78	97.62	98.78

Performance Analysis

The comparable performance was observed that on five performance measures: accuracy, sensitivity, specificity, and precision and F-score. Tables 4 and 5 contain the results of the eight datasets. Table 4 presents results on performance measure predicted class. Table 5 shows the accuracy, sensitivity, specificity, and precision performance measures, as well as the F-measure. Sensitivity is a measure of how well a test can identify true positives. At the same time, specificity measures how well a test can identify true negatives in a diagnostic test. There is always a trade-off between sensitivity and specificity in all diagnostic and screening testing, with higher sensitivities implying lower specificities and vice versa. The higher sensitivities implying lower specificities are observed in the result Table 5 Precision is the fraction of true positive examples among the model's examples classified as positive. It can be observed that precision is around 98%.

Figure 7. The comparison of an accuracy, sensitivity, specificity, precision and f-score of performance measure of medical datasets

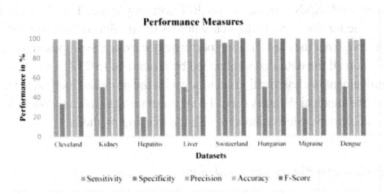

Although accuracy is important, it ignores the impacts of class imbalances and the costs of false negatives and false positives. We computed F-measure to consider these issues and found that the proposed models accurately consider class imbalances and the effects of false negatives and false positives. It is the geometric mean of precision and recall. The values for F-measure on eight datasets are around 0.98, and in percentage, it shows around 98% accuracy. Results are presented in Table 5. Figure 7 shows the performance measure of the FBNFC Method using the various medical datasets (i.e., Accuracy, Sensitivity, Specificity, and Precision, and F-measure.)

Observing Table 6 and Figure 8, we can state that the proposed approach outperforms with an accuracy of 98.33% compared to 81.89% accuracy on conventional ANN for the Cleveland dataset. The proposed AFBNFC achieves a 98.74% accuracy value for the Hungarian dataset, whereas the exiting ANN achieves 86.05% accuracy. The accuracy value of the Switzerland dataset is 97.64%, whereas the conventional neural network ANN provides an 82.40% accuracy value. The proposed technique attains a 98.40% accuracy value for the chronic kidney dataset, whereas the traditional neural network ANN reaches 82.74%. The accuracy value of the Hepatitis dataset is 98.17%, whereas the conventional neural network ANN provides an 85.17% accuracy value.

Table 6. The Comparison Shows the A_{FBNFC} and A_{ANN} Methods in the form of Accuracy Measured

Datasets	A_{NN}	A_{FBNFC}	Δ_2
Cleveland	81.89	98.33	20.07
Switzerland	82. 40	97.64	18.49
Hungarian	86.05	98.74	14.74
Chronic kidney	82.74	98.40	18.93
Hepatitis	85.17	98.17	15.26
Liver	86.19	98.94	14.79
Migraine	80.30	98.49	22.66
Dengue	85.27	97.62	14.49
The average accuracy			17.43%

The proposed technique attains a 98.94% accuracy value for the Liver dataset, whereas the traditional neural network ANN reaches 86.19%. The accuracy value of the Migraine dataset is 98.49%, whereas the conventional neural network ANN provides an 80.30% accuracy value. The proposed technique attains a 97.62% accuracy value for the Dengue dataset, whereas the traditional neural network ANN reaches 85.27%. It can be observed that the classification performance using the proposed method (on AFBNFC as compared to ANN) on all the datasets is enhanced by around 14 to 23%.

The average improvement in classification accuracy with the proposed method to the existing method is around 17.43% on the medical datasets used. From these results, we can conclude that our method achieves an improved accuracy value compared with the existing methods.

Figure 8. The comparison of accuracy measured of the A_{FBNFC} and A_{ANN} methods with medical datasets

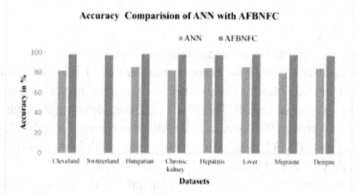

Hypothesis Testing

In Hypothesis testing, we have used two testing methods, the Wilcoxon rank-sum test and t-test. The Wilcoxon rank-sum test compares two paired groups and comes in two versions, the rank-sum and the signed-rank test. The goal of the test is to determine if two or more sets of pairs are different from one another in a statistically significant manner. A t-test is a statistical test used to compare the means of two groups. It is often used in hypothesis testing to determine whether a process or treatment affects the population of interest or whether two groups are different.

We have performed two tests in hypothesis testing, t-test and Wilcoxon rank-sum test. We have performed t-test on four hypothesis pairs (ANN, NFC), (NFC, BNFC), (NFC, FBNFC), and (BNFC, FBNFC). It is observed that the alternative hypothesis is true. We have completed a Wilcoxon rank-sum test on four hypothesis pairs (ANN, NFC), (NFC, BNFC), (NFC, FBNFC), and (BNFC, FBNFC). It is observed that the alternative hypothesis is true.

FUTURE RESEARCH DIRECTION

Medical data analysis has gained considerable significance in recent years. As discussed earlier, advances in computing methods and medical data processing are approaching their peak point. This data explosion requires new approaches to convert this data to information.

This research aims to solve some of the problems in studying medical data, including the processing of high-dimensional data, data noise, data imprecision and classification accuracy enhancement. This work can be enhanced in the following directions:

- It uses a different classifier instead of NFC for an integrated approach. It is expected to improve the classification performance of other classifiers.
- The approach can be implemented using parallel or distributed approaches to speed up the learning process.
- The approach can be implemented on large-sized data using a sampling approach to speed up the learning process.

CONCLUSION

Data selection and classification performance improvement are key challenges of medical data classification. This chapter needs other issues to address these problems, such as data noise, data limit selection, and inaccuracy. The authors also proposed two algorithms that incorporate multiple technologies to improve overall classification efficiency to tackle these problems. The authors used the Neuro-Fuzzy Classifier, BOW algorithm of the first BNFC technique. BOW prefers the best subset of functionality for fuzzy approaches in the Neuro-Fuzzy classifier to manage data inaccuracy, thereby maximizing classification performance. The proposed solution suits better according to existing methods. The second proposed FBNFC technologies also included three strategies for maximizing the performance of each classification. Filter with Bag of Words (FBOW) methods is used to capture subsets in three phases, including data filtering to extract noise data from training data and finally to identify the Neuro-Fuzzy process. Initially, this technique is used to exclude noise and imperfections from the raw medical information collection of the data filter. After this function, this range is made. The method for proper sorting of the feature subset is included in the suggested Bag Words framework. The combination NFC system is classified. According to the previous assumption, it handles data imprecision due to the use of fuzzy techniques and thus increases the quality of classification. Therefore, the proposed FBNFC methodology offers more reliable results than the methods currently in use. The comparative study of classification accuracy patient datasets reveals that the proposed method is more significant than existing approaches and improves around 17%. Moreover, the bag of words' efficiency is compared with the two methods used in the suggested scheme to choose LSFS and SFFS functions. We have performed two tests in hypothesis testing, t-test and Wilcoxon rank-sum test. It is observed that the alternative hypothesis is true.

REFERENCES

Alzubi, R., Ramzan, N., Alzoubi, H., & Amira, A. (2018). A Hybrid Feature Selection Method for Complex Diseases SNPs. *IEEE Access: Practical Innovations, Open Solutions, 6,* 1292–1301. doi:10.1109/ACCESS.2017.2778268

Anand & Neelanarayanan. (2019). Feature Selection for Liver Disease using Particle Swarm Optimization Algorithm. *International Journal of Recent Technology and Engineering, 8*(3).

Chimeno, Garcia-Zapirain, Gomez Beldarrain, Fernandez Ruanova, Garcia, & Carlos. (2017). Automatic Migraine classification via feature selection committee and machine learning techniques over imaging and questionnaire data. *Medical Informatics and Decision Making, 17*(1).

Chimeno, G. (2021). Stable Bagging Feature Selection on Medical Data. *Journal of Big Data, 8*(1), 2021.

Dasgupta, S., Sharma, N., Sinha, S., & Raghavendra, S. (2019). Evaluating The Performance of Machine Learning using Feature Selection Methods on Dengue Dataset. *International Journal of Engineering and Advanced Technology, 8*(5).

Do, Q. H., & Chen, J.-F. (2013). A Neuro-Fuzzy Approach in the Classification of Students. Academic Performance. *Computational Intelligence and Neuroscience, 2013,* 1–7. doi:10.1155/2013/179097

Dua, D., & Graff, C. (2019). *UCI Machine Learning Repository.* http://archive.ics.uci. edu/ml

Gamberger, D., & Lavrac, N. (1997). Conditions for Occam's Razor Applicability and Noise Elimination. *Proceedings of the Ninth European Conference on Machine Learning.* 10.1007/3-540-62858-4_76

George, J., Kohavi, R., & Pfleger, K. (1995). Irrelevant Features and the Subset Selection Problem. In *Machine Learning: Proceedings of the Eleventh International Conference* (pp. 121-129). Morgan Kaufmann Publishers.

Gorzałczany & Rudziński. (2016). Interpretable and Accurate Medical Data Classification-A Multi-Objective Genetic-Fuzzy Optimization Approach. Elsevier on Expert Systems with Applications, 1-17.

Guyon Weston, J., Barnhill, S., & Vapnik, V. (2003). Gene Selection for Cancer Classification Using Support Vector Machines. *Machine Learning, 46*(1-3), 389–422.

Harb & Desuky. (2014). Feature Selection on Classification of Medical Datasets based on Particle Swarm Optimization. *International Journal of Computer Applications, 104*(5), 14-17.

Husam, I. S. (2017). Feature Selection Algorithms for Malaysian Dengue. *Outbreak Detection Model, 46.* Advance online publication. doi:10.17576/jsm-2017-4602-10

Jayanthi & Sasikala. (2014). Naive Bayesian Classifier and PCA for WebLink Spam Detection. *Computer Science & Telecommunications, 41*(1), 3-15.

Juhola, M., Joutsijoki, H., Aalto, H., & Hirvonen, T. P. (2014). On Classification In The Case of A Medical Data Set with A Complicated Distribution. *Elsevier Applied Computing and Informatics, 10*(2), 52-67.

Khaleel, Pradhan, & Dash. (2013). A Survey of Data Mining Techniques on Medical Data for Finding Locally Frequent Diseases. *International Journal of Advanced Research in Computer Science and Software Engineering, 3*(8), 149-153.

Kumar & Minz. (2014). Feature Selection: A Literature Review. Smart Computing Review, 4(3), 211-229.

Kuncheva, L. I., & Faithfull, W. J. (2014). PCA Feature Extraction for Change Detection in Multidimensional Unlabeled Data. IEEE Transactions on Neural Networks and Learning Systems, 25(1), 69-80.

Little, R. J., & Rubin, D. B. (1989). The Analysis of Social Science Data with Missing Values. *Sociological Methods & Research, 18*(2-3), 292–326. doi:10.1177/0049124189018002004

Liu, X., Wang, X., & Su, Q. (2015). Feature selection of medical data sets based on RS-RELIEFF. *International Conference on Service Systems and Service Management (ICSSSM)*, 1-5.

Liu, Y., Zhang, H., Chen, M., & Zhang, L. (2016). A Boosting-Based Spatial-Spectral Model for Stroke Patients' EEG Analysis in Rehabilitation Training. IEEE Transactions on Neural Systems and Rehabilitation Engineering, 24(1), 169-179.

Murugesan, S., Bhuvaneswaran, R. S., Khanna Nehemiah, H., Keerthana Sankari, S., & Nancy Jane, Y. (2021). Feature Selection and Classification of Clinical Datasets Using Bioinspired Algorithms and Super Learner. Computational and Mathematical Methods in Medicine.

Park, H. W., Li, D., Piao, Y., & Ryu, K. H. (2017). A Hybrid Feature Selection Method to Classification and Its Application in Hypertension Diagnosis. *LNCS, 10443*, 11–19.

Patil, D.V., & Bichkar, R.S. (2012). Issues in Optimization of Decision Tree Learning: A Survey. *International Journal of Applied Information Systems, 3*(5), 13-29.

Peng, Y., Wu, Z., & Jiang, J. (2010). A novel feature selection approach for biomedical data classification. School of Informatics, University of Bradford. *UK Journal of Biomedical Informatics, 43*(1), 15–23. doi:10.1016/j.jbi.2009.07.008 PMID:19647098

Sánchez-Maroño, N., Alonso-Betanzos, A., & Tmobile-Sanromán, M. (2007). Lecture Notes in Computer Science: Vol. 4881. *Filter Methods for Feature Selection: A Comparative Study. Intelligent Data Engineering and Automated Learning - IDEAL 2007*. Springer.

Schafer & Graham. (2002). Missing data: Our view of state of the art. *Psychological Methods, 7*(2), 147-153.

Setiawan, D., Kusuma, W. A., & Wigena, A. H. (2017). Sequential Forward Floating Selection With Two Selection Criteria. *International Conference on Advanced Computer Science and Information Systems (ICACSIS)*, 395-400.

Sharma, S., Agrawal, J., Agarwal, S., & Sharma, S. (2013). Machine Learning Techniques for Data Mining: A Survey. *Proceedings of Computational Intelligence and Computing Research (ICCIC)*, 1 - 6. 10.1109/ICCIC.2013.6724149

Singha, B., & Kaurc. (2019). Software-based Prediction of Liver Disease with Feature Selection and Classification Techniques. *International Conference on Computational Intelligence and Data Science (ICCIDS 2019).*

Sofie & Anneleen. (2003). Ensemble Methods for Noise Elimination in Classification Problems. *Fourth International Workshop on Multiple Classifier Systems, 2709*, 317-325.

Sumalatha, G., & Muniraj, N. J. R. (2013). Survey on Medical Diagnosis Using Data Mining Techniques. *Proceedings of International Conference on Optical Imaging Sensor and Security*, 126-139. 10.1109/ICOISS.2013.6678433

Tarle, Tajanpure, & Jena. (2016). Medical Data Classification using different Optimization Techniques: A survey. *IJRET Journal, 5*(5), 101-108.

Tarle, Sanjay, & Jena. (2019). Integrating Multiple Methods to Enhance Medical Data Classification. *International Journal of Evolving Systems, 11*, 133–142.

Tarle & Akkalakshmi. (2019). Improving Classification Performance of Neuro Fuzzy Classifier by Imputing Missing Data. *International Journal of Computing, 18*(4), 495-501.

Tarle & Jena. (2019). Improved Artificial Neural Network (ANN) With Aid of Artificial Bee Colony (ABC) For Medical Data Classification. *International Journal of Business Intelligence & Data mining, 15*(3), 288-305.

Tuba, E., Ivana, S., Timea, B., Nebojsa, B., & Milan, T. (2019). Classification and Feature Selection Method for Medical Datasets by Brain Storm Optimization Algorithm and Support Vector Machine. *Procedia Computer Science, 162*, 2019. doi:10.1016/j.procs.2019.11.289

Xu, S., Dai, J., & Shi, H. (2018). Semi-supervised Feature Selection Based on Least Square Regression with Redundancy Minimization. *International Joint Conference on Neural Networks (IJCNN)*, 1-8.

Yahya, A. A., Osman, A., Ramli, A. R., & Balola, A. (2011). Feature Selection for High Dimensional Data: An Evolutionary Filter Approach. *Journal of Computational Science, 7*(5), 800–820. doi:10.3844/jcssp.2011.800.820

Zhao & Mao. (2018). Fuzzy Bag-of-Words Model for Document Representation. IEEE Transactions on Fuzzy Systems, 26(2), 794-804.

Chapter 13
Fetal ECG Extraction:
Principal Component Analysis Method for Extraction of Fetal ECG

Vidya Sujit Kurtadikar

Dr. Vishwanath Karad MIT World Peace University, India

Himangi Milind Pande

Dr. Vishwanath Karad MIT World Peace University, India

ABSTRACT

Fetal heart rate (FHR) monitoring is done for accessing fetal wellbeing during antepartum and intrapartum phases. Although noninvasive fetal electrocardiogram (NIfECG) is a potential data acquisition method for FHR, extraction of fetal electrocardiogram (ECG) from the abdominal ECG (aECG) is one of the major challenging research areas. This chapter proposed and assessed a method suitable for single channel based on principal component analysis (PCA) for extracting fetal ECG. Maternal R peaks and fetal R peaks were detected using Pan Tomkins algorithm (PTA) and improved Pan Tomkins algorithm (IPTA), respectively. Performance of fetal QRS detection is assessed using two open-access databases available online. The method shows satisfactory performance when compared with similar methods and makes it suitable for using a single channel system.

INTRODUCTION

According to World Health Organization's (WHO) health statistics published in 2018, globally 2.5 million neonatal deaths occurred in during year. Preterm births, intrapartum-related complications (such as birth asphyxia) are some of major causes of these deaths (World Health Statistics, 2018). Fetal monitoring performed during antepartum and intrapartum phase plays important role to determine fetal wellbeing which ultimately aims towards accurate and timely diagnosis of hypoxia which is considered to be early stage of asphyxia. Fetal Heart Rate (FHR) and heart rate variability are considered to be significant parameters and also critical to diagnose various pathological conditions such as fetal distress,

DOI: 10.4018/978-1-7998-9121-5.ch013

fetal asphyxia, fetal arrhythmias, bradycardia, and oxygen deficiency (Van Geijn et al., 1991), (Kennedy, 1998) and (Sameni R. et al., 2010).

Cardiotocograph (CTG) is the most common noninvasive fetal monitoring device widely used in clinics which captures FHR and uterine contractions. Although a CTG is normally used for FHR detection during antepartum and intrapartum phase (Rogers et al., 2010), repetition and long-time monitoring are not advisable due to ultrasound irradiation exposure is not completely safe for the fetus (Barnett et al., 2001). Another disadvantage of intrapartum FHR monitoring using the CTG is more maternal heart rate and FHR ambiguity compared to the electrocardiogram (ECG) (Reinhard, 2013).

FHR monitoring based on ECG can be alternative to CTG which can be done using invasive way which uses an invasive electrode attached to fetal scalp which is inserted through the dilated cervix. Although fetal ECG captured through scalp electrode provides a very good accuracy, it has apparent limitation that it requires dilated cervix therefore limited use during intrapartum phase and it also increases the chances of infection to both the fetus and the mother.

Figure 1. Power spectral density distribution (Burg method, order 20) for 5 min of scalp electrode ECG and 5 min of adult ECG. Notice the frequency overlap between the adult and fetal scalp ECG signals particularly in the frequency band of the QRS (Behar, 2016)

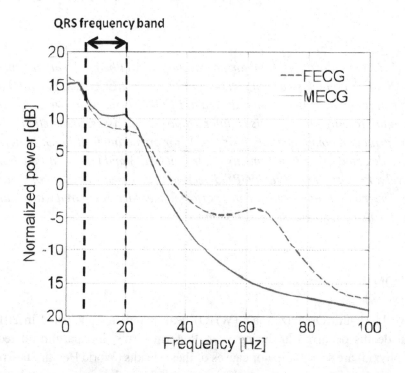

Alternative noninvasive method to detect fetal ECG is from maternal abdominal signal and is most suitable for long term monitoring of fetal health (Behar, 2016). We have also proposed Noninvasive fetal ECG (NIfECG) as potential data acquisition method for FHR. (Kurtadikar et al., 2021). Major components of abdominal ECG (aECG) are fetal ECG and maternal ECG (mECG), however fetal and maternal movements, mothers abdominal muscle artefacts, uterine contractions, maternal respiration, electrical noise from the device and power line affects quality of aECG. Extracting fetal ECG from aECG is challenging due to the fact that fetal ECG and mECG overlaps temporally as well as in the frequency domain as shown in Figure 1(Behar, 2016). The amplitude of mECG is 2-10 times that of fetal ECG, and the frequency of the QRS band of the ECG overlaps for the fetus and the mother which makes it difficult to separate these signals with simple signal processing techniques (Mujumdar et al., 2019).

The remainder of this paper is organized as section 2 describes related work, section 3 explains methods and materials, section 4 summarizes results, section 5 provides detailed discussion, section 6 provides future directions of research, and section 7 concludes paper.

RELATED WORK

There are numerous fetal ECG extraction methods explained in literature. These Fetal ECG extraction methods are divided into two classes:

- Abdominal electrode-sourced (AES) methods are those which require uses only abdominal electrodes
- Combined source (CS) methods are those which require both abdominal and chest electrodes

(Kahankova et al., 2020)

AES methods are further categorized into methods working in the temporal (time) domain and generates an mECG template which is subsequently subtracted from the aECG signal. These techniques include a variety of template subtraction methods as well as some hybrid methods. Template matching approach and the RR timeseries smoothing is used to detect fetal R wave using a single abdominal lead (H. Liu et al., 2019). Several combinations of methods such as Extended Kalman Filter (EKF), Extended Kalman Smoother (EKS), Adaptive Neuro-Fuzzy Inference System (ANFIS), and the differential evolution (DE) are tested and EKS-DE-ANFIS combination led to best result (Panigrahy, 2017). Attenuation of the mECG is done by filtering and wavelet analysis is used to find the locations of the fetal ECG, and fetal ECG is isolated based on locations. Two aECG signals collected at different locations are used. Only two signals of aECG are used without need of thoracic signal (Y.S. Alshebly et al., 2020). Selection of proper mother wavelet is key in wavelet method. Single channel abdominal recording is used to construct mECG artificial reference signal using singular value decomposition and smooth window techniques which further used to subtract mECG from aECG. Artificial signal avoids limitation that thoracic mECGs must be similar to abdominal mECGs in waveform (Zhang N. et al., 2017). Second category of AES methods uses spatial domain also called as blind source separation that includes the most well-known, include Principal Component Analysis (PCA), Independent Component Analysis (ICA), or nonlinear state-space projections. A multistep method based on PCA to eliminate mECG component, is used and best quality fetal ECG is selected based on features evaluation. Proposed method is suitable for single or multi-channel abdominal signals (Karimi et al., 2017). ICA assumes that fetal ECG, mECG, and the noise are statistically independent and non-Gaussian. Classical ICA algorithms such as JADE and FastICA are used to separate mECG, fetal ECG, and noise. Although ICA can be used to achieve comparatively good separation results, it needs multiple aECG channels. PCA is used for eliminating mECG component from aECG extracting fetal ECG from the aECG using a single electrode (Mujumdar et al., 2019). A fetal ECG extraction method based on clustering and PCA using only one aECG channel is implemented which will be suitable for portable monitoring equipment (Zhang Y et al., 2019). Combined source (CS) methods are those which require both abdominal and chest electrodes. Need of at least one chest electrode that can be discomforting for the patient is limitation of these methods. Fetal ECG extraction is highly dependent on quality of the reference chest signal. Additionally, the efficacy of these methods is significantly dependent on the configuration of the system (Kahankova et al., 2020). A dual dictionary framework that employs a learned dictionary for removing the mECG signals through sparse domain representation is proposed in addition to that wavelet dictionary for estimation of the fetal ECG signals is proposed (Furrukh et al., 2019).

In this paper, we have proposed PCA based method which falls in AES category. We have quantitatively assessed work done in (Mujumdar et al., 2019) and therefore current work can be thought of extension of the same. Proposed method is suitable for one aECG channel, which will make it appropriate for portable monitoring equipment. Another advantage is, it will be more conformable to patient as it does not require additional thoracic electrodes. We have used Pan Tomkins Algorithm (PTA) for detection of maternal R peak (Pan J. et al., 1985). An Improved Pan Tomkins Algorithm (IPTA) for fetal R peaks detection in fetal ECG is used here (Agostinelli et al., 2017).

METHODS AND MATERIALS

Following two datasets offered by PhysioNet (Goldberger AL et al., 2000) are used for the proposed method in this paper.

Dataset

Abdominal and Direct Fetal Electrocardiogram Database (ADFED) (Jezewski et al., 2012)

This database contains fetal ECG recordings which are obtained from 5 different women in labor. The women are between 38 and 41 weeks of gestation age. Each recording consists of four channel AECGs and additionally direct fetal ECG recorded concurrently from the fetal scalp. The signals are sampled at 1000 Hz, 16 bits resolution. More significantly, each recording has a reference annotation denoting fetal R-wave location. Each annotation is verified by a group of cardiologists (Agostinelli et al., 2017). All the five records are considered for experimentation in current study.

Physionet/CinC Challenge 2013 Set A (Challenge Set A)

The dataset contains total 75 recordings, each recording consists of four AECG channels which are sampled at 1000 Hz with 16 bits resolution. Each recording is 1 min long and also contains a reference annotation denoting fetal R-wave location (Goldberger AL et al., 2000). Total 20 records are considered for experiments in current study.

Steps Used for Fetal ECG Extraction

The following subsections explains steps used to extract fetal ECG from aECG. The sequence of steps is also represented in system block diagram in Figure 2.

Figure 2. System block diagram

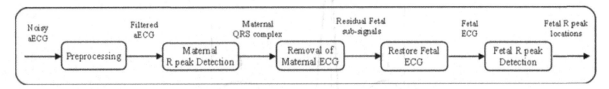

Preprocessing

The aECG contains a different component such as a fetal ECG component and mECG. Uterine contractions, respiration, maternal and fetal movement artifacts, power line interference, electronic devices noise and electrode contacts artifacts are different sources of interference and noise. Thus, preprocessing is essential step to reduce this noise. Firstly, the abdominal signal is filtered by using low and high-pass Butterworth filters with cutoff frequencies designed at 3 and 80 Hz to efficiently eliminate the wandering baseline and low frequency noise and to preserve necessary information appropriately. Afterwards, a notch filter with 50/60 Hz is applied to eliminate the power line interference subsequently, the signals are normalized to enable PCA to work on it. Preprocessing steps are summarized as follows:

Step 1: Band-pass filter with cutoff frequencies at 3 and 80 Hz
Step 2: Notch filter at 50/60 Hz to eliminate the power line interference
Step 3: Signal normalization as per following equation:

$$Sn(i) = \frac{S(i) - mean(S)}{Sd(S)} \tag{1}$$

Where *S*: Filtered signal; *i:* 1 to length(signal)
   Sn: Normalized signal; *Sd:* Standard deviation.

Step 4: Padding with mean value before first and after last element (P-R interval:200 ms and R-T interval: 300 ms as shown in Figure 3).

Figure 3. PQRST sub signal
(Mujumdar et al., 2019)

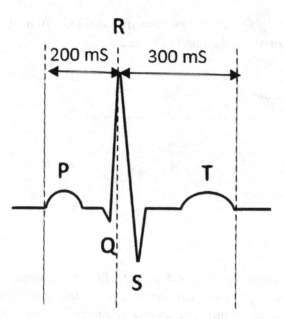

Maternal R-Peak Detection

The PTA (Pan J. et al., 1985) and (Sedghamiz, 2014) is used for detection of R-peaks in mECG. Despite the fact that it was proposed in 1985, PTA remains a well-known and normally used algorithm for R-peak detection (Agostinelli et al., 2017). PTA is one of the most dependable QRS detectors algorithm in which QRS complexes are recognized based on slope, amplitude and width of the wave. After detection of R-peaks in mECG, these QRS complexes are kept in a matrix size $n \times m$ where n represents R-peaks and m representing length of the PQRST complex (Mujumdar et al., 2019). The Matrix will look like as follows:

$$X = \begin{bmatrix} x_{11} & \cdots & x_{1m} \\ \vdots & \ddots & \vdots \\ x_{n1} & \cdots & x_{nm} \end{bmatrix} \qquad (2)$$

mECG Attenuation Using PCA

The PCA is one of the blind source separation methods which is based on second order statistics. PCA algorithm reduces the number of dimensions from a numerical measurement of several variables. Most importantly PCA is able to find the directions in the data with the highest variations and for aECG signals, the highest variation corresponds to the mECG. Hence, by carrying out PCA on the matrix of maternal complexes and removing the first few Principal Components (PC), we can suppress mECG signal to a good extent. The remaining PCs correspond to fetal ECG and noises. mECG attenuations steps are summarized as follows:

Step 1: Detection of R-peaks in mECG using PTA QRS detector algorithm
Step 2: Sub-signals of QRS complexes are created for mECG
Step 3: Highest variation corresponds to the mECG, PCA is applied and first few components are deleted.

Restoring Fetal ECG and Fetal R-Peak Detection

After removing first few PCs, fetal ECG can be reconstructed using following equations (3)-(5):

Equation (3) shows PCA projection matrix Z: $n \times k$ with n rows and k columns where X: $n \times m$ is normalized matrix as explained in equation (1) containing n number of maternal QRS complex each of length m whereas V: $m \times k$ is matrix of k eigenvectors

$$Z = XV \tag{3}$$

In order to be able to rebuild the fetal ECG in matrix X, we can map it back to m dimensions with V^T as mentioned in following equation (4), Where X^- is reconstructed fetal ECG

$$X^- = ZV^T = XVV^T \tag{4}$$

To get the final reconstruction $X\text{-}final$ we need to add the mean vector μ to equation (4)

$$X\text{-}final = ZV^T + \mu \tag{5}$$

Equation (5) can be written in general format as shown equation (6).

$$PCA\ reconstruction = PC\ scores.Eigenvectors^T + mean \tag{6}$$

Resulting sub-signals are aligned one after another creating the fetal ECG. Finally, IPTA is used for R peaks detection in fetal ECG (Agostinelli et al., 2017). These detected R-peaks are compared with reference annotations available in dataset as explained in results section.

Figure 4 shows a representative example for challenge dataset for record a08. Different processing stages such as a) Raw abdominal original signal, b) Preprocessed signal and c) Extracted fetal ECG.

Experimental Setup

The algorithm was implemented using MATLAB R2020b with following system Configuration: Intel R i5, RAM: 8 GB, 64-bit Operating System, x64 based processor and Operating System: Windows 10.

STATISTICAL ASSESSMENT

Statistical analysis is conducted to assess the performance of the method used in this paper. As mentioned in previous section, IPTA (Agostinelli et al., 2017) is used to detect the fetal QRS in this study.

Figure 4. a) Raw abdominal signal b) Preprocessed signal c) Extracted fetal ECG

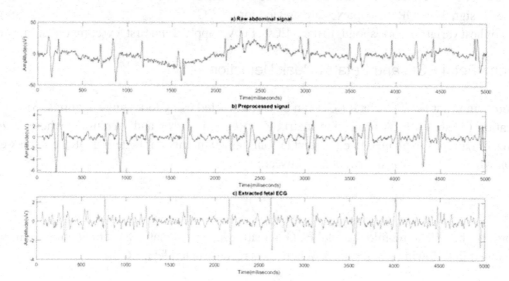

A window-based metric is used to assess the error for fetal QRS detection using (e.g., fetal QRS within ±XXX ms window). If a detected QRS is within 150 ms from the reference annotation for adults, it is considered a true positive. In the context of NIfECG extraction, a window of 50 ms is classically used to take into account the higher FHR than HR in adults (Behar et al., 2016). The performance of the fetal ECG QRS complex detection was assessed using window-based metric (beat-to-beat comparisons) between the detected fetal ECG QRS complex and the annotated. In accordance with the ANSI/AAMI guideline (ANSI/AAMI/ISO EC57, 1998/(R) 2008), sensitivity (Se), positive predictive value (PPV), and accuracy (ACC) metrics (Panigrahy, 2017) were used for the assessment and their formulae are presented below:

$$Se = \frac{TP}{\left(TP + FN\right)} \tag{7}$$

$$PPV = \frac{TP}{\left(TP + FP\right)} \tag{8}$$

$$Accuracy = \frac{TP}{\left(TP + FP + FN\right)} \tag{9}$$

$$F1 Score = 2 * \frac{PPV * Se}{\left(PPV + Se\right)} \tag{10}$$

As mentioned in previous section, two clinical databases, ADFED and Challenge Set A, are used to demonstrate the effect of the proposed method. In this work, records a33, a38, a47, a52, a54, a71, and a74 in Challenge Set A are excluded because they have inaccurate fetal QRS annotations (Zhang Y et al., 2019). Table 1-3 summarizes and compares results of FQRS detection and performance metrics generated considering method proposed in this paper on two datasets and results in (Zhang Y et al., 2019).

Figure 5. PPV comparison between proposed method and (Zhang Y et al., 2019) on ADFED dataset

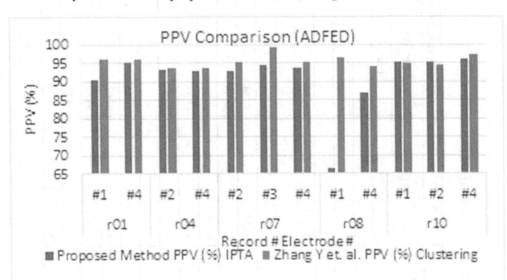

Figure 6. Se comparison between proposed method and (Zhang Y et al., 2019) ADFED dataset

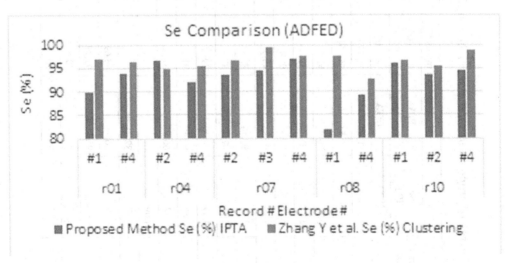

Table 1. Comparison of proposed method with method in (Zhang Y et al., 2019) on ADFED dataset

Record No.	Channel No.	Proposed method				(Zhang Y et al., 2019)		
		Se (%)	PPV (%)	Acc. (%)	F1 Score (%)	Se (%)	PPV (%)	F1 Score (%)
		IPTA	IPTA	IPTA	IPTA	Clustering	Clustering	Clustering
r01	#1	89.92	90.63	82.27	90.28	97.05	96.15	96.6
	#2	78.29	79.53	65.16	78.91	--	--	--
	#3	96.9	96.9	93.98	96.9	--	--	--
	#4	93.8	95.28	89.63	94.54	96.43	96.28	96.35
r04	#2	96.58	93.39	90.4	94.96	94.94	93.75	94.34
	#3	92.8	93.55	87.22	93.18	--	--	--
	#4	92	92.74	85.82	92.37	95.57	93.64	94.6
r07	#2	93.7	92.97	87.5	93.34	96.65	95.43	96.04
	#3	94.49	94.49	89.55	94.49	99.52	99.4	99.46
	#4	96.85	93.89	91.11	95.35	97.61	95.33	96.46
r08	#1	81.82	66.67	67.92	74	97.51	96.63	97.07
	#2	84.09	61.33	66.47	71	--	--	--
	#3	91.67	82.31	83.45	87	--	--	--
	#4	89.39	86.76	83.69	89	92.63	94.07	93.34
r10	#1	96.09	95.35	91.79	95.72	96.83	94.87	95.84
	#2	93.75	95.24	89.55	94.49	95.56	94.36	94.96
	#4	94.53	96.03	90.98	95.28	98.88	97.24	98.05

Table 2. Comparison of proposed method in (Zhang Y et al., 2019) on Challenge A dataset (Records a03-a20)

Record No.	Channel No.	Proposed Method					(Zhang Y et al., 2019)	
		Se (%) IPTA	PPV (%) IPTA	Acc. (%) IPTA	F1 Score (%) IPTA	Se (%) Clustering	PPV (%) Clustering	F1 Score (%) Clustering
a03	#1	96.88	96.12	93.23	96.5	95.31	96.06	95.68
	#2	93.75	95.24	89.55	94.49	-	-	-
	#4	94.53	96.03	90.98	95.28	-	-	-
a04	#1	96.12	96.88	93.23	96.5	96.9	96.15	96.52
	#3	95.35	96.09	91.79	95.72	-	-	-
	#4	94.57	94.57	89.71	94.58	96.12	95.38	95.75
a05	#1	89.92	90.63	82.27	90.28	95.35	96.09	95.72
	#2	77.52	78.74	64.1	78.13	-	-	-
	#3	96.9	96.9	93.98	96.9	-	-	-
	#4	93.8	95.28	89.63	94.54	94.57	93.13	93.84
a08	#1	94.57	96.83	91.73	94.21	100	100	100
	#3	96.12	99.2	95.38	97.26	-	-	-
	#4	95.35	96.85	92.48	94.62	99.22	96.21	97.69
a12	#1	96.38	97.79	94.33	96.03	94.2	94.2	94.2
	#2	92.75	92.75	86.49	89.52	93.48	94.85	94.16
	#4	92.75	90.78	84.77	87.68	-	-	-
a13	#2	93.65	93.65	88.06	90.77	95.24	94.49	94.86
	#3	95.24	90.23	86.33	88.24	-	-	-
	#4	96.83	91.73	89.05	90.38	-	-	-
a14	#1	95.97	97.54	93.7	95.59	-	-	-
	#2	91.13	90.4	83.09	86.6	-	-	-
	#4	87.9	87.2	77.86	82.27	-	-	-
a15	#1	95.52	95.52	91.43	93.44	98.51	97.78	98.14
	#3	96.27	95.56	92.14	93.82	-	-	-
a19	#2	93.7	92.97	87.5	90.16	93.7	95.2	94.44
	#3	94.49	94.49	89.55	91.96	94.49	93.02	93.75
	#4	96.85	93.89	91.11	92.49	95.28	93.8	94.53
a20	#2	95.42	93.28	89.29	94.34	94.66	95.38	95.02
	#3	91.6	90.91	83.92	91.25	-	-	-
	#4	95.42	93.98	89.93	94.7	-	-	-

Table 3. Comparison of proposed method in (Zhang Y et al., 2019) on challenge A dataset (Records a22-a72)

| Record No. | Channel No. | Proposed Method | | | | (Zhang Y et al., 2019) | | |
		Se (%) IPTA	PPV (%) IPTA	Acc. (%) IPTA	F1 Score (%) IPTA	Se (%) Clustering	PPV (%) Clustering	F1 Score (%) Clustering
a22	#1	87.3	91.67	80.88	89.43	98.41	97.64	98.02
	#3	92.86	94.35	87.97	93.6	-	-	-
	#4	97.62	98.4	96.09	98.01	94.44	94.44	94.44
a23	#2	93.65	93.65	88.06	93.65	96.03	96.03	96.03
	#3	92.86	91.41	85.4	92.13	95.24	94.49	94.86
	#4	96.03	92.37	88.97	94.16	-	-	-
a24	#2	96.75	94.44	91.54	95.58	93.5	95.04	94.26
	#3	96.75	95.2	92.25	95.97	95.93	96.72	96.32
	#4	96.75	96.75	93.7	96.75	95.93	93.65	94.78
a25	#2	89.6	92.56	83.58	91.06	92.8	92.8	92.8
	#3	92.8	93.55	87.22	93.17	-	-	-
	#4	92	92.74	85.82	92.37	92.8	93.55	93.17
a28	#1	81.93	85	71.58	83.44	97.01	94.19	95.58
	#2	84.34	84.34	72.92	84.34	-	-	-
	#3	83.13	83.64	71.5	83.38	-	-	-
a35	#1	89.57	90.12	81.56	89.85	96.93	95.76	96.34
	#2	90.18	91.3	83.05	90.74	95.09	93.94	94.51
	#3	91.41	91.41	84.18	91.41	95.09	93.94	94.51
	#4	89.57	90.68	82.02	90.12	95.71	93.98	94.84
a44	#1	95.09	98.1	93.37	96.57	-	-	-
	#2	91.41	91.98	84.66	91.69	96.93	96.34	96.63
	#4	-	-	-	-	-	-	-
a49	#1	-	-	-	-	-	-	-
	#2	89.86	88.67	80.61	89.26	96.62	93.46	95.01
a65	#2	93.06	95.04	88.74	94.04	99.31	96.62	97.95
	#4	93.75	95.07	89.4	94.41	-	-	-
a72	#1	86.23	89.44	78.26	87.8	-	-	-
	#2	89.22	92.55	83.24	90.85	97.01	95.29	96.14
	#3	-	-	-	-	-	-	-
	#4	66.47	68.94	51.15	67.68	-	-	-

Figure 7. F1 Score comparison between proposed method and (Zhang Y et al., 2019) ADFED dataset

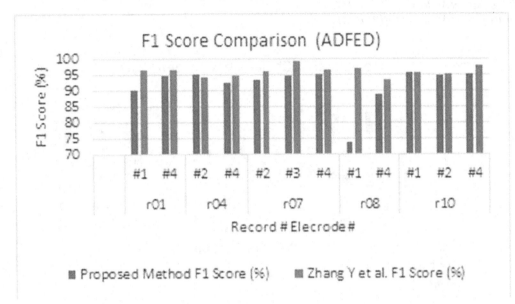

Figure 8. Acc of proposed method on ADFED dataset

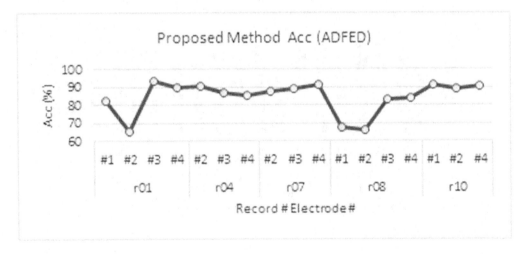

DISCUSSIONS

FHR is an important diagnostic indicator used to monitor fetal wellbeing during pregnancy and labor. Although CTG is widely used for fetal monitoring, it has its own limitations. As per our comprehensive comparison (Kurtadikar et al., 2021) between different fetal monitoring methods, we proposed NIfECG as data acquisition method for calculating FHR. Moreover, fetal ECG will be also useful for morphological analysis (Kurtadikar et al., 2021).

Figure 9. PPV comparison between proposed method and (Zhang Y et al., 2019)
a) (Challenge dataset A: Record # a03 to a15)
b) (Challenge dataset A: Record # a19 to a65)

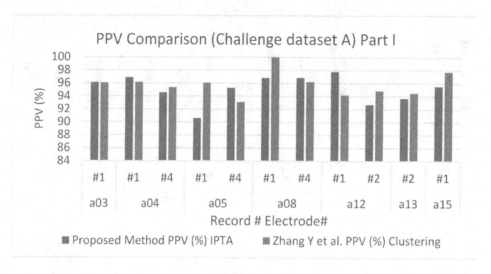

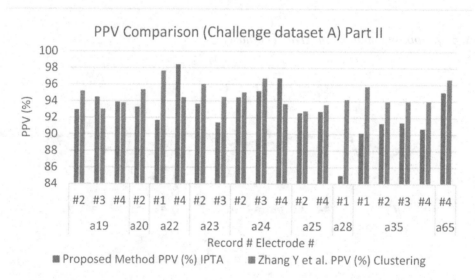

In this paper, we proposed and assessed PCA based fetal ECG extraction method which will be suitable for single channel. This method does not require any additional thoracic electrode thereby simplifies overall system and also comfortable to patient. We used IPTA to detect R peaks in extracted fetal ECG. As mentioned above, in the first step, preprocessing is done with a Butterworth filter with cutoff frequencies designed at 3 and 80 Hz for eliminating noise and this also preserves morphological information. This is followed by notch filter with 50/60 Hz is applied to eliminate the power line interference. PTA is used to detect maternal R peaks and then PCA is applied to eliminate first few components that attenuate mECG components. Fetal ECG is reconstructed by method explained earlier and fetal R peaks in restored ECG are detected using IPTA.

Figure 10. Se comparison between proposed method and (Zhang Y et al., 2019)
a) *(Challenge dataset A: Record # a03 to a15)*
b) *(Challenge dataset A: Record # a19 to a65)*

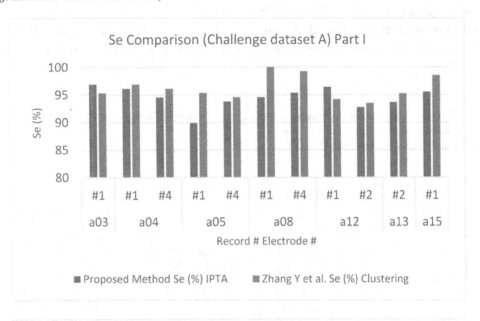

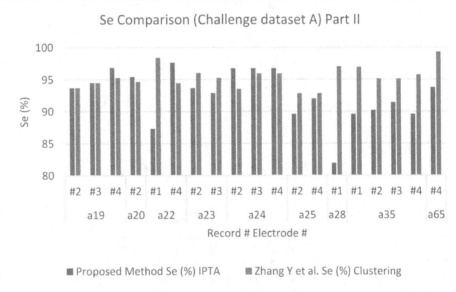

From interpretation of Figure. 7 and Figure 11, it is clear that, F1 score of resulted from method used in this paper is comparable with that of (Zhang Y et al., 2019) for most of the records considering both datasets. Moreover, F1 score is exceeding than (Zhang Y et al., 2019) for 6 cases: record r04 (Electrode #2) in ADFED dataset; record a03 (Electrode #1), a04 (Electrode #1), a12 (Electrode #1), a22 (Electrode #4), a24 (Electrode #4) in challenge dataset A. In addition to that this method has resulted F1 score equal to or more than 90% for total 16 cases (a03 (Electrode #2, #3), a04 (Electrode #3), a05 (Electrode #3), a03 (Electrode #2, #3) etc.) which are not shown in graphs as their corresponding F1 Scores are not available in (Zhang Y et al., 2019), for Challenge Set A dataset. Similarly, F1 score equal to or more than 90% for total 2 cases (r03 (Electrode #3), r04 (Electrode #3) where corresponding comparison is not available in (Zhang Y et al., 2019) for ADFED dataset.

The Acc of most of records is good enough for both databases, excluding record r01(Electrode #1), r08(Electrode #1, #2) for ADFED dataset; record a05(Electrode #2), a28(Electrode #1, #2, #3) for Challenge Set A dataset.

Figure 11. F1 score comparison between proposed method and (Zhang Y et al., 2019)
a) (Challenge dataset A: Record # a03 to a15)
b) (Challenge dataset A: Record # a19 to a65)

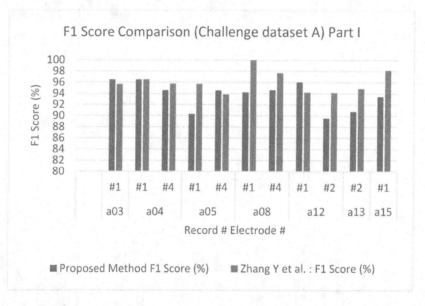

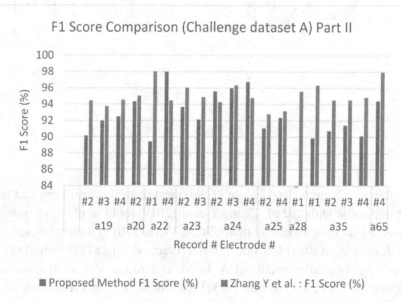

Figure 12. Acc of proposed method (Challenge dataset A)
a) (Challenge dataset A: Record # a03 to a20)
b) (Challenge dataset A: Record # a19 to a72)

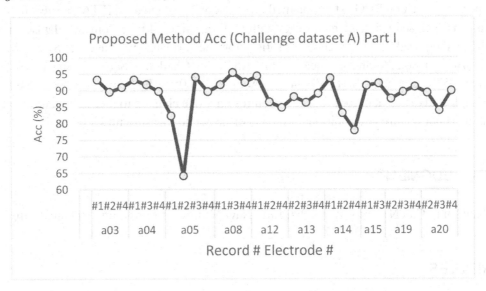

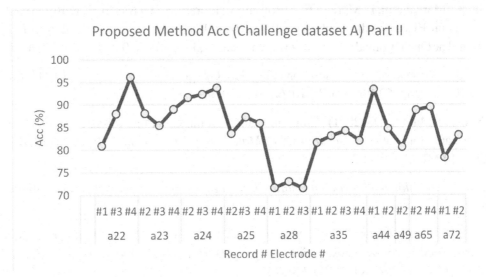

FUTURE DIRECTIONS

In this paper, we have considered two datasets: ADFED and Challenge Set A for experimentation. Although first dataset contains signals that lasts for 5 minutes, second dataset contains signals that lasts for 1 minute. Our future work will be focused on experimenting proposed method with additional fetal ECG datasets which are sufficiently large and recorded during antepartum phase and intrapartum phase (Sulas et al., 2021), (Matonia et al. 2020). We would like to work towards detection of fetal well-being during antepartum and intrapartum phases.

CONCLUSION

In this paper, we used fetal ECG extraction method based on PCA and used IPTA to detect fetal R peaks. Performance is assessed using 25 recordings with total duration 74 min from two datasets mentioned above. The method used in this paper shows satisfactory performance with average Se of 92.24%, PPV of 92.55%, Acc. of 86.22% and F1-measure of 91.57% for Challenge Set A. Using ADFED average results are: 91.57% (Se), 88.65% (PPV), 84.5% (Acc) and 90.05% (F1 Score). Proposed method in this paper is simple and convenient for users as it requires only one channel to measure maternal abdominal signal and does not require any additional thoracic electrode to measure mECG signal.

ACKNOWLEDGMENT

We are thankful to CareNx Innovations Pvt. Ltd., Navi Mumbai for providing technical support.

REFERENCES

Agostinelli, A., Marcantoni, I., Moretti, E., Sbrollini, A., Fioretti, S., Di Nardo, F., & Burattini, L. (2017). Noninvasive Fetal Electrocardiography Part I: Pan-Tompkins' Algorithm Adaptation to Fetal R-peak Identification. The Open Biomedical Engineering Journal, 11, 17–24. doi:10.2174/1874120701711010017

Alshebly, Y. S., & Nafea, M. (2020) Isolation of Fetal ECG Signals from Abdominal ECG Using Wavelet Analysis. *IRBM, 41*(5), 252-260. doi:10.1016/j.irbm.2019.12.002

Barnett, S. B., & Maulik, D. (2001). Guidelines and recommendations for safe use of Doppler ultrasound in perinatal applications. *The Journal of Maternal-Fetal Medicine, 10*(2), 75–84. doi:10.1080/jmf.10.2.75.84 PMID:11392597

Behar. (2016). *Extraction of clinical information from the non-invasive fetal electrocardiogram.* CoRR, abs-1606.01093.

Behar, J., Andreotti, F., Zaunseder, S., Oster, J., & Clifford, G. D. (2016). A practical guide to non-invasive foetal electrocardiogram extraction and analysis. *Physiological Measurement, 37*(5), R1–R35. doi:10.1088/0967-3334/37/5/R1 PMID:27067431

Goldberger, A. L., Amaral, L. A., Glass, L., Hausdorff, J. M., Ivanov, P. C., Mark, R. G., Mietus, J. E., Moody, G. B., Peng, C. K., & Stanley, H. E. (2000). PhysioBank, PhysioToolkit, and PhysioNet: Components of a new research resource for complex physiologic signals. *Circulation, 101*(23), e215–e220. doi:10.1161/01.CIR.101.23.e215 PMID:10851218

Jezewski, J., Matonia, A., Kupka, T., Roj, D., & Czabanski, R. (2012). Determination of fetal heart rate from abdominal signals: Evaluation of beat-to-beat accuracy in relation to the direct fetal electrocardiogram. *Biomedizinische Technik. Biomedical Engineering, 57*(5), 383–394. doi:10.1515/bmt-2011-0130 PMID:25854665

Kahankova, R., Martinek, R., Jaros, R., Behbehani, K., Matonia, A., Jezewski, M., & Behar, J. A. (2020). A Review of Signal Processing Techniques for Non-Invasive Fetal Electrocardiography. *IEEE Reviews in Biomedical Engineering*, *13*, 51–73. doi:10.1109/RBME.2019.2938061 PMID:31478873

Karimi Rahmati, A., Setarehdan, S. K., & Araabi, B. N. (2017). A PCA/ICA based Fetal ECG Extraction from Mother Abdominal Recordings by Means of a Novel Data-driven Approach to Fetal ECG Quality Assessment. *Journal of Biomedical Physics & Engineering*, *7*(1), 37–50. PMID:28451578

Kennedy, R. G. (1998). Electronic fetal heart rate monitoring: Retrospective reflections on a twentieth-century technology. *Journal of the Royal Society of Medicine*, *91*(5), 244–250. doi:10.1177/014107689809100503 PMID:9764077

Kurtadikar, V. S., & Pande, H. M. (2021). Comprehensive Study of Fetal Monitoring Methods for Detection of Fetal Compromise. In A. Joshi, M. Khosravy, & N. Gupta (Eds.), *Machine Learning for Predictive Analysis. Lecture Notes in Networks and Systems* (Vol. 141). Springer. doi:10.1007/978-981-15-7106-0_15

Liu, H., Chen, D., & Sun, G. (2019). Detection of Fetal ECG R Wave From Single-Lead Abdominal ECG Using a Combination of RR Time-Series Smoothing and Template-Matching Approach. *IEEE Access: Practical Innovations, Open Solutions*, *7*, 66633–66643. doi:10.1109/ACCESS.2019.2917826

Matonia, A., Jezewski, J., Kupka, T., Jezewski, M., Horoba, K., Wrobel, J., Czabanski, R., & Kahankowa, R. (2020). Fetal electrocardiograms, direct and abdominal with reference heartbeat annotations. *Scientific Data*, *7*(1), 200. doi:10.103841597-020-0538-z PMID:32587253

Mujumdar, R., Nadar, P., Bondre, A., Kulkarni, A., & Pathak, S. (2019). *Principal Component Analysis (PCA) based single-channel, non-invasive fetal ECG extraction*. https://fetosense.com/assets/publictions/PCA.pdf

Pan, J., & Tompkins, W. J. (1985). A real-time QRS detection algorithm. *IEEE Transactions on Biomedical Engineering*, *32*(3), 230–236. doi:10.1109/TBME.1985.325532 PMID:3997178

Panigrahy, D., & Sahu, P. K. (2017). Extraction of fetal ECG signal by an improved method using extended Kalman smoother framework from single channel abdominal ECG signal. *Australasian Physical & Engineering Sciences in Medicine*, *40*(1), 191–207. doi:10.100713246-017-0527-5 PMID:28210991

Reinhard, J., Hayes-Gill, B. R., Schiermeier, S., Hatzmann, H., Heinrich, T. M., & Louwen, F. (2013). Intrapartum heart rate ambiguity: A comparison of cardiotocogram and abdominal fetal electrocardiogram with maternal electrocardiogram. *Gynecologic and Obstetric Investigation*, *75*(2), 101–108. doi:10.1159/000345059 PMID:23328351

Rogers, L., Li, J., Liu, L., Balluz, R., Rychik, J., & Ge, S. (2013). Advances in fetal echocardiography: Early imaging, three/four dimensional imaging, and role of fetal echocardiography in guiding early postnatal management of congenital heart disease. *Echocardiography (Mount Kisco, N.Y.)*, *30*(4), 428–438. doi:10.1111/echo.12211 PMID:23551603

Sameni, R., & Clifford, G. D. (2010). A Review of Fetal ECG Signal Processing; Issues and Promising Directions. *The Open Pacing, Electrophysiology & Therapy Journal*, *3*, 4–20. doi:10.2174/1876536X01003010004 PMID:21614148

Sana, F., Ballal, T., Shadaydeh, M., Hoteit, I., & Al-Naffouri, T. Y. (2019). Fetal ECG extraction exploiting joint sparse supports in a dual dictionary framework. *Biomedical Signal Processing and Control, 48*, 46-60. doi:10.1016/j.bspc.2018.08.023

Sedghamiz, H. (2014). *Matlab Implementation of Pan Tompkins ECG QRS detector*. https://www.researchgate.net/publication/313673153_Matlab_Implementation_of_Pan_Tompkins_ECG_QRS_detect

Sulas, E., Urru, M., Tumbarello, R., Raffo, L., Sameni, R., & Pani, D. (2021). A non-invasive multimodal foetal ECG–Doppler dataset for antenatal cardiology research. *Scientific Data, 8*(1), 30. doi:10.103841597-021-00811-3 PMID:33500414

Van Geijn, H. P., Copray, F. J., Donkers, D. K., & Bos, M. H. (1991). Diagnosis and management of intrapartum fetal distress. *European Journal of Obstetrics, Gynecology, and Reproductive Biology, 42*, S63–S72.

World Health Statistics. (2018). https://apps.who.int/iris/bitstream/handle/10665/272596/9789241565585-eng.pdf

Zhang, N., Zhang, J., Li, H., Mumini, O. O., Samuel, O. W., Ivanov, K., & Wang, L. (2017). A Novel Technique for Fetal ECG Extraction Using Single-Channel Abdominal Recording. *Sensors (Basel), 17*(3), 457. doi:10.339017030457 PMID:28245585

Zhang, Y., & Yu, S. (2019). Single-lead noninvasive fetal ECG extraction by means of combining clustering and principal components analysis. *Med Biol Eng Comput., 58*(2), 419-432. doi:10.1007/s11517-019-02087-7

Compilation of References

Abdali, A. R., & Al-Tuma, R. F. (2019, March 27-28). *Robust real-time violence detection in video using CNN and LSTM* [Paper presentation]. 2019 2nd Scientific Conference of Computer Sciences (SCCS), Baghdad, Iraq.

Abdul-Kader, S. A., & Woods, J. C. (2015). Survey on chatbot design techniques in speech conversation systems. *International Journal of Advanced Computer Science and Applications*, *6*(7).

Accelerate and scale app development without managing infrastructure. (n.d.). *Firebase*. https://firebase.google.com/products-build

Adamopoulou, E., & Moussiades, L. (2020). An Overview of Chatbot Technology. In I. Maglogiannis, L. Iliadis, & E. Pimenidis (Eds.), *Artificial Intelligence Applications and Innovations. AIAI 2020. IFIP Advances in Information and Communication Technology* (Vol. 584). Springer. doi:10.1007/978-3-030-49186-4_31

Agangiba, W. A., & Agangiba, M. A. (2013). Mobile solution for metropolitan crime detection and reporting. *Journal of Emerging Trends in Computing and Information Sciences*, *4*(12), 916–921.

Agostinelli, A., Marcantoni, I., Moretti, E., Sbrollini, A., Fioretti, S., Di Nardo, F., & Burattini, L. (2017). Noninvasive Fetal Electrocardiography Part I: Pan-Tompkins' Algorithm Adaptation to Fetal R-peak Identification. The Open Biomedical Engineering Journal, 11, 17–24. doi:10.2174/1874120701711010017

Agrahari & Rao. (2007). Association Rule Mining using RHadoop. *Proceedings of the International Research Journal of Engineering and Technology*, *4*(10).

Akshita, V., Dhanush, J. S., Varman, A. D., & Kumar, V. K. (2021). Blockchain Based Covid Vaccine Booking and Vaccine Management System. In *Proceeding of 2nd International Conference on Smart Electronics and Communication (ICOSEC)*. IEEE.

Al Abri, A., Jamoussi, Y., AlKhanjari, Z., & Kraiem, N. (2020). PerLCol: A Framework for Personalized e-Learning with Social Collaboration Support. *International Journal of Computing and Digital Systems*, *9*(03).

Al-Kodmany, K. (2002). Visualization Tools and Methods in Community Planning: From Freehand Sketches to Virtual Reality. *Journal of Planning Literature*, *17*(2), 189–211. doi:10.1177/088541202762475946

Alkraiji, A. I. (2020). Citizen Satisfaction with Mandatory E-Government Services: A Conceptual Framework and an Empirical Validation. *IEEE Access: Practical Innovations, Open Solutions*, *8*, 117253–117265. doi:10.1109/ACCESS.2020.3004541

Alshebly, Y. S., & Nafea, M. (2020) Isolation of Fetal ECG Signals from Abdominal ECG Using Wavelet Analysis. *IRBM*, *41*(5), 252-260. doi:10.1016/j.irbm.2019.12.002

Alzubi, R., Ramzan, N., Alzoubi, H., & Amira, A. (2018). A Hybrid Feature Selection Method for Complex Diseases SNPs. *IEEE Access: Practical Innovations, Open Solutions*, *6*, 1292–1301. doi:10.1109/ACCESS.2017.2778268

Amaresan, S. (n.d.). *The Expert's Guide to Contextual Inquiry Interviews*. https://blog.hubspot.com/service/contextual-inquiry

Amit, M., Agrawal, A., Chouksey, A., Shriwas, R., & Agrawal, S. (2016, March). A Comparative Study of Chatbots and Humans. *International Journal of Advanced Research in Computer and Communication Engineering*, *5*(3).

Anand & Neelanarayanan. (2019). Feature Selection for Liver Disease using Particle Swarm Optimization Algorithm. *International Journal of Recent Technology and Engineering*, *8*(3).

Anindra, F., Supangkat, S. H., & Kosala, R. R. (2018). Smart Governance as Smart City Critical Success Factor (Case in 15 Cities in Indonesia). *Proceeding - 2018 International Conference on ICT for Smart Society: Innovation Toward Smart Society and Society 5.0, ICISS 2018*, 1–6. 10.1109/ICTSS.2018.8549923

Ansari, U. B., & Sarode, T. (2017). Skin Cancer Detection Using Image Processing. *International Research Journal of Engineering Technology*, 2875–2881.

Antoni, D., Bidar, A., Herdiansyah, M. I., & Akbar, M. (2017). Critical factors of transparency and trust for evaluating e-government services for the poor. *2017 Second International Conference on Informatics and Computing (ICIC)*, 1–6. 10.1109/IAC.2017.8280612

APA. (2021). *Operation Definition entry in APA Dictionary of Psychology*. American Psychological Association. Retrieved from: https://dictionary.apa.org/operational-definition

Appleton, K., & Lovett, A. (2005). GIS-based visualization of development proposals: Reactions from planning and related professionals. *Computers, Environment and Urban Systems*, *29*(3), 321–339. doi:10.1016/j.compenvurbsys.2004.05.005

Arsovski, S., Muniru, I., & Cheok, A. (2017). Analysis of the Chatbot open-source languages aiml and chatscript. *RE:view*. Advance online publication. doi:10.13140/RG.2.2.34160.15367

Avanzini, G. (1992). Pourquoi l'individualisation? AECSE, Individualiser les parcours de formation. Actes du colloque des 6 et 7 décembre 1991, Lyon.

Aydogdu, Ö. (2020). A Web Based System Design for Creating Content in Adaptive Educational Hypermedia and Its Usability. *Malaysian Online Journal of Educational Technology*, *8*(3), 1–24. doi:10.17220/mojet.2020.03.001

Bae, J. H., & Kim, A. H. (2014). Design and Development of Unity 3D Game Engine-Based Smart SNG (Social Network Game). *International Journal of Multimedia and Ubiquitous Engineering*, *9*(8), 261–266. doi:10.14257/ijmue.2014.9.8.23

Barak, B., Mathur, A., Lee, K., & Zhang, Y. (2001). Perceptions of age–identity: A cross- cultural inner-age exploration. *Psychology and Marketing*, *18*(10), 1003–1029. doi:10.1002/mar.1041

Barnett, S. B., & Maulik, D. (2001). Guidelines and recommendations for safe use of Doppler ultrasound in perinatal applications. *The Journal of Maternal-Fetal Medicine*, *10*(2), 75–84. doi:10.1080/jmf.10.2.75.84 PMID:11392597

Barnett, W. D., & Raja, M. K. (1995). Application of QFD to the Software development process. *International Journal of Quality & Reliability Management*, *12*(6), 24–42. doi:10.1108/02656719510089902

Barthes, R. (1966). Introduction à l'analyse structurale des récits. Communications, 8(1), 1–27. doi:10.3406/comm.1966.1113

Barthes, R. (1972). *Mythologies*. Jonathon Cape.

Batica, J., & Gourbesville, P. (2016). Resilience in Flood Risk Management-A New Communication Tool. *Procedia Engineering, 154*, 811–817. doi:10.1016/j.proeng.2016.07.411

Batime, C. & Weber, E. (2007). La formation ouverte et/ou à distance, un levier pour des dispositifs de formation en mutation. *Vie sociale, 4*(4), 127-150.

Batty, M., Dodge, M., Jiang, B., & Hudson-Smith, A. (2000). *New technologies for urban designers: the VENUE project.* Centre for Advanced Spatial Analysis Working Paper Series 21, University College London.

Baudrit, A. (2007). Apprentissage coopératif/Apprentissage collaboratif: D'un comparatisme conventionnel à un comparatisme critique. *Les Sciences de l'Education pour l'Ere Nouvelle, 40*(1), 115–136. doi:10.3917/lsdle.401.0115

Behar. (2016). *Extraction of clinical information from the non-invasive fetal electrocardiogram.* CoRR, abs-1606.01093.

Behar, J., Andreotti, F., Zaunseder, S., Oster, J., & Clifford, G. D. (2016). A practical guide to non-invasive foetal electrocardiogram extraction and analysis. *Physiological Measurement, 37*(5), R1–R35. doi:10.1088/0967-3334/37/5/R1 PMID:27067431

Bejaoui, R., Paquette, G., Basque, J., & Henri, F. (2017). Cadre d'analyse de la personnalisation de l'apprentissage dans les cours en ligne ouverts et massifs (CLOM). *Revue STICEF (Sciences et Technologies de l'Information et de la Communication pour l'Éducation et la Formation), 24*(2).

Bell, C., Fausset, C., Farmer, S., Nguyen, J., Harley, L., & Fain, W. B. (2013). Examining social media use among older adults. *Proceedings of the 24th ACM Conference on Hypertext and Social Media*, 158-163. 10.1145/2481492.2481509

Bertin, J., & Berg, W. J. (2011). *Semiology of graphics : Diagrams, networks, maps, 438* (1st ed.). ESRI Press.

Binu, M. R., Varghese, S., Joy, S. E., & Alex, S. S. (2019). Chatbot for Disease Prediction and Treatment Recommendation using Machine Learning. *Proceedings of the Third International Conference on Trends in Electronics and Informatics (ICOEI 2019).*

Bock, A., Isermann, H., & Knieper, T. (2011). Quantitative content analysis of the visual. In *The SAGE handbook of visual research methods* (pp. 265–282). SAGE Publications Ltd. doi:10.4135/9781446268278.n14

Boehm, B. W. (1988). A spiral model of software development and enhancement. *Computer, 21*(5), 61–72. doi:10.1109/2.59

Bolinger, J., Herold, M., Ramnath, R., & Ramanathan, J. (2011). Connecting reality with theory — An approach for creating integrative industry case studies in the software engineering curriculum. *Frontiers in Education Conference (FIE)*, T4G-1-T4G-6.

Bonchi, Castillo, Gionis, & Jaimes. (2011). Social Network Analysis and Mining for Business Applications. *ACM Transactions on Intelligent Systems and Technology, 2*(3).

Bonney, K.M. (2015). Case Study Teaching Method Improves Student Performance and Perceptions of Learning Gains. *Journal of Microbiology and Biology Education.* doi:10.1128/jmbe.v16i1.846

Boticario, J. G., Santos, O. C., & van Rosmalen, P. (2005). Issues in Developing Standard based Adaptive Learning-Management Systems. *EADTU 2005 Working Conference: Towards Lisbon 2010: Collaboration for Innovative Content in Lifelong Openand Flexible Learning.*

Bourdakis, V. (1996). From CAAD to VRML: London Case Study. In *The 3rd UK VRSIG Conference Full Paper Proceedings.* De Montfort University.

Bradeško, L., & Mladenić, D. (2012). *A survey of Chatbot systems through a loebner prize competition.* Academic Press.

Brahnam, S. (2005). Strategies for handling customer abuse of ECAs. *Proceedings of the INTERACT 2005 Workshop on Abuse: The darker side of Human-Computer Interaction.*

Brewer, N., & Chapman, G. (2002). The Fragile Basic Anchoring Effect. *Journal of Behavioral Decision Making, 15*(1), 65–77. doi:10.1002/bdm.403

Brusilovskiy, P. L. (1994). The construction and application of student models in intelligent tutoring systems. *Journal of Computer and Systems Sciences International, 32*(1), 70–89.

Brusilovsky, P. (2003). Developing adaptive educational hypermedia systems: From design models to authoring tools. In *Authoring tools for advanced technology Learning Environments* (pp. 377–409). Springer. doi:10.1007/978-94-017-0819-7_13

Burgos Solans, D. (2008). *Extension of the IMS Learnin Design specification based on adaptation and integration of units of learning.* Academic Press.

BuyuksalihI.BayburtS.BuyuksalihG.BaskaracaA.KarimH.RahmanA. (2017). 3D modelling and visualization based on the Unity game engine – advantages and challenges. *ISPRS Annals of Photogrammetry, Remote Sensing and Spatial Information Sciences.* doi:10.5194/isprs-annals-IV-4-W4-161-2017

Byrne, J., & Marx, G. (2011). Technological innovations in crime prevention and policing: A review of the research on implementation and impact. *Journal of Police Studies, 3*(20), 17–40.

Callahan, G. (1994). Excessive realism in GUI design: Helpful or harmful? Software Development.

Callejas, Z., Griol, D., & López-Cózar, R. (2011). Predicting user mental states in spoken dialogue systems. *EURASIP Journal on Advances in Signal Processing, 6*(1), 2011a. doi:10.1186/1687-6180-2011-6

Calvert, J. (2006). *Achieving Development Goals - Foundations: Open and Distance Learning.* Lessons and Issues.

Card, M. S. (2009). Readings in Information Visualization. *Using Vision to Think, 2,* 181.

Chandler, D. (2007). *Semiotics - the Basics* (2nd ed.). Routledge. doi:10.4324/9780203014936

Chan, R., Jepson, W., & Friedman, S. (1998). Urban Simulation: An Innovative Tool for Interactive Planning and Consensus Building. *Proceedings of the 1998 American Planning Association National Conference,* 43-50.

Chapter 2 Fundamentals I A Reader on Data Visualization. (n.d.). Retrieved September 9, 2021, from https://mschermann.github.io/data_viz_reader/fundamentals.html

Chasseneuil. (2000). *Formations ouvertes et à distance l'accompagnement pédagogique et organisationnel.* Collectif de Chasseneuil.

Chaves, A. P., & Gerosa, M. A. (2021). How should my chatbot interact? A survey on social characteristics in human–chatbot interaction design. *International Journal of Human-Computer Interaction, 37*(8), 729–758. doi:10.1080/10447318.2020.1841438

Chen, C. (2008). *Handbook of data visualization* (1st ed.). doi:10.1007/978-3-540-33037-0

Chen, C. M. (2008). Intelligent web-based learning system with personalized learning path guidance. *Computers & Education, 51*(2), 787–814. doi:10.1016/j.compedu.2007.08.004

Chen, C. M., Lee, H. M., & Chen, Y. H. (2005). Personalized e-learning system using item response theory. *Computers & Education, 44*(3), 237–255. doi:10.1016/j.compedu.2004.01.006

Chimeno, Garcia-Zapirain, Gomez Beldarrain, Fernandez Ruanova, Garcia, & Carlos. (2017). Automatic Migraine classification via feature selection committee and machine learning techniques over imaging and questionnaire data. *Medical Informatics and Decision Making, 17*(1).

Chimeno, G. (2021). Stable Bagging Feature Selection on Medical Data. *Journal of Big Data, 8*(1), 2021.

Ching-man. Yeung, & Iwata. (2011). Research on Social Network Mining and Its Future Development. *NTT Technical Review, 9*(11). doi:10.1088/1742-6596/1235/1/012111

CityZenith. (2021, December 5). *SmartWorldOS*. https://cityzenith.com/smartworldos-tm

Conlan, O., Wade, V., Bruen, C., & Gargan, M. (2002, May). Multi-model, metadata driven approach to adaptive hypermedia services for personalized elearning. In *International Conference on Adaptive Hypermedia and Adaptive Web-Based Systems* (pp. 100-111). Springer. 10.1007/3-540-47952-X_12

Connac, S. (2021). Pour différencier: individualiser ou personnaliser?. Éducation et socialisation. *Les Cahiers du CERFEE*, (59).

Connac, S. (2012). Analyse de contenu de plans de travail: Vers la responsabilisation des élèves? *Revue des Sciences de l'Education, 38*(2), 323–349. doi:10.7202/1019609ar

Connac, S. (2018). *La personnalisation des apprentissages: agir face à l'hétérogénéité, à l'école et au collège*. ESF Sciences Humaines.

Contextual Design. (n.d.). https://en.wikipedia.org/wiki/Contextual_design

Contextual Inquiry. (n.d.). https://en.wikipedia.org/wiki/Contextual_inquiry

Covid Vaccine Tweets | Kaggle. (n.d.). Retrieved June 29, 2021, from https://www.kaggle.com/kaushiksuresh147/covidvaccine-tweets

COVID-19 INDIA DATA | Kaggle. (n.d.). Retrieved September 9, 2021, from https://www.kaggle.com/ashkhagan/covid19-india-data

Cowan, G., & Siegen. (2019). Statistical data analysis. *Springer Series in Reliability Engineering, 0*, 53–81. doi:10.1007/978-3-319-92574-5_3 PMID:30691412

Creating an EC2 instance on AWS with Ubuntu 18.04. (n.d.). *CloudBooklet*. https://www.cloudbooklet.com/create-an-ec2-instance-on-aws-with-ubuntu-18-04/

CSSEGISandData GitHub. (n.d.). Retrieved September 9, 2021, from https://github.com/CSSEGISandData

d'Ortun, F., & Jézégou, A. (2005). Formations ouvertes. Libertés de choix et autodirection de l'apprenant. Paris, France: L'Harmattan. doi:10.7202/018979ar

Darmawan, A. K., Siahaan, D. O., Susanto, T. D., Umam, B. A., & Bakir, B. (2020). Exploring Factors Influencing Smart Sustainable City Adoption using E-Government Services Effectiveness Evaluation Framework (E-GEEF). *2020 3rd International Conference on Information and Communications Technology (ICOIACT)*, 234–239. 10.1109/ICOIACT50329.2020.9332140

Dasgupta, S., Sharma, N., Sinha, S., & Raghavendra, S. (2019). Evaluating The Performance of Machine Learning using Feature Selection Methods on Dengue Dataset. *International Journal of Engineering and Advanced Technology, 8*(5).

Data Visualization | Microsoft Power BI. (n.d.). Retrieved September 9, 2021, from https://powerbi.microsoft.com/en-us/

De Bra, P., Houben, G. J., & Wu, H. (1999, February). AHAM: A Dexter-based reference model for adaptive hypermedia. In *Proceedings of the tenth ACM Conference on Hypertext and hypermedia: returning to our diverse roots: returning to our diverse roots* (pp. 147-156). 10.1145/294469.294508

De Souza, C. (2005). *The Semiotic Engineering of Human-Computer Interaction* (1st ed.). The MIT Press. doi:10.7551/mitpress/6175.001.0001

Depover, C., De Lievre, B., Decamps, S., & Porco, F. (2014). *Analyse et conception des scénarios d'apprentissage*. Le Département des Sciences et de la Technologie de l'Education Université de Mons.

Desurvire, H. W. (1994). Faster, cheaper!! Are usability inspection methods as effective as empirical testing? In J. Nielsen & R. L. Mack (Eds.), *Usability inspection methods* (pp. 173–202). John Wiley & Sons, Inc.

Domino's Pizza. (n.d.). https://play.google.com/store/apps/details?id=com.Dominos&hl=en_IN

Do, Q. H., & Chen, J.-F. (2013). A Neuro-Fuzzy Approach in the Classification of Students. Academic Performance. *Computational Intelligence and Neuroscience, 2013*, 1–7. doi:10.1155/2013/179097

Doyle, M. (2008). *How to setup your own domain name*. https://www.elated.com/set-up-your-own-domain-name/

Doyle, S., Dodge, M., & Smith, A. (1998). The potential of web-based mapping and virtual reality technologies for modelling urban environments. *Computers, Environment and Urban Systems, 22*(2), 137–155. doi:10.1016/S0198-9715(98)00014-3

Drettakis, G., Roussou, M., Reche, A., & Tsingos, N. (2007). Design and Evaluation of a Real-World Virtual Environment for Architecture and Urban Planning. *Presence: Teleoperators and Virtual Environments, 16*(3), 318–332. doi:10.1162/pres.16.3.318

Dua, D., & Graff, C. (2019). *UCI Machine Learning Repository*. http://archive.ics.uci. edu/ml

Durachman, Y., Harahap, D., Rodoni, A., Faisal Bakti, A. M., & Mansoer, M. (2020). Analysis of Factors That Affect The Quality of E-Government Services: A Case Study in Ombudsman of the Republic of Indonesia. *2020 8th International Conference on Cyber and IT Service Management (CITSM)*, 1–7. 10.1109/CITSM50537.2020.9268796

Ebook | Visualize It!: A Comprehensive Guide to Data Visualization. (n.d.). Retrieved September 9, 2021, from https://www.netquest.com/en/download-ebook-data-visualization

El-Kechai, H. (2008). *Conception collective de scénarios pédagogiques dans un contexte de réingénierie: Une approche par la métamodélisation située* (Doctoral dissertation). Université du Maine.

Elkheshin, S., & Saleeb, N. (2017). A conceptual model for E-government adoption in Egypt. *Proceedings of 2016 11th International Conference on Computer Engineering and Systems, ICCES 2016*, 254–259. 10.1109/ICCES.2016.7822010

Faasos. (n.d.). https://play.google.com/store/apps/details?id=com.done.faasos&hl=en_IN

Febriliantina, R., & Ristekawati, S. F. (2016). The Study of e-Government Implementation in Improving the Quality of Public Services. *2016 International Conference on ICT For Smart Society, July*, 105–110.

Ferrucci, Brown, Chu-Carroll, Fan, Gondek, Kalyanpur, Lally, Murdock, Nyberg, Prager, Schlaefer, & Welty. (2010). The AI Behind Watson – The Technical Article. *AI Magazine*.

Few, S. (2005). Dashboard Design: Beyond Meters, Gauges, and Traffic Lights. *Business Intelligence Journal, 10*(1), 18–24.

Few, S. (2007). *Data Visualization - Past*. Present, and Future.

Fitriani, W. R., Handoyo, I. T., Rahayu, P., & Sensuse, D. I. (2017). Intention to use smart city system based on social cognitive theory. *2016 International Conference on Advanced Computer Science and Information Systems, ICACSIS 2016*, 181–188. 10.1109/ICACSIS.2016.7872747

Flutter documentation. (n.d.). *Flutter.* https://flutter.dev/docs

FoodPanda. (n.d.). https://play.google.com/store/apps/details?id=com.india.foodpanda.android&hl=en_IN

Franklin, R., Heesom, D., & Felton, A. (2006). A Critical Review of Virtual Reality and Geographical Information Systems for Management of the Built Environment. *Proceedings of Information Visualization*, 1-6. doi:10.1109/IV.2006.6

Frunza, O., Inkpen, D., & Tran, T. (2011). A Machine Learning Approach for Identifying Disease Treatment Relations in Short Texts. *IEEE Transactions on Knowledge and Data Engineering*, 23(6), 801–814. doi:10.1109/TKDE.2010.152

Gamberger, D., & Lavrac, N. (1997). Conditions for Occam's Razor Applicability and Noise Elimination. *Proceedings of the Ninth European Conference on Machine Learning.* 10.1007/3-540-62858-4_76

Garrison, D. R., & Shale, D. (1987). Mapping the boundaries of distance education: Problems in defining the field. *American Journal of Distance Education*, 1(1), 7–13. doi:10.1080/08923648709526567

George, J., Kohavi, R., & Pfleger, K. (1995). Irrelevant Features and the Subset Selection Problem. In *Machine Learning: Proceedings of the Eleventh International Conference* (pp. 121-129). Morgan Kaufmann Publishers.

Ghadirian, P., & Bishop, I. D. (2008). Integration of augmented reality and GIS: A new approach to realistic landscape visualisation. *Landscape and Urban Planning*, 86(3-4), 226–232. doi:10.1016/j.landurbplan.2008.03.004

Gibson, J. (1974). *The Perception of the Visual World.* Greenwood Press.

Gibson, J. (1978). *The Ecological Approach to the Visual Perception of Pictures.* MIT Press. doi:10.2307/1574154

Giri & Saravanakumar. (2017). Breast Cancer detection using Image processing Techniques *Oriental. Journal of Computer Science and Technology*, 391–399.

GitHub - CSSEGISandData/COVID-19_Unified-Dataset: Unified COVID-19 Dataset. (n.d.). Retrieved September 9, 2021, from https://github.com/CSSEGISandData/COVID-19_Unified-Dataset

Goldberg, A., & Zhu, X. (2004). Seeing stars when there aren't many stars: Graph-based semi supervised learning for sentiment categorization. *HLT-NAACL 2006 Workshop on Textgraphs: Graph-based Algorithms for Natural Language Processing.*

Goldberger, A. L., Amaral, L. A., Glass, L., Hausdorff, J. M., Ivanov, P. C., Mark, R. G., Mietus, J. E., Moody, G. B., Peng, C. K., & Stanley, H. E. (2000). PhysioBank, PhysioToolkit, and PhysioNet: Components of a new research resource for complex physiologic signals. *Circulation*, 101(23), e215–e220. doi:10.1161/01.CIR.101.23.e215 PMID:10851218

Gordon, E., & Manosevitch, E. (2010). Augmented deliberation: Merging physical and virtual interaction to engage communities in urban planning. *New Media & Society*, 13(1), 75–95. doi:10.1177/1461444810365315

Gorzałczany & Rudziński. (2016). Interpretable and Accurate Medical Data Classification-A Multi-Objective Genetic-Fuzzy Optimization Approach. Elsevier on Expert Systems with Applications, 1-17.

Gregory, R. (1970). *The Intelligent Eye.* Weidenfeld and Nicolson.

Gu, N., Kim, M. J., & Maher, M. L. (2011). Technological advancements in synchronous collaboration: The effect of 3D virtual worlds and tangible user interfaces on architectural design. *Automation in Construction*, 20(3), 270–278. doi:10.1016/j.autcon.2010.10.004

Guo, Y., Du, Q., Luo, Y., Zhang, W., & Xu, L. (2008). Application of augmented reality GIS in architecture. International Archives of the Photogrammetry, Remote Sensing and Spatial Information Sciences XXXVII, 331-336.

Gupta, K., & Chawla, N. (2019). Analysis of Histopathological Images for Prediction of Breast Cancer Using Traditional Classifiers with Pre-Trained CNN. *International conference on Computational Intelligence and Data science(ICCIDS 2019)*, 878-889.

Gupta, M. (2019). A Study on Impact of Online Food Delivery App on Restaurant Business Special Reference to Zomato and Swiggy. *International Journal of Research and Analytical Reviews*, *6*(1).

Guyon Weston, J., Barnhill, S., & Vapnik, V. (2003). Gene Selection for Cancer Classification Using Support Vector Machines. *Machine Learning*, *46*(1-3), 389–422.

Haake, M. (2009). *Embodied Pedagogical Agents: From Visual Impact to Pedagogical Implications* (Doctoral thesis). Lund University.

Hahm, Y., Kim, J., An, S., Lee, M., & Choi, K.-S. (2018). Chatbot who wants to learn the knowledge: kb-agent. *Semdeep/NLIWoD@ISWC*, 4.

Hamad, Y. A., Simonov, K., & Naeem, M. B. (2018). Breast Cancer Detection and Classification using Artificial Neural Networks. *1st Annual International conference on Information and Sciences (AICIS)*, 51-57. 10.1109/AiCIS.2018.00022

Han, J., & Kamber, M. (2006). Data Mining: Concepts and Techniques (2nd ed.). Academic Press.

Han, Kamber, & Pei. (2012). *Data Mining: Concepts and Techniques*. Morgan Kaufmann. doi:10.1016/C2009-0-61819-5

Han, Z., Wei, B. Z., Zheng, Y., Yin, Y., Li, K., & Li, S. (2017). Breast Cancer Multi-classification from Histopathological Images with Structured Deep Learning Model. *Scientific Reports*, *7*(1), 1–10. doi:10.103841598-017-04075-z PMID:28646155

Harb & Desuky. (2014). Feature Selection on Classification of Medical Datasets based on Particle Swarm Optimization. *International Journal of Computer Applications*, *104*(5), 14-17.

Hendler, J. (2009). Web 3.0 Emerging. *Computer*, *42*(1), 111–113. doi:10.1109/MC.2009.30

Henri, F., & Lundgren-Cayrol, K. (1997). *Apprentissage collaboratif à distance, téléconférence et télédiscussion. Rapport interne no 3* (version 1.7). Montréal: LICEF. http://www.licef.teluq.uquebec.ca/Bac/fiches/f48.htm

Herold, M., Bolinger, J., Ramnath, R., Bihari, T., & Ramanathan, J. (2011). Providing end-to-end perspectives in software engineering. *Frontiers in Education Conference (FIE)*, S4B-1-S4B-7.

Hilburn, T. B., Towhidnejad, M., Nangia, S., & Shen, L. (2006). A Case Study Project for Software Engineering Education, *Proceedings, Frontiers in Education. 36th Annual Conference*, 1-5. 10.1109/FIE.2006.322302

Hill, J., Ford, W. R., & Farreras, I. G. (2015). Real conversations with artificial intelligence: A comparison between human–human online conversations and human–chatbot conversations. *Computers in Human Behavior, Elsevier*, *49*, 245–250. doi:10.1016/j.chb.2015.02.026

Hodge, R., & Kress, G. (1988). *Social Semiotics*. Polity.

Hollis, R. (1994). *Graphic design - A concise history* (1st ed.). Thames and Hudson.

Holmes, S., Moorhead, A., Bond, R., Zheng, H., Coates, V., & Mctear, M. (2019). Usability testing of a healthcare chatbot: Can we use conventional methods to assess conversational user interfaces? In *Proceedings of the 31st European Conference on Cognitive Ergonomics (ECCE 2019)*. ACM. 10.1145/3335082.3335094

Honest, N. (2017). Applying case study based approach as part of problem based learning student development. *International Journal of Advanced Research in Computer Science, 8*(9). doi:10.26483/ijarcs.v8i9.4962

How John Burn-Murdoch's Influential Dataviz Helped The World Understand Coronavirus | by Jason Forrest | Nightingale | Medium. (n.d.). Retrieved September 9, 2021, from https://medium.com/nightingale/how-john-burn-murdochs-influential-dataviz-helped-the-world-understand-coronavirus-6cb4a09795ae

How Much Data Is Created Every Day? [27 Powerful Stats]. (n.d.). Retrieved September 9, 2021, from https://seedscientific.com/how-much-data-is-created-every-day/

Husam, I. S. (2017). Feature Selection Algorithms for Malaysian Dengue. *Outbreak Detection Model, 46.* Advance online publication. doi:10.17576/jsm-2017-4602-10

Hussain, F. (2012). *E-Learning 3.0= E-Learning 2.0+ Web 3.0?* International Association for Development of the Information Society.

IBM. (2017). *How Chatbots can help reduce customer service costs by 30%.* Retrieved from https://www.ibm.com/blogs/watson/2017/10/how-Chatbots-reducecustomer-service-costs-by-30-percent/

Ilham, N., WuriHandayani, P., & Azzahro, F. (2017). The Effects of Pictures, Review Credibility and Personalization on Users Satisfaction of Using Restaurant Recommender Apps. *2nd International Conference on Informatics and Computing (ICIC).*

Imran, H., Belghis-Zadeh, M., Chang, T. W., & Graf, S. (2016). PLORS: A personalized learning object recommender system. *Vietnam Journal of Computer Science, 3*(1), 3–13. doi:10.100740595-015-0049-6

Inan, F., & Grant, M. (2011). Individualized web-based instructional design. In *Instructional Design* (pp. 375–388). Concepts, Methodologies, Tools and Applications. doi:10.4018/978-1-60960-503-2.ch212

Ingram, M. (2017). *Medical Students are using Augmented Reality to Study Patients in 3D.* Retrieved from: https://fortune.com/2017/05/03/medical-augmented-reality/

Internet Usage in India. (n.d.). https://www.statista.com/topics/2157/internet-usage-in-india

Ismail, A. (2016). Utilizing big data analytics as a solution for smart cities. *2016 3rd MEC International Conference on Big Data and Smart City (ICBDSC),* 1–5. 10.1109/ICBDSC.2016.7460348

Ittelson, W. H., & Kilpatrick, F. P. (1951). Experiments in Perception. *Scientific American, 185*(2), 50-56.

Izard, C. (1977). *Human Emotions.* Springer Science+Business Media, LLC.

Jackson, M. O. (2010). *Social and economic networks.* Princeton University Press.

Jalote, P. (n.d.). *Software Engineering: A Precise Approach.* Wiley India.

Jayanthi & Sasikala. (2014). Naive Bayesian Classifier and PCA for WebLink Spam Detection. *Computer Science & Telecommunications, 41*(1), 3-15.

Jeremy Wolfe and Lynn Robertson. (n.d.). *From Perception to Consciousness: Searching with Anne Treisman - Oxford Scholarship.* Retrieved September 9, 2021, from https://oxford.universitypressscholarship.com/view/10.1093/acprof:osobl/9780199734337.001.0001/acprof-9780199734337

Jezewski, J., Matonia, A., Kupka, T., Roj, D., & Czabanski, R. (2012). Determination of fetal heart rate from abdominal signals: Evaluation of beat-to-beat accuracy in relation to the direct fetal electrocardiogram. *Biomedizinische Technik. Biomedical Engineering, 57*(5), 383–394. doi:10.1515/bmt-2011-0130 PMID:25854665

Jia, J. (2009). CSIEC: A computer assisted English learning Chatbot based on textual knowledge and reasoning. *Knowledge-Based Systems*, 22(4), 249–255. doi:10.1016/j.knosys.2008.09.001

Jitsi meet security & privacy. (n.d.). *Jitsi.* https://jitsi.org/security/

Johnson, D. W., & Johnson, R. T. (1994). *Learning Together and Alone (ouvrage original publié en 1975).* Allyn and Bacon.

Johnson-Laird, P. N. (2013). Mental models and cognitive change. *Journal of Cognitive Psychology*, 25(2), 131–138. doi:10.1080/20445911.2012.759935

Jongerius, C. (2018). Quantifying Chatbot Performance by using Data Analytics. Center for Organization and Information Department of Information and Computing Sciences, Utrecht University.

Josephine, M. (2019). *Understanding hot reload in Flutter.* https://medium.com/podiihq/understanding-hotreload-in-flutter-2dc28b317036

Juhola, M., Joutsijoki, H., Aalto, H., & Hirvonen, T. P. (2014). On Classification In The Case of A Medical Data Set with A Complicated Distribution. *Elsevier Applied Computing and Informatics*, 10(2), 52-67.

Kahankova, R., Martinek, R., Jaros, R., Behbehani, K., Matonia, A., Jezewski, M., & Behar, J. A. (2020). A Review of Signal Processing Techniques for Non-Invasive Fetal Electrocardiography. *IEEE Reviews in Biomedical Engineering*, 13, 51–73. doi:10.1109/RBME.2019.2938061 PMID:31478873

Kale, P., Bhutkar, G., Pawar, V., & Jathar, N. (2015). Contextual Design of Intelligent Food Carrier in Refrigerator: An Indian Perspective. In *IFIP Working Conference on Human Work Interaction Design*. Springer. 10.1007/978-3-319-27048-7_15

Karimi Rahmati, A., Setarehdan, S. K., & Araabi, B. N. (2017). A PCA/ICA based Fetal ECG Extraction from Mother Abdominal Recordings by Means of a Novel Data-driven Approach to Fetal ECG Quality Assessment. *Journal of Biomedical Physics & Engineering*, 7(1), 37–50. PMID:28451578

Kaschesky, M., Sobkowicz, P., & Bouchard, G. (2011). Opinion Mining in Social network: Modelling, Simulating, and Visualizing Political Opinion Formation in the Web. *Proceedings of 12th Annual International Conference on Digital Government Research*.

Kay, J. (2000). User modeling for adaptation. *User Interfaces for All, Human Factors Series*, 271-294.

Keegan, D. (1986). *The foundations of distance education.* Croom Helm.

Kennedy, R. G. (1998). Electronic fetal heart rate monitoring: Retrospective reflections on a twentieth-century technology. *Journal of the Royal Society of Medicine*, 91(5), 244–250. doi:10.1177/014107689809100503 PMID:9764077

Kenny, P., & Parsons, T. D. (2011). Embodied Conversational Virtual Patients. In Conversational Agents and Natural Language Interaction: Techniques and Effective Practices. IGI Global. doi:10.4018/978-1-60960-617-6.ch011

Keraj, B. (2020). *Analysis, design and implementation of the Albanian Vaccination Managemnet Syatem.* Epoka University.

Kerly, A., Hall, P., & Bull, S. (2007). Bringing Chatbots into education: Towards natural language negotiation of open learner models. *Knowledge-Based Systems*, 20(2), 177–185. doi:10.1016/j.knosys.2006.11.014

Kerr, P. (2015). Adaptive learning. *ELT Journal*, 70(1), 88–93. doi:10.1093/elt/ccv055

Kettle, S. (2017). *Distance on a sphere: The Haversine formula.* https://community.esri.com/t5/coordinate-reference-systems/distance-on-a-sphere-the-haversine-formula/ba-p/902128

Khaleel, Pradhan, & Dash. (2013). A Survey of Data Mining Techniques on Medical Data for Finding Locally Frequent Diseases. *International Journal of Advanced Research in Computer Science and Software Engineering, 3*(8), 149-153.

Khanna, A., Pandey, B., Vashishta, K., Kalia, K., Bhale, P., & Das, T. (2015). A study of today's A.I. through Chatbots and rediscovery of machine intelligence. *International Journal of U- and e-Service Science and Technology, 8*(7), 277–284. doi:10.14257/ijunesst.2015.8.7.28

Khan, R. (2017). Standardized architecture for conversational agents a.k.a. Chatbots. *International Journal of Computer Trends and Technology, 50*(2), 114–121. doi:10.14445/22312803/IJCTT-V50P120

Khurana, D., Koli, A., Khatter, K., & Singh, S. (2017). *Natural language processing: State of the art, current trends and challenges.* Retrieved from https://arxiv.org/abs/1708.05148

Kim, J., Park, S., Yuk, K., Lee, H., & Lee, H. (2000). Virtual reality simulations in physics education. *Interactive Multimedia Electronic Journal of Computer-Enhanced Learning.* http://imej.wfu.edu/articles/2001/2/02/index.asp

Kim, P. (2006). *The Forrester Wave: Brand Monitoring, Q3 2006.* Forrester Wave.

Kirby, S. D., Flint, R., Murakami, H., & Bamford, E. (1997). The Changing Role of GIS in Urban Planning: The Adelaide Model Case Study. *International Journal for Geomatics, 11*(8), 6–8.

Kitchin, R., Young, G., & Dawkins, O. (2021, online first) Planning and 3D spatial media: Progress, prospects, and the knowledge and experiences of local government planners. *Planning Theory & Practice.* Advance online publication. doi:10.1080/14649357.2021.1921832

Kodinariya, T. M., & Makwana, P. R. (2013). Review on determining number of Cluster in K-Means Clustering. *International Journal of Advance Research in Computer Science and Management Studies, 1*(6), 90–95.

Koninger, A., & Bartel, S. (1998). 3D-GIS for Urban Purposes. *GeoInformatica, 2*(1), 79–103. doi:10.1023/A:1009797106866

Koper, R. (2001). *Modeling units of study from a pedagogical perspective-the pedagogical meta-model behind EML.* http://eml. ou.nl/introduction/docs/ped-metamodel. pdf

Kowalski, S., Pavlovska, K., & Goldstein, M. (2013). *Two Case Studies in Using Chatbots for Security Training.* Information Assurance and Security Education and Training, IFIP Advances in Information and Communication Technology. doi:10.1007/978-3-642-39377-8_31

Kress, G. (2010). *Multimodality A social semiotic approach to contemporary communication* (1st ed.). Routledge.

Kress, G., & van Leeuwen, T. (1996). *Reading images - The grammar of visual design.* Routledge.

Krippendorff, K. (2004). Reliability in Content Analysis. *Human Communication Research, 30*, 411–433.

Kuligowska, K. (2015). Commercial Chatbot: Performance evaluation, usability metrics and quality standards of embodied conversational agents. *Professionals Center for Business Research, 2*(02), 1–16. doi:10.18483/PCBR.22

Kumar & Minz. (2014). Feature Selection: A Literature Review. Smart Computing Review, 4(3), 211-229.

Kuncheva, L. I., & Faithfull, W. J. (2014). PCA Feature Extraction for Change Detection in Multidimensional Unlabeled Data. IEEE Transactions on Neural Networks and Learning Systems, 25(1), 69-80.

Kurtadikar, V. S., & Pande, H. M. (2021). Comprehensive Study of Fetal Monitoring Methods for Detection of Fetal Compromise. In A. Joshi, M. Khosravy, & N. Gupta (Eds.), *Machine Learning for Predictive Analysis. Lecture Notes in Networks and Systems* (Vol. 141). Springer. doi:10.1007/978-981-15-7106-0_15

Laforcade, P. (2004). Modélisation et méta-modélisation UML pour la conception et la mise en oeuvre de situations problèmes coopératives. Doctorat de l'Université de Pau et des Pays de l'Adour. *International Journal of Computer Trends and Technology, 69*(6), 28–35. doi:10.14445/22312803/IJCTT-V69I6P105

Lamya, Kawtar, Mohamed, & Mohamed. (2020). Personalization of an educational scenario of a learning activity according to the learning styles model David Kolb. *Global Journal of Engineering and Technology Advances, 5*(3), 99-108. doi:10.30574/gjeta.2020.5.3.0114

Langner, B., Vogel, S., & Black, A. (2010). *Evaluating a dialog language generation system: Comparing the MOUNTAIN system to other NLG approaches. Academic Press.*

Larman, C., & Basili, V. R. (2003). Iterative and Incremental Development: A Brief History. *Computer, 36*(6), 47–56. doi:10.1109/MC.2003.1204375

Laumans. (2016). *Visualizing Data.* Academic Press.

Law, E. L. C., & Sun, X. (2012). Evaluating user experience of adaptive digital educational games with Activity The01·y. *International Journal of Human-Computer Studies, 70*(7), 478–497. doi:10.1016/j.ijhcs.2012.01.007

Lee & Chen. (2013). Understanding social computing research. *IT Professional, 15*(6), 56-62.

Lefevre, M., Broisin, J., Butoianu, V., Daubias, P., Daubigney, L., Greffier, F., ... Terrat, H. (2012). *Personnalisation de l'apprentissage: comparaison des besoins et approches à travers l'étude de quelques dispositifs.* Academic Press.

Lewis, J., Zheng, D., & Carter, W. (2017). *Effect of encryption on lawful access to communications and data.* Rowman & Littlefield.

Li, L., Lee, K. Y., Emokpae, E., & Yang, S.-B. (2019). What makes you continuously use Chatbot services? Evidence from Chinese online travel agencies. *Electronic Markets.* Advance online publication. doi:10.100712525-020-00454-z

Little, R. J., & Rubin, D. B. (1989). The Analysis of Social Science Data with Missing Values. *Sociological Methods & Research, 18*(2-3), 292–326. doi:10.1177/0049124189018002004

Liu, Y., Zhang, H., Chen, M., & Zhang, L. (2016). A Boosting-Based Spatial-Spectral Model for Stroke Patients' EEG Analysis in Rehabilitation Training. IEEE Transactions on Neural Systems and Rehabilitation Engineering, 24(1), 169-179.

Liu, F., & Lee, H. J. (2010). Use of social network information to enhance collaborative filtering performance. *Expert Systems with Applications, 37*(7), 4772–4778. doi:10.1016/j.eswa.2009.12.061

Liu, H., Chen, D., & Sun, G. (2019). Detection of Fetal ECG R Wave From Single-Lead Abdominal ECG Using a Combination of RR Time-Series Smoothing and Template-Matching Approach. *IEEE Access: Practical Innovations, Open Solutions, 7,* 66633–66643. doi:10.1109/ACCESS.2019.2917826

Liu, X., Wang, X., & Su, Q. (2015). Feature selection of medical data sets based on RS-RELIEFF. *International Conference on Service Systems and Service Management (ICSSSM),* 1-5.

Lopes, A., Valentim, N., & Moraes, B. (2018). Applying user-centered techniques to analyze and design a mobile application. *J Softw Eng Res Dev, 6.* doi:10.1186/s40411-018-0049-1

Lowry, J. (2015). *Augmented reality is the future of design.* Retrieved from https://thenextweb.com/augmented-reality/2015/08/31/augmented-reality-is-the-future-of-design/

Lytras, M. D., & Şerban, A. C. (2020). E-Government Insights to Smart Cities Research: European Union (EU) Study and the Role of Regulations. *IEEE Access: Practical Innovations, Open Solutions, 8,* 65313–65326. doi:10.1109/ACCESS.2020.2982737

MacPhedran, S. (2018). *Augmented Manufacturing: The Big Six Hololens Use Cases for Manufacturers.* Retrieved from https://blog.smith.co/2018/Augmented-Manufacturing

Madyatmadja, E. D., Nindito, H., Verasius, A., Sano, D., & Sianipar, C. P. M. (2010). *Data Visualization of Priority Region Based On Community Complaints in Government.* Academic Press.

Madyatmadja, E. D., Olivia, J., & Sunaryo, R. F. (2019). *Priority Analysis Of Community Complaints Through E-Government Based On Social Media.* Academic Press.

Maha, K., Omar, E., Mohamed, E., & Mohamed, K. (2021). Design of educational scenarios of activities in a learning situation for online teaching. *GSC Advanced Engineering and Technology, 1*(1), 49-64.

Mann, S., Furness, T., Yuan, Y., Iorio, J., & Wang, Z. (2018). *All Reality: Virtual, Augmented, Mixed (X), Mediated (X,Y), and Multimediated Reality.* CoRR. abs/1804.08386.

Marietto, M., Varago de Aguiar, R., Barbosa, G., Botelho, W., Pimentel, E., Franca, R., & Silva, V. (2013). Artificial intelligence markup language: A brief tutorial. *International Journal of Computer Science and Engineering Survey, 04*(3), 1–20. Advance online publication. doi:10.5121/ijcses.2013.4301

Martin, J. (1991). Rapid application development. Macmillan Publishing.

Masche, J., & Le, N.-T. (2018). *A review of technologies for conversational systems.* doi:10.1007/978-3-319-61911-8_19

Masud, M., Alhumyani, H., Alshamrani, S. S., Cheikhrouhou, O., Ibrahim, S., Muhammad, G., Hossain, M. S., & Shorfuzzaman, M. (2020). Leveraging Deep Learning Techniques for Malaria Parasite Detection Using Mobile Application. Wireless Communications and Mobile Computing, 1-15.

Matonia, A., Jezewski, J., Kupka, T., Jezewski, M., Horoba, K., Wrobel, J., Czabanski, R., & Kahankowa, R. (2020). Fetal electrocardiograms, direct and abdominal with reference heartbeat annotations. *Scientific Data, 7*(1), 200. doi:10.103841597-020-0538-z PMID:32587253

Mat, R. C., Shariff, A., Zulkifli, A., Rahim, M., & Mahayudin, M. (2014). Using game engine for 3D terrain visualisation of GIS data: A review. *7th IGRSM International Remote Sensing and GIS Conference and Exhibition.* 10.1088/1755-1315/20/1/012037

Mcclees, E. (2019). *How the police use cell phone data in criminal investigation.* https://www.mctexaslaw.com/how-do-police-use-cell-phone-data-in-criminal-investigations

McCoy, E. (2018) *Storytelling Strategies for Augmented and Virtual Reality.* Retrieved from https://killervisualstrategies.com/blog/storytelling-strategies-for-augmented-and-virtual-reality.html

Meiyanti, R., Misbah, M., Napitupulu, D., Kunthi, R., Nastiti, T. I., Sensuse, D. I., & Sucahyo, Y. G. (2018). Systematic review of critical success factors of E-government: Definition and realization. *Proceedings - 2017 International Conference on Sustainable Information Engineering and Technology, SIET 2017,* 190–195. 10.1109/SIET.2017.8304133

Meiyanti, R., Utomo, B., Sensuse, D. I., & Wahyuni, R. (2019). E-Government Challenges in Developing Countries: A Literature Review. *2018 6th International Conference on Cyber and IT Service Management, CITSM 2018,* 1–6. 10.1109/CITSM.2018.8674245

Merleau-Ponty, M. (1945). *Phenomenology of Perception* (C. Smith, Trans.). Éditions Gallimard, Routledge & Kegan Paul.

Messinger, Stroulia, Lyons, Bone, Niu, Smirnov, & Perelgute. (2009). Social computing: An overview. *Communications of the Association for Information Systems, 19*(1), 37.

Messinger, P. R., Stroulia, E., Lyons, K., Bone, M., Niu, R. H., Smirnov, K., & Perelgut, S. (2009). Virtual worlds—past, present, and future: New directions in social computing. *Decision Support Systems, 47*(3), 204–228. doi:10.1016/j.dss.2009.02.014

Mikolov, T., Sutskever, I., Chen, K., Corrado, G. s., & Dean, J. (2013). Distributed representations of words and phrases and their compositionality. *Advances in Neural Information Processing Systems*, 26.

Mislevics, A., Grundspenķ, K., Is, J., & Rollande, R. (2018). *A systematic approach to implementing Chatbots in organizations—RTU leo showcase*. BIR Workshops.

Mkhwanazi, K., Owolawi, P. A., Mapayi, T., & Aiyetoro, G. (2020, August 6-7). *An automatic crime reporting and immediate response system* [Paper presentation]. *2020 International Conference on Artificial Intelligence, Big Data, Computing and Data Communication Systems (ICABCD)*, Durban, South Africa.

Mödritscher, F., Garcia-Barrios, V. M., & Gütl, C. (2004). The Past, the Present and the Future of adaptive E-Learning. *Proceedings of ICL 2004*.

Moore, J. L., Dickson-Deane, C., & Galyen, K. (2011). e-Learning, online learning, and distance learning environments: Are they the same? *The Internet and Higher Education, 14*(2), 129–135. doi:10.1016/j.iheduc.2010.10.001

Mujumdar, R., Nadar, P., Bondre, A., Kulkarni, A., & Pathak, S. (2019). *Principal Component Analysis (PCA) based single-channel, non-invasive fetal ECG extraction*. https://fetosense.com/assets/publictions/PCA.pdf

Murugesan, S., Bhuvaneswaran, R. S., Khanna Nehemiah, H., Keerthana Sankari, S., & Nancy Jane, Y. (2021). Feature Selection and Classification of Clinical Datasets Using Bioinspired Algorithms and Super Learner. Computational and Mathematical Methods in Medicine.

Mushtaq, J. (2016). Different Requirements Gathering Techniques and Issues. *International Journal of Scientific & Engineering Research, 7*(9).

Mwiya, M., Phiri, J., & Lyoko, G. (2015). Public crime reporting and monitoring system model using GSM and GIS technologies: A case of Zambia police service. *International Journal of Computer Science and Mobile Computing, 4*(11), 207–226.

Nagarhalli, T., & Vinod Vaze, N. K. (2020). A Review of Current Trends in the Development of Chatbot Systems. *6th International Conference on Advanced Computing & Communication Systems (ICACCS)*. 10.1109/ICACCS48705.2020.9074420

Nanayakkara, Kumara, & Rathnayaka. (2021). A Survey of Finding Trends in Data Mining Techniques for Social Media Analysis. *Sri Lanka Journal of Social Sciences and Humanities, 1*(2), 37–50.

Nasution, M. K. M. (2019). Social Network Mining: A discussion. *Journal of Physics: Conference Series*, ●●●, 1235.

Natrajan, B., & Jacob, S. (2018). Provincialising Vegetarianism putting Indian Food Habits in Their Place. *Economic and Political Weekly, 53*(9), 54–64.

Navita. (2017). A Study on Software Development Life Cycle & its Model. *IJERCSE, 4*(9).

Negandhi, P., Chauhan, M., Das, A. M., Neogi, S. B., Sharma, J., & Sethy, G. (2016). Mobile based Effective Vaccine Management Tool: An m health Initiative Implemented by UNICEF in Bihar. *Indian Journal of Public Health, 60*(4), 334–340.

Nicholson, P. (2007). A history of e-learning. In *Computers and education* (pp. 1–11). Springer. doi:10.1007/978-1-4020-4914-9_1

Nie, P., Zhou, X., Wang, C., Zheng, H., & Zeng, Y. (2021). Design and Implementation of Coronavirus Vaccines Information Traceability System based on Blockchain. *Proceeding of International Symposium on Artificial Intelligence and its Application on Media (ISAIAM).*

Nimavat, K., & Tushar, C. (2017). Chatbots: An Overview Types, Architecture, Tools and Future Possibilities. International Journal for Scientific Research & Development, 5(7).

Nimavat, K., & Champaneria, T. (2017). Chatbots: An overview types, architecture, tools and future possibilities. *International Journal for Scientific Research and Development*, 5(7), 1019–1024. http://www.ijsrd.com/

Norval, C. (2012). Understanding the incentives of older adults' participation on social networking sites. *ACM Sigaccess Accessibility and Computing*, 102(102), 25–29. doi:10.1145/2140446.2140452

Nt, T. (2016). *An e-business Chatbot using AIML and LSA.* doi:10.1109/ICACCI.2016.7732476

Onyesolu, M. O. (2009a). Virtual reality laboratories: The pedagogical effectiveness and use in obtaining cheap laboratories using the computer laboratory. *Journal of Science Engineering and Technology*, 16(1), 8679-8689.

Onyesolu, M. O., & Akpado, K. A. (2009b). Virtual reality simulations in computer engineering education. *International Journal of Electrical and Telecommunication Systems Research*, 3(3), 56-61.

Paar, P. (2006). Landscape visualizations: Applications and requirements of 3D visualization software for environmental planning. *Computers, Environment and Urban Systems*, 30(6), 815–839. doi:10.1016/j.compenvurbsys.2005.07.002

Pang, B., & Lee, L. (2008). Using very simple statistics for review search: An exploration. *Proceedings of the International Conference on Computational Linguistics (COLING).*

Panigrahy, D., & Sahu, P. K. (2017). Extraction of fetal ECG signal by an improved method using extended Kalman smoother framework from single channel abdominal ECG signal. *Australasian Physical & Engineering Sciences in Medicine*, 40(1), 191–207. doi:10.100713246-017-0527-5 PMID:28210991

Pan, J., & Tompkins, W. J. (1985). A real-time QRS detection algorithm. *IEEE Transactions on Biomedical Engineering*, 32(3), 230–236. doi:10.1109/TBME.1985.325532 PMID:3997178

Paquette, G. (2002). *L'ingénierie du téléapprentissage: pour construire l'apprentissage en réseaux.* Sainte-Foy: Presses de l'Université du Québec.

Paquette, G., Aubin, C., & Crevier, F. (1997). Design and Implementation of Interactive TeleLearning Scenarios. *Proceedings of ICDE'97 (International Council for Distance Education).*

Paramythis, A., & Loidl-Reisinger, S. (2003). Adaptive learning environments and e-learning standards. In *Second European conference on e-learning* (Vol. 1, No. 2003, pp. 369-379). Academic Press.

Parashar, N., & Ghadiyali, S. (2017). *A Study on Customer's Attitude and Perception towards Digital Food App Services. Amity Journal of Management.*

Park, H. W., Li, D., Piao, Y., & Ryu, K. H. (2017). A Hybrid Feature Selection Method to Classification and Its Application in Hypertension Diagnosis. *LNCS*, 10443, 11–19.

Parmenter, D. (2010). *Key performance indicators* (2nd ed.). Wiley.

Patel, Gandhi, & Shetty, & Tekwani. (2017). Heart Disease Prediction Using Data Mining. *International Research Journal of Engineering and Technology*, 04, 1705–1707.

Patil, D.V., & Bichkar, R.S. (2012). Issues in Optimization of Decision Tree Learning: A Survey. *International Journal of Applied Information Systems, 3*(5), 13-29.

Paulson, L. D. (2001). Adapting methodologies for doing software right. *IT Professional, 3*(4), 13–15.

Pawar, S., & Bhutkar, G. (2021). Usability Testing of Twitter App with Indian Users. *Human-Computer Interaction and Beyond, 1*, 35–73. doi:10.2174/9789814998819121010006

Payne, S. (2003). Users' Mental Model: The Very Ideas. In J. Carroll (Ed.), *HCI Models, Theories, and Frameworks - Toward a Multidisciplinary Science* (pp. 135–156). Morgan Kaufmann. doi:10.1016/B978-155860808-5/50006-X

Peirce, C. S. (Ed.). (1883). *Studies in Logic, by Members of The Johns Hopkins University.* Little Brown. doi:10.1037/12811-000

Pemin, J.-P. (2005). Langages de modélisation de situations d'apprentissage: l'approche Leaming Design. Séminaire du Groupe Rhône Alpes d'Initiative sur les Normes et Standards dans les Technologies d'Information et de Communication pour l'Education, Lyon, France.

Peng, Y., Wu, Z., & Jiang, J. (2010). A novel feature selection approach for biomedical data classification. School of Informatics, University of Bradford. *UK Journal of Biomedical Informatics, 43*(1), 15–23. doi:10.1016/j.jbi.2009.07.008 PMID:19647098

Perera, R., & Nand, P. (2017). Recent advances in natural language generation: A survey and classification of the empirical literature. *Computer Information, 36*(1), 1–31. doi:10.4149/cai_2017_1_1

Pernin, J.-P., & Lejeune, A. (2004). Dispositifs d'apprentissage instrumentés par les technologies: vers une ingénierie centrée sur les scénarios. Dans Actes du colloque TICE, 407-414.

Perraton, H. (1988). A theory for distance education. In D. Sewart, D. Keegan, & B. Holmberg (Eds.), *Distance education: International perspectives* (pp. 34–45). Routledge.

Perrenoud, P. (1995). *La pédagogie à l'école des différences.* ESF.

Pietsch, S. M. (2000). Computer visualisation in the de- sign control of urban environments: A literature review. *Environment and Planning. B, Planning & Design, 27*(4), 521–536. doi:10.1068/b2634

Pimplapure, M. (2019). Consumer Behavior towards Food Delivery App. *Indian Journal of Applied Research, 9*(7).

Portman, M. E., Natapov, A., & Fisher-Gewirtzman, D. (2015). To go where no man has gone before: Virtual reality in architecture, landscape architecture and environmental planning. *Computers, Environment and Urban Systems, 54*, 376–384. doi:10.1016/j.compenvurbsys.2015.05.001

Pressman, R. S. (n.d.a). *Software Engineering: A practitioners approach* (5th ed.). Mc-Graw Hill Publication.

Pressman, R. S. (n.d.b). *Software Engineering: A Practitioner's Approach* (7th ed.). Mc-Graw-Hill.

Principles of grouping - Wikipedia. (n.d.). Retrieved September 9, 2021, from https://en.wikipedia.org/wiki/Principles_of_grouping

Przegalinska, Ciechanowski, Stroz, Gloor, & Mazurek. (2019). *In bot we trust: A new methodology of Chatbot performance measures.* Kelley School of Business, Indiana University. / doi:10.1016/j.bushor.2019.08.0050007-6813

Quintin, J. J., Depover, C., & Degache, C. (2005, May). Le rôle du scénario pédagogique dans l'analyse d'une formation à distance. In Analyse d'un scénario pédagogique à partir d'éléments de caractérisation définis, actes du colloque EIAH, Montpellier.

Radziwill, N. M. & Benton, M. C. (2017). *Evaluating Quality of Chatbots and Intelligent Conversational Agents*. Academic Press.

Rainer, G., Scheibehenne, B., & Kleber, N. (2010). Less may be More When Choosing is Difficult: Choice Complexity and Too Much Choice. *Acta Psychologica*, *133*(1), 45–50. doi:10.1016/j.actpsy.2009.08.005 PMID:19766972

Ramesh, K., Ravishankaran, S., Joshi, A., & Chandrasekaran, K. (2017). A survey of design techniques for conversational agents. In *Information, communication and computing technology* (Vol. 750, pp. 336–350). Springer. doi:10.1007/978-981-10-6544-6_31

Rasanayagam, K., Kumarasiri, S., Tharuka, W., Samaranayake, N., Samarasinghe, P., & Siriwardana, S. (2018, December 21-22). *CIS: An automated criminal identification system* [Paper presentation]. *IEEE International Conference on Information and Automation for Sustainability (ICIAfS)*, Colombo, Sri Lanka.

Razaghi, M., & Finger, M. (2018). Smart Governance for Smart Cities. *Proceedings of the IEEE*, *106*(4), 680–689. doi:10.1109/JPROC.2018.2807784

RealSim. (2021). *Jersey 3D*. https://realsim.ie/realsim-city/

Reinhard, J., Hayes-Gill, B. R., Schiermeier, S., Hatzmann, H., Heinrich, T. M., & Louwen, F. (2013). Intrapartum heart rate ambiguity: A comparison of cardiotocogram and abdominal fetal electrocardiogram with maternal electrocardiogram. *Gynecologic and Obstetric Investigation*, *75*(2), 101–108. doi:10.1159/000345059 PMID:23328351

Rivas, P., Holzmayer, K., Hernandez, C., & Grippaldi, C. (2018). Excitement and Concerns about Machine Learning-Based Chatbots and Talkbots: A Survey. *IEEE International Symposium on Technology in Society (ISTAS) Proceedings*. 10.1109/ISTAS.2018.8638280

Rogers, L., Li, J., Liu, L., Balluz, R., Rychik, J., & Ge, S. (2013). Advances in fetal echocardiography: Early imaging, three/four dimensional imaging, and role of fetal echocardiography in guiding early postnatal management of congenital heart disease. *Echocardiography (Mount Kisco, N.Y.)*, *30*(4), 428–438. doi:10.1111/echo.12211 PMID:23551603

S., R., & Balakrishnan, K. (2018). Empowering Chatbots with business intelligence by big data integration. *International Journal of Advanced Research in Computer Science*, *9*(1), 627–631. doi:10.26483/ijarcs.v9i1.5398

Sagar & Saini. (2016). Color Channel Based Segmentation of Skin Lesion from Clinical Images for the Detection of Melanoma. *2016 IEEE 1st International Conference on Power Electronics, Intelligent Control and Energy Systems (ICPEICES)*, 1-5.

Salter, J. D., Campbell, C., Journeay, M., & Sheppard, S. (2009). The digital workshop: Exploring the use of interactive and immersive visualisation tools in participatory planning. *Journal of Environmental Management*, *90*(6), 2090–2101. doi:10.1016/j.jenvman.2007.08.023 PMID:18558460

Sameni, R., & Clifford, G. D. (2010). A Review of Fetal ECG Signal Processing; Issues and Promising Directions. *The Open Pacing, Electrophysiology & Therapy Journal*, *3*, 4–20. doi:10.2174/1876536X01003010004 PMID:21614148

Samsudeen, M. (2020). *Easily visualize OpenStreetMaps and Bing maps in Flutter*. https://www.syncfusion.com/blogs/post/easily-visualize-openstreetmaps-and-bing-maps-in-flutter.aspx

Sana, F., Ballal, T., Shadaydeh, M., Hoteit, I., & Al-Naffouri, T. Y. (2019). Fetal ECG extraction exploiting joint sparse supports in a dual dictionary framework. *Biomedical Signal Processing and Control*, *48*, 46-60. doi:10.1016/j.bspc.2018.08.023

Sánchez-Maroño, N., Alonso-Betanzos, A., & Tmobile-Sanromán, M. (2007). Lecture Notes in Computer Science: Vol. 4881. *Filter Methods for Feature Selection: A Comparative Study. Intelligent Data Engineering and Automated Learning - IDEAL 2007.* Springer.

Sandler, E. (2018). *Zara Stores Target Millennials with Augmented Reality Displays.* Retrieved from https://www.forbes.com/sites/emmasandler/2018/04/16/zara-stores-targets-millennials-with-augmented-reality-displays/#7ec8a40c2315

Santhana Lakshmi, V. (2020). A Study on Machine Learning based Conversational Agents and Designing Techniques. *Proceedings of the Fourth International Conference on I-SMAC (IoT in Social, Mobile, Analytics and Cloud) (I-SMAC).*

Saranya, P., Monica, V., & Priyadarshini, J. (2017). Comparative Study of Software Development Methodologies. *International Research Journal of Engineering and Technology.*

Sari, A. M., Hidayanto, A. N., Purwandari, B., Budi, N. F. A., & Kosandi, M. (2018). Challenges and issues of E-participation implementation: A case study of e-complaint Indonesia. *Proceedings of the 3rd International Conference on Informatics and Computing, ICIC 2018,* 1–6. 10.1109/IAC.2018.8780467

Sarker, M. N. I., Khatun, M. N., Alam, G. M. M., & Islam, M. S. (2020). Big Data Driven Smart City: Way to Smart City Governance. *2020 International Conference on Computing and Information Technology (ICCIT-1441),* 1–8. 10.1109/ICCIT-144147971.2020.9213795

Sawant, Bhandari, Yadav, & Yele, & Bendale. (2018). Brain Cancer Detection from Mri: A Machine Learning Approach (Tensorflow). *International Research Journal of Engineering and Technology, 5,* 2089–2094.

Saxena, A. (2019). An Analysis of Online Food Ordering Applications in India: Zomato and Swiggy. *4th National Conference on Recent Trends in Humanities, Technology, Management & Social Development (RTHTMS).*

Schafer & Graham. (2002). Missing data: Our view of state of the art. *Psychological Methods, 7*(2), 147-153.

Schreyer, A. C. (2013). *Architectural Design with SketchUp: Component-Based Modelling, Plugins, Rendering and Scripting.* John Wiley & Sons.

Sedghamiz, H. (2014). *Matlab Implementation of Pan Tompkins ECG QRS detector.* https://www.researchgate.net/publication/313673153_Matlab_Implementation_of_Pan_Tompkins_ECG_QRS_detect

Sekhri, A. (2020). *The criminal law blog: Mobile phones and criminal investigations.* https://criminallawstudiesnluj.wordpress.com/2020/05/07/mobile-phones-and-criminal-investigations/

Semeraro, G., Andersen, H. H., Andersen, V., Lops, P., & Abbattista, F. (2002). Evaluation and Validation of a Conversational Agent Embodied in a Bookstore. In N. Carbonell & C. Stephanidis (Eds.), *Universal access.* doi:10.1007/978-3-642-23196-4

Setiawan, D., Kusuma, W. A., & Wigena, A. H. (2017). Sequential Forward Floating Selection With Two Selection Criteria. *International Conference on Advanced Computer Science and Information Systems (ICACSIS),* 395-400.

Shanthi, D., Maheshvari, P. N., & Sankarie, S. (2020). Survey on Detection of Melanoma Skin Cancer Using Image Processing and Machine Learning. *International Journal of Research and Analytical Reviews,* 237-248.

Sharda, R., Delen, D., & Turban, E. (2018). Business intelligence and analytics. *Higher Education Strategy and Planning.* doi:10.4324/9781315206455-12

Sharma, S., Agrawal, J., Agarwal, S., & Sharma, S. (2013). Machine Learning Techniques for Data Mining: A Survey. *Proceedings of Computational Intelligence and Computing Research (ICCIC),* 1 - 6. 10.1109/ICCIC.2013.6724149

Shinde, P., & Jadhav, S. (2014). Health Analysis System Using Machine Learning. *International Journal of Computer Science and Information Technologies*, 3928–3933.

Shiratuddin, M. F., & Thabet, W. (2011). Utilizing a 3D game engine to develop a virtual design review system. *Journal of Information Technology in Construction, 16*, 39–68.

Shneiderman's Eight Golden Rules of Interface Design. (n.d.). *Capian.* https://capian.co/shneiderman-eight-golden-rules-interface-design

Shute, V. J., & Psotka, J. (1994). *Intelligent Tutoring Systems: Past, Present, and Future (No. AL/HR-TP-1994-0005).* Armstrong Lab Brooks AFB TX Human Resources Directorate.

Shylesh, S. (2017). *A Study of Software Development Life Cycle Process Models.* SSRN: https://ssrn.com/abstract=2988291

Silva, R., Oliveira, J. C., & Giraldi, G. A. (2003). *Introduction to augmented reality.* National Laboratory for Scientific Computation.

Singapore, V. (2021). *National research foundation.* https://www.nrf.gov.sg/programmes/virtual-singapore

Singha, B., & Kaurc. (2019). Software-based Prediction of Liver Disease with Feature Selection and Classification Techniques. *International Conference on Computational Intelligence and Data Science (ICCIDS 2019).*

Sitowise. (2021). *AURA.* https://www.sitowise.com/references/aura-user-interface

Sjödén, B., Silvervarg, A., Haake, M., & Gulz, A. (2011). Extending an Educational Math Game with a Pedagogical Conversational Agent: Facing Design Challenges. *Communications in Computer and Information Science, 126.* doi:10.1007/978-3-642-20074-8_10

Skyline. (2021). *TerraExplorer for desktop.* https://www.skylinesoft.com/terraexplorer-for-desktop/

Sleeman, D., & Brown, J. S. (1982). *Intelligent tutoring systems.* Academic Press.

Smith, S. (2018). *Overview of ASP. NET Core MVC.* https://docs.microsoft.com/en-us/aspnet/core/mvc/overview?view=aspnetcore-5.0

Smitha, P., Shaji, L., & Mini, M.G. (2011). A Review of Medical Image Classification Techniques. *IJCA Proceedings on International Conference on VLSI, Communications and Instrumentation (ICVCI)*, 34–38.

Sofie & Anneleen. (2003). Ensemble Methods for Noise Elimination in Classification Problems. *Fourth International Workshop on Multiple Classifier Systems, 2709*, 317-325.

Song, Y., Wong, L. H., & Looi, C. K. (2012). Fostering personalized learning in science inquiry supported by mobile technologies. *Educational Technology Research and Development, 60*(4), 679–701. doi:10.100711423-012-9245-6

Sparta, J., Alsumait, S., & Joshi, A. (2019). Marketing Habituation and Process Study of Online Food Industry (A Study Case: Zomato). *Journal of Community Development in Asia.*

Spring, J. (2012). *Education networks: Power, wealth, cyberspace, and the digital mind.* Routledge. doi:10.4324/9780203156803

Stojanovski, T. (2018). City Information Modelling (CIM) and Urban Design: Morphological Structure. Design Elements and Programming Classes in CIM. *City Modelling & GIS, 1*(36), 507-516.

Stolte, C., Tang, D., & Hanrahan, P. (2002). Polaris: A system for query, analysis, and visualization of multidimensional relational databases. *IEEE Transactions on Visualization and Computer Graphics, 8*(1), 52–65. doi:10.1109/2945.981851

Sulas, E., Urru, M., Tumbarello, R., Raffo, L., Sameni, R., & Pani, D. (2021). A non-invasive multimodal foetal ECG–Doppler dataset for antenatal cardiology research. *Scientific Data*, 8(1), 30. doi:10.103841597-021-00811-3 PMID:33500414

Sumalatha, G., & Muniraj, N. J. R. (2013). Survey on Medical Diagnosis Using Data Mining Techniques. *Proceedings of International Conference on Optical Imaging Sensor and Security*, 126-139. 10.1109/ICOISS.2013.6678433

Sunassee, K., Vythilingum, T., & Sungkur, R. K. (2017). Providing improved services to citizens, a critical review of E-government facilities. *2017 1st International Conference on Next Generation Computing Applications (NextComp)*, 129–134. 10.1109/NEXTCOMP.2017.8016187

Suta, Lan, Wu, Mongkolnam, & Chan. (2020). An Overview of Machine Learning in Chatbots. *International Journal of Mechanical Engineering and Robotics Research, 9*(4).

Swiggy. (n.d.). https://play.google.com/store/apps/details?id=in.swiggy.android&hl=en_IN

Tabassum, K., Shaiba, H., Shamrani, S., & Otaibi, S. (2018, April 4-6). *E-cops: An online crime reporting and management system for Riyadh city* [Paper presentation]. 2018 1st International Conference on Computer Applications & Information Security (ICCAIS), Riyadh, Saudi Arabia.

tableau-visual-guidebookTableu. (n.d.). Retrieved September 9, 2021, from https://www.tableau.com/learn/whitepapers/tableau-visual-guidebookTableu

Tadlaoui, M. A., & Khaldi, M. (2020). Concepts and Interactions of Personalization, Collaboration, and Adaptation in Digital Learning. In M. Tadlaoui & M. Khaldi (Eds.), *Personalization and Collaboration in Adaptive E-Learning* (pp. 1–33). IGI Global. doi:10.4018/978-1-7998-1492-4.ch001

Tan, A.-H. (1999). Text mining: The state of the art and the challenges. *Proceedings of the Pakdd 1999 Workshop on Knowledge Disocovery from Advanced Databases, 8*, 65–70.

Tandon, A., Kaur, P., Bhatt, Y., Mantymaki, M., & Dhir, A. (2021). Why do People Purchase from Food Delivery Apps? A Consumer Value Perspective. *Journal of Retailing and Consumer Services, 63*, 63. doi:10.1016/j.jretconser.2021.102667

Tarle & Akkalakshmi. (2019). Improving Classification Performance of Neuro Fuzzy Classifier by Imputing Missing Data. *International Journal of Compu*ting, 18(4), 495-501.

Tarle & Jena. (2019). Improved Artificial Neural Network (ANN) With Aid of Artificial Bee Colony (ABC) For Medical Data Classification. *International Journal of Business Intelligence & Data mining, 15*(3), 288-305.

Tarle, Sanjay, & Jena. (2019). Integrating Multiple Methods to Enhance Medical Data Classification. *International Journal of Evolving Systems, 11*, 133–142.

Tarle, Tajanpure, & Jena. (2016). Medical Data Classification using different Optimization Techniques: A survey. *IJRET Journal, 5*(5), 101-108.

Tepper, A. (2012). *How much data is created every minute?* https://mashable.com/2012/06/22/datacreated-every-minute/

Thakkar, J. (2021). *End-to-end-encryption: The good, the bad and the politics.* https://www.thesslstore.com/blog/end-to-end-encryption-the-good-the-bad-and-the-politics/

Thompson, E. M., Greenhalgh, P., Muldoon-Smith, K., Charlton, J., & Dolník, M. (2016). Planners in the Future City: Using City Information Modelling to Support Planners as Market Actors. *Urban Planning, 1*(1), 79–94. doi:10.17645/up.v1i1.556

Total data volume worldwide 2010-2025 | Statista. (n.d.). Retrieved September 9, 2021, from https://www.statista.com/statistics/871513/worldwide-data-created/

Treisman, A. (1985). Preattentive processing in vision. *Computer Vision Graphics and Image Processing, 31*(2), 156–177. doi:10.1016/S0734-189X(85)80004-9

Tuba, E., Ivana, S., Timea, B., Nebojsa, B., & Milan, T. (2019). Classification and Feature Selection Method for Medical Datasets by Brain Storm Optimization Algorithm and Support Vector Machine. *Procedia Computer Science, 162*, 2019. doi:10.1016/j.procs.2019.11.289

Tucci, C. E. (2007). *Urban Flood Management*. World Meteorological Organization. http://www.apfm.info/pdf/Urban_Flood_Management_En_high.pdf

Tutorial: How to determine the optimal number of clusters for k-means clustering. (n.d.). Retrieved January 14, 2022, from https://blog.cambridgespark.com/how-to-determine-the-optimal-number-of-clusters-for-k-means-clustering-14f27070048f

Vaishnavi & Girarddi. (2019). *Detection of Brain Tumour Using Image Classification*. https://www.researchgate.net/publication/327497285_Detection_of_Brain_Tumor_using_Image_Classification

Van Geijn, H. P., Copray, F. J., Donkers, D. K., & Bos, M. H. (1991). Diagnosis and management of intrapartum fetal distress. *European Journal of Obstetrics, Gynecology, and Reproductive Biology, 42*, S63–S72.

Van Vugt, H., Bailenson, J., Hoorn, J., & Konijn, E. (2010). Effects of facial similarity on user responses to embodied agents. ACM Transactions on Computer-Human Interaction, 17(2). doi:10.1145/1746259.1746261

Vantroys T. (2003). *Du langage métier au Langage technique, une plateforme flexible d'exécution de scénarios pédagogiques*. Doctorat de l'université Lille.

Velmourougan, S., Dhavachelvan, P., Baskaran, R., & Ravikumar, B. (2014). Software development Life cycle model to build software applications with usability. *International Conference on Advances in Computing, Communications and Informatics (ICACCI)*, 271-276. doi: 10.1109/ICACCI.2014.6968610

Vijayalakshmi, M. (2019), Melanoma Skin Cancer Detection using Image Processing and Machine Learning. *International Journal of Trend in Scientific Research and Development (IJTSRD)*, 780-784.

Vijayaraghavan, Cooper, & Leevinson. (2020). Algorithm Inspection for Chatbot Performance Evaluation. *Procedia Computer Science, 171*, 2267–2274.

Villegas, W., Arias-Navarrete, A., & Palacios, X. (2020). Proposal of an architecture for the integration of a Chatbot with artificial intelligence in a smart campus for the improvement of learning. *Sustainability*, 12(1500), 1500. Advance online publication. doi:10.3390u12041500

Villiot-Leclercq, E. (2007). *Modèle de soutien à l'élaboration et à la réutilisation de scénarios pédagogiques*. Academic Press.

Visual Mapping – The Elements of Information Visualization I Interaction Design Foundation (IxDF). (n.d.). Retrieved September 9, 2021, from https://www.interaction-design.org/literature/article/visual-mapping-the-elements-of-information-visualization

Volume of data generated in a single year for various sources. The size... I Download Scientific Diagram. (n.d.). Retrieved September 9, 2021, from https://www.researchgate.net/figure/olume-of-data-generated-in-a-single-year-for-various-sources-The-size-of-Single_fig1_271839316

VU City. (2021). *London*. https://www.vu.city/cities/london

Wahyu Sulistya, A. Q., Bastian Sulistiyo, B., Aditya, F., Aritonang, I. D., Amos Simangunsong, S., Shihab, M. R., & Ranti, B. (2019). A case study of Indonesian government digital transformation: Improving public service quality through E-government implementation. *Proceedings - 2019 5th International Conference on Science and Technology, ICST 2019*. 10.1109/ICST47872.2019.9166234

Walkington, C., & Bernacki, M. L. (2020). *Appraising research on personalized learning: Definitions, theoretical alignment, advancements, and future directions*. Academic Press.

Wallace, R. S. (2009). The anatomy of a.l.I.C.e. In R. Epstein, G. Roberts, & G. Beber (Eds.), *Parsing the turing test: philosophical and methodological issues in the quest for the thinking computer* (pp. 181–210). Springer Netherlands. doi:10.1007/978-1-4020-6710-5_13

Wang, Wang, Liao, & Wang. (2020). Supervised Machine Learning Chatbots for Perinatal Mental Healthcare. *International Conference on Intelligent Computing and Human-Computer Interaction (ICHCI)*.

Wang, F.-Y. (2008). Social computing: fundamentals and applications. In *2008 IEEE International Conference on Intelligence and Security Informatics*. IEEE. 10.1109/ISI.2008.4565016

Wang, F.-Y., Carley, K. M., Zeng, D., & Mao, W. (2007). Wang, Fei-Yue (2008). "Social computing: From social informatics to social intelligence. *IEEE Intelligent Systems, 22*(2), 79–83. doi:10.1109/MIS.2007.41

Wani, N., Bhutkar, G., & Ekal, S. (2017). Conducting Contextual Inquiry of Twitter for Work Engagement: An Indian Perspective. *International Journal of Computer Applications, 168*(9), 27-36.

Ware, C. (2020). Information visualization : Perception for design (4th ed.). Academic Press.

Watson Assistant |IBM Cloud. (2020). https://www.ibm.com/cloud/watson-assistant/

Webley, K. (2013). The adaptive learning revolution. *Time Magazine*, 6.

Weibelzahl, S. (2003). Evaluation of adaptive systems. *User Modeling, 2003*, 292–294.

What are Word Clouds? The Value of Simple Visualizations | Boost Labs. (n.d.). Retrieved September 9, 2021, from https://boostlabs.com/blog/what-are-word-clouds-value-simple-visualizations/

White, T. (2017). Symbolization and the Visual Variables. *Geographic Information Science & Technology Body of Knowledge, 2017*(Q2). doi:10.22224/GISTBOK/2017.2.3

Wilcox, B., & Wilcox, S. (2014). Making it real: Loebner-winning Chatbot design. *Arbor, 189*(764), a086. Advance online publication. doi:10.3989/arbor.2013.764n6009

Wilke, C. O. (2019). Fundamentals of data visualization Aitor Ameztegui Data visualization (1st ed.). Academic Press.

Wissen, U. (2011). Which is the appropriate 3D visualization type for participatory landscape planning workshops? A portfolio of their effectiveness. *Environment and Planning. B, Planning & Design, 38*(5), 921–939. doi:10.1068/b36113

World Health Statistics. (2018). https://apps.who.int/iris/bitstream/handle/10665/272596/9789241565585-eng.pdf

Wu, Y., Wu, W., Xing, C., Zhou, M., & Li, Z. (2016). *Sequential matching network: A new architecture for multi-turn response selection in retrieval-based Chatbots*. Retrieved from https://arxiv.org/abs/1612.01627

Xiao, J., Stasko, J., & Catrambone, R. (2007). The Role of Choice and Customization on Users' Interaction with Embodied Conversational Agents: Effects on Perception and Performance. *Proceedings of CHI 2007*. 10.1145/1240624.1240820

Xu, S., Dai, J., & Shi, H. (2018). Semi-supervised Feature Selection Based on Least Square Regression with Redundancy Minimization. *International Joint Conference on Neural Networks (IJCNN)*, 1-8.

Yahya, A. A., Osman, A., Ramli, A. R., & Balola, A. (2011). Feature Selection for High Dimensional Data: An Evolutionary Filter Approach. *Journal of Computational Science*, *7*(5), 800–820. doi:10.3844/jcssp.2011.800.820

Yarandi, M., Jahankhani, H., &Tawil, A. (2013). A personalized adaptive e-learning approach based on semantic web technology. *Webology, 10*(2).

Young, D. (2013). *Software Development Methodologies.* https://www.researchgate.net/publication/255710396

Yu, J. (2018). Research Process on Software Development Model. *IOP Conf. Ser.: Mater. Sci. Eng, 394*, 032045. doi:10.1088/1757-899X/394/3/032045

Zhang, Y., & Yu, S. (2019). Single-lead noninvasive fetal ECG extraction by means of combining clustering and principal components analysis. *Med Biol Eng Comput., 58*(2), 419-432. doi:10.1007/s11517-019-02087-7

Zhang, J., Jin, & Liu. (2015). Study of Data Mining Algorithm in Social Network Analysis. *3rd International Conference on Mechatronics, Robotics and Automation (ICMRA 2015).*

Zhang, J., & Li, J. (2010). Teaching Software Engineering Using Case Study. *International Conference on Biomedical Engineering and Computer Science*, 1-4.

Zhang, N., Zhang, J., Li, H., Mumini, O. O., Samuel, O. W., Ivanov, K., & Wang, L. (2017). A Novel Technique for Fetal ECG Extraction Using Single-Channel Abdominal Recording. *Sensors (Basel), 17*(3), 457. doi:10.339017030457 PMID:28245585

Zhao & Mao. (2018). Fuzzy Bag-of-Words Model for Document Representation. IEEE Transactions on Fuzzy Systems, 26(2), 794-804.

Zhou, H., Huang, M., Zhang, T., Zhu, X., & Liu, B. (2017). *Emotional chatting machine: emotional conversation generation with internal and external memory.* Academic Press.

Zhou, L., Gao, J., Li, D., & Shum, H.-Y. (2019). *The design and implementation of xiaoice, an empathetic social Chatbot.* Retrieved from https://arxiv.org/abs/1812.08989

Zhou, Y., Huang, C., Hu, Q., Zhu, J., & Tang, Y. (2018). Personalized learning full-path recommendation model based on LSTM neural networks. *Information Sciences, 444*, 135–152. doi:10.1016/j.ins.2018.02.053

Zniber, N. (2010). *Service-Oriented Model for Personalized Learning Process Design* (Doctoral dissertation). Université Paul Cézanne-Aix-Marseille III.

Zomato - Restaurant Finder and Food Delivery App. (n.d.). https://play.google.com/store/apps/details?id=com.application.zomato&hl=en_IN

Zongmei, H., Xiaoping, X. U., Lihua, G. U., Aizhen, P., & Minhong, L. (2020). A SWOT analysis of vaccine management in Zhejiang Province. *Journal of Preventive Medicine, 12*, 655–658.

Zumstein, D., & Hundertmark, S. (2017). Chatbots – an interactive technology for personalized communication. *Transactions and Services. IADIS International Journal on WWW/Internet, 15*, 96–109.

About the Contributors

Abhijit Banubakode is currently working in the capacity of Principal at MET Institute of Computer Science, Mumbai and Head Institute of Information Technology Centre for Development of Advanced Computing(C-DAC), Mumbai, India. A has 23+ years of Academic, Training and Industrial experience. Received Ph.D. degree in Computer Studies from Symbiosis International University (SIU), Pune and ME degree in Computer Engineering from Pune Institute of Computer Technology (PICT) affiliated to Savitribai Phule Pune University in 2005. He is the Member of Board of Studies, Academic Council of various universities. He is also Member of National and International Professional bodies like International Association of Computer Science and Information Technology (IACSIT), IEEE, ISTE and CSI. A researcher - teacher of Theory of Computation, Data Base Management System his current research areas are Data Science, Query Optimization, Object -Oriented Database and delivered a wide range of subjects in Computer Engineering and IT to various universities. He is a PhD guide to distinguished Indian Universities and presented 100+ research papers at international journal and conferences. Authored a world class International textbook of "Springer", "Bentham Science Publishers" and IGI Global Publication along with Patents and Copyright to his credit.

Ganesh Bhutkar is a Usability Researcher and Academician. He is a Coordinator, Centre of Excellence in Human-Computer Interaction (HCI) and also, Assistant Head (Research) & Associate Professor at Department of Computer Engineering at Vishwakarma Institute of Technology (VIT), Pune, India. His research work is mainly focused on HCI, Artificial Intelligence, Medical Usability and Assistive Technology. He has a PhD in HCI from Indian Institute of Technology (IIT), Bombay. He is an active member of ACM as well as SIGCHI and also, a Vice Chair of a work group - IFIP 13.6 – Human Work Interaction Design (HWID). He has delivered invited talks in research events across Europe, Africa, and Asia. He is a Secretary of Shirwal Gymkhana, a sports academy training students. His research team has recently completed a research project on bicycle safety, with OFFIS, Germany.

Yohannes Kurniawan has more than 10 years of experience in academics and industries, he has helped a lot of organizations to accelerate their digital transformation. Yohannes' extensive expertise in Information System Development, Knowledge Management, Digital Business, Business Analytics, and User Experience. It's make him become the Subject Matter Expert for UX and Educational Technology at BINUS CREATES. His research interests vary from Implementing Human Information Behaviour Concept for Design, Knowledge Management System, and Analysis and Design of Information System. Apart from his work in digital transformation, Yohannes currently holds a strategic role as the Dean of School of Information Systems at BINUS UNIVERSITY, as well as prestigious positions in various associations as such co-founder and Vice Chair of AsosiasiSistemInformasi Indonesia (ASII), and Chair of Indonesia ACM SIGCHI. His recent experiences also hold the role as a Chair of International HCI and UX Conference. He has contributed on various projects related to UI/UX such as Principle UX Consultant for Start-Up Company in Indonesia

Chhaya S. Gosavi has completed her graduation. in Computer Engineering from Vishwakarma Institute of Technology, Pune, and Post-graduation in Computer Engineering from Pune Institute of Computer Technology, and Ph.D. in Computer Engineering from Savitribai Phule Pune University. For the last 20+ years, she has been working in the Computer Engineering Department of MKSSS's Cummins College of Engineering for Women, Karvenagar, Pune. She is a life member of the Computer Society of India. Her areas of interest include Machine Learning. Image Processing, Multimedia, Operating Systems and Compilers. She received Cambridge International Certificate for Teachers and Trainers, by Wipro. She has more than 25 International journals and conferences publications. She has a copyright on her name and filed a patent in India. She has conducted many expert sessions at various institutes. She was an organizing committee member, session chair and reviewer for various national and international conferences. She was a part of the Guinness World Record event on "Training programming in 24 hrs" organized by AICTE and GUVI.

* * *

Bharati Ainapure has completed B.E. in Computer Science and Engineering from Karnataka University and M. Tech in Computer Science and Engineering from Vishweshryaya Technological University, Kanataka, in 2008. She did her Ph.D from JNTU, Anatapur, India. Currently, she is working as Associate Professor in Computer Engineering Department, Vishwakarma University, Pune, India. She has more than 20 years of experience in teaching and industry and has published more than 30 research papers in renowned international journals and conferences. She has got an Australian patent grant in 2020. Her research interests include Cloud Computing, Parallel Computing and high-performance computing.

Muddana Akkalakshmi is a Professor in the Department of Computer Science and Engineering at GITAM (Deemed to be University) Hyderabad. Her areas of interest include Artificial Intelligence and Security. She gives training to undergraduate, postgraduate students and guides research scholars in these areas.

Lamya Anoir is a PhD candidate in Computer sciences, and member of Research team in Computer Science and University Pedagogical Engineering Higher Normal School, Abdelmalek Essaadi University, Tetouan, Morocco. She has a Master degree in Instructional design Multimedia engineering at Higher Normal School of Martil, Morocco in 2019. The current research focuses on: Personnalized E-learning, Adaptive Hypermedia Systems, Artificial Intelligence.

Sushama Deshmukh is an Assistant Professor in Computer Science and Engineering, Maharashtra Institute of Technology, Aurangabad, Maharashtra India. She is awarded with Infosys - Bronze Partner Faculty award. She worked as a member of peer reviewer committee Nationally for Virtual Lab development, a project by Ministry of Human Resource Development. Along with this working as a reviewer of reputed International Journals, she has also contributed to the educational domain by developing an educational tool- virtual lab simulator to perform experiments of Software Engineering and also registered copyright in Software Category for "Software Engineering Virtual Lab with the User's Performance Evaluation Report for the Experiment: Identify Appropriate Software Process Model for the Given Scenario and Comparison of Basic Software Process Models". Sushama has patent and copyrights under her credit. She is life member of Computer Society of India and Indian Society for Technical Education. Her interest area is Software Engineering, Database Management System, AI ML and Security, also like to work for healthcare domain. She has guided and supervised various sponsored and research projects.

Mohamed Erradi is a professor at Higher Normal School Tetouan, and member of Research team in Computer Science and University Pedagogical Engineering Higher Normal School, Abdelmalek Essaadi University, Tetouan, Morocco.

Smita Kasar is Associate Professor and Head, Dept. of Computer Science and Engineering, at Maharashtra Institute of Technology, Aurangabad, Maharashtra India. She is institute Coordinator of Outreach Programme, Indian Institute of Remote Sensing (ISRO), Dehradun. She has worked as a reviewer in many international conferences and also published a patent. Registered copyright for Biomedical Waste Management Audit Software Tool. She is life member of Computer Society of India, Indian Society for Technical Education and IETE. She is working on international projects. Her area of interest includes Machine Learning, and Security.

Mohamed Khaldi is a professor at Higher Normal School Tetouan, and member of Research team in Computer Science and University Pedagogical Engineering Higher Normal School, Abdelmalek Essaadi University, Tetouan, Morocco.

Rob Kitchin is a professor in Maynooth University Social Sciences Institute and Department of Geography. He was the PI of The Programmable City project funded by the European Research Council and co-PI of the Building City Dashboards project funded by Science Foundation Ireland. He is the (co)author or (co)editor of 31 academic books and (co)author of over 200 articles and book chapters. He has been an editor of Dialogues in Human Geography, Progress in Human Geography and Social and Cultural Geography and was the co-Editor-in-Chief of the 12-volume International Encyclopedia of Human Geography.

Nina Lyons is a graphic designer with over 15 years of experience in the industry. She holds a BDes from the Limerick School of Art & Design, Ireland, a Masters in Design Practice from the Dublin Institute of Technology Dublin (now TU Dublin) and HDip in Science in Computing from the Institute of Technology Blanchardstown (now TU Dublin). She has recently taken up a lecturing position in the Creative Digital Media course in TU Dublin. She is currently completing a Ph.D. that examines AR as a visual communication medium.

Evaristus Didik Madyatmadja received a Master's degree in Computer Science from Gadjah Mada University, Yogyakarta, Indonesia, in 2005 and the Ph.D. degree in Computer Science from Bina Nusantara University, Jakarta, Indonesia, in 2019. From 2010 until now, he was a Researcher and Lecturer in School of Information Systems, Bina Nusantara University, Jakarta, Indonesia. Since 2016, he has been an Associate Professor. He is the author of more than 50 journals and publications. He is an Editor in Chief of the Computer, Mathematics and Engineering Applications Journal (Comtech). He is a General Chair of 6th International Conference on Information Management and Technology and Technical Committee of 5th International Conference on Education and E-Learning in 2021. His interests are in e-government, big data, data mining and business intelligence. Author is a member of IEEE and International Association for the Engineers and the Computer Scientists (IAENG).

Neelam Naik has received her PhD degree (Computer Science) from Department of Computer Science, University of Mumbai, Maharashtra, India in 2019. She has around 17 years of industrial and teaching experience. Her teaching experience includes teaching to graduate and post graduate students of Computer Applications and Information Technology. Her research interests are Data Science, Big Data Analytics, Machine Learning, and Data Mining. She has published her research work in many International Journals.

Varsha Pimprale has completed B.E. in Computer Engineering from Nagpur University, M.E. in Computer Networks from Savitribai Phule Pune University (SPPU). She is an Assistant Professor in Computer Engineering Department at Cummins College of Engineering for women, Pune. She is having teaching experience of 15 years. Her area of interest include Machine learning ,object oriented programming and operating systems.

Reshma Pise has completed B.E. in Computer Engineering from Karnataka University, M.E. in Computer Engineering from Savitribai Phule Pune University (SPPU) in 2004 and currently pursuing Ph.D. at Vishwakarma University, Pune. She is working as Assistant Professor in Computer Engineering Department, Vishwakarma Univerisry, Pune, India. She has more than 20 years of experience in teaching. Her research interests include Machine Learning, Data Science and Compiler Design.

Sonal Shilimkar is a Computer Engineering background student. She is a hard working and sincere. She is honest and good leader to work in a team. she take initiatives and having innovative ideas. Her areas of interest includes Image processing,programming.

Matt Smith is an academic who has been a researcher and lecturer for over 30 years at the University of Aberdeen, the Open University, Winchester University and Middlesex University in the UK, and most recently at Technological University Dublin, Ireland. His work involves investigating the design, development and evaluation of interactive multimedia interfaces, especially for systems that formally, or informally, support learning. In recent years Matt has targeted the exploitation of game technologies (he is author of Unity Cookbooks published by Packt), and novel interface techniques including Virtual and Augmented Reality.

Balasaheb Tarle is presently working as an Associate Professor of the Computer Engineering department, MVPS's KBTCOE Nasik. He has more than 17 years of teaching and research experience. He completed AMIE in 2000, BE from KKWIEER Nasik in 2002 and ME Computer Engineering 2007 from IET-DAVV Indore. He is doing PhD from GITAM (Deemed to be University), Hyderabad. His research area is Data Mining, and he has published more than 20 papers in international journals and conferences. Mr. Tarle has worked as a reviewer and chairperson of international conferences.

Tomasz Zawadzki (PhD) is currently an Assistant Professor in the Department of Digital Game Design at ARUCAD, Cyprus.

Index

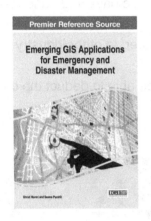

IGI Global Author Services

Providing a high-quality, affordable, and expeditious service, IGI Global's Author Services enable authors to streamline their publishing process, increase chance of acceptance, and adhere to IGI Global's publication standards.

Benefits of Author Services:

- **Professional Service:** All our editors, designers, and translators are experts in their field with years of experience and professional certifications.

- **Quality Guarantee & Certificate:** Each order is returned with a quality guarantee and certificate of professional completion.

- **Timeliness:** All editorial orders have a guaranteed return timeframe of 3-5 business days and translation orders are guaranteed in 7-10 business days.

- **Affordable Pricing:** IGI Global Author Services are competitively priced compared to other industry service providers.

- **APC Reimbursement:** IGI Global authors publishing Open Access (OA) will be able to deduct the cost of editing and other IGI Global author services from their OA APC publishing fee.

Author Services Offered:

English Language Copy Editing
Professional, native English language copy editors improve your manuscript's grammar, spelling, punctuation, terminology, semantics, consistency, flow, formatting, and more.

Scientific & Scholarly Editing
A Ph.D. level review for qualities such as originality and significance, interest to researchers, level of methodology and analysis, coverage of literature, organization, quality of writing, and strengths and weaknesses.

Figure, Table, Chart & Equation Conversions
Work with IGI Global's graphic designers before submission to enhance and design all figures and charts to IGI Global's specific standards for clarity.

Translation
Providing 70 language options, including Simplified and Traditional Chinese, Spanish, Arabic, German, French, and more.

Hear What the Experts Are Saying About IGI Global's Author Services

"Publishing with IGI Global has been *an amazing experience* for me for sharing my research. The *strong academic production* support ensures quality and timely completion." – **Prof. Margaret Niess, Oregon State University, USA**

"The service was *very fast, very thorough, and very helpful* in ensuring our chapter meets the criteria and requirements of the book's editors. I was *quite impressed and happy* with your service." – **Prof. Tom Brinthaupt, Middle Tennessee State University, USA**

Learn More or Get Started Here:

For Questions, Contact IGI Global's Customer Service Team at cust@igi-global.com or 717-533-8845

www.igi-global.com

www.igi-global.com

Publisher of Peer-Reviewed, Timely, and Innovative Academic Research Since 1988

IGI Global's Transformative Open Access (OA) Model:
How to Turn Your University Library's Database Acquisitions Into a Source of OA Funding

Well in advance of Plan S, IGI Global unveiled their OA Fee Waiver (Read & Publish) Initiative. Under this initiative, librarians who invest in IGI Global's InfoSci-Books and/or InfoSci-Journals databases will be able to subsidize their patrons' OA article processing charges (APCs) when their work is submitted and accepted (after the peer review process) into an IGI Global journal.

How Does it Work?

Step 1: **Library Invests in the InfoSci-Databases:** A library perpetually purchases or subscribes to the InfoSci-Books, InfoSci-Journals, or discipline/subject databases.

Step 2: **IGI Global Matches the Library Investment with OA Subsidies Fund:** IGI Global provides a fund to go towards subsidizing the OA APCs for the library's patrons.

Step 3: **Patron of the Library is Accepted into IGI Global Journal (After Peer Review):** When a patron's paper is accepted into an IGI Global journal, they option to have their paper published under a traditional publishing model or as OA.

Step 4: **IGI Global Will Deduct APC Cost from OA Subsidies Fund:** If the author decides to publish under OA, the OA APC fee will be deducted from the OA subsidies fund.

Step 5: **Author's Work Becomes Freely Available:** The patron's work will be freely available under CC BY copyright license, enabling them to share it freely with the academic community.

Note: This fund will be offered on an annual basis and will renew as the subscription is renewed for each year thereafter. IGI Global will manage the fund and award the APC waivers unless the librarian has a preference as to how the funds should be managed.

Hear From the Experts on This Initiative:

"I'm very happy to have been able to make one of my recent research contributions *freely available* along with having access to the *valuable resources* found within IGI Global's InfoSci-Journals database."

– **Prof. Stuart Palmer,**
Deakin University, Australia

"Receiving the support from IGI Global's OA Fee Waiver Initiative *encourages me to continue my research work without any hesitation.*"

– **Prof. Wenlong Liu**, College of Economics and Management at Nanjing University of Aeronautics & Astronautics, China

Printed in the United States
by Baker & Taylor Publisher Services